MAY 2 4 2011

P9-CRR-476

Homesteading
in the 21st Century

Homesteading
in the 21st Century

How One Family Created
a More Sustainable,
Self-Sufficient, and
Satisfying Life

George Nash & Jane Waterman

The Taunton Press

DISCARDED
BRADFORD WG
PUBLIC LIBRARY

BRADFORD WG LIBRARY
425 HOLLAND ST. W.
BRADFORD, ON L3Z 0J2

Text © 2011 by George Nash
Photographs © 2011 by George Nash (except where noted)
Illustrations © 2011 by The Taunton Press, Inc.
All rights reserved.

The Taunton Press, Inc.
63 South Main Street, PO Box 5506
Newtown, CT 06470-5506
e-mail: tp@taunton.com

Editor: Deborah Cannarella
Copy editor: Seth Reichgott
Indexer: Jay Kreider
Cover and interior design: Alison Wilkes
Layout: Sandra Mahlstedt
Illustrator: Graham Blackburn
Photographers: All photos by George Nash except photos by © Les Jorgensen on
pp. ii, iv, vi, 2, 6 (right), 12–13, 15 (top), 48, 54, 65, 89, 98, 115 (bottom left),
126 (left), 132–133, 135, 149 (left), 152 (bottom right), 162 (top left),
167 (top & left bottom), 185, 202 (top right & bottom), 217, 223 (top left &
bottom), 226 (right), 235, 244 (top & bottom left), 262–263, 265, 276 (top),
284, 329, 331, 334 (top & bottom left), 339 (top), 360 (top & bottom left), 377
(top left), 382 (bottom left), 399.

The following names/manufacturers appearing in *Homesteading in
the 21st Century* are trademarks: Alaskan®, Ball®, Corn Huskers®,
Craigslist℠, eBay®, ElectroStop®, ENERGY STAR℠, Garn®, Goodwill®,
Harbor Freight Tools®, Hardieplank®, Hearthstone®, Husqvarna®, iPad®,
Kevlar®, KitchenAid®, Lava® soap, Lehman's℠, Mantis®, Miracle-Gro®,
Mirro®, Peeps®, Port-O-Let®, Presto®, Pyrex®, Römertopf®, Roundup®,
Sears®, Stihl®, Walmart®, Windex®, Wonder Bar®

Library of Congress Cataloging-in-Publication Data
Nash, George, 1949-
  Homesteading in the 21st century : how one family created a more sustainable,
self-sufficient, and satisfying life / George Nash & Jane Waterman.
       p. cm.
  Includes index.
  ISBN 978-1-60085-296-1
  1. Agriculture--United States. 2. Home economics, Rural--United States. 3.
Gardening--United States. 4. Country life--United States. I. Waterman, Jane. II.
Title.
  S501.2.N37 2011
  640--dc22

                              2010054357

Printed in the United States of America
10 9 8 7 6 5 4 3 2 1

dedication

To our grandchildren, Olive, Henry, Genevieve, Dela,
Cecilia, Eli, Roscoe, Jack, and Georgia, in the hope that at least
one among you will plant the seeds for the third generation.

acknowledgments

We'd like to thank our editorial crew: Peter Chapman for having the vision
and tenacity to believe in this book and for convincing the good people at
The Taunton Press to push the boundaries of the how-to-book far beyond
their comfort zone; Katy Binder, our photo editor, and Alison Wilkes,
our art director, for putting it all together with such panache; and Deb
Cannarella, our editor, for her skill pruning and seamlessly stitching
together our sprawling manuscript, preserving our voices without doing
violence to the letter and spirit. And most of all, we'd like to thank our
farm apprentice, Daniel Keeney. Though he didn't contribute so much
as a comma to this book, he tended our garden and animals throughout
the spring and summer while we were chained to our computer keyboards.
Without him, this book would not exist. Thanks also to Les Jorgensen,
whose vibrant images bring the text to life.

If you want to be happy for one day,
get drunk.
If you want to be happy for one week,
go traveling.
If you want to be happy for one month,
get married.
If you want to be happy for a lifetime,
become a gardener.

—Old Chinese proverb,
related by Rémy Bousquet, Quebec agriculturalist

contents

Meet George & Jane

W'e're not ashamed to admit it. We were part of that back-to-the-land migration of the late 1960s and early '70s that reshaped the landscape of rural America. Inspired by Helen and Scott Nearing's *Living the Good Life* (Schocken Books, 1970) and navigating by the light of the *Whole Earth Catalog* and Lloyd Khan's *Shelter* (Shelter Publications, 1973), we each sought our own version of the "good life" in the hinterlands of northern Vermont, where our paths crossed and our fates entwined.

Jane   Unlike the majority of those refugees from middle-class suburban and urban privilege, I grew up poor on a real, working New Hampshire dairy farm. Gardening and animal husbandry were my native skills.

Shortly after (just barely) graduating from high school, I got married and lived on The Farm in Summerland, Tennessee—Stephen Gaskin's 1,000-acre experiment in American Maoism and soybean–based spirituality. It wasn't a great fit. My then husband and I returned to New England. We eventually parked our school bus at the edge of a field in Elmore, Vermont, and began building our homestead.

By then I had two babies, both born at home (or, actually, on the bus, as a house was still in the works). We built the house with lumber that had been recycled from an old barn. I hauled water, dipped from a hand-dug spring, with buckets and a yoke. I heated the water on the wood cookstove by the light of a kerosene lantern, to boil beans for supper and wash diapers for the babies.

My garden provided us with all our food, including soybeans and cornmeal. I canned and dried food for winter storage. Like the Nearings, we boiled the sap from our maple trees to make syrup. We even went the Nearings one better: Not only did we live off-grid, we lived off-road. The house was a quarter-mile back from the town road. Summers, the field was mostly drivable, but it was long sledding come winter. Living hand to mouth, buttressed somewhat only by my husband's sporadic outside work, we couldn't afford a driveway.

George   I grew up outside of New Haven, Connecticut. I was about 10 years old when they bulldozed the last of the apple orchards to make room for the shopping centers, but I did not spend my childhood entirely insulated from the natural world.

There was the annual family expedition to the Long Island potato farm my great uncle owned. I got to glean potatoes behind the harvester until I had to run, shrieking in terror, from a vicious rooster in pursuit. East Rock Park, a 450-acre preserve of woodland, trails, and 300-ft. basalt cliffs, with a river running through it, was a short walk up the street from our house. My parents allowed me the run of the entire park. You could say I grew up in those woods.

My dad built our house, and my grandfather was a roofer. So I grew up comfortable and confident with tools, which might be why—armed with my degree in English from the requisite Ivy League university and after a stint as a theater technician at Sarah Lawrence College, which lasted just long enough to acquire a trust-funded girlfriend—I went back to the woods instead of pursuing a career in the city. My girlfriend and I moved to Wolcott, Vermont, just across the valley from Elmore. She purchased the dauntingly decrepit old farmhouse that I spent the next two years restoring to a habitable state, while, at the same time, honing my carpentry skills and building a contracting business.

Our personal relationship ended at about the same time the house was finished. She kept the house, and I got the truck. The truck collateralized my down payment on 68 soggy acres of worn-out and overgrown pasture at the dead end of a rough road four-tenths of a mile from the last house and power pole. Almost at the exact center of the property, a mere truck's length from the road, was a level clearing where I dumped gravel and poured a concrete slab.

In ten days, working alone, with a borrowed generator and a circular saw, salvaged timbers and boards, scrounged windows and steel roofing, and rough-sawn lumber from the local sawmill, I put up a 16-ft. by 20-ft. one-room cabin with a sleeping loft. I hired a backhoe operator to pipe the waterline down from a spring on the hillside and paid the electric company to extend the power lines. I dug a pit and built an outhouse, installed a wood-stove and a metal chimney, and moved in just before the snowfall.

I never intended for the cabin to be my house. The plan was to live in the cabin until I could afford to build a "real" house higher up on the hillside, which had a seriously breathtaking view of the mountains and valleys rolling away to the southeast. The cabin, I thought, would then become my workshop. There was room enough for a barn to house my future livestock, too.

Then I met Jane, who was recently divorced—the legendary queen of the local back-to-the-landers, the real deal. I suspect that electricity, running water, proximity to the town road, and a reliable truck were at least a part of what attracted her to me.

By the time she and I met, Jane had three children, some or all of whom would live with us at least part of the year. Not too long thereafter, we had another on the way. The cabin-cum-workshop sprouted additions and attachments and enhancements and evolved into an actual house. My construction company continued to grow. I acquired a partner, equipment, overhead, and the standard headaches of any successful small businessman.

Jane I stayed home and oversaw our huge garden. Eschewing my vegetarianism, I agreed to raise pigs, lambs, and beef to store in the freezer, which, occasionally, George would top off with fresh venison. We kept a cow for milk, butter, yogurt, and cheese. I also raised hundreds of loaves of bread. I started a home bakery business

shortly after the birth of our youngest daughter.

All of my children had been born at home, and, as word spread, I found myself invited to attend at home births throughout the county. Back then, trained midwives who were willing to help at home births were few and far between. At the time, a nascent apprenticeship program, which later became the Vermont Independent Midwives Association, was gaining ground. I completed the training and went on to deliver hundreds of babies throughout the northeastern part of the state. One consequence of that career choice was that I needed reliable transportation. So we bought a brand new Chevette and, with it, acquired our first car payment.

George Measured against the standards of the mainstream consumer economy, our consumption during that time wouldn't register a blip on the radar. Our house was furnished with castoff and hand-me-down furniture, our couture was Goodwill®, and we didn't own a television. The food we didn't raise ourselves we bought in bulk from the local co-op. We brewed our own beer and wine and, like almost everyone we knew, we were chronically cash-strapped.

Winter work in construction was pretty scarce. A goodly portion of the profit went back into the business to acquire more tools and equipment. Given the equally marginal finances typical of her clientele, Jane's midwifery career ran at a loss. With both of us working away from home to pay the mortgage, taxes, and homeowner's,

medical, and auto insurance, we were stretched between the needs of family and the demands of our chosen lifestyle—growing and harvesting a large garden, cutting and putting up cords of firewood, tending animals, and buying their feed.

Living the "good life" was not simple, and we certainly weren't "living off the land." We realized that there was a big difference between raising our own food and supporting ourselves by homesteading. Turns out, homesteading is an expensive hobby, especially if you're trying to do it on a worn-out, unproductive piece of overgrown hillside and don't have a trust fund to help you buy a tractor and build a house and barn. At least one of us needed to find satisfying and decent-paying work.

Jane had once mentioned to her first husband that she wanted to attend nursing school. He told her that she wasn't smart enough to be a nurse (which might have been one of the reasons she left him). I told her that she was too bossy to be a nurse and that she should become a doctor instead.

Jane   It truly did seem like a good idea at the time. At age 30, with four children, the youngest just 2, and a teenage foster son, I enrolled as a freshman at nearby Johnson State College. Five years later, I became one of the 93 out of 3,000 applicants to be admitted to the University of Vermont College of Medicine Class of 1990. At the time, I was the second-oldest

student ever admitted and had the most children of anyone ever admitted, too—the very definition of nontraditional student. I graduated from medical school on my 40th birthday.

George   With Jane rooming an hour-and-a half away in the big city of Burling-ton, the garden and the livestock collection back at the homestead grew smaller and smaller. With five kids needing my atten-tion (three of them now teenagers), the construction business grew smaller, too. I sold my share to my erstwhile partner and took on small and sporadic projects so that I could be home for the kids after school. By Jane's last year in medical school, I stopped working in construction entirely

and started writing about it instead. I was also building up my part-time business selling Christmas trees in New York City. My goal was to earn the bulk of the family income in a short burst of intense activity, and so have more time to spend on my writing and with my family.

By the time Jane graduated from medical school, our eldest son and daughter and our foster son were no longer living at home. Together with the two youngest, we relocated to Scottsdale, Arizona, where Jane began her residency in family practice. We rented the farmland in Vermont and later sold the house and ten acres. We bought a concrete-block ranch house in Scottsdale that had a patio and hot tub. In the small backyard grew a fig tree and a grapefruit tree. We grew prodigious quantities of cherry tomatoes and peppers in a little plot along the side fence, struggling with strange insects and alien dirt.

Upon completion of her residency, Jane was recruited to set up a practice in a small town on Penobscot Bay in Maine. So we moved again. Back on more or less familiar ground, we enjoyed getting back into serious gardening. Meanwhile, our youngest son, who was by then married and had a daughter, informed us that our old Vermont property was on the market. He said he'd like to live there. So we bought it back.

We moved to an elderly house on a one-third-acre lot in the small village of Northport, Maine, not far from Jane's office. We put in a 25-square-ft. raised-bed garden and converted the single-car garage at the back edge of the property into a chicken coop and a pig barn. We raised 50 meat chickens, a small flock of egg layers, and two pigs. We raised plenty of fresh vegetables in season and put up the surplus for winter. We installed a woodstove to cut down on the fuel oil bill.

Jane   Our son's tenure at the Vermont homestead lasted only as long as his marriage. For various and sundry reasons, our circumstances had also changed. We sold the house in Maine and moved back to Vermont, not yet as homesteaders, but as "snowbirds." We wintered in Arizona and, later, in California, where our eldest son and family had settled. I became a "temp" doc, working short-term assignments in rural emergency rooms. George

continued writing and selling Christmas trees and, during our Vermont sojourns, kept the house from falling down while I tended the garden and the grandkids.

It turned out that shoveling chicken manure and weeding out witchgrass was a lot more enjoyable than playing politics with hospital administrators and hassling insurance companies for reimbursements. Like a fungus insidiously sucking the vitality out of a living tree, the business of medicine ate away at the satisfactions of doctoring. Disillusioned and just plain sick and tired, I eventually gave up practicing medicine.

George and Jane   We now live full-time on the Vermont homestead with our eldest daughter and her husband and two children. We are once again raising our own vegetables, berries, eggs, meat, and fuel. We're actively restoring the overgrown and neglected pastures, cleaning up the woodlot, rehabilitating apple trees, and producing pastured poultry and pork for local markets. We're looking forward to milking a cow again and dream of launching a business making sausages and other value-added meat products. We're just getting started. It feels good.

And, along the way, we think we have gained some experience and knowledge that might be useful to anyone who is thinking about how to live a more satisfying and self-sufficient life—which is why we've written this book.

Toward a
Self-Sufficient Life

Only a small minority of folks—whether striving for self-sufficiency or not—are actually seriously considering pulling up stakes and moving out to the country. Of that number, only a few will actually do it; others will try and fail and go back to the city, both poorer and richer for the experience. Regardless of these outcomes, the bottom line is that a lot of folks (many of whom are reading this book, we hope) are thinking about ways to become self-sufficient or at least to do a little more for themselves. They may entertain notions of growing some portion of their food (whether for cost savings, safety, or pleasure), brewing a backyard batch of biodiesel, or installing a woodstove in the living room or solar panels on the roof (motivated to do more than just recycle bottles and newspapers to fight global climate change). In times of increasing uncertainty, it's understandable that many of us would want to feel a little more secure, a little more in control of our lives and livelihoods, and a little less at the mercy of distant corporations or the tectonic upheavals of the economy. Keeping

a few chickens or raising some herbs and tomatoes may be all it takes.

The goal of "homesteading" is to live a more satisfying life, insofar as that can be defined as freeing yourself from the burden of useless possessions and obsessions, raising kids that grow up curious and hopeful, forging strong family ties, and gathering together around the dinner table to celebrate good food and good living. When you cultivate a garden, you not only cultivate the fruits and vegetables you grow, you cultivate the ability to enjoy small pleasures and to find gratification in honest work. In a sense, when you're homesteading, manual labor becomes a sort of life sport.

Ultimately, in this book, our intent is to show you how to appreciate and celebrate the enduring realities of life—food, shelter, livelihood, family, and community—and how to work with your hands to reclaim and reconnect with the natural world. A homesteader's life is sufficient unto itself—sustaining, satisfying, and successful. What more does anyone really need? Whether you're a city dweller, live in a suburban setting,

B.F. Peck Farm, East Bethany, N.Y., c. 1876

or have (or are about to invest in) plenty of land for a small farming enterprise of your own, the self-sufficient good life is within reach.

You don't have to live in the country to homestead—your mindscape is more important than your landscape. You might, for example, convert a city lot or an apartment rooftop into a small "homestead" or create an oasis of relative solitude in the middle of a suburban desert. With intensive gardening techniques, you can grow a significant part of your year's vegetables in a very small area. Even in most major cities, you can keep a small flock of chickens for eggs or broilers, bees for honey, a dairy goat for milk or cheese, and rabbits or

even a pig for meat. You can certainly brew your own beer or make your own wine and maybe plant a couple of dwarf fruit trees or berry bushes on the front lawn. Throughout this book, you'll find occasional sidebars entitled "Homesteading Wherever You Are," which will provide some tips and guidelines for the approach that is most practical for your living situation.

Scott and Helen Nearing—homesteading gurus and authors of the homesteader's bible, *Living the Good Life*—believed in self-reliance, healthy exercise and diet, social cooperation, and environmental awareness. Whatever else it might be, homesteading is an excellent vehicle for achieving those goals. Reducing superfluous consumption and paring down your list of wants to your list of needs doesn't mean that you have to live a life of privation. It just requires you to find more in less. The goal of homesteading is to live deep, not wide. In practice, this approach translates into deciding what you can and can't live without. Healthy food? Health insurance? Cable TV? Peace of mind? Some choices may seem like no-brainers; other decisions are not even on the table—or maybe not until you really begin to think about them.

As you'll learn in this book, there are degrees of commitment and different possibilities along the continuum from total dependence to total self-reliance. You can find your niche wherever you are most comfortable at the moment and ramp your efforts up or down as suits your circumstances or goals. We don't believe that self-sufficiency has got to be all or nothing. A little bit is a lot better than none.

It takes a lifetime to learn how to homestead. Our purpose is to demystify the process and point you in the right direction. We will touch on as many subjects as we can to help you get started and give you a map for where to go once you embark on a particular path. Fortunately, you can learn as you go. You don't need to know everything up front. So, indeed, read everything you can. Build a library, subscribe to magazines, do research online. Once you begin, you'll discover that there's somehow always a mentor somewhere along the way—a neighbor, a friend of a friend—who can show you how to do whatever it is you need to know how to do. Eventually, you will become that mentor for somebody else. Until then, you can take pride in each new accomplishment, even as you accept that there will always be so much more to learn and do.

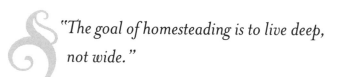
"The goal of homesteading is to live deep, not wide."

The Seven Virtues of the Highly Successful Homesteader

As you strive to achieve a degree of self-sufficiency you inevitably strengthen your self-reliance. The character traits that enable you to work toward that goal in the first place also provide great rewards after you finally reach it.

1. Resourcefulness. It's pretty hard to become self-sufficient without being resourceful. You won't know much when you begin, but eventually you will gain the skills, knowledge, and self-confidence you need—as long as you're willing to read, learn, and take advice from people who "know a thing or two." Learn how to change a light bulb rather than call an electrician. When something needs building, find out how to do it yourself. Above all, learn from your mistakes.

2. Fearlessness. Security is an illusion. The best way to overcome obstacles and deal with setbacks is by cultivating the ability and flexibility to shift course and embrace new possibilities. Master the art of "getting by." Remember, when you reach the bottom of one barrel, you've arrived at the top of the next one.

3. Equanimity. This quality fosters the ability to take delight in small things and enjoy mind-numbingly repetitive physical labor. Weeding the vegetable garden can be very satisfying if you have the proper, Zen attitude. The process of reaching that state of mind is a kind of mental and physical meditation, achieved by sinking deeply into the task at hand, moving below the pain of protesting muscles.

4. High tolerance for frustration. Equanimity (see #3 above) is easy to maintain when things are going right, but it can take all day to get your truck out of the ditch it slipped into as you backed down the icy driveway. The ten-minute job turns into a nine-hour nightmare. Persevere.

5. High tolerance for the absence of novelty or entertainment. Stimuli, such as concerts, plays, social encounters with new people, interesting restaurants, etc., are literally far and few between when you're living in the country. Potlucks, church suppers, the country fair, and your daughter's sixth-grade play will be the height of your social season. Eventually, you'll come to love those moments, embracing them without a shred of irony. Irony is toxic to joy; the antidote is humility. (A constitutional deficiency in jadedness is also helpful.)

6. Consciousness. Living a sustainable life presupposes an awareness of the interconnectedness of life and the importance of acting responsibly within the community and toward the rest of the planet—sometimes referred to as "seeing the big picture." Pay attention to details. Your choices matter.

7. Contemplation. Enjoy the sunset, the dance of the fireflies on a July night, the warmth of the woodstove on a winter's eve. Find purpose in fitting your life into the cycle of the seasons, within the great wheel of generations of friends and family. Find satisfaction in the stewardship of your own small piece of the earth, in making your garden, and building your humble empire.

PART I

The Homestead

"It is possible, as I have learned again and again, to be in one's place, in such company, wild or domestic, and with such pleasure, that one cannot think of another place that one would prefer to be—or of another place at all." —Wendell Berry

chapter i

Finding the Right Location

In July 1975, while I stood on an outcropping of bare ledge, warmed by the slanting golden light of the late afternoon sun, my gaze soared eastward across serried ridges quilted with the greens of pasture and forest to mountains purpling in the haze. There, in the gap between the hump of Buffalo and the rump of the Stannard Mountains, I could barely discern the ghostly smudge that was Mt. Washington, 60 miles in the distance. Below me, across the rough track of the old town road, the steep hillside reclined into 20 acres of unkempt meadowland that was in the first stages of reverting back to forest.

At that moment, convinced that I had found my dream homestead, I wrote a check for the "earnest money" to cement the purchase, and so embarked on the ambitious, misbegotten, foolish, demanding, rewarding, and more or less satisfying adventure that is now my life's work. If I had it to do over again, I would have kept looking. My only excuse is that, at age 27, heart was pretty much guaranteed to trump head—and, as a city boy, I didn't know any better.

Seduced by the view from that ledge, it never occurred to me that slightly more than half of the 68.5 acres that I had just committed to buy was the face of a 300-ft.-high hill. Somehow, in the glow of the vision, I failed to notice the alders and willows that sprouted in the meadow, or the ubiquitous thickets of alder interspersed with the stubble of saplings of ash and sugar maple that covered the slope since its cleared pastures were abandoned 20 years before. I simply ignored the fact that the stage for my homestead dream was basically a 33° swamp. Luckily, it did have a favorable southeastern exposure—but I'm pretty sure that, even if it had faced due north, I would have found a way to ignore that shortcoming, too.

Consider Your Goals

Homesteading in the 21st century does not necessarily mean that you must be a farmer or totally self-sufficient. There

Top: Home sweet homestead. Bottom left: Are we there yet? Bottom right: Good neighbors are a big part of the "good life."

Living Off the Land: A Few Cardinal Rules

If you want to live off the land, it helps to have livable land. All too often during the last four decades, I've been reminded of the truth of this maxim and the consequences of ignoring it. In fact, when selecting my homestead, I sinned against every one of the cardinal rules for choosing good land put forth by good ol' Maurice G. Kains, author of *Five Acres and Independence* (Dover, 1973):

1. *"In choosing a farm, therefore, it is essential that not the total area conveyed by the deed or contract be considered, but the area available for profitable use. Any additional land may be really a liability instead of an asset, since often the returns do not pay the taxes."*

Contemplating almost 70 acres at the dead end of a dirt road, a half-mile beyond the nearest neighbor, envisioning a cozy hole in a doughnut of protected woodlands, my own lost world, I was too far gone to hear Kains's distant warning.

2. *"If the land is steep or broken it is not practical to use improved machinery and it is difficult to harvest crops by older methods. Such fields may possibly be worked but the cost of production is necessarily higher than on fields which permit efficient use of labor and machinery."*

Had I cared to pay attention, it would have been all too obvious that most of the field I was envisioning as productive pasture and hay land was another textbook example of the kind of land least likely to succeed.

3. *"A person choosing a farm should make assurance doubly sure on this point; first as to the natural drainage of the fields and second as to the possibility of draining if artificial drainage is necessary."*

Granted, that summer had been unusually dry. As I was to soon discover, in a normal year, you couldn't step anywhere on the front half of that field without getting your shoes wet.

Alders and willows like to keep their feet wet. Cows and sheep don't. The "artificial drainage" necessary to rehabilitate my soggy field would turn out to be both extensive and expensive.

I admit that the 60 acres that my wife, Jane, and her former husband had bought in nearby Elmore some years before had a lot more "actual" virtue than potential. Their property had 15 or so acres of well-drained south-sloping tillable pasture, and the balance was mixed woodlot, which included a working sugar bush—a stand of sugar maples suitable for producing maple syrup. All that property lacked was a driveway, electric power, and a well. It would have cost a lot less to put in that infrastructure than it cost us to drain and rehabilitate my would-be farm. I should have listened to Jane, years later, when she suggested selling my place and buying hers.

are degrees of commitment and different possibilities along the continuum—whether you're an urban dweller or a committed back-to-lander. You might devote yourself, for example, to creating an oasis of relative solitude in the middle of a suburban desert or converting a city lot or

states at least once. Almost everywhere we went, a particular landscape, a peculiar quality of light and sky, the comfort of a village nestled into its valley would reach out and pluck a harmonious chord on our heartstrings. "Yes," we'd say to each other, "wouldn't this be a fine place to live!"

 "Farming looks mighty easy when your plow is a pencil and you're a thousand miles from the corn field." —Dwight D. Eisenhower

apartment rooftop into a self-sufficient homestead. You don't have to leave the city to live in the country. Your mind-scape is more important than landscape.

"Property Size" at the end of this chapter provides an overview of guidelines to consider, depending on the type and scale of "homesteading" you decide to pursue.

The Search

You don't have to meander too far from the interstate to realize that there's a lot of country out there. In fact, once you've cleared the clotted urban cores and their dendritic suburbs, you'll see a lot of country from the interstate, too—mile upon mile of soybeans and corn, hour after hour of wheat and grass prairie, thousands of miles of alleys arrowing through plantations of yellow pine, mountain vistas as breathtaking as the view from God's picture window, deserts as vast and empty as death. There's definitely a lot of country out there.

During our snowbird years, we drove through every one of the 48 continental

After having lived for a time in places as diverse as northern Vermont, southeastern Arizona, coastal Maine, and the Santa Barbara foothills, we've learned that it's possible to live quite happily ever after in any number of places. So how do you find the place that suits you best?

The "best" place is a matter of temperature and temperament, that is, the degree of alignment between a place and your predilections. We suggest you begin by choosing a climate and terrain that appeal to you. This process isn't as obvious or as easy as it seems, especially for would-be urban emigrants. City dwellers don't really "register" weather, at least not like country folks do. When you live in a city, your exposure to the great outdoors is a short dash from the doorway to the subway stop or taxi stand. Unless you are homeless, dressing for the weather is more a matter of fashion than of survival.

This phenomenon may help to account for the curious fact that, only a few seasons after settling into their new rural environs, many ex-urbanites discover that

. . . .

the local weather actually sucks. Much to their dismay, the truth is revealed: The rainy season fuels suicidal ideation, winters are soul-crushing, summers enervating, the fog constant, the mosquitoes ravenous. The imagined endless supply of those perfect days they recall from their first visit is so depleted that they have to consider going somewhere else very expensive to enjoy them.

Even without the extra-continental adjuncts of Hawaii and Alaska, a landmass as sprawling as the United States offers an astounding variety of climes and terrains, every one of which has its attractions and drawbacks for the would-be homesteader. Climates run the gamut from arid to humid, subtropical to subarctic, temperate to tempestuous. Every sort of terrain— from alpine peaks to littoral wetlands, landscapes of woodlands, grasslands, chaparral, and desert—has its particularities of soils, growing seasons, insects, weeds, and vermin. In some regions, soils are predominantly acidic; in others, alkaline. Soils may be deep, thin, stony, sandy, or clayey. All these variables influence the types of agricultural enterprises that will succeed there.

The Climate

While it's true that a change of scene can improve your outlook, we caution anyone who is considering a really big change of scene, like moving from a wet and cold climate to a hot and dry one, or vice versa —especially those who might have spent some years gardening or farming in their native milieu: The growing experience you've had won't necessarily be relevant to the practice of horticulture or agriculture in a radically different environment.

When we moved from Vermont to Arizona, our first attempts at gardening were less than productive. The growing season was almost reversed 180°. Plantings had to be scheduled for harvest before the onset of the summer inferno. Soil, such as we knew it, did not exist, so we had to build it, molecule by molecule, from scratch. We had to learn about automatic irrigation systems. We watched in dismay as our feeble crops withered under the punishing sun and were ravaged by strange insects. None of our familiar gardening books and accumulated lore applied to gardening in the desert.

Just before we moved back to the Northeast, rescued by David Owens's book *Extreme Gardening: How to Grow Organic in the Hostile Deserts* (Poco Verde Landscape, 2000), we were just starting to get the hang of it. It helps, when you put down new roots, to do so in familiar ground.

On the other hand, something entirely new and different may be exactly what you're looking for. The challenge of learning new skills and acquiring knowledge may be one of the factors motivating you to make the move in the first place. Just remember, a garden that fails because you're unfamiliar with the specific characteristics of the region is not necessarily a disaster, but a farming business that fails due to that sort of ignorance can be ruinous. Irritating cliché that it is, the admonition to wade rather than dive into unfamiliar waters is, unfortunately, often the last thing that urban emigrants with cash on hand and dreams of bucolic bliss want to hear as they set out on their way to organic bankruptcy.

The Lifestyle

Relocating to a small town or village in the country can offer many intangible benefits, the chief of which is a sense of community. It is a lot easier to maintain a self-reliant lifestyle in a place where people have always been self-reliant. At the very least, you shouldn't have to worry that a neighbor will complain that your compost pile stinks. Country neighbors are often a source of useful lore about country ways and, more than likely, appreciative to have an audience. Unless you are a total misanthrope or paranoid survivalist, the value of friendly and helpful neighbors cannot be overestimated. There are still places where doors are left unlocked, keys are left in the ignition, and business agreements are made with a nod and handshake.

These benefits aren't duty-free, however. You might find that your rural community has a lack of decent schools and a dearth of cultural amenities. If you agree with Dr. Laurence J. Peter that "a cultured person is one who can entertain himself, entertain guests, and entertain ideas," you might find opportunities for satisfying cultural exchange in the countryside. All sorts of interesting people

inhabit the backwoods, but you can only talk about pig killings and listen to deer stories for so long. Keep in mind that the activities in the daily life of a homesteader can be so all-consuming and exhausting that there may be little time for flights of fancy or opportunities to "take a break." The mind—like old bread—can grow stale and mold over. I suggest that if you don't already know how to play a musical instrument, learn to—before you move.

Even though I prefer to spend winter evenings by the woodstove, enthroned on my favorite chair, reading the latest *New Yorker*, I realize that a certain amount of stimulus is necessary in order to lead a satisfying life. How much amusement are you willing or able to provide for yourself, relying on your own imaginative resources? How much help will you require from other people?

Keep in mind that you're likely to revise this estimate of your stimulus budget after your first few winters in the country. There are seasons of the spirit whose only solace is a guilty foray into the world you forsook, moods whose only relief is an expensive meal at a fancy restaurant (hopefully one that serves locally grown food). As summarized in Nash's Wife's Law, "A night on the town becomes a fixed cost of homesteading in direct proportion to the number of winters spent homesteading." Chances are that people who are capable of uprooting themselves from their lives, casting aside the chimera of security, radically changing careers, and trading financial slavery for a tenuous

Earning the Rest of Your Living

It's a lot harder to make a living in the country. Job opportunities can be, as they say, "scarcer than a hen's teeth." Before you move, make an inventory of your marketable skills. How many openings for marketing analysts or financial counselors are there in your prospective new locale? (You may discover that there are actually more than you think.)

Light industry has discovered the benefits of rural life, particularly its large and willing (and nonunionized) labor pool. So has corporate America. (Vermont's largest private employer is IBM.) The market for skilled nurses, medical technicians and assistants, and social services workers is nearly bottomless anywhere you might consider relocating. If you have to depend on the general job market, however, the jobs, if any, are usually unskilled, seasonal, and low paying, especially in tourist areas. The best jobs typically require a lengthy commute to an urban center. Because public transportation is pretty much nonexistent in rural America, families are burdened with the added cost of maintaining at least one and, more often, two or even three unevenly reliable vehicles. That's the trade-off when you opt for independent living.

Many urban and suburban émigrés think that they can support themselves through self-employment in a skilled trade. So do the carpenters, plumbers, electricians, masons, and mechanics that already live there. In many rural areas, tourism is the engine of economic development. Towns surrounding ski or other seasonal recreational areas are often economic anomalies, islands of prosperity and opportunity within the economic backwaters.

As a newcomer, you'll have to compete against well-established operators. Forget about that ad in the Yellow Pages. In the country, work comes through word of mouth. Keep in mind that the work that eventually filters down to you may not be enough to keep your boat afloat until your brilliant craftsmanship is discovered. Fortunately, the farther out into the boondocks you go, the less intense the competition will be for those nonexistent jobs.

Of course, a good idea will sell anywhere—eventually. Cottage industries and successful small enterprises are ubiquitous throughout rural America, although the market for your product or service will be limited by low population density. You may make a living, but you probably won't get rich. Country folk have mastered the art of "gettin' by," a combination of ingenuity and frugality that allows them to survive, by reducing their needs to the point where episodic employment and/or a steady trickle of cash flow and an occasional jacked deer pays the bills and fills the larder.

Nowadays, there's also eBay® and other Internet-based entrepreneurial opportunities available to the intrepid. (Or, like Jane and me, you could try to become a famous writer.) It won't be too long before the newcomer begins to resemble the native in at least one respect—defined by one local fellow as "someone who's too poor to leave."

independence already have the resourcefulness needed to adapt to country life
and will prosper in spades.

But not always. Peaceful solitude can
sometimes turn into grinding isolation.
Running out of half-and-half for your
morning coffee becomes a major crisis
when the nearest corner store is 8 miles
down a washboarded gravel road. Long
winters without outside diversions irritate
those personal sore spots, which blister
and eventually erupt in outbursts. The
casualty rate can be high. One person's
chafing is another's winnowing.

"Six of one, half-dozen of t'other," as
they say. It's all about trade-offs. The
closer to civilization you locate, the more
you have to deal with its discontents. In a
nutshell, the overhead is higher. Hired
labor, contractors, materials, and pretty
much everything else costs more, including the property taxes that pay for your
police and fire protection, better schools,
and bigger bureaucracies. If your dream
includes building or renovating a house,
you'll spend more time and money
dealing with permits, fees, inspections,
and codes in town than you will out in the
sticks. You may, for example, discover
that your plan to keep a flock of hens runs
afoul of local zoning ordinances.

On the other hand, you might consider
better schools and more frequent and
varied cultural and entertainment events
to be benefits that are worth paying for.
You might actually welcome and enjoy the
opportunities that are available within easy
distance of a city. Rather than fleeing
from civilization, some people might find

satisfaction in working within it to
humanize their environs.

The Neighbors

It's commonplace that country folk, while
not exactly unfriendly, take a while to warm
to a newcomer. It's usually not a personal
thing or a response to any perceived
fecklessness of character. Instead, this
holding back is a kind of social weather.
Here in northern Vermont, there are
ponds that the ice won't go out of until the
end of May. Spring is a slow and halting
season, a minuet of advance and retreat,
always holding back the surrender of
summer's favors. Like old maples, deeply
rooted into the bedrock, the natives have
seen newcomers come and go, dry leaves
blowing across stubble fields.

Neighboring and visiting use up a lot of
energy. A body's got enough to do without
squandering goodwill on every bunch that
comes driving up the hill in their brand-
new SUV. Better to wait and see if they're
stayin' or leavin' come winter before you
open too many doors. Oh sure, you'll be
there to help if they have need of it. You'd
do the same for anyone, neighbor or
stranger. Got to around here. You never
can tell when it's your turn to get stuck
in a snow bank and him that'll be pullin'
you out. But just so. Keep to yourself. Let
them be. So long as they're honest as they
appear. Well, wait and see . . .

Summer has to be earned. So does the
respect of the neighbors, always measuring—the measured nod and the finger lifted slightly in greeting when passing on the
road, until that day when the crickets sing

Before You Pack

When searching for the perfect place to be, would-be homesteaders and, especially, farmers need to consider the natural climate and terrain. Yet regardless of the appeal of the landscape or weather, they also need to carefully consider the social terrain.

Don't move somewhere where you won't fit in. Whenever possible, spend some time visiting the area before making your move. If you can afford it, consider a vacation rental there or consider renting a place before you buy. In any case, get to know the neighbors and the locals as best you can before settling in.

A good place to start is with a virtual tour of the prospective location. Check out the websites of state, regional, and local tourism agencies and associations. Almost any hamlet of more than 12 people has its own online presence, too. Keep in mind, however, that, although you can glean a fair amount of helpful socioeconomic and climate data from these sites, the overall image may tend to be glossier than the reality. Let's call it the Lake Wobegon Effect.

Every municipality touts itself as the best of all possible places to live, with excellent schools, bustling businesses, and solid folk nestled in the bosom of prosperity, blessed with every amenity, and smiled upon by the weather gods. These websites are designed to seduce you to visit. Even if you never return, at least you'll have left some dollars behind.

their summer cadence and the neighbor's wife doesn't stop the gossip when you call at her kitchen door.

There's a story about a woman from "down country" who, having lived in her small village for more than 20 years, running the local store, serving on the school board, doing all she could to adapt to the ways and mores of her adopted home, was frustrated that her native Vermont neighbor still considered her a "flatlander." Over coffee in her kitchen, she remarked to the neighbor, "Maybe I won't ever be a real Vermonter, but you can't say that about my children." To which the neighbor replied, "Well, if the cat had kittens in the oven, you wouldn't call them muffins now, would you?"

Like the native trees you find, the neighbors likely have lived on their land for generations. They know how to get by and to prosper. Otherwise they wouldn't be there. As a newcomer, respect this. It takes a whole lifetime to learn how to farm, even if it's the wrong way. A subscription to *Mother Earth News* or *Hobby Farm* and a compost pile doesn't make you a farmer or make you someone others should take seriously. Your neighbors might have a bit to teach if you stop trying to impress them with how much you already know.

Considering Cost

The cost of land is, for most would-be homesteaders, a major limiting factor as to where to relocate. Unless you are fortunate enough to have accumulated a good-size nest egg or happen to inherit a going operation, good land—that is, dirt that is rich enough to produce or is already producing a decent income—will likely be too rich for your budget. In other words, it's unlikely that you'll find your ideal homestead in Westchester County, New York, or Santa Barbara, California, or Silver Spring, Maryland, or within an easy day's drive of any major metropolitan center, for that matter.

In a better-organized world (organized in the way that much of Europe is), however, small farmsteads and market gardeners would be in those exact locations—just beyond the urban centers, the market they would supply with fresh produce and meat. Here in the New World, unfortunately, the barrier reef of concentric suburban sprawl, the concentration of food production on far-distant factory farms, and the high cost of land all limit the availability of fresh food and the opportunities for local production. Most of the small operations that supply the big-city farmer's markets must make a three- or four-hour drive from the "boonies" to the "burg."

If your goal is to eventually support yourself by some sort of market gardening or livestock operation, proximity to the market is an important consideration. Fortunately, farmer's markets are becoming increasingly common in small cities and towns throughout the country, even in rural areas. In regions where tourism is the economic engine, restaurants that buy locally grown products now support a growing number of small farmers.

Rules of thumb Even if you have no desire to do any sort of farming whatsoever and all you want is a small plot of land, a house, and a garden off a quiet road somewhere, the most affordable land is still going to be found "out back of beyond." I'm thinking of places like Aroostook County in the northeastern corner of Maine, the "Southern Tier" where western New York State straddles the border with Pennsylvania, regions along the Ohio River Valley, or any of the small towns that cling like dying leaves to the veins of those red and blue highways—U.S. Routes 2, 20, 36, 40, 50, 54, 180, 380, and 395—made obsolete by the interstates they parallel.

My rule of thumb for finding affordable land is to look around any place that's at least 50 miles from the nearest Walmart®. These places are generally a long way from anywhere most people want to be—places too cold, remote, barren, or empty; places that people move away from; places that never bounced back from the Great Depression. In some of these places, the land you find might be not only affordable but fertile, with a tolerable or even pleasant climate. Zoning regulations and permit requirements, if they exist at all, typically will be far less onerous in rural areas.

Buy the best Wherever you choose to locate, try to buy the best land you can afford. Even then, it won't likely be the best land you can find. Top-quality tillable land will be expensive. Like everything else, it's a question of supply and demand. Except for the deep and stone-free soils of the Midwest, most parts of the country had precious little naturally rich land to begin with. The short-lived satis-

If "Oleo Acres" (the lower-priced spread) is all you can afford, at least you'll have a good idea of what you'll be doing for the next ten years or so. Poor-quality land is an uncertain investment, hanging like the Sword of Damocles over your head for the rest of your life, while you wait for the day when the land will finally pay off.

"My rule of thumb for finding affordable land is to look around any place that's at least 50 miles from the nearest Walmart."

faction of tilling the rocky residue of the last Ice Age was one reason why so many New England farmers migrated westward after the Civil War.

Since the last half of the 20th century, too much of our precious prime soils has been lost to commercial and residential developments. Level, fertile bottomland produces more income growing house lots than growing potatoes. Without the protective shield of some kind of conservation easement or agricultural-use tax abatement, even beyond the compass of densely populated areas, tillable open land is just expensive real estate.

Buying good land that has a high per-acre cost could prove to be more economical in the long run than buying land of marginal quality at a lower initial cost—especially if you intend to put the land into production. Prime agricultural land at $5,000 an acre is going to cost you $5,000 an acre. If you buy worn-out land at $2,000 an acre, you'll likely put at least $3,000 into rehabilitating each acre.

If, however, you don't intend to earn part of your living "off the land" (it's damn-near impossible these days to earn *all* of a living from land that is worth more per acre as house lots than cropland), then buying prime land may not be important to you. Given enough humus and handwork, a productive vegetable garden can be wrung from the most intractable plot.

Farming

If you really want to farm, buy a farm, either an operating one, with machinery and livestock, if possible, or a bare farm (just the land and buildings) that is suitable for your intended crops without the need for major restructuring. If you can afford it, buying an existing farm will cost you a lot less than bringing abandoned or poor land back into production or building from scratch the infrastructure that every working farm requires.

Whatever your intentions, don't even think you can jump right into farming fresh out of the city. Contrary to the

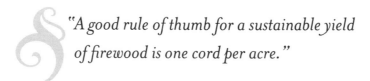

stereotype as an occupation for hayseeds, farming has been a highly skilled and sophisticated occupation since the late 19th century. The most successful modern farmers grow up farming, and many go to vocational schools or colleges to hone their management and technological expertise. Before you try to get into farming, spend some time working as an apprentice on the type of farm that you think you'd like to eventually have yourself.

When you do buy that big chunk of tillable land, start off small and slow. You don't want to put yourself out on the limb by having to make your operation pay from the get-go. Start with hobby farming. As you begin to learn what you're doing and figure out what type of farming will work best within the limitations of your land and market—and your temperament and predilections—you can grow your hobby farm into a real farm. Or not. Maybe a hobby farm will be real enough for you, especially after you tack on farm tours, a petting zoo, a bed and breakfast, and other income-generating extras.

Renting

You don't necessarily need to own a farm in order to farm. As Mr. Maurice G. Kains says, "Renting is chiefly valuable for the opportunities it affords to gain experience before making a permanent investment."

There are a surprising number of landowners—often wealthy, absentee owners—who want to keep their land open and productive and are willing to rent it on a long-term basis for very little more than the amount of the taxes. Along with tillable and productive land, the rental property may include a house, outbuildings, and even some equipment. Conservation trusts sometimes buy farms and are willing to lease them to young farmers or even sell them outright on very favorable terms.

Some rich folk enjoy having a "pet" farmer, which presents another option. Given the difficulty of making farming pay enough to carry a mortgage and ongoing improvements, playing that role is a pretty good deal. Just make sure you get all the terms of the lease spelled out in detail, especially those concerning which party is responsible for improvements and the disposition of those improvements after the lease term ends. Seek competent legal advice, however, before you sign anything.

Productive Land

Fortunately, not everyone yearns for a security blanket of myriad acres or dreams of ruling over rustic realms, as I did. How much land do you really need? The answer depends on where you're at and where you want to be—in other words, what, exactly, are your intentions?

Tillable land No matter how many acres you own, no matter how wide the extent of your realm, the key concept in evaluating land is whether or not it is tillable. Tillable land is land that is readily worked (with or without machinery) and can be planted to grow crops for home use or market sale. Ideally, your tillable land would be level or gently sloping, with deep, rich, well-drained soil, or, as is more often the case, exhausted soil that can be restored to vitality with "good handling," as Mr. Kains suggests. Managing 5 to 10 acres of productive cropland is a major commitment and will require at least some machinery and supplemental labor.

Pastureland Although you may choose to reserve some portion of your tillable land for pasturing livestock, pastureland doesn't have to be tillable. Fields that are too steep, rocky, or wet for efficient cropping can still support livestock. Careful management and pasture rotation will keep the land in grass and, over time, will greatly improve its quality, too.

Woodlot Arguably, one of the most essential components of a self-sufficient homestead property is a woodlot that is large enough to supply your annual firewood. The point is arguable because, depending on the severity of your winters and the size and snugness of your house, you might be able to supply all your firewood by scrounging scrapwood or harvesting wood from public forests by permit. You may even decide that it makes more sense to buy or barter for your firewood than to buy and pay taxes on a piece of land that includes a woodlot

that is sufficient to your needs. If, on the other hand, filling your woodshed with renewable fuel that you've harvested from your own land is ethically and economically important to you, make sure that the woodlot on your homestead is large enough to supply all your firewood, year after year.

A good rule of thumb for a sustainable yield of firewood is one cord per acre. This calculation assumes that you have a stand of young adult hardwoods. On my place, that means 20- to 30-year-old white ash and red maple, with a 6-in. to 10-in. DBH (diameter at breast height; that is, about 5 ft.). My trees are about 30 ft. to 40 ft. tall, which is what an abandoned pasture looks like a generation after the cows have gone home. If your hardwood lot includes a stand of sugar maple trees, even better—you'll have maple syrup on the table and possibly another source of income for your homestead.

Other virtues Even the best and richest landholding usually encompasses a few marginal areas of little or no commercial potential, but keep in mind there are many different kinds of productive land. Swamps, wetlands, and cutover softwood scrub might not produce any cash crops, but they do provide habitats for wildlife. The value of the privacy provided by that dense thicket of alders and shrubs that sits between your place and your neighbor's just might be worth the taxes that you pay on it.

Property Size

Not everyone wants or needs to be a farmer. You don't even need to move to the country to improve the quality of your life or increase your quotient of self-sufficiency. For example, you can "homestead" your suburban backyard. Even city-dwellers can make a difference, without ever leaving the city.

You can find your homesteading niche wherever you're most comfortable and always later decide to move up and down as suits your changing circumstances and preferences.

Halfway to a market garden: We grow vegetables for three families in our 50-ft. by 150-ft. garden.

Urban Homesteading

Urban gardeners can grow astounding quantities of vegetables in a very small space. Select compact or bush varieties of vegetables, take advantage of highly productive raised beds, and utilize walls and vertical supports to garden in three dimensions.

The careful selection of plant varieties is the key to successful compact gardening. For example, potatoes and sweet corn require a lot of space relative to yield—and they are readily available and inexpensive to buy at farmer's markets. The sprawling vines of winter squash and pumpkin likewise claim too much ground.

An urban mini-garden

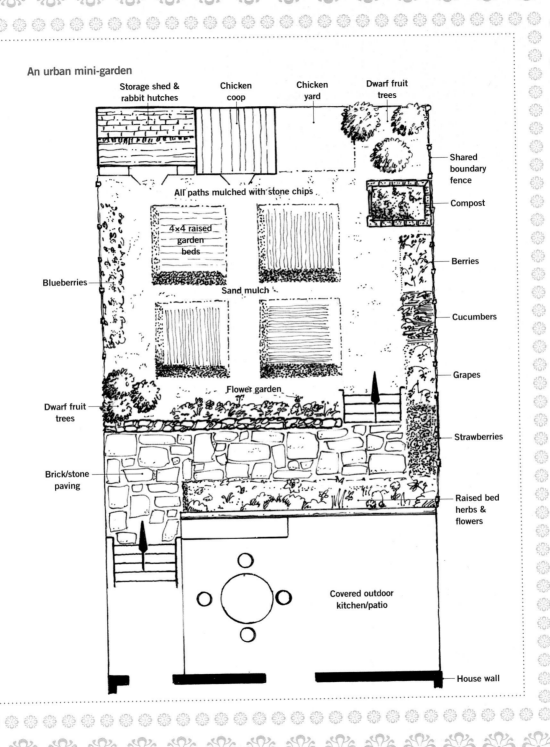

Storage shed &
rabbit hutches

Chicken
coop

Chicken
yard

Dwarf fruit
trees

Shared
boundary
fence

Compost

All paths mulched with stone chips

4×4 raised
garden
beds

Berries

Blueberries

Cucumbers

Sand mulch

Grapes

Flower garden

Dwarf fruit
trees

Strawberries

Brick/stone
paving

Raised bed
herbs &
flowers

Covered outdoor
kitchen/patio

House wall

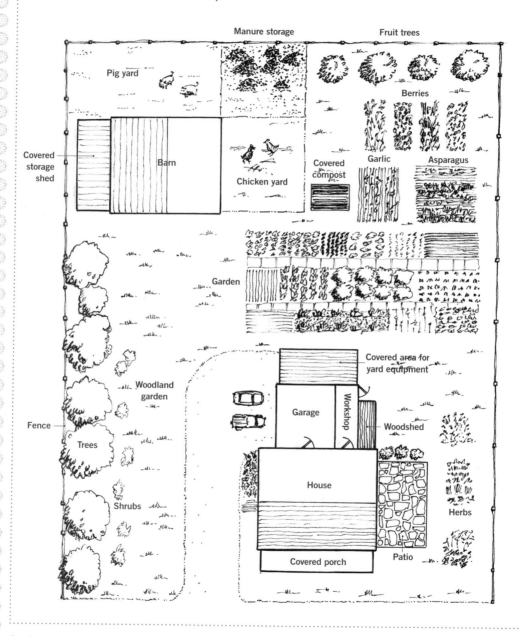

Third-acre suburban homestead plot

Manure storage

Fruit trees

Pig yard

Berries

Covered
storage
shed

Barn

Covered
compost

Garlic

Asparagus

Chicken yard

Garden

Woodland
garden

Covered area for
yard equipment

Garage

Workshop

Fence

Woodshed

Trees

House

Herbs

Shrubs

Covered porch

Patio

You'll certainly have room for a couple of bush-type summer squashes, however. Devote a goodly part of urban beds to salad and other leafy greens. Pole beans take up less space than bush beans and provide room for low-growing plants in their understory. The drawing on p. 25 shows the layout for a 20-ft. by 20-ft. rooftop or reclaimed backyard mini-garden that will yield a bounty of crops and still have room to accommodate a rabbit hutch, small chicken coop, or beehive.

Suburban Homesteading

The Dervaes of Pasadena, California, created a self-sufficient homestead on a tiny (132 ft. by 66 ft.) plot of land. They grew three tons of vegetables in their tenth-of-an-acre (66 ft. x 66 ft.) garden. Their house site is one-half of their city lot; the other half is occupied by the chickens, goats, rabbits, and ducks that produce their eggs, milk, and manure. (Vegetarians, they raise no animals for meat.)

Of course, in California, they are blessed with the advantage of a nearly year-round growing season, which doubtless contributes to their bountiful harvest. Yet even in climates in which four-season gardening is impractical, it's still possible to grow enough vegetables to get a family of four through the winter on a similar or even smaller-size plot—as long as you have room for a chest or upright freezer and a cool attic or basement area to store the harvest.

In many small cities, the suburban lots or backyards of multifamily houses are considerably larger than the Dervaes's homestead. Many suburban homesites encompass from ½ acre to a full acre or more—which nearly qualifies the property for true mini-farm status.

Managed to its full productive capacity, almost any suburban backyard could furnish all the vegetables and animal protein you might want or need. You'll likely have more than enough area to keep chickens for eggs and meat, possibly a dairy goat or two, a beehive for honey, or a few rabbits (in lieu of meat birds where local ordinances restrict the size of backyard poultry flocks). As shown in the drawing on the facing page, you'll probably still have space left over for fruit trees, berry bushes, and even a small fish pond. If you have a large lot—an acre or more—you could keep a dairy cow and a couple of pigs and even raise some of the forage for your assorted livestock.

The Mini-Farm

In some cases, size does matter. If your goal is to earn part of your living from market gardening or to grow the bulk of your livestock forage and fodder, your own fruits and vegetables, and possibly even some grains, you'll need a 5-acre plot. If you have more tillable acreage than this, you have officially made the transition from homestead to farmstead.

chapter ii

Land & Climate

The idea of owning a piece of land is so mesmerizing that it can easily overwhelm one's critical judgment. "Look, trees! Look, rocks! Look, water!" The newly minted country squire, traversing his dominions, looks upon the old pasture, now given over to hardhack, birches, and boulders, and instead sees meat and potatoes leaping from the earth, working in grateful harmony with the beaming sun and gentle rains, a vision not in the least obscured by the thin hiss of wet, driven snow. As, over time, that vision darkens, in that same purview, he sees dairy goats, fitted with snorkels, browsing dispiritedly among the swamp alders; his windmill, cobbled together from a salvaged methane generator, hangs limp in the powerless heat of day. With his spectacles buttered with black flies and bug dope, he's wondering if his toddler fell into the latrine pit or was carried off by hungry mosquitoes.

The view from my rocky ledge was undeniably soul stirring, but, given that my gaze would more often be scouring the tired ground at my feet than soaring out over the ridges and valleys, a great view was probably not the best reason to buy the place. Aesthetics are undeniably important (who wants to look out at a junkyard or cutover scrub or into the neighbor's backyard?), but a homestead or house site is more than a piece of land with a view.

There's a lot to good land that meets the eye, if you know what you're looking at. In this chapter, we'll discuss some of the features of soil, water, slope, vegetation, and microclimate that determine what you can do with your land and how practical it will be to bring your schemes and dreams to fruition.

On-Site Insight

The obvious and not-so-obvious attributes of any site have myriad practical and monetary consequences. In addition to determining the ease and feasibility and, ultimately, profitability of any future

Top: For homesteaders, hope always springs eternal. Bottom left: Boulders for a retaining wall. Bottom right: Nutsedge and ferns: a sure sign of wet ground.

farming enterprise, soil type is literally the ground zero of design. Soil type determines the kind of building foundations you need and how to repair or whether to replace an existing foundation.

Unless the property is connected to a municipal sewer line, soil type also determines the design of the on-site disposal system—or, in the worst case, whether the land is legally habitable at all. For example, a light, well-drained sandy loam (an ideal soil for crop production) poses no problems for building and sewage disposal, but very sandy or gravelly soils do, because they drain too fast. Soil that won't hold moisture may eliminate the problems of wet basements and cracked foundation slabs and reduce drainage costs, but it will definitely complicate the design of your leach field. Without a lot of remedial supplements, sand won't grow much of anything you'd want to grow, because water and nutrients will leach right through it.

Clay soil is at the opposite end of the soil spectrum. Plant roots rot and nutrients remain locked up in cold, wet, heavy clay. In cold regions, when water trapped in the interstices between clay particles freezes, the resulting ice lenses expand upward and laterally with a force so powerful that no ordinary foundation wall can withstand it. A frost heave literally can—and does—heave buildings out of the ground and break apart foundations. Like heavy clay, rock ledge that is too close to the ground surface precludes having a standard leach field and also complicates excavation for cellar holes.

The general lay of the land—whether it is forested or open, level, gently or steeply sloping—and its compass orientation also limit or enhance agricultural possibilities and construction options. Furthermore, these factors have a direct effect on seasonal heating and cooling requirements. The breathtaking view from that high, exposed site means that there's no protection against winter winds (and the tax assessors will like that view almost as much as you do; one landowner I know groused that his taxes amounted to $10 per sunset). Even at more modest altitudes, the prospect and the proximity of neighbors and roadways will affect the design of the house on your property, particularly its orientation and window placement, and may also necessitate a privacy fence or hedge.

Added Value

Some sites may contain useful or marketable materials, such as softwood species for construction lumber, hardwoods for firewood and high-value lumber, or even a neglected stand of Christmas trees that could be improved or left to mature into pulpwood. You might have a meadow that is too steep for crops but would make good livestock pasture or a "cut your own" Christmas tree lot. (Woodland—particularly a large forested tract only tentatively connected to roads and services—often costs far less than open land, so tree farming may be a good way to make the place pay for itself. See "Natural Resources" (pp. 98–131) for ideas about woodlot management, making your own lumber, and harvesting firewood.)

Building with Stone

A pile of stones does not always a wall make. Stones that have regular flat faces and edges are best for building well-made walls or other permanent structures. The rounded boulders found along riverbeds are good for building facing, but not for walls. Stones like shale, which are easy to split because of their pronounced cleavage planes (like stuck-together pages of a book), are useful for dry-laid stonework or flagging—although those desirable cleavage planes also make them vulnerable to fracture from frost.

Any old stone walls on the property are the most obvious and accessible source of relatively high-grade building stone. If the wall is still standing at all, it's because some long-dead farmer sorted through a field's worth of stones to make sure the wall he built would stay there. Previous generations of farmers took pride in a well-laid-up stone wall. They often tossed the reject stones into a pile, which you may find somewhere half-buried at the edge of a field.

Look for a low hummock, overgrown with birches or chokecherries. Pull back the thin scab of sod, and you may unearth a truckload or more of stones. You can use fist-size and smaller stones as fillers in a rubble wall or as thermal mass for a passive-solar heat-storage system (see pp. 125–129).

You might find another source of recycled building stone in the foundation that's falling apart beneath your old house. If you're pouring a new concrete foundation, all that stone has to be dug out to make room. If you can't find an immediate use for the stone, don't bury or haul it away. Leave it piled up in an unobtrusive spot until you have a use for it—every homesteader can use a stone bank.

If your master plan includes a mortgage-free homestead, and you have a place to live while the work slowly proceeds, building a stone house may be part of the strategy. You don't necessarily need to build the entire structure with stone. One Indiana couple built a chicken coop with the stone from their land. A novice stone mason might start by building stone piers, a fireplace and chimney, or the visible (above-grade) portion of a cellar wall.

Another valuable building material that you might find on your site is stone. Although building with stone is extremely labor-intensive and takes a toll on your time and your back, the material (other than the cost of mortar and lumber for formwork) is free for the hauling. The really big stones, which you might find along a field border or tucked out of sight at the margin of the woodlot, will be too heavy to lift or move without a team of workhorses or heavy equipment. Assisted by a backhoe, excavator, or a log truck grapple, you can artfully set and stack them to make beautiful retaining walls. Or, your local landscape contractor might be willing to pay you good money to haul them away. There's a brisk trade in ORs (ornamental rocks).

Even the ground beneath your feet can make a useful building material. Mixed with chopped straw, that pestilent hard clay, which melts into a viscous sticky pudding whenever it rains, is perfect for casting adobe bricks. It also makes an excellent mud plaster, to serve as a base coat beneath a waterproof gypsum topcoat. There are many proven alternative technologies—such as rammed earth, stacked soil bags, and stabilized soil cement—that can turn clay and silty loam soils into structurally sound walls, in any climate.

Sand and gravel are often overlooked as building materials, but they are valuable and fairly ubiquitous. Excavation may reveal that an entire hillside is nothing but a gravel pile under a shrubby toupée. You may even have a visible gravel pit. If not, either the locals or your soil map can

tell you if there is usable gravel beneath your land. A lot of sand and gravel go into roadbeds, foundation backfill, utility and drainage trenches, and, of course, leach fields. Most of the cost of gravel, stone, and sand is in the trucking, so the end cost of any materials mined from your on-site pit could literally be dirt-cheap.

The Real Dirt

At the most basic level, all soils can be classified according to their mode of formation. Soils are either residual or transported. Residual soils are derived from the weathering and disintegration of their parent (underlying) bedrock or the decay of vegetable matter. Transported soils have been deposited by water, wind, or glaciers.

The two soil types are sorted on a continuum of texture, that is, particle size. They range from clay (45 billion particles per gram), which is the finest, to silt (65 million per gram), through increasingly coarser grades of sand (1.6 million to 1,700), to fine gravel (about 250 particles per gram). They are further sorted into various classes or family groups, according to the percentages of each type of particle and any humus (decomposed plant matter) they contain. (These gross divisions are further broken down into a complex taxonomy based on particle size, composition, depth, slope, and other factors, which, however fascinating it may be to soil scientists or civil engineers, is more than anyone else needs to know.)

The crux of the matter is that the mix of these components is responsible for

Hands-On Soil Testing

Laboratory analysis determines the relative proportions of each type of soil particle that make up a standard soil type, but there's a simple hands-on way to test your soil texture right there on your land. Moisten a bit of soil and rub it between your thumb and fingers. Heavy clay soil will feel greasy or sticky. Silty soils will feel slippery. Not surprisingly, sandy soils will feel gritty, like grains of Lava® bar soap.

You can confirm your initial crude analysis with an additional test. Squeeze a handful of the soil between your fingers to form a lump. Then roll it out between your palms to form a "rope" that is about the same thickness as your little finger.

If the soil crumbles before you can roll it out, the soil is very sandy. If the rope holds together, squeeze it between your thumb and forefinger. If you can extrude a flat noodle of soil, you've got heavy clay or very silty loam. If the rope crumbles as you squeeze it, you've got sandy loam. If you're fortunate, you'll get a ribbon that almost holds its shape, but then breaks apart—that's evidence of good garden-grade loam.

the physical properties of the soil and the kinds of plant life it can sustain. An ideal loam (the technical term for a tri-partite mixed soil), comprised of nearly equal portions of sand, silt, and clay, will hold just the right amount of water for just long enough to grow happy plants. It is pretty much your ideal all-purpose agricultural soil. There are also other types of loams that have one component dominating the others—for example, sandy loam, clay loam, and silt loam. There's also sandy clay, silty clay, and silty sand, which are soil types with primarily two particle sizes. The primary component in *muck* (also known as *peat*) soils is organic, not mineral—for example, humus derived from rotted vegetation.

The only good thing about muck soil is that—if you can drain it, lime it, pick out the surface stones, and seed in a grass mix adapted for wet ground—it could eventually make an "improved" pasture. Over a period of three or four years, we've probably put our excavator's children through college in our quixotic quest to do just that. The (probably wiser but less satisfying) alternative would have been leaving it as an "unimproved" pasture, where livestock (outfitted with rubber booties) could graze whatever grass they didn't tread into the squishy ground.

The soil's particle size pretty much determines its water-holding capacity. The coarser the texture (larger particles), the faster water moves through it—and vice versa. The inability to retain water makes

"An ideal loam . . . comprised of nearly equal portions of sand, silt, and clay, will hold just the right amount of water for just long enough to grow happy plants."

sandy soils unsuited for most cultivated crops. Also, the plant nutrients will rapidly leach out of the root zone.

Too much water in a soil is just as injurious to vegetative growth as too little. The much smaller particles of heavy clay and silt soils are packed so tightly together that there is almost no room between the particles for water to drain through. Instead, the water is held in a thin film that coats the surface of the particles (which gives clay its greasy texture). This film acts like a lubricant, allowing the particles to slip past each other under pressure, trapping the water (this effect explains why clay soils provide poor bearing for building foundations). When the voids between clay particles fill with water instead of air, the beneficial microbial life that creates humus suffocates.

In *Five Acres and Independence*, Maurice G. Kains advises that "one should distinguish between soils which cannot easily be corrected because of naturally poor physical condition and those which through improper management are in poor physical condition but which can be restored by good handling." Whereas compensating for deficiencies in soil nutrients or pH levels is relatively simple, improving a poorly drained soil to the point where it can be used productively is anything but simple. You can ditch and drain the land, but, in most cases, it would be hard to justify the expense.

Soil Maps

The Natural Resources Conservation Service (NRCS) has compiled a downloadable digital database of soil maps for almost every square foot of the United States, including the land you either own or are considering buying. The level of detail on these maps is astounding. Pockets of distinct soils in 3 acres or less are clearly delineated. The maps are keyed to databases that describe the properties of each soil type: its structure, composition, depth, acidity or alkalinity, drainage, and suitability for various types of agriculture, recreational facilities, wildlife habitat, on-site sewage disposal, roadbed, building foundations, and more. You can download interactive maps from the NRCS website (http://websoilsurvey.nrcs. usda.gov/app/HomePage.htm) or visit the local office of the United States Department of Agriculture (USDA) or your county extension service. These agencies will download the map you need and provide you with a hard copy of the soil survey for your county, with all the descriptive charts you'll need to interpret your soil map. As a bonus, you'll also get to meet your county agent, a useful person to know.

Obviously, if your farming enterprise is limited to a home vegetable garden, you really don't need a soil map. Just about any soil can be improved or adapted to support a small garden plot. (Think of the vacant, rubble-strewn urban lots that have been converted into verdant community gardens. With raised beds, you can build productive soil on top of the most inhospitable substrate.) If you intend to do any kind of actual farming, however, or develop a campground, plant an orchard or Christmas trees, install an on-site sewage system, or select a house site, consulting a soil map might spare you a lot of future trouble—and the expense of engineering consultants. At the very least, if you have a soil map, you'll gain a general understanding of what your land is best suited for.

People have always depended upon shade trees to keep themselves, their livestock, and their buildings comfortable in hot weather. The cooling effects of evapo-transpiration are especially well suited to passive solar houses, which characteristically feature large areas of south-facing glass. Leaving one or more full-grown deciduous trees on the south and west sides of a building will block most of the undesirable summer sun. On southern walls, a tree makes a better sunscreen than a roof overhang because it blocks reflected and diffuse sunlight and direct radiation. On west-facing walls, where overhangs are useless, trees are the only effective way to screen out glare and heat.

Unlike a wind screen, solar shading doesn't require a solid wall of trees to be effective, so it won't necessarily obstruct a pleasant view. The shadows of a few properly placed tall pines can block plenty of sun without blocking your line of sight. Conifers are best suited for screening western exposures. Deciduous trees are more appropriate for moderating south-facing windows; their branches are barren in the winter, when the maxi-

Subsoils at a Glance

Reddish and yellowish subsoil	Rich in iron and tends to be well drained; typical of warm climates
Bluish grey heavy clay subsoil	Lacks oxygen; poor drainage
Medium brown subsoil	Well drained
Dark brown subsoil	High in organic content; former wetlands
Acidic whitish to grey subsoil	Nutrients and organic matter leached out
Subsoil and topsoil of same color	Likely lacking topsoil; disturbed or excavated ground

mum amount of solar radiation is desirable, and, in summer, the leaves provide superior shade and noticeable natural air conditioning.

Soil Horizons

Soil can be divided into three distinct layers, called horizons. The uppermost layer, the A horizon, is the dark layer that holds the bulk of the organic matter and microbial life and, hence, the nutrients. The lighter-colored B horizon is a reservoir of nutrients and minerals leached from the upper layer or drawn from below that also stores water. The deepest layer, the C horizon, is the mineral layer derived from the weathered bedrock that is the parent material of the soil. Some deep-rooted trees and desert plants have taproots that reach well into the lowest horizon to pull up water and minerals.

The permeability and thickness of each horizon affects its ability to hold water, transport nutrients, and, ultimately, support plant life. The composition of the bedrock itself determines the pH (acidity or alkalinity) of the overlying, uncultivated soil.

Telltale Vegetation

Trees and other native vegetation can be a reliable rough indicator of the general quality of the underlying soil. For example, hardwoods like apple, ash, black walnut, sugar (aka hard) maple, hickory, and burr-oak require relatively good and well-drained soil for robust growth. The predominance of beech and softwoods like hemlock and spruce suggests relatively acidic and poorly drained soils.

Although they are adaptable to drier soils, balsam fir, black ash, and yellow

Soil Horizons

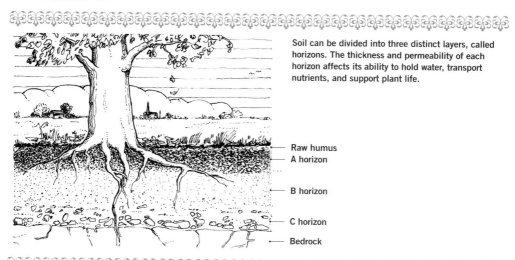

Soil can be divided into three distinct layers, called horizons. The thickness and permeability of each horizon affects its ability to hold water, transport nutrients, and support plant life.

Raw humus
A horizon

B horizon

C horizon

Bedrock

What Is pH and Why Does It Matter?

The Danish chemist Søren Sørenson first advanced the concept of pH in 1909 as a measure of the molar concentration of hydrogen ions in a solution. Solutions rich in hydrogen ions are said to be *acidic*, and those with a low concentration are *basic, or alkaline*. The numbers on the pH scale range from 1 (most acidic) to 14 (most alkaline).

The pH of a solution has important consequences for living systems because the acidity of a solution affects such things as the functioning of proteins, the conduction of nerve impulses, and the ability of plants to take up dissolved nutrients. Animal blood is slightly alkaline. Water has a pH of 7 and is considered neutral. Most plants are happiest in a neutral or slightly acidic environment (pH 6.4 to 6.8). The soil bacteria that fix nitrogen into a form that plants can utilize and that foster the decomposition of organic matter also thrive at that pH. It's also the optimal pH level for the efficient uptake of dissolved mineral nutrients.

birch prefer wet ground, as do northern white cedar and paper birch. Alders, pussy willows, and other willow species positively thrive in swampy ground. Pines do best in very sandy soils. In the Southwest, a lush mesquite thicket is a sure sign that there's underground water within 20 ft. of the surface.

The presence or absence of certain herbaceous plants and grasses is also an indicator of soil fertility and general condition. Ferns, sorrel, and wild blueberries indicate acidic soil. Dandelions, plantain, and wild strawberries are indicative of slightly less acidic conditions. In arid regions, salt grass, greasewood, and creosote bushes thrive in alkaline soils, whereas sages suggest more neutral conditions. The presence of little or no vegetation and a crusty white appearance

signal highly alkaline soil. Hydrangeas are a natural litmus test: The blossoms are red in alkaline soil and blue in acidic soil.

Sedges will predominate on soils that are too poor and wet to support vigorous grasses. (Had I known that the coarse, grasslike plant dominating my front field was nut sedge, I would have known that I was standing upon chronically wet ground. The marsh marigolds that emblazoned that same piece each spring were another obvious clue—as were the horsetails, wiregrass, and, of course, the cattails and rushes.)

Wild carrot, Indian paintbrush, and daisy tend to thrive on depleted ground, whereas Canada thistle, ragweed, clover, pigweed, and lamb's quarters require fertile soils, which is why they are perennial pests on cultivated cropland and gardens.

Legumes, such as clover, are another sign of rich, mellow soil. Some plants, like goldenrod, will colonize any type of ground. Here, rankness of growth—in other words, the degree to which the weed is robust or stunted—correlates with soil quality.

The lesson here is that, while no one plant in particular will provide a definitive indicator of soil fertility or condition, by observing both the species of vegetation and the vigor of its growth, you can reliably judge the relative fertility of your land and its general suitability for various types of agricultural enterprises. Subsequent soil testing refines this initial impression, pinpointing specific nutrient deficiencies and pH values that you'll need to remedy.

Because the mineral composition of the parent bedrock is largely responsible for the pH of the overlying soil, it would seem that you could correct pH problems and nutrient deficiencies with supplements of soluble acidic or alkaline minerals and with fertilizers that contain the proper ratio of the three essential plant nutrients (nitrogen, phosphorus, and potassium). This logic led to the conversion of former munitions plants into fertilizer factories after World War II, fueling the explosive growth of our current system of chemical-dependent industrial agriculture.

If soil were nothing more than an inert mix of mineral particles providing anchorage for plant roots, this industrialized approach would stand, but it's not that simple. Fertile soil is more than just the right ratio of mineral nutrients. It is

Because our garden slopes 10° to the southeast, we generally miss the late spring and early fall frosts.

....

an incredibly complex and multifarious ecosystem—a web of bacterial, mycorrhizal, and invertebrate communities, subtly interlinked in symbiosis with plant roots, soil minerals, and organic matter —and one that biologists have only begun to unravel. Contemporary organic and biodynamic farming methods foster the health of this community through the use of traditional preindustrial farming practices, such as incorporating animal and green manures, composting, crop rotations, and fallowing. The bottom line: A healthy soil grows healthy plants and animals. You've got to feed your soil if you want to feed yourself.

Climate Considerations

The prevailing weather conditions at your site also strongly influence the difficulty of farming and gardening, the parameters of new construction, and the comfort of an existing house. There are two kinds of climate: macro and micro.

Macroclimate encompasses all those elements determined by latitude and longitude: minimum and maximum temperatures, amounts and forms of precipitation, wind speed and direction, sunshine and cloud cover, number of frost-free days, and so on—basically, all the factors that we call "the weather." Microclimate refers to the macroclimatic conditions modified by local topographical features, such as slope, altitude, and shade.

Slope Slope is in fact one of the major microclimate modifiers (the word "climate" comes from *klima*, the Greek word for slope). Air behaves like a liquid. Cold, heavy air flows downhill to puddle in the hollows and ditches. Therefore, frost always strikes the valleys first and last.

means the ground will warm faster in spring. Laying out your garden on a 10° slope is the same as moving it 700 miles southward. Pass the sweet potatoes please!

The benefits of "earth sheltering" present another compelling reason to site a new house, barn, or root cellar

"Anyone who's grown up on a farm can tell a lot about the soil just by looking at what's growing on it."

Exposed hilltops cool off quickly and are further chilled by exposure to the wind, but air movement limits condensation, so hilltops and slopes are less likely to experience a frost. As any short-season gardener knows, this factor makes all the difference in determining whether tomatoes ripen on the vine or on the windowsill.

The orientation of a slope is just as important as its altitude. A south-facing slope receives more direct sunshine than any other orientation. Eastern slopes get morning sun; western slopes get the most afternoon sun. More direct sunshine means the ground receives more solar energy per square foot, so it will warm during the day and cool off slowly at night. The steepness of a slope is a factor in determining the amount of sunlight energy it receives (the energy is greatest when its sunlight strikes perpendicular to the ground's surface). Each degree of increase in a south-facing slope is equivalent to a southward shift of 70 miles—which

on a slope. If part or all of the north, west, and east walls are tucked into the slope, the bulk of the earth piled against them will, with proper insulation, keep the building warmer in winter and cooler in summer. Our root cellar—dug into the hillside, capped with a guest cabin, and sheltered by a storage room and woodshed along its exposed face—never freezes in winter and is remarkably cool during the summer (see pp. 249–250).

Shade trees If you've ever strolled under a forest canopy, you've experienced another moderating effect of microclimate. Trees absorb sunlight and shade the ground. They work like a giant air conditioner. The water taken up by the tree's roots evaporates from its leaf surfaces and cools the surrounding air. By blocking direct solar radiation, the forest shade cools the ground during the day and, by slowing the escape of heat, keeps the ground warmer at night.

At the Foundation

Wet, poorly drained soil is not only detrimental to healthy plants, but it also complicates pretty much anything else you might wish to do with your land, from building roads and foundations to flushing your toilet. Whether you intend to build from scratch or move into an existing house, the soil, slope, and drainage conditions can profoundly affect where, what, and how you build—or, in the case of an old house, the need for major remediation.

When it comes to foundations, not all terra is firma. I used to believe that the heavy clay soils of northern New England were the builder's ultimate bugbear. I built a career retrofitting drainage systems and replacing the heaved-in cellar walls of old farmhouses.

Then I met the adobe shale soil of California. When wet, this

Load-Bearing Capacity of Soils	
Soil Type	PSF (pounds per sq. ft.)
Rock ledge, bedrock	30,000
Compacted sand, gravel	12,000
Loose gravel, dry clay, compacted coarse sand	6,000
Fine wet sand, firm clay hardpan	4,000
Soft clay	2,000
Muck, organic fill	1,000 (or less)

peculiar soil greatly expands; when dry, it shrinks. On level ground that lacks proper drainage, this type of soil might cause a foundation to crack or tilt. In the case of my eldest son's hillside Santa Barbara ranch house, the effect of these contractions and expansions was to push the entire house 14 in. southeast and 4 in. out of plumb over 8 ft., a condition nearing fatal instability.

The cure was to remove the existing foundation and anchor

the house to bedrock some 20 ft. deeper by boring a number of 2-ft.-wide holes and filling them with reinforced concrete to support concrete beams and a structural slab—basically, slipping a tabletop and legs beneath the house. From a professional's point of view, it was a pretty impressive operation; from a homeowner's, a pretty expensive one. From a rational point of view, it was not the best site on which to build a house.

Building the Soil

Homesteading is not a lifestyle. It is a life, a way of living and a means of making a living, a lifelong occupation and a vocation. Homesteading is all about grasping the radical notion that—no matter where you live—you can reclaim, to whatever degree possible, the hands-on responsibility for producing your own sustenance and creating your own shelter, wresting control away from the faceless corporations and anonymous experts to which other people have surrendered it. Homesteading is, therefore, a seriously subversive activity—wherever and however you do it.

Urban Homesteading

Throughout most of history, the typical urban household included at least a small garden, fruit trees, and various small livestock. Today, in small, midsize, and even some large cities, surviving 19th- and early-20th-century properties still have sufficient backyards to accommodate a good-sized garden, a few fruit trees, and a flock of chickens or a rabbit hutch.

Whether by squat, stealth, or official beneficence, vacant lots in every city are being transformed into verdant community gardens and urban mini-farms. Because many of these plots are on formerly blighted ground, it's a good idea to test for lead and other toxic residues before planting anything. After rubble and detritus are removed,

An enterprising homeowner turns a sidewalk apron into a mini-garden.

in most cases, you must build the soil from scratch, a bucket or pickup load at a time. Intensive composting and vermiculture are two of the best ways to build soil fertility.

Soil is a precious commodity in the urban setting, and deep-raised-bed gardening is one of the most practical, economical ways to utilize it. You can build beds from brick, concrete block, or scrounged timbers (scrounging is a crucial skill for an urban homesteader). Fill the raised beds with 18 in. or more of compost-enriched soil, and they will support extremely high-density, productive plantings. You'll also be more comfortable as you cultivate and harvest the beds. Raised beds allow more light and are well drained and more resistant to drought than conventional garden beds. They make the best use of limited space—and are also very pretty.

Suburban Homesteading

Even though the contemporary suburban lot is more likely to be $\frac{1}{10}$ to $\frac{1}{2}$ acre, by city standards, that's still a pretty good-size spread. Properly managed, a lot that size is more than enough to provide for the bulk of one's food—animal and vegetable. You can't assume, however, that a large plot of ground is a large plot of productive ground. In many suburban developments, most of the original topsoil was stripped off to facilitate construction. Later, just enough was put back to support a thin graft of lawn grass. So you'll likely need to build topsoil from scratch.

In some ways, it can be more difficult to homestead the wide-open backyards of the suburbs than the pocket plots of the city. Although no one will take umbrage if you put in a garden, converting your lawn into a pasture might get you a citation for failure to maintain your property. The restrictions on the keeping of poultry and other domestic livestock are often more stringent and more likely to be enforced in a suburban environment. (Most towns allow a small flock of laying hens, but roosters are definitely not welcome.)

The Mini-Farm

Acreage is seductive. Deep in the kernel of the homestead dream—beneath the skin and pith of considerations of soil, site, and suitability—lies a seed of sheer irrational desire: a lust for land and lots of it, acres of acreage.

A cautionary tale: When I first moved to Vermont, I lived in an old farmhouse set back from the town road on 5 acres of level, fertile, open land. The property had a garage, a workshop, and a small barn with enough space to house a pair of pigs, a few chickens, some sheep, and a milk goat. There was also an apple tree, a small pond, and just enough meadow for hay and pasture. It was—or could have been—a perfectly suitable small homestead, the ideal 5-acre mini-farm, a plug-and-play operation. I should have been happy there. Every square foot met the three essential criteria of size, soil suitability, and location, but there were only 218,405 of them. Envisioning my own private empire, I imagined that my heart's content could only be satisfied by at least ten times that much ground. So, when the offer to buy came, I turned it down.

Thirty years later, with tens of thousands of dollars plowed into 60-plus acres of steep, stony, soggy ground, I have realized that desire, as the Buddhists say, is definitely the cause of all suffering. Downsize your dreams.

chapter iii

Water & Water Systems

One of the criteria our ancestors used in selecting a good building site for their homestead was the ready availability of clean drinking water. Rainwater percolates into the ground and accumulates in an aquifer, which is basically a layer of porous sand, gravel, or shattered rock lying over impermeable material. The amount of water the aquifer contains will naturally rise and fall with seasonal variations in rainfall and snowmelt and also, unnaturally, as water is withdrawn by pumps. The water table is the surface of this subterranean reservoir.

A well is the shaft of a water mine. The only difference between a surface spring, a shallow-dug well, and a drilled well is how deep you've got to go before you find water and what it will take to bring it up to the surface. A seep, a chronic wet spot, or, better yet, an actual trickling spring—signs of an intersection of the water table and the ground—are all good candidates as areas for a shallow well. In most cases,

The farm pond can serve many useful purposes besides recreation.

clues to the whereabouts of the water table are hidden from view, deep beneath the ground, divinable only by luck or the dowser's art.

Modern science has no explanation for the uncanny accuracy with which the predictions of dowsers are borne out and hasn't been able to offer any technology superior to "water witching" for locating an underground source. Based on the recorded depths of neighboring wells, your well driller might be willing to hazard a guess as to the likely depth at which he'll strike water on your site. The dowser we hired to locate our well not only assured us that we would find water at around 120 ft., but also that there would be a lot of it. He was confident enough in his prediction to base his remuneration on the number of gallons per minute that the well would deliver. When the drill rig reached 125 ft., water began to gush from the bore hole. It was the best $23 we ever spent.

Convinced that dowsing was no more certain than blind chance, our skeptical neighbor didn't see any point in wasting money on such foolishness. When, however, hardly 200 yd. from our well, after drilling almost 250 ft. deep, he finally tapped into a half-gallon-per-minute trickle, he sheepishly admitted that perhaps he might have felt better if he could at least blame the dowser.

Shallow-Dug Wells

In northern New England, current prices for drilled wells typically run about $3 per foot plus an additional $3 per foot for each length of steel casing (to prevent the sides of the hole from caving in until it reaches solid rock). Wells in this part of the

residues, oil, gas, and chemical spills) and from pathogens from animal or human sources carried by groundwater. Of course, there's no guarantee that a deep well won't be contaminated. Industrial pollutants, legal and illegal, have a nasty habit of insinuating themselves into underground aquifers of all depths. Because deep aquifers are inhospitable to bacteria growth, water samples from deep wells are unlikely to test positive for E. coli, the common bacterium that testing labs use to indicate hazardous contamination. In many parts of the country, water drawn from aquifers

"In most cases, clues to the whereabouts of the water table are hidden from view, deep beneath the ground, divinable only by luck or the dowswer's art."

world usually run 100 ft. to 250 ft. deep, so a drilled well will set you back anywhere from $3,000 to $7,500, before you add in the cost of the pump, piping, and installation.

There's a big advantage in developing a natural spring into a shallow-dug well rather than drilling a deep well. Because the source lies close to the surface, the shallow-dug well is much less expensive. Shallow wells suffer from two main drawbacks, however: pollution and unreliability.

Risk of pollution Because shallow-dug wells draw from porous strata close to the surface, even when they are well constructed, they are much more susceptible than a deep well is to pollution from contaminants (such as fertilizer and herbicide

adjacent to hot springs, volcanic activity, or certain rock formations often naturally contains high concentrations of corrosive acids or foul-smelling sulphur, staining iron, toxic arsenic, carcinogenic radon gas, and other dissolved minerals that are difficult to remove.

In areas where "hard" water is endemic, a water-softening system is necessary. By removing the dissolved calcium, magnesium, and iron salts, water softeners extend the life of water heaters, washing machines, and hydronic systems and pipes. Although there are point-of-entry units on the market designed to treat all incoming water, water softeners are usually plumbed only to treat the hot-water supply, where corrosion is most problematic.

Digging a Shallow-Dug Well

Once you've decided on a likely spot, simply begin digging with a backhoe until you strike water-bearing gravel or a crack in the rock. On some sites, you'll hit the water table just about anywhere you dig a hole. On others, the water will lie beyond your reach, no matter where you dig. (Even dowsers can be wrong sometimes.) Underground springs are most often found where water trickles between cracks in buried rock ledges. The overlying hardpan will be as dry as dust until, suddenly, with the next bite of the shovel, muddy water is everywhere. A pencil-thin trickle will deliver more than enough water to supply a household, as long as you contain the water within a large-enough reservoir.

1. Once you've located your source, dig at least 2 ft. below with the backhoe or shovel and clear the bottom of loose mud and debris.

2. Line the excavation with filter fabric and spread about 6 in. of clean, washed, 1-in. to 2-in. "chestnut" stone on the bottom.

3. Set the first 3-ft.-dia. concrete well tile into the stone. Mortar the joints between successive tiles.

4. Drill or chisel out the flange of the joint to accept a supply pipe and set the inlet about 2 in. above the bottom. For a pumped supply, attach a foot valve at the inlet to prevent the pump from losing its prime (which is what otherwise happens when the pump shuts off and the water drains back down the pipe into the spring). Gravity-fed supplies don't need a foot valve, because their flow is always one way.

5. Backfill with more crushed stone to the source or first tile, whichever is higher. Then fold the filter fabric over the stone and up against the tiles. The fabric prevents fine particles from clogging the stone.

6. Continue backfilling with clean washed gravel to within 1 ft. or so of the finished grade. The gravel helps keep frost heave in the native soil from cracking or dislocating the well tiles.

7. Seal the excavation to minimize groundwater infiltration by capping it with impermeable, compacted heavy clay. Slope the clay to drain off the surface water.

8. Set the concrete cover. It's also a good idea to fence out any grazing animals within a 50-ft. radius of the spring box.

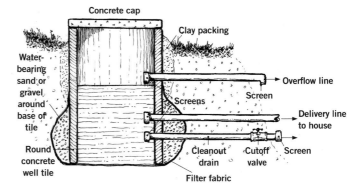

water & water systems **51**

Softened water isn't the same thing as safe water, however. Water softeners alone can't remove pathogens, toxic metals, or organic pollutants. There is no single treatment or device that can correct every type of problem. You'll need to find the right type of treatment for your particular condition. For example, some types of activated charcoal filters are effective at trapping giardia cysts and cryptosporidium organisms, asbestos fibers, and lead. Reverse-osmosis filters strain out inorganic contaminants, so a point-of-use system is a good way to purify drinking water and remove the extra sodium contributed by the water softener.

Unreliability The second disadvantage of a shallow-dug well is unreliability, a facet of country life with which I've had more than enough personal experience. An old farmhouse I once lived in had a spring that the neighbors told me had *hardly ever* run dry, that is, until the year we had a serious drought. After two months of hauling water from the neighbor's spring—which didn't *ever* run dry—I resolved to find a better spring. Several hundred feet from the house, down by the pond, I excavated along the face of a rock ledge and did, indeed, find a usable trickle. I built a spring box and, soon after I began drawing water from that new source, I noticed that the level of the water in the pond was dropping. By summer's end, the pond had shrunk to a puddle.

One of the advantages of my homestead site was the old stone-lined spring box high up on the hill. According to the old-timer who had farmed the place (before he and

the place wore each other out), that spring had never run dry in anyone's memory. I dug out the old well, replaced the stones with concrete tiles, and ran 400 ft. of $1^{1}/_{4}$-in. polyethylene pipe downhill to my cabin, unearthing fragments of the old lead water pipe along the way.

For the next two years, all the water I could ever want flowed effortlessly by gravity into my kitchen sink. The following summer we had a severe drought, and the once-robust flow shrank to an anemic trickle until the fall rains replenished the water table. The next summer followed on the heels of a virtually snowless winter. My spring ran dry. Loath to abandon my gravity-fed water supply, I squandered several hundred scarce dollars on surgical excavations intended to deepen the spring and increase its storage capacity—but, as they say, you can't squeeze water from a stone. There wasn't any water in the ground to fill the spring tiles. By disturbing the underlying strata, my attempt to improve the spring may well have had the opposite effect.

My neighbor had an interesting theory as to why that erstwhile infallible spring had gone dry. When he was farming the place, the entire 35-acre hillside was open pasture. By the time I came upon it, the slope, while not exactly forest primeval, had reverted to a dense forest of maple saplings and swamp alders. He supposed that a good deal of the surface runoff, which would have otherwise recharged my spring, had been commandeered by the transpirational needs of my stand of sugar maples. Could be. My theory was that the failure

Testing the Water

Just because your water is supplied by a public utility doesn't mean it's safe to drink. Reservoirs are excellent catch basins for toxic runoff. Cement-asbestos pipe was once used for public water mains throughout the country, so there's a chance that carcinogenic asbestos fibers are in your water.

Ideally, water should be tested for dissolved solids and minerals, and, where local conditions merit, for radon and any other compounds of concern. There's no blanket test for the witch's brew of the hundreds of potentially harmful industrial chemicals, toxic minerals, and viral and microbial organisms that can find their way into the water table. A meaningful, broad-spectrum water test performed by a certified public lab would cost thousands of dollars. So, unless you have reason to suspect a particular pollutant, water tests must necessarily settle for targeting the most likely suspects.

Unfortunately, the medicine-show huckster of yesteryear has been reincarnated as the water-purifier salesman of today. It's almost impossible to sort out the truth from the hype. Beware of sales agents offering free water testing. Almost without exception, any such tests are bogus, designed to scare you into signing a contract for an overpriced and not necessarily effective cure. Get a second and even third opinion and solicit proposals from more than one company before you buy any water-treatment system. In many cases, the problem may be more of an annoyance than a health hazard, and the solution no more complicated than an inexpensive water-filtering pitcher.

Private water systems need to test free of E. coli before your local building inspector or mortgage lender will sign off on a newly built house. If you intend to conduct any sort of home-kitchen or farm-based business that involves baking or food or meat processing, you'll also need clean-water test results before you can obtain a license. Test results notwithstanding, most states won't license a home business that draws its water from a shallow-well source. (We learned that when we tried to start a homestead bakery business. Not only were we required to abandon our perfectly good gravity-fed spring, but the outhouse was out, too. We needed a drilled well, indoor toilet, and approved on-site septic system. Talk about unanticipated startup costs.)

was caused by the three drilled wells of the four new families that had moved onto the other side of the hill. Those wells tapped a vein some 100 ft. to 150 ft. deep. My spring, 50 ft. above my house, was probably on a branch of that same vein. In any case, there didn't seem to be enough water to go around. Several thousand dollars later, I had cold, clear water from my own drilled well, a few feet behind my cabin.

Tales of springs and wells drying up in response to new construction, dynamiting,

A reliable source of fresh clean water is just as important for livestock as it is for the household. (Setting the pan in an old tire makes it harder for the pigs to overturn it.)

and changes in land use are a stock subject in rural conversation. What may have seemed an ideal water source can, for no apparent reason, suddenly disappear, while a neighbor's spring is completely unaffected. Deep-drilled wells go dry, too, but not quite as often. Developing a spring, although initially less costly, could lead to future problems and the need to drill a well after all. Well drilling is a kind of gamble. The driller gets paid, whether or not the drill finds water. Be aware that some well drillers charge a minimum equivalent to the cost of drilling 100 ft., so even if you strike all the water you need at 35 ft., you're still paying for a deep well. Of course, there's no maximum charge—or rebate—for a dry hole.

Tapping the Aquifer

Most wells need the assistance of some kind of powered pump (powered by wind, the sun, or electricity) to bring the water to the surface and into the house. The type of pump depends on how high the water has to be lifted and whether it will be collected in a storage tank or pumped directly into the house. A gravity-fed water supply or an artesian well (in which the water tapped from a deep aquifer is under so much natural pressure that it erupts from the wellhead like an oil gusher) is an uncommon bonus.

Blessed be they who have a gravity-fed water system. Power failure or not, water will flow from the tap for as long as the planet continues to tumble through space. Water flows downhill, so if your kitchen sink is lower than your water source, water will come out of the faucet. The rough rule of thumb is that the pressure at the tap will be half the difference between your source and its outlet (actually, 1 lb. of pressure for every 2.3 ft.). So, if your spring box is 40 ft. above your kitchen, you can figure on a bit less than 20 lb. of pressure at the sink tap (the standard minimum operating pressure for household systems), which is not quite enough to operate a modern washing machine unless you locate the machine in the basement to gain a few more pounds of pressure.

Several conditions affect the performance of a gravity-fed system. First, the delivery pipe must be larger in diameter than it needs to be for pressurized systems ($1^1/4$-in.-dia. polyethylene pipe is good). Otherwise, friction against the pipe walls will cause an undesirable pressure drop, especially as the length of the pipe run increases. Second, because pressure is a function of hydraulic head (the difference between the inlet and outlet), if your upstairs showerhead is only 2 ft. lower than the level of the outlet at the bottom of your well, you won't enjoy a very luxurious shower. One way to compensate for the low head is to bring the water into a cellar cistern or large storage tank by gravity and then pressurize it for distribution to the upper floors with a small centrifugal pump.

Where the Water Goes

In a corner of the basement in the house I grew up in, there was a pipe that entered through the wall and fit into a pear-shaped brass casting that had a clocklike dial. The apparatus, which could have been salvaged from the wreck of Captain Nemo's *Nautilus*, was, my dad told me, the water meter. A man from the water company was supposed to come to look at the hands pointing to the numbers to see

To Drill or Not to Drill

Although installing a deep well pump yourself isn't prohibitively difficult, it may be a pennywise-pound-foolish economy. If something goes wrong, even ten years down the road, you're the one stuck with the repair and backing up the warranty. Having gone down both roads (as a former building contractor and fairly skilled, code-savvy amateur plumber and electrician), my advice is to at least let the well driller install the pump in the well. Whether you decide to take it from there depends on your confidence, experience, and ability to find and follow good directions. As an owner-builder, in most states, you can legally do your own plumbing and wiring—but that doesn't absolve you of the responsibility to meet code and pass inspection.

how much water we had used. I never saw the man come, and none of us ever gave a moment's thought to how much water we might have used—and, until very recently, it appears, neither did most Americans, no matter whether they lived in the water-soaked Pacific Northwest, the well-watered East, or the irrigated Southwest deserts.

the tap wide open. Don't forget the in-sink garbage disposer, the weekly car wash in the driveway, or the swimming pool in the backyard. To meet the demands of normal modern domestic life requires a water system that can deliver at least 10 gallons per minute (gpm) at a steady pressure of 50 lb. per sq. in. (psi).

"Plumbers and designers calculate that a standard American household uses 75 to 100 gallons of potable water per person per day."

Water was just there. There was as much as you cared to use, whenever you felt like it. Open a tap, out it came, and down the drain it went.

Plumbers and designers calculate that a standard American household uses 75 to 100 gallons of potable water per person per day. In places outside of the developed world, that amount would be considered an almost inconceivable quantity of a precious resource. Your clothes washer uses up to 40 gallons per load; your dishwasher uses 20 gallons; and your daily shower or bath soaks up 30 gallons. It's at least another 500 gallons every time you water your lawn.

Flushing a pint of urine down the toilet used to require 6 gallons of water, until building codes mandated the 1.6-gallon flush. (The typical first-generation low-volume toilet had to be flushed two or three times to clear its load, so, in those cases, that old number is still more or less valid.) Figure 2 or 3 gallons just for shaving or brushing your teeth, even without

Don't think that, as a homesteader or subsistence farmer, you can claim moral superiority to the prisoners of suburbia. Sprinkling your 1,000-sq.-ft. vegetable garden with 1 in. of water requires at least 600 gallons. Agriculture is water intensive —as the water wars between developers and farmers have shown—even without irrigation. A milking cow drinks 35 gallons of water per day. Beef cattle, dry cows, and horses require 6 to 12 gallons. A flock of 100 chickens needs 5 to 10 gallons per day, and turkeys need twice that. Hogs are more parsimonious; they drink 2 to 4 gallons each. Sheep and goats get by on 2 gallons each, more if they're milking. Although you might be able to cut back on toilet flushings or daily showers, you can't stint farm animals (or crops and vegetables) of their drinking water if you want them to grow or produce.

Ducks must have a constant supply of clean drinking water. They also enjoy dabbling in the overflow.

How Much Water Do You Need?

When you're drawing the water at your tap from your own private well, the question you need to answer is not, as the conservation-minded among us might ask, "How much water do you need?" but "How much water do you have?" The bulk of the 75 to 100 gallons per person per day that your family uses must be supplied during those few hours when everyone is flushing, brushing, showering, cooking, and washing up. This peak-demand-period factor has consequences for each component of your water system—pump size, pipe diameter, storage capacity, and pressure maintenance. Basically, to calculate the peak demand in gallons, you'd refer to a table that correlates the total usage in gallons for all the fixtures in use with the number of bathrooms in the house. Then assume this level of demand lasts for 7 minutes, to find the minimum pump size for the gallons per minute (gpm) that will keep everyone happy.

What if you determine that you need to pump 10 gpm, and

your well only provides 3 gpm? Does that mean you'll pump the well dry? Not necessarily. Whether deep or shallow, wells are more than a water source; they're also a water supply— that is, to a greater or lesser degree, they also provide water storage.

For example, a standard 6-in.-dia. well casing holds 1.5 gallons per foot. So if the well is 150 ft. deep, you've got 225 gallons stored in the well to draw upon. If you're pumping out reserve at a rate of 10 gpm, and the well is recharging itself at 3 gpm, then the actual drawdown is 7 gpm, which means you can run that pump full tilt for a little more than half an hour before you'd suck the well dry and fry the pump (7 gmp x 30 minutes = 210 gallons).

Remember, this 7-minute peak flow is a largely theoretical construct. It's unlikely that you'd ever open all those valves and faucets simultaneously or leave them open for more than a few minutes. Also, most of the time, that 10-gpm pump is supplying water to a fixture that

only has a 1.5 to 5 gpm flow rate. So, you're free to enjoy your low-flow showerhead for as long as it takes to run out the hot water, with no possibility of emptying your well. If you forget to turn off your ¾-in. garden hose, however, that 6 gpm flow will tap out your 225-gallon reserve in about 1 hour and 15 minutes. Of course, if your well is like ours and delivers 23 gpm, you could leave the garden hose and every faucet in the house wide open day and night and not even begin to lower the reservoir.

These scenarios assume that the well provides the only reserve of water, and that there's a high-capacity pump to utilize it. Obviously, with a very slow recharge rate, storage capacity versus demand is an issue. The solution is to add secondary storage—typically a concrete, steel, wood, or plastic tank. The configuration of a secondary storage system depends on the terrain of the site, the motive source and capacity of the pump, and the needs of the household.

A Pump Primer

The simplest mechanical pump is the **piston pump**. Lifting a piston in a chamber causes a drop in the air pressure of the space behind it. This principle causes atmospheric pressure to push up the column of water in a well pipe. Normal air pressure at sea level is 14.7 lb. pounds per square foot (psf). The weight of the water column increases as it rises (1 lb. psi for every 2.3 ft. of height). So, if a perfect vacuum could be maintained in a frictionless pipe, atmospheric pressure alone would theoretically lift the water to almost 40 ft. In the real world, friction and other factors limit the practical lift of a suction pump to no more than 25 ft. and about 1 ft. less for every gain of 1,000 ft. in altitude.

Replacing the old fashioned hand-powered "pitcher pump" with an electric motor will save on elbow grease, but it can't increase the amount of a suction pump's lift. The only limiting factor on horizontal pull is the friction of the pipe walls, which is why pipe diameter needs to increase as the horizontal distance between the pump and well increases.

A **centrifugal pump** employs rotating vanes (impellers) in a circular chamber (the volute) to pull water. This type of pump is more powerful and efficient than a piston pump, which means that it can deliver a greater volume of water with less energy expended. It can't develop more than a single atmosphere of suction, however, so its draw is likewise limited to about 25 ft.

The least-expensive pump installation for deeper wells (25 ft. to 150 ft.) is the **centrifugal jet pump**. This type of pump gets around the suction limitation by utilizing a principle known as the Venturi effect. A portion of the water drawn by the pump is directed downward through a separate pipe (inside of the main draw pipe or parallel to it) and into a high-velocity nozzle near the bottom of the well, where it causes a pressure drop and pushes water upward. This pushing force isn't limited by atmospheric pressure, so it augments the suction developed by the pump's impellers. As depth increases, so does the weight of the water column, until it becomes greater than the added boost of the jet can overcome.

The solution is the **submersible pump**, which is compact enough to fit down the well casing, suspended a few feet above the bottom by the drop pipe. The cylindrical pump casing contains a watertight motor that powers a stack of a dozen or more impellers and diffusers, which develop a force powerful enough to rapidly push large volumes of water up from depths as great as 500 ft. Properly installed, modern submersible pumps are amazingly trouble-free and will run for decades with no maintenance, as long as the well never runs dry (in which case, they're toast).

Wind Pumps

Windmills (or, more accurately, wind pumps) were an icon of the North American landscape until the Rural Electrification Program (REA) program of the 1930s made them obsolete. They employed a submersible piston pump at the bottom of the well, which was powered by the up-

and-down motion of a long "sucker" rod that was connected to the mill's gearbox. The moving rod would slowly and steadily push a small volume of water up the drop pipe and into a holding tank, where it was stored until needed and replenished whenever the wind was up (on the Great Plains, this was pretty much all of the time).

Supplemental Storage

Whatever the motive power of the pump, a secondary storage tank of some kind is necessary whenever the reserve capacity of the well is insufficient to meet household demand. In cold climates, where freezing would be a problem, it's best to bury the tank partially underground, locate it in

"Television is like the invention of indoor plumbing. It didn't change people's habits. It just kept them inside the house." —Alfred Hitchcock

A wind pump delivers only a slow and steady trickle of water, so the water had to be stored. The classic wind pump was often erected directly over an above-ground storage tank. The tanks were either covered (for supplying water to the house and barn) or uncovered (for watering livestock). Often, the storage tank was mounted on top of a tower to pressurize the system. The same wind-powered water systems that were state of the art for rural Victorian-era homesteads and railroads (when wind pumps and water towers were built every 3 miles along the tracks to supply water for locomotive boilers) today supply off-grid homesteads and Third World–village water systems throughout the world. With a proven track record of more than 130 years (700 or so, if you include the wind-sail mills of medieval Europe), wind-powered water pumps are anything but an "alternative" technology.

the cellar under the house, or enclose it in an insulated and heated shed (passive solar heated, possibly).

Cisterns To distinguish them from elevated tanks, underground or in-cellar storage tanks are referred to as cisterns. Cisterns should be covered to keep the tank dark and the water clean. Translucent plastic tanks are problematic, because exposure to light fosters the growth of algae.

Concrete tanks must be waterproofed on the inside with a double coat of trowel-polished mortar parging (a thin coat of mortar or concrete) or other approved nontoxic lining. A removable manhole or access hatch and a drain line (to enable occasional draining, cleaning, and disinfecting) are also necessary accoutrements of the well-designed cistern. You need to protect an inground tank against contamination from surface water by setting it on a raised site and allowing at least 4 in. of the tank (or the manhole cover) to project above grade. Provide a screened vent pipe to permit air to escape when the cistern is filling and to permit air to enter when water is drawing off—and also to keep out insects and vermin.

In regions characterized by long dry periods with sporadic or seasonal bursts of rain or in temperate zones where a well, for whatever reason, is impractical or unproductive, you have options. You can use a paved parking lot; a shingled, tiled or metal-clad roof; or any large sloping, impervious surface as a rainfall catchment. Then just fill a cistern that is large enough to store the bulk of a household's annual amount of water. Divert the initial runs of rainfall, either manually or automatically, until the surface of the catchment is thoroughly clean. You can route the unclean diverted water to a secondary, nonsanitary storage tank for garden irrigation.

As long as the cistern is carefully disinfected (along with the well itself and the rest of the plumbing system) and is kept covered, the water it holds is potable. Cisterns that store rainwater should not be considered safe to drink without supplemental filtration or further treatment.

If it so happens that your site features a hill of sufficient elevation above your house site, a hilltop cistern, working in tandem with a wind-powered or other low-volume pump, will function like an elevated storage tank to pressurize your water system. Cisterns at or below ground level require a second pump to pressurize the system. The well pump's control box is wired to a pair of sensors mounted to the inside of the well casing. The upper sensor turns the pump on when the water recovers to its level; to protect the pump, the lower sensor turns the pump off when the water drops down to its level. A float switch mounted in the cistern turns the pump off to prevent overfilling. A second pump on or near the cistern delivers pressurized water to the plumbing fixtures. For good measure, install a hand-operated piston pump to a tap at the kitchen sink as a backup in case of a power outage.

Drilled wells The average drilled well is generally deep enough and recharges itself fast enough so that supplemental storage isn't required. The water column in the well is the only reservoir. A hydropneumatic pressure tank maintains water pressure within useful limits so that the pump doesn't have to operate each time there is a demand for water, which would cause it to burn out.

The pressure tank—that familiar, squat, blue metal cylinder in the basement, connected to the incoming line from a deep well or next to (or underneath) a shallow well pump—is wired to the pump control with a pressure switch that turns the pump on when the pressure drops to minimum operating level (20 lb. psi) and off when it reaches the high limit (typically 50 lb. psi). A cushion of compressed air within the tank, separated from the water by a rubber diaphragm, maintains the pressure within those preset limits. The storage capacity of the pressure tank must be large enough to supply demand long enough to keep the pump from cycling too frequently.

Do-It-Yourself Perc Test

The absorptive capacity of the native soil is the key to how well and safely a septic system works. You can estimate that capacity—and thereby the requisite area of your leach field—by digging a 1-sq.-ft. hole in the general area where you want to install the field. The hole should be to the depth of the bottom of the absorption trench (typically about 3 ft.).

Fill the hole with 6 in. of water. Then time how long it takes for the water level to drop 1 in. The result will help you calculate the required area of the bed in square feet (SF) per bedroom (a minimum of 150 SF per bedroom is required).

This DIY "perc" test will give you some idea of whether your land can support a conventional system and where to put it, but you'll still have to hire a licensed civil engineer to perform the official test and design your system based on the results. The slope of the site and the soil profile of the test pit (which reveals depth to bed rock and the height of the seasonal water table) are also critical design factors.

Percolation Rate and Required Leach Field Area

Minutes for water to fall 1 in.	Absorption area (SF per bedroom)
< 2	85
3	100
4	115
5	125
10	165
15	190
30	250
60	330
> 60	Requires special design

On-Site Sewage Treatment

To paraphrase the observation of a good friend about beer, "You can't buy water, you can only rent it." Bringing water into your house is only the first part of the transaction. Returning it to the ground after you use it completes the cycle.

Chances are, if you have an on-site water source, you'll also have an on-site sewage system. Even in suburban areas linked to the umbilical pipe of a public water supply, it's not uncommon to find a septic tank in the backyard. Extending water mains is a lot easier and cheaper than extending sewer lines.

The standard on-site sewage disposal system that safely and efficiently handles about one-quarter of all household sewage in the United States consists of a septic tank and leach field. Poorly drained soils create problems for this type of system. Soils suitable for a leach field must be sufficiently porous to allow percolation of septic-tank effluent (the partially digested liquid portion, which still presents a health hazard) throughout the field. At the same time, the soil must not be so porous that it permits migration into the water table before the naturally occurring soil microbes can digest and neutralize the pathogens. Pathogens in the water table could cause pollution and disease for hundreds of yards or even miles from the source (depending on the extended area of the water table).

The leach field must always be above the seasonal water table if it is to work at all, so the presence of unsuitable soils typically requires the construction of an expensive mound system—basically, a leach field built on top of the ground, up to which the effluent is pumped. There are a number of other alternative on-site systems, some of which are still considered experimental and others that have been accepted by health officials in most parts of the country. Regulations and code acceptance are determined at the state and county levels.

Some states (Massachusetts, Maine, North Carolina, Washington, Minnesota, and New Mexico) accept alternative systems, including composting toilets. If you live in other states or municipalities, the process of obtaining acceptance of an alternative system, particularly a home-built system, will require a protracted campaign with no guarantee of success. The biggest drawback of these alternative systems— besides the difficulty of getting approval to install one—is their high cost, which runs several to many times that of standard systems. For an informative discussion of some options, check out the New Alchemy Institute's *Journal of the New Alchemists 6,*

"On-Site Wastewater Treatment Systems" (http://www.thegreencenter.net/).

Composting Toilets

Waterless composting toilets arrived on the U.S. scene in the 1970s in response to a growing awareness of the problem of wastewater pollution. There were a few manufactured units—most famous, the Clivus Multrum—and a plethora of plans for homemade composters. Unfortunately, many of these early systems were faulty in both design and installation and often were difficult to maintain or manage. Problems with odors, flies, and incompletely digested compost, compounded by the refusal of most local authorities to permit them, prevented their widespread integration into the flush-it-and-forget-it mainstream.

Since then, the technology and reliability of these alternative systems have been greatly improved, and composting toilets have begun to be more widely approved (albeit reluctantly). This grudging acceptance applies mostly to manufactured units; very few officials will even allow owner-built systems. Some counties consider systems only on a case-by-case basis. The real stumbling block to wider acceptance isn't a prejudice against dry toilets per se. (After all, pit privies, the venerable outhouses, are still permitted for on-site waste disposal in most rural areas, as long as they're constructed according to approved designs.) The concern of your local health officer is with contamination from water-borne waste, also known as grey water. Those considering the installation of a composting toilet are often surprised to learn that they will still need to install a conventional septic tank and leach field to process the household grey water. In recognition of the reduced load, however, some states allow a 40-percent reduction in the leach field area. The well-

> "If I had my life to live over again, I'd be a plumber." —Albert Einstein

founded concern is that there's no guarantee that the present or future homeowners won't, at some point, abandon the system and install a conventional flush toilet.

The problem with alternative grey water systems is that, in most states, getting one approved is even harder than getting a composting toilet approved. Contrary to what you might think, grey water can, and often does, carry the same pathogens as black water. The question is not whether grey water needs treatment, but which methods will accomplish it safely. Most systems employ a grease trap and a sand filter to remove solids and cleanse the effluent. Then the effluent is released into a drip or subsurface irrigation system, where aerobic bacteria in the upper layer of the soil purify it, and deliver the nutrients to the root zone of vegetables planted in a raised bed on top of the drainfield. Caution: Never plant root crops near a grey-water system.

Despite the increased awareness of the need to conserve water and the pollu-

tion potential of failed septic systems, it's doubtful that composting toilets and alternative grey-water systems will ever replace the flush toilet. For one thing, it takes an especially conscientious and dedicated individual to maintain the level of involvement with one's own excrement that the successful operation of a composting toilet requires. The thrill and novelty wear off fast. Most people just aren't that into it. For another, legal off-the-shelf systems are costly. Like an imported solar yogurt maker, a composting toilet is more a moral, eco-chic statement than a cost-effective alternative.

For the less-well-heeled but equally dedicated homesteader, a 5-gallon bucket, a scoop of sawdust, and a daily trek to the compost pile is an even more morally superior and satisfying statement and costs a lot less money. (There is an absolutely serious book devoted to the question of why, if animal manure is valued as fertilizer, is human manure considered toxic waste? *The Humanure Handbook: A Guide to Composting Human Manure* by Joseph C. Jenkins [Jenkins Publishing, 2006] aims to radically shift the paradigm.)

About Ponds

In the fall of 1974, when I began building the one-room cabin that eventually metastasized into our home, I hired an excavator to trench my water line and bury the rotted ruins of the old farmhouse in

its cellar hole. Across the road from the house site, in the southwest corner of my swampy meadow, was a bowl of pushed-up ground maybe 40 ft. in diameter and 5 ft. high, enclosing a small knee-deep puddle. The berm was broken with a notch that kept the bowl from filling. Apparently, the previous owner of the land had started building a pond and then quit. It took all of 15 minutes for the backhoe to repair the breach. That winter I had my own skating pond. For the next twelve years, until we dug deep (into ground and pockets both) and turned our little swimming pool into a full-sized pond, our family

We'd wager that most folks build ponds—unchlorinated, back-forty versions of the backyard swimming pool—for fun.

and friends spent many a summer day splashing around in its refreshing waters.

You typically get a lot more bang for your buck with a pond than with a swimming pool. Ponds can cost significantly less to build and almost nothing to maintain, and a pond increases property values.

Enhancing the possibilities for family recreation aside, there are good, practical, and ecological reasons to build a pond. Ponds create a niche for wildlife, such as frogs, turtles, and fish, and provide a stopover for migrating waterfowl. Fish-stocked ponds can help fill the larder with high-quality protein or provide supplemental income from a fish-farming operation. Ponds store irrigation water for field, nursery, or orchard crops; drinking water for livestock; and, with proper filtration and treatment, backup water for the household. If there's a way to quickly move the impounded water, a pond can also provide fire protection, which could save you money on your fire insurance (and save your house if you live a stretch too far from the firehouse).

There are two basic ways to build a pond: excavation or embankment—in other words, digging down or building up. The method you choose depends on the lay of the land and the properties of the underlying soil. The first step is to dig an 8-ft.- to 12-ft.-deep test hole at the pond site to expose the soil profile and see if it will hold water.

If you are digging out a wet or marshy area, the odds are that the subsoil will be a thick bed of impervious clay, which is the reason the wet spot is there in the first place. If so, your pond will certainly hold water and will be easy and relatively inexpensive to dig, because all the material pushed up out of the basin can be used to berm up the sides. If the soil is too gravelly or loose to hold water, you'll have to haul in better-quality dirt or waterproof the excavation with a synthetic membrane, akin to an aboveground pool,

or with a layer of bentonite, an expansive (and expensive) volcanic clay. (Or, in this case, it might make more sense and save more dollars to simply abandon the project.)

The dam for an embankment pond is built up on top of the pond site rather than dug down into it. This approach is most often used for sites that are deficient in suitably watertight soils and for special-purpose ponds, such as cranberry bogs, aquaculture installations, and stock or irrigation water storage. An added advantage is that draining a pond whose bottom is at ground level can be done by gravity rather than by pumping. Also, unlike an excavated pond, whose surface is often below the surrounding ground level, an embankment pond is less exposed to pollution from surface runoff (which might provide the main water source for an excavated pond).

The source water for ponds is easily polluted. Ponds that fill from ground-water seepage or from an actual spring are much less susceptible to contamination and much more likely to maintain their water level than ponds that rely mainly upon surface runoff. Take care to isolate the pond watershed so it is free from contamination by fertilizer runoff or animal manure. Fence out livestock. An encircling drainage swale, installed far enough away from the pond so as not to create a de facto embankment, will divert surface contamination. For the same reason, no matter how picturesque the temptation, never let ducks or geese swim in a people pond.

Before You Begin Digging

Before you call the excavator, call your local county extension office and talk to a USDA Soil Conservation Service staff member. He (or she) will design your pond (usually for free)—if, in fact, you can disturb the ground of your proposed pond site in the first place. The U.S. Army Corps of Engineers (USACE) has jurisdiction over wetlands, which it defines as "those areas that are inundated or saturated by surface or ground water at a frequency and duration sufficient to support and that under normal circumstances do support, a prevalence of vegetation typically adjusted for life in saturated soil conditions." So, simply bulldozing those bulrushes and cattails that are lining the scummy puddle in your meadow might land you in really deep federal doo-doo. There are also state and county water-quality regulations entwined with the federal protections.

Understanding what is or is not allowed and what, if any, permits are required isn't a job for the faint of heart. If you are, even for a moment, tempted to "dredge or dam a stream or wetlands to create a pond or lake," you are definitely within the purview of the permit process. Under the Swampbuster provision of the Food Security Act of 1985, you could even lose any USDA benefits or subsidies if you do bust one. In Western states, where there is a long tradition of wrangling over water rights, you could also run afoul of riparian law if you attempt to divert a watercourse to fill your pond. Contact the USACE's district office to schedule a site inspection from the local field office scientist—but don't assume that a pass at the federal level is also a pass at the state level.

Fish, on the other hand, are another matter. If your piscine preference is for trout, you'll need to build the deepest pond you can afford. Trout thrive only in cold water (30°F to 70°F), which requires a depth of at least 12 ft. to maintain year-round. A shallower pond will support warm-water species, such as bass, bluegills, and catfish, which thrive in water temperatures of 80°F to 90°F. Unlike trout, which must be restocked from year to year as pond water is too turbid for them to spawn, warm-water fish will breed. Bass are particularly desirable for keeping the frog population in check. They'll also do a number on juveniles of other species that normally would eat mosquitoes, so if you stock your pond with bass, you'll have a good ecological excuse to go fishin', too.

Water Conservation

Wherever you live, access to a reliable source of clean, safe drinking water is likely to become a growing problem, and water conservation will become an increasingly important issue. As Kelly Coyne and Erik Knutzen, authors of *The Urban Homestead* (Process, 2010), advise: "Take control of both your plumbing and your rainwater, whether you live in a suburban house in Phoenix or an apartment in Manhattan. By reducing our dependence on city water, we'll prepare our homesteads for possible water uncertainties on the horizon."

Urban Homesteading

There's much more that you can do to conserve water and reduce your dependence on municipal supplies than just fixing leaks and installing low-flow fixtures and water-saving, ENERGY-STAR℠ washing machines.

Capturing and storing rainwater for garden irrigation and other nonpotable household uses will increase your water self-sufficiency. You can also recycle grey water from the kitchen sink, bathtub, and washing machine to irrigate fruit trees, ornamentals, and sections of your garden. (Code-enforcement officials universally regard grey water with an alarm wildly disproportionate to any actual health threat, so your reclamation project will have to be under the table [or sink, as it were]). You need only minimal plumbing skills to extend the drain from the washing machine standpipe to a storage barrel outside the house. Stored grey water will become anaerobic quickly, so use any stored quantity within 24 hours.

When you tap into any drain line, install a three-way diverter valve or two standard PVC globe valves to retain the option of routing excess grey water to your sewer line as needed. If you plan to irrigate with grey water, make sure your laundry detergent is compatible with a grey-water system and is not just biodegradable. Phosphorus, in this case, is a desirable plant nutrient.

Suburban Homesteading

Roughly 60 percent of all residential water use is for "landscape purposes" (for watering the lawn and thirsty ornamental plants). In the arid Southwest, xeriscaping (with ornamental gravel and native water-hoarding plants) goes a long way toward curtailing this waste, but gardening on any but the smallest scale is just as water-intensive as that impractical green suburban sward.

The principles of permaculture will help you reduce your dependence on city water. With just a hand shovel, you can build a system of low berms and shallow swales that will turn your yard into a "rain farm," capturing water that would otherwise run off into the storm sewer. The dikes and ditches will impound the rainwater long enough for it to soak slowly into the ground, nourishing the roots of the vegetables and ornamentals planted on top of the berms.

The actual shutoff valve of a frost-free hydrant is located at the bottom of the standpipe, below frost depth.

In dry country, plant your vegetables in "depressed beds," the inverse of the raised beds that gardeners favor in wet climates. Form shallow troughs by dragging up soil from the centers of the rows to the sides. After the plants are established, mulch heavily. Flood the trenches every three days or so. The mulch will conserve water by slowing evaporation, which will retain soil moisture and reduce the need for watering. Gutters and downspouts feeding into an array of 55-gallon salvaged plastic drums, tapped with boiler drain valves at their bottoms, will supply free irrigation water during dry spells.

The Mini-Farm

One major logistical hassle for any small farming operation is getting adequate fresh, clean drinking water to livestock or poultry that are housed 100 yd. or more from the house or barn or are out on summer pasture. If you have only a few animals, it's not a big deal to haul one or two 5-gallon buckets on a garden tractor wagon. But if your chickens go through four 8-gallon waterers daily and the cows slurp up a bathtub full, you can spend a lot of time doing nothing but supplying your critters with fresh water.

Hoses—yards and yards of them—are the quick and dirty solution during the summer months. Black plastic polyethylene pipe is an expensive (albeit less flexible) alternative to daisy chains of hoses. Lay hoses directly on the ground or cable-tie them to a stretched-wire support. There's virtually no limit to the horizontal distance you can run your water line. Because pressure drops with height, vertical distance is another story. Whenever possible, run hoses or pipe downhill from the source. If you do, above ground lines will be usable until the hard freeze sets in (if you shut the water off and allow the hose to drain before nightfall). To have remote water year-round, bury the water line below frost level and attach it to a frost-proof hydrant at the outlet end. Having free-running water in the middle of winter sure beats breaking the ice out of frozen buckets.

BRADFORD WG LIBRARY
425 HOLLAND ST. W.
BRADFORD, ON L3Z 0J2

chapter iv

·················

Home Base

There's a lot more to homesteading than just the land—there's the "home" part of the stead. If you blow your entire budget on undeveloped land, how will you afford to build a house—or the barns, sheds, outbuildings, and fences that any small farming operation must have? Unfortunately, the cost of the land is still only a fraction of the cost of building a house from scratch, so there's good reason to look for an affordable piece of land that includes a standing house in at least marginally habitable condition.

The property you buy will probably bear little resemblance to the homestead of your dreams, especially if, like most folks seeking to move back to the land, you lack the capital and credit it takes to buy that fully realized ideal place. Even the proverbial "handyman's special," requiring only a dollop of "tender loving care" to reclaim its original glory, may be more "potential" than you can afford. But if you know where to look—and how to look beyond what you're looking at—your homestead dream may be more attainable than you might think.

The least-expensive real estate is, of course, the least appealing. We're talking about that shabby, single-wide mobile home rotting away in a weed-grown field, amidst the junk cars and sorry detritus of a rural meth-lab lifestyle—the sort of real estate that's just about 100 percent pure "potential." There are warts like this all over the face of rural America. Because most people just drive right on by, the asking price is likely to scrape the bottom of the local market. The seller may be desperate (or, as real estate agents put it, "motivated") to free himself from the tax burden or other carrying costs. The property may be in foreclosure, and the bank willing to cut a serious deal to clear it off their books.

Look beyond that run-down trailer, through the rusting scrap and old tires, to the land beneath it. Is there power and water? A good well? A functioning septic

···

Top: Our outbuilding complex.   Bottom left: Geraniums and a found driftwood sculpture grace the entry to our homestead.   Bottom right: One good reason to build your own home is for the fun of it.

system? Are there shade trees? Are there any trees or shrubs? Is the parcel just a lot or is there a bit of acreage? Is it tillable? Is there enough land for gardens and some livestock? What about the neighbors? Are their places in the same condition or worse? The goal is to find hospitable ground hidden beneath hideous real estate at a bargain-basement price.

Taking On an Old House

If the price is right, buying an abandoned or even working farmstead that includes an old house—slouching toward horizontal, but not yet so far gone that you can't live in it while restoring it to its former glory as time and finances permit—makes a lot of sense. If you're lucky, there's also a usable barn, shed, workshop, or other outbuilding.

More than likely, the plot on which the old farmhouse sits also includes some vestigial remnants of the old farmstead itself—a garden plot, flower beds, fruit and nut trees, a berry patch, a pond, an overgrown pasture with good fences, plantings of rhubarb, asparagus, horseradish, or perennial herbs. These remnants are gifts, not so much for what they are but for what they represent in terms of saving you time and effort. Each and every bit of infrastructure already in place is one more item checked off of your list of Things to Do, one less obstacle on the road to making your homestead dream a reality. If the buildings are already there, you can focus your attention on building your soil, raising your food, and creating a livelihood.

Keep in mind that, as the many horror stories about old-house "money pits" suggest, sometimes trying to renovate an old house can be an expensive and frustrating mistake. Any house can be fixed if you spend enough time and money, but unless you have more dollars than sense, you should know the difference between problems that are so bad that they make renovation unfeasible and problems that are formidable but worth the effort. As I point out in my book *Renovating Old Houses* (The Taunton Press, 2003), unless a house has actually started to collapse or its frame has rotted to powder or been digested by termites, there is rarely an old house so derelict that it isn't worth saving.

What to look for outside How to distinguish between an old house that will respond to a spoonful of TLC (Tender Loving Care), one that is in need of a major dose of TL (Tough Love), or one whose only hope is a TD (Teardown)? The rule of thumb is, a square house is a sound house.

Begin on the outside. Stand back some distance and look at the shape of the house. Sight along the ridgeline of the roof—is it straight or swaybacked, sagging noticeably in the middle? Does the edge of the roof hump upward or curve outward? Do the walls bow out or in? Are they parallel, or do they tilt at oddly skewed angles at the corners? "Read" the lines of clapboard siding. They were installed level, so any deviation is a sure sign of foundation settlement or other structural problems.

Foundation settlement is a serious problem. When the underlying foundation

The Importance of Being on the Same Page

Homesteading, whether in the suburbs or way out in the "puckerbush," is not normally a sport for singles. It's usually a joint venture, a partnership of like-minded persons in a committed relationship. Even the most well-funded venture will fail miserably in short order if both partners aren't "together," both in the sense of having it together and keeping it together personally and, more important, in the sense of being on the same page regarding the homesteading lifestyle.

Although superficially gender-specific, husbandry is a unisex vocation. If one of you doesn't share the other's passion for nurturing plants and animals, if one of you secretly believes that dirt is dirty or that life beyond the range of cell phone towers is intolerable, if one of you yearns for the distractions and actions of city life and despises the small talk of small towns or believes that children raised in the backwoods grow up backward, while the other can think of no greater happiness and satisfaction than knocking the ice out of the chicken's water pail in the dark of dawn or curling up on a bone-crunchingly cold winter's night in front of the woodstove with *War and Peace* and would rather have a finished barn and frost-proof water supply than nice furniture and clean floors, your venture is doomed to miserable failure. It may take only a single season, or it make take several years, but if you don't wear each other smooth, you'll eventually rub each other raw. The time to discuss your goals and dreams is before you make the move, not after, when you might discover, to your dismay, that your dream is your partner's nightmare.

---

gives way, the house above has no choice but to follow. Rotted sill beams produce the same results. Check the above-grade portion of the foundation walls for cracks and other signs of settlement. The exact extent of the condition can be confirmed by an internal examination of the cellar.

As is true of house walls, foundation walls should not bow in or out. Cellar bulkheads or entryways are a common trouble spot. Unless they were properly constructed to minimize frost damage and the cellar hatch was kept watertight, cellar walls can fail and push in the main foun-

dation. The grade should slope away from the foundation. If not, surface runoff will flow back against the walls and into the cellar. Examine any window wells and/or cellar vent windows to be sure they don't allow water into the cellar.

Except for the northernmost or highest altitudes, termite infestation is a potential problem throughout the continental United States. Termites can be hard to detect, let alone to prevent or repair their damage. These insects build earthen tubes from the soil up the foundation walls in search of edible wood—you might spot

"A city man is at home anywhere, for all big cities are much alike. But a country man has a place where he belongs, where he always returns, and where, when the time comes, he is willing to die."
—Edward Abbey

them, but most termite infestations go undetected until major damage is done. Make sure your purchase agreement includes a guarantee that the house was inspected and found to be free of active termites. Even so, when you gut the walls during renovation, you may uncover framing, subflooring, and structural framing that have been riddled by the excavations of exterminated colonies. This sort of unwelcome discovery is what turned our son's tough-love renovation in Santa Barbara into a total teardown.

Carpenter ants and other wood-boring or consuming insects, such as powder-post beetles, damage framing and sheathing in regions too cold to support termites. Deposits of coarse sawdust at the entrance of a tunnel are a sign of damage by carpenter ants. Piles of frass (fine powdery sawdust) indicate infestation by wood-boring beetles. Most infestations can be arrested with good ventilation to dry out damp cellars. If you suspect insect problems (and the seller has provided no documentation of a recent inspection), make the closing of the sale contingent upon professional certification that the house is bug free.

While you are still poking around the outside of the house, examine the windows.

The glass more than likely will be in need of reglazing, which is time-consuming and tedious but not expensive or difficult. Examine the sash (the wood frames that hold the glass), particularly along the bottom edges and corners. If there is rot that is not too severe, it can be dug out and filled with epoxy patching or replaced with new milled sash.

Also check the windowsills. There's likely to be at least some rot where the sill abuts the casing boards and sash. Often, water works its way down behind the sill or the drip cap at the top of the window. If left unchecked, the underlying wall sheathing—and even the wall studs and sill beam—may have rotted away. If the clapboards at the bottom of the wall appear rotten, there's a good chance that the underlying structure has rotted away, too. Sills under door thresholds are especially vulnerable to rot, as are wall areas behind steps or any other locale that traps water or snow. Fortunately, repairing localized areas of decay isn't expensive or especially difficult.

Be especially wary of "buttress" walls. In the attempt to shore up a heaved foundation or to prevent surface runoff and wind from infiltrating, some old-time builders would pour a sloped concrete wall directly against the unmortared stones of the above-grade portion of the foundation. Because the wall seldom extended more than a few inches below ground, frost action could easily push up the wall and break it. Even worse, because the builder often poured the concrete directly against the siding or sheathing boards, the wall is an ideal incubator for rot. If you can easily penetrate the sheathing boards with an ice pick, extensive sill replacement is almost guaranteed.

Evaluate any attached sheds, ells, or porches. These structures were often tacked onto a main structure as an afterthought, in a lackadaisical manner, with inferior materials. They often rest on unstable foundations, sometimes little more than a jumble of rough stones lying directly on the ground. The addition will likely have racked and settled noticeably and may even have pulled away from the main house. Water entering into the resulting open wound will have done its damage. Depending on how far gone the structure is, the only sensible fix is often demolition and rebuilding.

Assess the roof. Note the roofing material and its condition. Moss-covered crumbling wood shingles and asphalt shingles that are cracked, swollen, and brittle will have to be removed and replaced. If the underlying metal is still sound, rusted steel roofing can be restored to years of useful life with an asphalt-based coating or antirust paint. Check the vertical seams between the roofing sheets. Over the years, the contraction and expansion of the metal will work the old style "lead head" nails loose to the point where they are no longer

watertight and no longer anchored in the underlying wood. You'll have to pull the old nails and secure the roofing with leak-proof neoprene-gasket hex-head roofing screws. Slate roofing lasts a very long time, but eventually it weathers away. Long before that, individual slates will break or split from ice damage or internal faults. You can replace broken slates to prolong the life of the roof. As long as you're not afraid of heights and are comfortable working from "chicken" ladders or narrow staging planks, re-roofing is something any moderately skilled do-it-yourselfer can easily manage.

Try to determine the condition of the chimneys, with the help of binoculars or the zoom lens of your camera. Look for obvious signs of trouble—for example, cracks, missing and loose bricks, or deteriorated or missing flashing metal between the chimney and the roofing. Look for signs of a tile flue liner, which you should see projecting an inch or two above the top of the chimney cap. (A four- or six-brick-per-course chimney will almost always be unlined. More than six bricks per course indicate multiple flues or a very large single flue. As a rule, old chimneys lacked flue tiles; mortar parging sealed the flue.) An unlined chimney is a fire and carbon-monoxide-poisoning hazard. You'll either have to retrofit the chimney with a liner and seal the chimney or tear the chimney down and replace it— in any case, it's a big, expensive job. Flue liners are proprietary systems installed by licensed professionals. Retrofitting flue tiles is best left to a skilled mason.

Examine the siding and exterior trim. Bear in mind that, like an undertaker's cosmetic, a fresh coat of paint is a notoriously effective sleight-of-hand technique for boosting the selling price while avoiding basic repairs. The condition of the paint is a clue as to possible problems with insulation and moisture within the wall cavities. If a wall is inadequately insulated or vapor retardant, water vapor moves through it and eventually loosens the bond between the paint film and the siding, causing it to blister. If you see several courses of small, circular plastic plugs at regular intervals in the siding, the wall cavities have been filled with cellulose or fiberglass insulation, blown in from the outside. That's a good thing. The only drawback is that it's seldom possible— working blind, as it were—to find and fill every cavity hidden behind the walls. (Some professionals use infrared scans to detect voids.)

If the clapboards or wood shingles are so badly split and weathered that they reveal the underlying sheathing, they have outlived their usefulness. Removing a small section of deteriorated wood siding without escalating the damage requires finesse and experience. If more than small areas have decayed, wholesale removal and re-siding are probably in order. "Clear" paint-grade clapboard in particular and most wood siding in general are labor intensive and costly to repair. Asphalt composition and aluminum or vinyl siding were often applied directly over original clapboards, which may still be quite sound but for a coat of paint.

Cement-asbestos shingles were a siding "improvement" widely used during the 1930s and '40s. Although brittle, they are also fireproof, freeze-thaw stable, and will basically last forever. You can safely repair or replace individual damaged or missing shingles. They're no longer manufactured, but specialty roofing suppliers carry them or gypsum-cement replacements. If your cement-asbestos shingles are in good shape, it's better to leave them alone than to replace them with more handsome siding. Although they are not considered hazardous by the Occupational Safety and Health Administration (OSHA) or the Environmental Protection Agency (EPA), because these shingles contain asbestos, their removal and disposal are regulated by most states. In effect, you'll need to hire an expensive licensed asbestos-abatement contractor to remove them.

The various elements of decorative trim at the edges of the roof that form the cornice serve as more than mere embellishment. The eave (bottom edge) and rake (side edge) overhangs help divert the water that drains off the roof away from the walls and foundation. Deteriorated trim allows water to seep into the walls, fostering mold and decay. Squirrels, birds, bats, and other pests can sneak into the attic and wall cavities through holes in rotten trim. Reconstructing a cornice, particularly at the "return," where the cornice meets the corner trim, is a skilled and finicky job that requires expensive "clear" lumber, if you intend to do it properly.

Finally, check the condition of the service drop, the overhead cable that runs

Service Drop Inspection

Check the condition of all elements at the house end. The span from the power pole to the weatherhead is the electric company's responsibility.

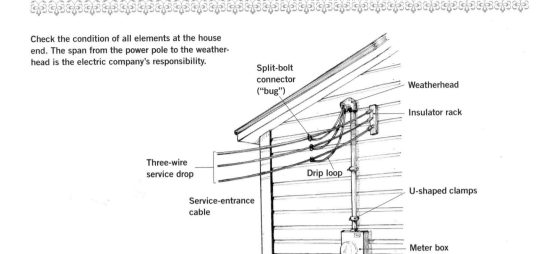

Split-bolt connector ("bug")

Weatherhead

Insulator rack

Three-wire service drop

Drip loop

Service-entrance cable

U-shaped clamps

Meter box

Service mast

from the transformer at the utility pole to the weatherhead (the metal pipe above the electric meter box). Check the cable either at an attachment insulator high up on the gable wall of the house or at the service mast along an eave. Make sure the cable doesn't rub against any tree limbs. It should be at least 18 ft. above any public roadway, 12 ft. above a driveway, 10 ft. above a sidewalk, 8 ft. above any porches or other flat roofs, and 3 ft. above any roof slope of 4/12 or more. Check that the service mast is straight and braced to the roof or that the attachment insulator is likewise securely anchored to the building wall. From the power pole to the splice at

the weatherhead, the service drop is the exclusive province of the electric company, and they must make any changes or repairs. The homeowner is responsible for the rest of the drop—from the weatherhead on down into the meter box and from there into the house. Check that the plastic jacket of the service-entrance cable is intact. Old-fashioned cloth-covered, rubber-insulated cable is likely to be frayed and cracked and should probably be replaced for safety's sake. Connectors at the meter socket and building penetrations should be watertight.

What to look for in the cellar If your outside inspection failed to reveal any deal killers, move on to the next step, the internal exam. Pay no attention to the charming "country" details, the cheerful wallpaper, or the beautifully refinished wide floorboards that the real estate agent is pointing out. Proceed, instead, directly to the cellar, where the true condition of the house will be revealed. Bring a flashlight. The cellars in most old houses lack adequate or even working lights—and you'll need the flashlight for close examination of the sills and joists, in any case.

Are the cellar stairs too steep or narrow to allow safe or convenient passage? Are the treads and stair carriage sound or rotten? If so, don't be alarmed—just take note. What you are really looking for are signs of water infiltration and the true extent of any suspected foundation problems. If you see standing water on the cellar floor, venture no further. Water in the cellar is a big black mark on the scorecard. Unless you are prepared to sink a great deal of time and money into a new foundation or a retrofitted perimeter drain system, look for another old house to play with.

There's good reason to go house hunting in the spring when the water table is at its highest level. Any seasonal infiltration problems should be obvious, although after a spell of dry weather they may not be. If the cellar appears to be dry, look for high-water marks or mineral stains on the walls and cellar posts or for signs of rot at the bottom of posts. You have to replace rotted posts. Examine the foundation walls. Check that the masonry or poured concrete is free of extensive

cracks, indicators of settlement or heaving. If there are cracks, are parts of the wall bowed in or tilted? If the walls are mortared or dry-laid (unmortared) stone, are they intact or have portions fallen in? Look for evidence of earth that's washed through the wall joints and onto the cellar floor. The settlement or heaving of the foundation wall almost always necessitates replacement, in whole or in part.

Water in the basement is not always a guaranteed sign of foundation trouble. An earth-floored cellar is always likely to be damp in the spring. (There isn't much you can do about it, short of covering the floor with a layer of crushed stone, topped with a filter fabric, an inch of sand, a vapor barrier, and a poured concrete slab.) Basement water can also indicate runoff that is saturating the ground adjacent to the exterior of the foundation wall and percolating through it—especially true with dry-laid stone foundations. If you're lucky, regrading to divert that water away from the foundation will solve the problem, but in most cases the only permanent cure may be to excavate down to the footings and install perimeter drain pipes.

If you haven't found signs of water trouble, continue the cellar inspection. Check the cellar beams, joists, and underside of the floorboards for insect damage and rot. Look for active frass deposits, which will be light colored with a flour-like texture; inactive frass is yellowish and caked. Probe the extent of the decay with an ice pick.

Dry rot (which might more properly be called "wet rot," as it's caused by a fungus that requires moisture to survive) turns wood into something that resembles soft, reddish charcoal. Dry rot is a particular problem on the bottom of sills, where the wood absorbs moisture via capillary action from the stones or concrete. Finding significant decay on the cellar side of a sill is a sure sign that the problem will be even worse on the outside of the sill. Replacing sills isn't as difficult or costly as replacing the foundation, but it's not a pleasant way to spend a summer's worth of weekends. If the ends of carrying beams, floor joists, and sections of floor are also rotted or insect damaged, there had better be something truly special about the property and its price, with the house thrown in basically as a "freebie" to sweeten the deal. It's a question of how you prefer to squander your resources.

remove the panel cover. The terminals on the service-cable side of the main breaker are always "hot," even when the breaker is switched off. (It's a good idea to stand on a piece of plywood or a plastic pail,

> "Short of having a baby, . . . there's little else most of us can do in our lives that involves a greater commitment, requires more energy and expense, or is potentially more rewarding than building one's own house."
>
> —George Nash, Do-It-Yourself Housebuilding

especially in a damp, earth-floored cellar, when doing any work around live electrical panels.)

When you're poking at the beams, take a look at the service panel. This gray steel box is the heart (or, to be more metaphorically precise, the brain) of the electrical system. Open the door to check the rating of the main breaker and the number of circuits—100 amps with 24 available circuits is the bare minimum for a modern house. Very carefully unscrew and

Look for signs of obvious problems—burned or corroded terminals, charred wire, cracked or chipped breakers, evidence of water damage. Rust in the panel or on steel-jacketed cables or steel outlet boxes are all danger signs. Electrical connections that are exposed to moisture corrode. Corroded connections create increased resistance, and resistance creates heat. Corroded connections are more than just a fire hazard. They also cause a faulty ground, which could, under the wrong conditions, electrocute someone.

Although there is no requirement to replace old electrical work just because it's old, the National Electrical Code (NEC) does quite sensibly require you to correct any potentially life-threatening deficiencies. The most likely culprit is the wiring itself. Until the adoption of plastic insulation in the late 1940s and early '50s, electrical-cable conductors were insulated with rubber, which begins breaking down after 25 years or so. You'll still find old houses with some parts of the original rubber-insulated cable still in use. Be aware that, when the house owner or real-estate agent attests that the electrical system has been upgraded, it's likely that the old fuse panel has been replaced with modern circuit breakers but the old cable and most of the original wiring hidden behind walls and ceilings hasn't been touched. If the insulation on the cable conductors is plastic and not rubber, however, the original components might not present a danger.

The number and kinds of possible wiring defects in an old house can easily fill a book (in fact, a very good book, *Your Old Wiring* by David E. Shapiro [McGraw-Hill, 2000], is a must-have if you are thinking of buying an old house with old wiring). If the house's existing system must be replaced, most electricians will insist on ripping everything out and starting over rather than attempting piecemeal repairs. That's a good strategy, particularly if you intend to do the work yourself. It is a lot easier and safer (and cheaper, if you're paying an electrician) to wire from scratch than to troubleshoot and repair existing wiring. As a homeowner, you can legally rewire your own residence as long as the work you do meets code and passes inspection (even without inspection, the work should still meet code for safety's sake).

The cellar is also a good place to ascertain the condition of the plumbing system. The history of the system is evident in the successive accretions of materials and methods, especially those in the drain-

Buyer Beware

If your old house is not connected to a public sewer line, the seller's disclosure documents must indicate the type of on-site disposal system and the presence of any problems. The same disclosure is required for the water supply and, depending on the state and the real estate forms, a host of other information, such as asbestos and radon pollution. Sellers can be liable for fraud if they knowingly make a false statement, so you can safely assume that if the documents claim that there is a septic tank and leach field on the property, there probably is.

There is a potentially troubling loophole, however. Sellers must state whether they are "aware" of any problems with the item in question. It's not altogether inconceivable for a seller to be "unaware" of a problem that has no paper trail or that was never tested. *Caveat emptor.* If there's a lush patch of vegetation or, worse, foul-smelling water seeping out of the ground in the general area where the leach field is supposed to be, no matter what the disclosure documents say, there's a problem with the septic system (and it's likely a very expensive one to fix).

age system. The original cast-iron bell-and-spigot drain line with its caulked and leaded joints may still be intact. At some point, copper or galvanized iron pipe may have been grafted onto it. During more recent renovations, most if not all of the original drain lines may have been replaced with PVC (white/tan) or ABS (black) pipe and fittings. Whether these changes and upgrades were done according to code or not is the question. Although improperly vented drains or fixture traps can allow noxious (and flammable) sewer gas to infiltrate the house, unlike electrical problems, defects in domestic plumbing aren't usually life-threatening. (Although there are situations in which potable water can be contaminated by waste water or toxic leachate from old lead pipes or solder. In the case of the former, you could get a very nasty case of diarrhea; in the latter, you'll eventually go mad.) Corroded or clogged old pipes also leak, drain slowly, or back up into sinks and tubs. Ultimately, an old house's plumbing problems are caused either by obsolete or deteriorated materials or by illicit and improper work by unlicensed contractors or ignorant home handymen, who are responsible for the unique and often bizarre examples of creative plumbing so often found in old houses.

High-quality cast-iron pipe can last a century or more, which means that any surviving cast-iron drainpipe in an old house plumbed before 1930 is on its last legs. Corrosive minerals in the water, grease buildup and settlement that traps water, and low-grade iron in the original manufacture all conspire to rust out the pipe from the inside. Look for signs of patching. Tap the pipe with a hammer—sound pipe will ring, rotten pipe will produce a dull tone (or shatter, so be careful!). Make sure hangers adequately support the drains and prevent sagging. Check the leaded joints for signs of leaks.

You can pretty much assume that any galvanized-steel supply lines are afflicted by some stage of blockage and will eventually have to be replaced. Copper tubing is a lot less vulnerable to the buildup of mineral deposits that clog steel pipe. Look for corrosion at connections between these (and other) dissimilar metals. In cold climates, if the water is turned off, look for bulges, splits, or separated joints—all of which are signs of frozen pipes. If the water supply is turned on, open a tap and check for adequate flow. The hallmark of a low-budget installation is the use of $1/2$-in. tubing throughout. Better systems use $3/4$-in. main lines with $1/2$-in. fixture risers (which prevents you from being scalded while showering if someone flushes a toilet or opens the kitchen faucet).

Given the cost of replumbing an entire house professionally, it's probably easier to live with a deficient system that is still functional and fix only those things that absolutely need fixing. Or you may want to gut the house, tear out the old system, and replace it with a new, legal, and more-efficient system. You can plumb your own house, too, as long as you follow the code and satisfy the inspector.

Note the condition of the furnace or boiler (a furnace heats air; a boiler heats

water). Unless there are service records to the contrary, you can safely assume that it's been some time since either has had a tune-up or inspection. You need a professional to assess the condition and overall performance of a heating system, but there are a few obvious symptoms of trouble. A dirty air filter suggests that regular maintenance was not a high priority. A blower fan that squeaks or vibrates excessively indicates worn shaft bearings. Old units are less efficient than modern ones, but it usually doesn't pay to replace a functioning furnace or boiler just because it is old and inefficient. The payback just takes too long, and there are cost-effective fixes that can boost the efficiency of the existing unit. The normal service life of a furnace or boiler is about 20 years. Beyond that, there's no harm in just waiting for it to die—but be aware that the old thing is most likely to give up the ghost on the coldest night of the year.

Cooling systems are even more opaque to the inquiring amateur than furnaces, but you can at least check the cooling fins of the outside compressor unit. They should be clean and free of clogging debris. Note the condition of the insulated coolant lines, too. Let the system run long enough to deliver maximum cooling. If the temperature drop is insufficient, the refrigerant probably needs to be recharged—another job for the service person. In the arid Southwest, many homes employ evaporative coolers (called swamp coolers) in tandem with or in lieu of air conditioners. These typically roof-mounted units require regular maintenance. The cool-

ing pads must be replaced when clogged with the mineral plaque deposited by the evaporated cooling water. The plug-in water pump module requires periodic replacement, too, and the fan belt and motor pulleys also require attention. When the galvanized-steel cooler enclosure eventually rusts out, the entire unit will need to be replaced. It's always a good idea to climb up onto the roof to inspect the swamp cooler up close.

Water heaters have a much shorter service life than furnaces and boilers, especially when located in a damp basement. Depending on the quality of the tank liner and the mineral content of the water, 7 to 12 years is considered a normal life span. If the heater doesn't have a dated installation tag, your local plumbing and heating distributor may be able to establish its age from the make, model, and serial number. Look for rust and signs of leakage at the bottom of the tank. Remove the element covers of electric heaters (carefully, because the exposed terminals on the thermostat are "hot") and look for corrosion and leakage around the fittings. For gas-fired heaters, remove the burner access plate at the bottom of the unit to check for rust and leaks. Check the flue pipe for corrosion, too.

What to look for in the attic If your tour of the cellar hasn't convinced you to abandon all hope, proceed to the attic, the second most important stop on your inspection itinerary. Is the attic accessible via stairwell or a hatch in the ceiling? (Converting an unfinished attic into living space is a lot easier if you don't have to rearrange rooms and hallways to get to it.) Check for signs of daylight or water leakage (stains, molds, or rot) on the underside of the roof-sheathing boards and along the rafter bottoms and tops of the walls. Do the roof rafters sag noticeably at midspan? Are they spaced more than 2 ft. apart? Is the attic floored over or open? Is there any insulation between the attic floor joists? Keep in mind that the attic is the easiest and cheapest part of the house in which to retrofit insulation, so if there's no insulation in the attic, there's probably none in the walls either. Chances are good that if there is insulation, it isn't thick enough. Does the insulation block air circulation at the soffit (the underside of the cornice along the eaves)? Unless the previous owner already retrofitted a soffit vent, it will be up to you to provide this crucial component of proper attic ventilation. If heating and cooling air ducts are routed through the attic, are they properly insulated to reduce energy loss?

If there is a masonry chimney in the attic, does it appear sound? Creosote stains on the brickwork indicate dangerously deteriorated mortar and an unlined chimney. The chimney will either have to be relined or demolished and rebuilt. There are a number of proprietary systems for safely relining chimneys with cementitious materials or with flexible stainless-steel flue pipe. A skilled mason can also retrofit an unlined chimney with fire-clay flue tiles. The process of relining a chimney is typically an expensive proposition that requires materials and equipment that are unavailable to the homeowner. Demo-

lition of an unsound chimney is messy but straightforward. If you're a skilled do-it-yourselfer, building a new chimney isn't necessarily something you couldn't attempt, but working within the confines of existing walls or removing walls for access can get complicated and expensive.

What to look for inside Now look through the rest of the house. Are the walls plastered or covered with generic wood paneling? One of the strongest arguments in favor of a total demolition is the presence of significant areas of bulging, loose, crumbling, or fallen plaster on walls and ceilings. You can patch and repair small areas of unsound plaster. Are there original floorboards buried beneath the carpet or plywood underlayment? Vintage, wide floorboards are a treasure, and refinishing them is worth the effort.

Any house built before 1979 probably has asbestos and lead paint in it somewhere. Depending on the composition of the native bedrock, there's a possibility of radon contamination in the cellar, too. The disclosure documents must report the date and results of any tests or attest to the seller's knowledge or lack thereof of the presence of these substances. Asbestos pipe and boiler insulation would be obvious sources. Asbestos in textured ceiling finishes, floor tiles, and drywall joint compound is less obvious. The good news is that asbestos is only harmful if it is friable, that is, loose and crumbly enough to release airborne particles that can be inhaled. As long as the material is intact, it isn't a hazard and should be left alone. The bad news is, if you have

The Bottom Line

The usual advice is to avoid houses with major defects, such as failed foundations or extensive structural rot that would require difficult and expensive repairs. That's good advice indeed, but if the "stead" portion of a questionable homestead property is otherwise ideal, and the price is right, and you have the necessary skill set and confidence to pull it off, I wouldn't necessarily recommend against signing on the dotted line.

We've been there, more than once. Our Maine homestead had gently sloping open fields with rich, well-drained soil, mature apple trees, a grape arbor, decent pasture, an extensive stand of fence-post cedars and mixed hardwoods, a large greenhouse and attached heated workshop, and—the cherry on the sundae—almost 900 ft. of frontage on the tidal estuary of the Penobscot River, with the requisite soul-stirring sunset view. Situated at the end of a long drive, the property was private, yet only a short drive from the town center and shopping.

The house was habitable, but not by much. The real estate agent's "cute and cozy" was code for "cramped and crooked." Fortunately, most of the wiring had been upgraded, the plumbing was adequate, and the furnace worked (at least that first winter). The airtight woodstove that had been retrofitted into the fireplace opening grudgingly kept the house from freezing. The dirt-floored cellar barely had enough headroom to stand up in, and rivulets came through the unmortared foundation stones whenever it rained. The well pressure tank was a bladderless galvanized tank on its last legs, and, as we discovered the following spring, the leach field was a lush patch of grass at the end of a straight pipe. Although the core of the house was a basically solid 1830s timber frame, the dormers, porches, and other subsequent accretions were of uniformly shoddy construction. The wood-shingle siding was badly weathered, and the exterior trim needed replacement.

We went back and forth over whether it was wiser to renovate and add on or just to get by until we could build a new house elsewhere on the property. We were looking at a considerable outlay of time and money either way, on top of a budget we had pretty well maxed out buying the place. So, for the next few years, the question was moot. We had no choice but to live in the house we had and focus our energy on our gardens and grounds. (Sadly, we never did resolve the dilemma. Following a prolonged illness, a business setback, and a change of employment, we sold our ideal homestead and moved onto a 1/3-acre village lot and into a circa 1900 house that needed little more than new paint, refinished floors, and a few other cosmetic repairs.)

friable asbestos, dealing with it will be very expensive.

Like asbestos, lead paint causes no ill effects until it deteriorates. Lead is chronically released onto household surfaces by abrasion at the edges of moving window sashes and door casings, and sporadically released whenever surfaces are scraped for repainting. Because the exterior of most houses is routinely repainted at least once every decade, any surviving layers of lead paint are safely buried under at least one coat of lead-free paint. Lead-laden chips and dust from previous painting prep, however, likely lie buried in the soil next to the house walls and is in the dust that blows into the house through open windows. (There are definite downsides to renovating old houses.)

Taking the plunge Now you need to face the demon. How badly do you want this place? If the foundation has fallen in, the sill beams are rotten, the mechanical systems antiquated and corroded, the roofing threadbare, the walls a tissue, any reasonably sane person would stop, not pass "Go," and look for a kinder, gentler house to fall in love with. But what's love got to do with it when the price is right?

The character of an old house is more than the sum of its architecture. Bringing a house back to useful life, delving into the grain and gristle of its structure, connecting with the spirits of its former inhabitants, who, like wood smoke from the kitchen stove, have been absorbed into the plaster on the walls, has got to be worth something. A restored old house can be a restorative island of peace amidst the chaotic storm of overwhelming details and mindless, grinding labors.

Take heart. Although it may require major structural repairs that must be finished before other more cosmetic work can commence, very few structural repairs—other than patching a leaky roof—must be undertaken immediately. After all, unless the house has been abandoned for a long time, someone had been living in it until you decided to buy it. It may not be comfortable, it certainly won't be *House Beautiful* worthy, but it is, at least, livable. In the meantime, you can focus on more important projects, such as fixing up the old barn out back, fencing the pasture, and putting in the garden.

Developing a realistic long-term plan based on your priorities and goals will go a long way toward preserving your sanity. So will cultivating a certain Zen-like sense of acceptance when it dawns on you that things will be going pretty well if you can finish up your June work by the end of September.

Building from Scratch

For many folks, building their own house is a major, and sometimes the most important, part of their homesteading dream. The literature of do-it-yourself house building has always echoed the tropes of self-discovery: home improvement as self-improvement. There are many good reasons to build a house from scratch rather than move into an existing house. For example, your potential homestead site may be blessed with all the features and qualities you desire but not have any buildings on it (a minor detail, when viewed through suitably rose-tinted spectacles).

Building a house presupposes a great deal of infrastructure, which, if not already on-site, must be built, installed, or otherwise provided by the would-be builder—or, more precisely, by the various subcontractors who have the knowledge, equipment, and licenses to do the job. The vital necessities (a road or driveway, utili-

house all by yourself can take a very long time. A period of two or three years is not unusual. In my case it was 12 years before the last few "details" were finally finished. If one could monetize the endless hours of worry, stress, and yes, strife, endured over the course of the enterprise and charge it against the putative savings of owner building, the "sweat equity" would be a net loss.

"Warmed by the fire from wood you cut and split, you sit down at the table in the house you built, to eat the food you grew, and you suddenly realize, 'Hey, I made this, and it's good!'"

ties or easy access to them, a drilled well or other water source, a septic system or at least approved plans for one, a cleared and accessible building site), whose absence can really complicate your quest for the simple life, make up a big chunk of the building budget.

The time spent scaling the learning curve can also be expensive. Unlike contractors, who build houses for their livelihood, few ordinary folks have the luxury of suspending their lives to dedicate at least nine months, and more likely twice that, exclusively to the work of building their house. Squeezed between the need to earn a living (or at least pay the subcontractors and building supply dealer) and the need to maintain some semblance of ordinary life (tending to family, children, and spouse), building your own

Reasons to build There are good reasons to build your own house, however, even with the added costs of infrastructure (such as roads, driveways, utility services, and water supply and waste-disposal systems) and of the passage of time. With common sense, judicious "book learning," and a bit of luck, you can save a substantial amount of money just by doing your own contracting. As an added bonus, the more of your own labor you can contribute, the more you can save in the costs of subcontractors and carpenters.

Off-the-shelf building materials account for roughly 60 percent of the cost of a modest modern home, so if you do all the work yourself (but for excavation —including the septic system—and well drilling), you can theoretically realize an overall savings of up to 40 percent.

If you build with logs, lumber, or stone that you've harvested from your own land or with homemade adobe brick or cordwood, you can save a lot more (although "alternative" construction techniques—as opposed to standard "stick framing"—tend to be extremely labor-intensive). Straw-bale construction, however, which initially provided both labor and cost savings, has become popular enough to drive the cost of straw bales through the roof.

One of the best reasons for building your own house is quality control or, to put it another way, getting your money's worth. Doing it yourself frees you (to some extent) from the pressures of tight scheduling and a locked-in contract agreement, so you can make changes as better ideas occur or as mistakes become obvious. You can scrounge used materials, shop for bargains, and incorporate serendipitous finds and inspirations into the structure as they arise. Unlike contractors, you can afford to take all the time you need to do it right. With the caution that comes from inexperience, you'll likely tend to overbuild, rather than cut corners.

Unlike renovating an existing house, building from scratch also allows you to design a house specifically tailored to your needs. Like a nautilus, you can build your house in stages, starting with a small, affordable core, designed for future expansion and additions as circumstances demand or allow. You can easily incorporate passive-solar space- and water-heating systems and state-of-the-art energy-efficient and sustainable materials and technologies into the construction—much

Our workshop garage sits between the garden and the house.

harder to do with an old house. If you intend to live "off the grid," in fact, it's best to build from scratch.

Ultimately, the very best reason to build your own house is for the pleasure of it. As I've said elsewhere, by giving public shape to private dreams, the act of home-building is a creative, challenging, and socially valued form of applied art. The reward of your hard labor is in the satisfaction of standing back and looking at the results. Warmed by the fire from wood you cut and split, you sit down at the table in the house you built, to eat the food you grew, and you suddenly realize, "Hey, I made this, and it's good!"

Temporary housing Ideally, that mobile home you've found on the property will still be, if not exactly well appointed, at least habitable, so you can live in it while you build your dream house. (Or, at the very least, you can use the likely considerable cost of demolition and removal of it as a bargaining chip with the seller.) Even if it's too far gone for human habitation, an old mobile home can still house livestock or store equipment and supplies. A mobile home is also quick and easy to renovate. Gut the walls down to the frame, rip up the moldy carpeting, install new insulation, drywall, and floor tile, and you've got tolerable coach-class accommodations.

If there are not other habitable structures on the property you buy, you might

consider buying a mobile home. Vintage, single-wide mobile homes in conditions ranging from "owned by a little old lady who only drove it on Sundays" to "teenage boy learned to drive on it" can often be had for a few hundred to a few thousand dollars or best offer. The same money that

our site to live in while we were building our house. When we were done with it, we purchased a building lot, moved the trailer there, and completely renovated it, adding a pitched roof, real wood siding, a deck, new interior finishes, and trim work. Then we sold it as a low-cost "starter

"Down in the jungle/Living in a tent/Better than a prefab/No rent!"
—*Iona & Peter Opie,* Language and Lore of Schoolchildren

buys you a run-down mobile home can also net you a 15- to 20-year-old travel trailer in even better shape.

The term "single-wide mobile home" is something of a misnomer, as their 8-ft. width is rather narrow, which works in your favor. Eight feet is the legal limit for moving a structure along public roads. Beyond that, you need a wide-vehicle permit (or one of the expensive professional mobile-home transport companies that has them). You can tow an 8- by 48-footer onto your site with a farm tractor or a standard four-wheel-drive pickup truck. With a little advance planning, you can lay out the mobile home's power, phone, and water hookups so they'll convert to permanent hookups with a minimal disruption of service. Chemical toilets, rented Port-O-Lets®, or a properly constructed pit privy will postpone the immediate need for a conventional on-site waste-disposal system.

We moved the 14 by 70 mobile home that we inherited from Jane's father onto

home." Our modestly profitable foray into real-estate development convinced us that mobile homes, like turkeys, often suffer from a bum rap.

Building an outbuilding to live in temporarily is another strategy that allows you to build your house free from the pressures of time. This rude shelter, the simplest and most utilitarian cabin you can afford, can eventually become a garage, workshop, guest house, rental or apprentice apartment, or livestock shelter.

One option for temporary housing or storage is a recycled fiberglass or steel shipping container. These rugged, waterproof, stackable 8-ft.-wide modules are available in 20-ft. or 40-ft. units. Set on concrete blocks or treated timbers, they provide an instant livestock shelter or storage facility. With a little ingenuity and a reciprocating saw (to cut openings for windows and door), some rigid-foam panel insulation and drywall, basic wiring (or not), and a small wood or propane gas heater, you can transform one into a utilitarian, postmodern-style homestead-er's cabin. Because of its durability and the high demand, the price of a container is considerably higher than that of a much larger and more functional used mobile home.

The trouble with "temporary" houses is that they sometimes morph into per-manent ones before you get around to building your "real" house. Trust me on this. My present house began as a 16 by 20 roadside workshop, a rough-framed structure built on a concrete slab. It had running water but no indoor toilet, a sheet-metal woodstove, minimal wiring, and salvaged window sashes. I threw it together in less than two weeks, working with a generator and hand-held power tools. The plan was to live in it until I could build my castle upon the hillside pasture. Thirty-six years, three major and several minor additions, multiple renovations (with more still to come), and thousands of hours and dollars later, the hillside is still pastured, and my former cottage is the dining room of a housing complex that contains two stories, four bedrooms, a wrap-around greenhouse/sunspace, attached garage, root cellar, woodshed, decks, studio apartment, and a 500-plus-sq.-ft. workshop shed.

This process would have been perfectly satisfactory had I built my future work-shop on my future homesite—but, like a tumor, it took root where it had no busi-ness being. The hillside offered breath-taking and spiritually uplifting vistas of ridges and valleys lapping against the shores of distant mountains. The roadside location had industrial conveniences and a truncated prospect of a field, obscured by forest walls.

My exculpatory explanation is extenuat-ing circumstances: Jane entered my life with three children from her first mar-riage. Small as they were, they were too large to sleep in the laundry hamper or under the desk. I built the first addition almost as a reflex. I established momen-tum, and Plan A faded like a blueprint left out in the rain. Sometimes the fabric of your life seems to unravel faster than you can knit it back together.

Rule of thumb? If you decide to opt for temporary housing, stick to a mobile home or travel trailer. If you don't want to convert it for other purposes, it can be sold or hauled away when the house is finished. Failing this, at least build your temporary housing in the right place and design it intentionally, as the seed of fu-ture additions. If you adhere to this plan, you'll be honoring a venerable home-steading tradition. Many a sprawling old farmhouse is a one-room cabin at heart.

Staying Sane

At first, building your house is a welcome thing. Full of energy and enthusiasm, blissfully unaware of how much work lies ahead, you embrace the idea, constantly measuring in your mind's eye where to hang the curtains, how high to mount the shelf in the pantry, how big to build the wood box you'll place next to the old iron cook stove. As the days wane and the nights grow sharp and clear, your hori-zons shrink. Getting the place closed in for winter becomes a hectoring worry that swallows every waking thought. You sit down at the breakfast table and eat insulation that's fallen into your corn flakes. A rainy day is a personal insult from what you consider a sadistic god. You begin to sympathize with Sisyphus and wonder why

between you and your loved ones. More than one relationship has run aground on the reef of a building project.

How do you avoid getting caught in this vise? The advice seems easy enough but is sometimes hard to implement. Begin by trying to state clearly what you expect

 *"No man but feels more of a man in the world if he have a bit of ground that he can call his own. However small it is on the surface, it is four thousand miles deep; and that is a very handsome property." —Charles Dudley Warner*

he just didn't let that rock roll back down the hill. At night, lying in bed, your head is in the attic, running wires for circuits you don't quite understand. Your spouse is wondering where you went and why you never even send a postcard.

Whether you're building the house yourself or hiring a builder, you'll find yourself inexorably drawn into a project that becomes increasingly all-encompassing, until it devours you.

The house-building obsession is also potentially harmful to family and spouse (or "significant other," wife, husband, "special friend," or any other conceivable variation on the designation for the other person within a committed relationship). Whatever latent tensions there may be in the relationship are exacerbated, like the scab on your knuckle that is constantly sloughed off every time you pick up a tool. Daily life becomes an incubator for a host of increasingly virulent strains of discord

of each other. A house is not built in a vacuum of time and space. The chores and needs of daily life are not suspended during the house-building period—and they are every bit as important as framing walls. Negotiate responsibilities, create a job description for each of you for the coming months, with the provision that the agreement is subject to review and renegotiation after each stage of the work is accomplished.

Building your house is a means, not the end. When you feel overwhelmed or discouraged, take a break and do something different, something small and discrete and whimsical, something that isn't on that oppressive, omnipresent List of Things to Do. Find something you want or need to do but that you always put off in deference to the "important" building tasks. Landscape a small corner of the property, plant a fruit tree, build a doghouse, or hang those bird feeders and wind chimes in the maple tree. Clean up the site and haul the debris to the transfer station. Take what a farmer I know calls a "two-hour vacation." Whatever activity you decide to do, you and your partner should do it together, to make it a special treat. There are times when you should put the hammer down, say "To hell with it," and go out to dinner. Buy a bottle of wine, crawl into your tent or mobile home, and get seriously reacquainted.

You'll need to rely on these rebalancing techniques again and again as your homesteading adventure unfolds. Building your house is just the first of many steps on the road to self-sufficiency. Rest assured, there will be no shortage of future critical projects equally constrained by lack of time and money to pick at those old scabs of discontent, to tug you awake in a nauseous predawn sweat, no matter how much you strive to live in the moment and maintain your fragile equanimity.

Making hay when the sun shines is more than metaphor. How do you do what inarguably needs doing and still manage to sustain a satisfying quality of life, one that leaves you time to eat, rest, exercise, and work the way you want to? In medieval peasant societies, a plethora of holy days (holidays) punctuated the calendar, offering respite from the grueling labors of serfdom. In later agricultural communities, potluck dinners, barn raisings, corn shucking, square dances, and quilting bees transformed individual chores into communal celebrations. The ways in which our ancestors dealt with the ceaseless and inescapable rounds of farm work

offer a clue for us. We modern homesteaders need to create rituals and observe them scrupulously. These rituals may be activities as small as sharing a morning cup of coffee or enforcing a Sunday moratorium on any type of work beyond basic chores. How about a family walk? Include the family dogs (they like ritual even more than people do). Occasionally, you may be tempted to declare an emergency that overrides the ritual. Don't fall into that trap. Catch yourself and resolve to keep on keepin' on.

Living Off the Map

In 1974, when I bought that homestead at the end of the road 8 miles from town, I was not thinking about how my choice could close off options that I might later wish were open. The 1970s in northern New England was a time of frenzied real-estate speculation. Slick operators were buying and chopping up worn-out old hill farms and logged-off woodlots to "flip" to the influx of well- and not-so-well-heeled "flatlanders" (aka "folks from down-country" or "folks from away") who were seeking land on which to build their dreams (or their vacation homes). At the top of my list of priorities was a degree of isolation from those surrounding environs. My fantasy of a self-sufficient homestead was hermetic.

I imagined that at some point I would no longer need to support myself with "outside" work, at least not year-round. My ultimate goal was to become a subsistence farmer, growing as much of my own food as possible and having as little

Road Building 101

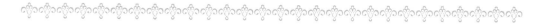

In places like the arid Southwest, you can more or less successfully drive across hard bare ground anywhere except for a few days after one of those rare times when it rains and the surface turns into a morass of sticky, sucking mud. In the rest of the country, the process of building a four-season road begins with stripping off the surface vegetation and topsoil down to subsoil. Then you spread and shape a layer of slightly silty gravel (at least 12 in. thick and 14 ft. wide) to form the road surface. Depending on the character of the subsoil (the percentage of gravel versus clay) and the seasonal water table, you may also need a base layer of coarse gravel or stone to improve drainage. In any case, install road fabric over the subsoil to keep the roadbed from gradually sinking into the ground. On slopes, use water bars, ditches, and culverts as needed to prevent erosion and washout during floods.

If your house site is set far back from the nearest town road, you'll have to build a road to get to it. Building roads is expensive, whether you hire an excavator or are skilled and experienced enough to do the work yourself. Renting a bulldozer can theoretically save about half the cost of hiring, but if you are only casually experienced in operating heavy machinery, a lot of those potential savings will be squandered on the learning curve. You can make an awful mess with a bulldozer if you don't really know what you're doing.

In either case, you'll have to pay for truckloads of gravel for the road surface and for culverts to drain the ditches. After the road is built, it will have to be maintained. The surface must be graded and crowned regularly. You also need to periodically add new gravel and clean ditches and culverts.

Then there's the matter of keeping the road open in snow country. Depending on the length of the road and how often it snows, at $50-plus per shot, the bill for hired plowing can pile up higher than the snowbanks along the roadside. If you already own a tractor with a loader and rear-mounted scraper blade, your costs will only be the fuel and the time it takes to do the work yourself. The cost savings is also a great excuse to justify buying that ultimate boy's toy. Otherwise, just accessorize your pickup truck with a snowplow. Snowplowing is brutally hard on the front end and frame, so many folks plow with a "beater" truck (unregistered, uninsured, too rusted out to pass inspection, but still strong enough to push snow once you get it to start) and save their street-legal, "good" truck for kinder and gentler tasks.

interaction with the consumer economy as possible. Part of that fantasy was a vague notion of growing some sort of (legal) cash crop. In retrospect, had I given any thought to what that crop might be and how I might market it, it might have occurred to me that a farmstand at the end of a bumpy and dusty 20-minute drive from town was unlikely to attract many customers and that I would spend many future hours of my life pounding vehicles into scrap by driving them continually back and forth to town. Building a livelihood and a lifestyle upon a fossil-fuel commuter foundation is ultimately neither self-sufficient nor sustainable.

By location and vocation, I had unwittingly set myself up to be absolutely dependent on reliable transportation. Between parental livery service and multiple vehicle maintenance, living the simple life can get very complicated and expensive. Insurance, fees, fuel, maintenance, monthly car payments, or periodic purchase—one way or another, the care and feeding of an automobile, new or used, adds at least $5,000 to the homestead overhead annually. Back then, when gasoline cost less than 40¢ a gallon, driving a truck that averaged 12 mpg to distant job sites barely registered as overhead.

Now that we do actually earn part of our living by selling the products we raise, I've often wished I'd looked for land closer to town, a place where a roadside stand would be more convenient for customers. At the very least, a shorter drive to town would save some time and extend the life of our vehicles. I wouldn't want to front a

state highway, but life abutting a secondary road, a village main street, or even a gravel road could strike a reasonable balance between privacy and convenience (as long as the house was set far enough back from the road).

No matter how much you may desire and enjoy the solitude and relative inaccessibility of a location "a ways out" from town, there is one additional circumstance that may cause you to regret the choice: You'll be a long way from the fire station. By the time the pumper truck arrives at your burning house or barn, the place will be beyond saving. Even if the truck does arrive quickly, unless there is a nearby pond or river, the pumper may run out of water before extinguishing the fire. There are no fire hydrants beyond the municipal water lines, which is why rural householders pay substantially higher premiums for their fire insurance policies. A fire pond or water-storage cistern is a wise addition to the infrastructure of a homestead located where wildfires are endemic.

There are definite advantages to living in or close to the village, where you can have high-speed Internet access and kids and parents can walk or bicycle to and from school and work. It's just something to think about when you're dreaming that backwoods dream.

Resourcefulness

In 1970, my first wife and I settled in Oakland, California, after a cross-continental odyssey in a Volkswagen bus. I guess you could say we were urban home-steaders of a sort. We lived in a low-rent apartment in a squalid building. Our only heat during the damp chill of winter was the open oven door of the gas stove. I scraped together a down payment on 10 acres of second-growth redwood forest scrub off a steep and muddy dirt road with a vague plan to somehow homestead it while working in the city to pay it off. That winter, it rained every day from Thanksgiving until New Year's Day. Discouraged, we moved back East to more tolerably miserable weather and traded in our California homestead dream for a Vermont version. This time, we decided to make a real plan.

Urban Homesteading

One of the upsides of life in a consumer society is that people throw out an amazing amount of perfectly usable stuff. Dumpster diving is the urban equivalent of foraging for wild foods. Apartment-house dumpsters are a veritable thrift store, offering a selection of clothing, furnishings, and furniture that the original owners were too lazy to haul to Goodwill. Restaurant, bakery, and supermarket dumpsters are a reliable source of gourmet feed for pigs and poultry—and edible, albeit bruised or overripe, fruit and produce. You'd be amazed at the building materials you can find in dumpsters on construction sites—everything from window sash, doors, and cabinets to piles of usable lumber. You'll have all this, plus the frisson of a slightly outlawish activity.

Although it's generally not illegal to salvage discarded items (unless you disregard fences and "No Trespassing" signs), the savvy dumpster diver should have the courtesy not to leave any of the pickings strewn about. If animal feed is what you're after, for the best yield—and to avoid any problems—develop a regular route and schedule; introduce yourself to the chef or restaurant owner and apprise him or her of your intentions.

Suburban Homesteading

We all live downstream from someone else. When we design our houses and choose our materials, we have a responsibility to ask, "Is this the best material for the job or is there something else that will do, something that will cause less long-term environmental damage or have less embedded energy?" Almost always, the best material is one that is "natural" and native or locally manufactured—wood, stone, brick, adobe, and bamboo. Unlike their synthetic analogues, these materials age gracefully and are generally renewable, recyclable, or biodegradable. When you have no better alternative, select processed materials that contain the least amount of embedded energy or will last the longest (for example, choose steel roofing instead of asphalt shingles; gypsum plaster instead of gypsum drywall).

Some modern or petroleum-based building materials are, however, a great improvement over their natural antecedents, and some are manufactured from the waste of industrial processes. Fiberglass and rigid-foam plastic insulation, for example, reduce overall energy consumption and keep homes more comfortable than sawdust, seaweed, or corncobs do. Plywood sheathing and subflooring is much stronger than board sheathing (and reduces the number of trees cut to frame a house). Plastic pipe and plastic-jacketed electrical cable have radically simplified household plumbing and wiring and have also increased safety—a justifiable use of petrochemicals. Cement board siding (such as Hardieplank®) is fireproof, dimensionally stable, and impervious to insects, rot, and moisture. It's virtually immortal and doesn't look too bad, either.

The Mini-Farm

The decision to live off the grid entirely is more a philosophical/political/moral/ethical decision than it is an attempt to lower your utility bills. As Dave Black, author of *Living Off the Grid* (Skyhorse, 2008), writes, "Becoming self-sufficient costs a lot of money." He reminds the casual dreamer that even though going off-grid may eliminate monthly utility bills, there are still ongoing maintenance costs—even after the system is bought and paid for. Storage batteries have to be replaced every three or four years, and backup generators eventually break down, too.

Life in an off-grid household, whether powered by photovoltaic (PV), wind, or hydro power—or a combination of all three—presupposes some major lifestyle adjustments. The so-called average American family uses (squanders) 850 kilowatt-hours (kWh) per month (10,200 kWh annually). This amount of energy is almost exactly twice the annual output of a midsize PV array, so it would be virtually impossible to feed the electrical appetite of the modern American lifestyle with this affordable and feasible "alternative" power system.

Resistance loads (water heaters, electric ranges and ovens, space heaters, electric clothes dryers, dishwashers operated on heated dry cycles) scarf down big gulps of power, as do electric motors and compressors (freezers, refrigerators, air conditioners, washing machines, dishwashers, and water pumps). Eliminate some of these appliances or replace them with versions fueled by liquefied petroleum (LP) gas or with very efficient ENERGY-STAR appliances. Stationary power tools or submersible deep-well pumps can run on supplemental power from a backup generator. The first step is to conserve as much energy as you can. Living off the grid will quickly raise your awareness of your daily energy consumption.

chapter v

....

Natural Resources

For many folks, the word "homestead" conjures up a vision of a remote mountainside cabin, far from the nearest road, solar panels on the roof, and a windmill on a tall tower turning in the breeze. Energy self-sufficiency is the holy grail of the full-blown homestead dream. There you'll be, safe and secure in your bright and cozy cabin, while the rest of the world freezes in the dark.

It's an appealing idea, and certainly one that is becoming increasingly affordable and practical, even if your homestead is no farther from the grid than the nearest utility pole on a suburban street. As long as you have unobstructed access to the southern sun at some place on your rooftop or lawn, you can generate some portion of your household electricity and/or hot water from the sun wherever you live. At the very least, you can use building orientation, natural shading,

....

Top: Clearing an overgrown hillside pasture provided enough firewood to fill our woodshed for two years.
Bottom: Just some of the many accessories of a functioning homestead.

structural mass, sunspaces, and other passive solar strategies to carry some portion of your heating and cooling loads. Every little bit helps.

The farm woodlot is arguably as necessary for a self-sufficient homestead as is tillable land—not only as a source of firewood, but as a source of saw logs for building your home and other structures and as logs for market. The income from tree farming can supplement, or even supersede, the income from agriculture. Depending on your mix of species and the quality of the trees, you could harvest valuable hardwood logs to mill into flooring and cabinet-grade boards, softwood logs for building lumber or timbers, or, ideally, some of both. The leftover limb wood and the "tops" of hardwood trees can fill your firewood quota.

Harvesting Trees

Harvesting trees for firewood is also a means of Timber Stand Improvement (TSI). Culling the crooked, crowded, clumpy, dead, and diseased trees for firewood boosts the growth of the remaining straight-trunked trees. With standing deadwood and culls, a good hardwood woodlot can provide a sustainable yield of 1 cord per acre per year, without depleting the stock of more valuable trees. If the soil is such that the woodlot is chronically wet and hardpan is close to the surface, the resulting shallow root system will be starved of nutrition. Stressed trees grow slowly and often succumb to disease. Blowdowns are common. Under such conditions, any sustainable yield will be much smaller.

Softwoods (conifers) are useful for lumber but, whenever possible, avoid using them for firewood. They are usually less dense and more resinous than hardwoods (deciduous trees), so softwoods burn hot and fast, without producing the long-lasting coals that sustain the fire. (If you live amidst a boreal forest, however, you may not have the option of burning hardwoods, although alders and birches do grow near the timberline. Fortunately for wood burners, the slow growth rate of softwoods in harsh environments creates very dense wood.) Back in the 1970s, we neophyte wood burners obsessed over charts and tables of the BTU (British Thermal Units, the measure of heat output) content of various firewoods, trying to determine which woods would yield the most heat. All that quantification was just explaining the obvious. Burning a pound of dry wood produces about 7,000 BTUs, no matter which kind of wood it is. (One BTU equals the amount of heat it takes to raise the temperature of 1 lb. of water 1°F at sea level.)

Because the weight of wood corresponds to its density, a greater volume of a light wood is required to produce the same amount of heat as a smaller volume of a denser wood. Softwoods, which are less dense, produce less heat than an equivalent volume of hardwoods. There are some species, like yellow pine, however, that, although technically softwood, are much denser than some hardwoods, such as poplar or basswood. Rule of thumb: Hardwoods are denser than softwoods and therefore burn longer and produce more heat for the same-size load. If the wood is not thoroughly dry, some goodly number of those BTUs will be squandered in boiling away the water before the wood will burn, so burn only dry firewood.

Tree Farming 101

Turning your own trees into value-added lumber is a very good way to increase the value of your forest land. One of the real advantages of living in a rural area (at least in forested regions) is the availability of local sawmills. "Native" lumber (sawn from locally harvested trees) purchased directly from the mill typically costs about 30 percent less than "imported" lumber from the building-supply depot in town.

One might, then, reasonably conclude that harvesting timber from your own land and milling it yourself would yield even greater savings. Not necessarily. There are several types of roller-bar chainsaw mills (the Alaskan® Roller Bar Mill is the prototype) that are touted as the homesteader's ideal personal sawmill. The problem with roller-bar mills is that it takes a good while

> *"Happiness belongs to the self-sufficient."*
> —Aristotle

and a powerful chainsaw (as in, heavy and very expensive) to convert a log into a pile of 1-in. or 2-in. boards. I would venture to say that, unless you are situated way back in the woods, on a track inaccessible to motor vehicles (in the Alaskan bush, for example), the best use of this tool might be squaring off the faces of logs to make timbers for framing or constant-depth (as opposed to naturally tapered) logs for cabin building.

Logs are heavy. They don't move easily. It takes heavy equipment to skid (drag) a log from where the tree has been felled and limbed to the landing, where it can be loaded onto a truck for transport to the local sawmill or market. (Many old-timers moved logs with horses or with stronger and more placid oxen.) You could rent a tractor to skid your logs yourself or hire a logger to haul them to the landing with his skidder and then also possibly load and truck them to the sawmill, too. Depending on the terms of the deal, the charge may be a flat rate for each load or accrue by the hour, by the cord, or by estimated board foot. If you're on good terms with a farmer neighbor, you might work out a trade or cash deal to skid your logs to the landing with his tractor, which might otherwise be idle during the winter, which is the season when most logging is done.

If you can drive anywhere close to them, you could also skid your logs with a four-wheel-drive truck or all-terrain vehicle. A bumper-mounted electric winch will greatly extend your reach. Given enough cable (you can hook multiple lengths together) and a pulley block or two to ease the cable around corners, you could easily pull logs out of otherwise inaccessible areas. There are also three-point, hitch-mounted, power-take-off-powered logging winches that allow your tractor to safely and efficiently pull logs over a considerable distance of difficult terrain.

Once you've gotten your logs to the landing, the first half of the battle, and probably the easiest half, is over. Loading the logs onto some sort of conveyance to haul them to the sawmill is the second and more-challenging task. Loading requires you to lift the log up onto something, which is a lot harder than dragging it along the ground. If you have a substantial quantity of logs—a truckload or more—the easiest way to get them to the mill is to pay a logger to load them onto his log truck. For less than a full truckload (typically about 7 cords), the value of the lumber (after the costs of sawing) won't pay for the cost of trucking.

A short-bed (6-ft.) pickup truck with the tailgate down can carry logs up to 12 ft. long. A standard (8-ft.) bed truck can haul 14-footers. The trick is getting the logs over the sideboards and onto the bed. (To estimate the weight of a log, multiply the weight

Muscle-powered Log Loading

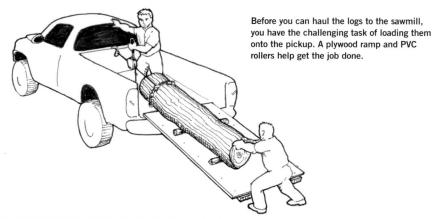

Before you can haul the logs to the sawmill, you have the challenging task of loading them onto the pickup. A plywood ramp and PVC rollers help get the job done.

of a 1-ft. cross section of a given diameter by the length. See the chart on p. 103.) The "green" (fresh-cut and water-saturated) weight of common domestic hardwoods varies from about 45 lb. to 65 lb. per cubic foot. Live oak tops out at a hefty 76 lb. The bantam-weight poplar (at 38 lb.) is closer to softwood species like spruce and eastern white pine, which weigh in around 35 lb. Water-soaked woods like larch (tamarack) and hemlock fall on the low end of the hardwood scale, at around 50 lb.

You could easily lift a 440-lb., 10-ft.-long, 12-in.-dia. sugar maple log with a chain that's been secured to the bucket (or fork attachment) of a smaller farm tractor. If you increase the diameter of that log to 18 in., the weight more than doubles, putting it well beyond the lift capacity of the tractor hydraulics—

and close to the load limit of the pickup truck, too.

The ancient Druids that built Stonehenge didn't have tractors or boom trucks to raise those multiple-ton monoliths. They used ramps, rollers, and muscle power. In comparison, manhandling a half-ton log onto the bed of a pickup truck is pretty small potatoes. A sheet of plywood, screwed to roughsawn 2x12 or 3x12 planks serves as the ramp. A couple of 2-ft.-long sections of Schedule 80 PVC pipe serve as rollers. A come-along, hitched to the end of the log, provides the pull (and the safety to prevent backsliding) while you and a helper supply the push. The height of the bed from the ground makes for a steep incline, however.

The deck of a utility or landscape trailer is half as high off the ground as the bed of a pickup truck, and the drop-down tail-

Log Weight Calculator

(Weight in Pounds per 1-ft. Cross-Section of Green Logs)

To estimate the weight of a log, by species, determine the log's average diameter. Multiply the log's length by the number (found here) for the weight of a 1-ft. cross-section of a log of that diameter.

Species	Pounds per cubic foot	Average diameter (in.)							
		10	12	14	16	18	20	22	24
Spruce	34	19	27	36	47	60	74	90	106
White Pine	36	20	28	39	50	64	78	95	113
Poplar	38	21	30	40	53	67	83	99	119
Basswood	42	23	33	45	59	74	92	111	132
Black Gum, Black Cherry	45	25	35	48	63	79	98	119	141
Silver Maple, Butternut	46	25	36	49	64	81	100	121	144
Tamarack	47	26	37	50	65	83	102	124	147
White Ash	48	26	38	51	67	85	104	126	150
Cottonwood	49	27	38	52	68	86	107	129	154
Paper Birch, Red Gum, Hackberry	50	27	39	53	70	88	109	132	157
Red Maple, Eastern Hemlock, Sycamore	52	28	41	55	72	97	113	137	163
Elm, Beach	54	29	42	58	75	95	118	142	169
Apple	55	30	43	59	77	97	120	145	173
Sugar Maple	56	31	44	60	78	99	122	148	176
Yellow Birch	57	31	45	61	80	101	124	151	179
Black Walnut	58	32	45	62	81	102	126	153	182
Honey Locust	61	33	48	65	89	113	140	169	201
Black Oak, White Oak	62	34	48	66	86	109	135	163	194
Osage Orange, Red Oak	63	34	49	67	88	111	137	166	200
Shagbark Hickory	64	35	50	68	89	113	140	169	201
Live Oak	76	41	60	81	106	134	166	200	238

International ¼-in. Scale Log Rule

Adapted from *Reference Handbook for Foresters* by Burl S. Ashley (USDA Forest Service, 2001)

Diameter (in.)	Length of Log (ft.)					
	6	8	10	12	14	16
	Contents in Board Feet					
6	5	10	10	15	15	20
7	10	10	15	20	25	30
8	10	15	20	25	35	40
9	15	20	30	35	45	50
10	20	30	35	45	55	65
11	25	35	45	55	70	80
12	30	45	55	70	85	95
13	40	55	70	85	100	115
14	45	65	80	100	115	135
15	55	75	95	115	135	160
16	60	85	110	130	155	180
17	70	95	125	150	180	205
18	80	110	140	170	200	230
19	90	125	155	190	225	260
20	100	135	155	175	210	290
21	115	155	195	235	280	320
22	125	170	215	260	305	355
23	140	185	235	285	335	390
24	150	205	255	310	370	425
25	165	220	280	340	400	460
26	180	240	305	370	435	500
27	195	260	330	400	470	540
28	210	280	355	430	510	585
29	225	305	385	465	545	630
30	245	325	410	495	585	675

gate does double duty as a loading ramp, which will make the entire operation safer and easier. The longer bed of the trailer can carry longer logs. Also, if the trailer has removable sideboards, the logs can be loaded parallel to the bed rather than perpendicularly. This way, the log itself becomes a roller and can be more safely and readily pulled up a pair of timber or steel-pipe skid rails from the opposite side of the trailer. (For safety, insert chocks under the log as it moves up the rails.)

When the logs finally end up on the truck or trailer, the load should be secured at both ends with a log chain (5/16-in. or 3/8-in. high-strength steel links) and a load binder or 2-in. nylon ratchet straps. Otherwise, if the load shifts, you could lose control of the vehicle or the logs could spill onto the highway.

When loggers bring a load of logs to a sawmill, the sawyer will "scale" the logs according to one of several different (more or less regional) "rules" to figure the payment based on the market rate per board foot. (Board foot is a unit measure of volume. One board foot is equivalent to a block of wood that is 1 ft. square and 1 in. thick.) Board-foot measure facilitates pricing lumber at a constant rate, regardless of dimension. If a log is rectangular or cylindrical, estimating the volume is fairly easy and accurate—not so if it's irregularly conical. The various log "rules" will approximate the volume of lumber in the cone-shaped log after deducting some volume to compensate for the saw kerf (width of the cut) and the squared-off edge slabs. Whether you're paid for scaled logs or fin-

ished lumber depends on the mill. There is no standard. It's a lot easier to haul logs home once they're sawn into boards.

Air drying versus kiln drying Like green, fresh-cut firewood, "pond-dried" (as my neighbor calls it) lumber is best seasoned (dried) before use. The cells of a living tree are saturated with water. Depending on the species, water can comprise as much as 200 percent of the weight of a fresh-cut log.

Whether the log is air- or kiln-dried, the goal is to remove as much water as it takes to dry the wood to the same moisture level as the ambient air (measured as Equilibrium Moisture Content, or EMC). For hundreds of years, seasoning meant stacking the fresh-cut lumber under a protective roof, separating the layers with thin "stickers" of waste wood to encourage air circulation. The alternative—enclosed temperature- and atmosphere-controlled drying kilns—have only been in wide use for little more than a century. They offer precise control and a much faster drying period than air drying does. The high temperature also kills insects and fungus.

The real advantage of kiln drying, however, is economic, facilitating the rapid sale of large volumes of standardized lumber by middleman brokers. The disadvantage is that you have to pay someone to season the wood for you. Also, the kilns are fossil fueled and not at all carbon neutral (unlike air drying), even before you add in the trucking to and from the kiln. Air drying requires a lot more time than kiln drying, usually up to six months, sometimes longer—if you begin the process in winter, it barely proceeds at all—but it's free, and you can do it at home. If you're planning to use the wood for outdoor construction (barns, sheds, general framing), as soon as it reaches the EMC for

supply paper mills. Brokers pay by the cord at roadside or at an accessible landing. Check with your local extension forestry service to find the current price for pulp and to learn which species of pulpwood is in demand. The market fluctuates wildly

"Bottom line: If you have a chainsaw and own or can borrow a pickup truck or small utility trailer, you can harvest your own firewood, no matter where you live."

your climate, it's good to go. If you plan to use the wood indoors, dry it, then restack it inside, and leave it to dry further until it reaches the indoor EMC.

With all this hauling, heaving, hiring, skidding, sawing, and stacking, you might find that the final cost of your lumber isn't much less than what it would have been if you purchased it directly from the mill. Instead of bringing your logs to the sawmill, consider bringing the sawmill to your logs. Some contractors operate portable sawmills, which they will bring to your log pile (even in urban areas). Come to think of it, if you had money to invest in a trailer-mounted mobile dimension saw, and were a fair mechanic to boot, you might manage to earn a good part of your living milling logs.

The wood pulp option Even a large woodlot might contain relatively few saw-log-grade trees, but you can monetize even a second-rate woodlot. Depending on the market cycle, there may be a strong demand for hardwood or softwood pulp to

from year to year and even within a season.

Consider yourself lucky if there is a demand for balsam pulp. This short-lived fir usually succumbs to "butt rot" (a fungus that destroys the wood at the base of the trunk first) once it reaches 1 ft. in diameter. In any case, its wood is too weak to make good lumber (although you may find some balsam mixed in with a load of spruce and hemlock boards or studs from your local mill). Although many mills now buy only 8-ft. logs, you may still find buyers for traditional 4-ft. pulp logs.

The winter of 1979 was unusual for a double delight of deep cold and a dearth of snow. Swampy ground wasn't the only thing that froze up that winter—there was no work for carpenters like me, either. Softwood pulp was selling for $35 a cord, and, on a good day, working alone, felling 8-in. to 12-in. balsams, limbing and sawing them into 4-ft. lengths, I could load a full cord onto the long narrow trailer behind the tractor. The check for the first few 7-cord loads kept the wolf from our door. By winter's end, I had cut and hauled 60 cords out of that balsam swamp—and had blown up a $400 chainsaw to boot. I stopped cutting when the broker told me the market was glutted. Apparently, I wasn't the only one taking advantage of that once-in-a-generation opportunity to cut where no one could cut before.

Stumpage contracting If you're determined to "do" something with the marketable wood growing on your land but you lack the equipment and expertise—or you're just too damn busy caring for animals, gardens, and family—the simplest option is to arrange a stumpage contract with a professional logger, preferably one who is supervised by or working in tandem with a forester. Essentially, you'll agree to sell any harvestable timber for a set fee, per cord or per board foot, either "on the stump" or at the landing.

The terms of stumpage contracts can be notoriously vague, and there is a long tradition of their disregard by "outlaw" loggers, so get references and check them out. If a particular logger has a reputation for leaving behind a mess or "accidentally" cutting the most valuable trees on the neighbor's side of the line, chances are you'll hear about it.

If you have enough wood that is worth harvesting sustainably, you will most likely already have enrolled in the USDA TSI Program to qualify for subsidies and property-tax abatements (if any). If so, contact the forestry consultant you paid to draw up your management plan for help in drawing up a stumpage contract. Ask the consultant to recommend a responsible and honest logger or perhaps to oversee the operation. Timber cruising, the art of marking trees for removal and estimating the volume of stumpage on a given lot, is one of the more valuable services provided by a forestry consultant.

Be sure that your contract specifies which trees will be taken and whether the "tops" will be left behind to provide wildlife habitat (as many experts favor) or stacked and burned or chipped for market (less favored). What will be done with the culls (the unmarketable defective logs)? The logger may cut them into firewood-length blocks at the landing in return for a discount on the stumpage payment.

The heavy equipment that modern mechanized logging depends on can, and often does, make an awful mess of the woods. Deep ruts in wet ground will pollute streams and seriously erode slopes. (The potential damage is one reason why many landowners prefer to work with horse-powered loggers. A team of horses leaves only the faintest scars, and those heal quickly. Horses are ideally suited to low-volume, selective-cutting operations. Nearly the only disadvantage of horse logging is that a small team can't always skid the longer and thicker logs that command a premium at the mill.) Conscientious mechanized loggers build good, properly drained roads and quit using them when their hard-frozen surface begins to soften. They'll wait and finish the job when the ground dries out in summer. Make sure your contract specifies.

Heating with Wood

Pros	Cons
Felling, chopping, and toting provide physical exercise	Harvest and handling is physically demanding and potentially hazardous
Wood is a renewable fuel (but requires good management for sustainability)	Wood cords require protected storage area
Available from local sources (so less expensive to transport than fossils fuels)	Must be "seasoned" for extended period for best use
Supports local economy (firewood dealers, loggers, foresters, etc.)	Inconvenient in that must be handled repeatedly
Economical (as compared to oil or gas heat)	House-sitter or backup heating system required to keep house from freezing when you're away from home
Increases self-sufficiency and utilization of land	Older wood burners present pollution and air-quality issues
No loss of heat during power outage (unless you heat with electrically controlled wood boiler)	Fire hazard if chimney maintenance is neglected
Resulting ash is valuable garden additive	Ash disposal can present problem

Finally, be sure you and your forester are on the same page regarding management philosophy. There are still professional foresters who look at a forest with a resource-extraction rather than a sustainable-harvest point of view. Your woodlot deserves the same husbandry that sustains your livestock and gardens.

From Woodlot to Woodstove

"Wood heats you three times: once when you cut it, twice when you split it, and thrice when you burn it." This old adage pretty well sums up the virtues of wood as a heating fuel. Even if you have firewood delivered to your door, heating with wood requires at least some level of involvement on the part of the consumer, even if it's only stacking the logs and carrying them to the woodstove.

There are a number of ways to get firewood, often free or for a nominal cost. Arborists and tree surgeons often have to pay to dump tree leftovers in a municipal facility (too large to fit into the chipper, which is the fate of smaller-limbed wood). The company may be happy to drop off the remnants from their job in your driveway or even load you up at the job site.

Municipal facilities for disposal of trees that were removed because of storm damage, disease, or development (known as stump dumps) may sell firewood or allow you to haul away a supply of logs. Sawmills often sell bundles of slabs and edgings left from squaring off logs. (If you can, find a mill that produces hardwood rather than softwood lumber.)

Finally, there are programs that allow residents to cut marked trees in state or municipal forests or on other public lands for free or for a nominal fee as part of ongoing TSI management. You might also find a landowner who is willing to let you cut wood on his property as part of a private management program. Just be sure

§ *"People love chopping wood. In this activity one immediately sees results."—Albert Einstein*

that you put the arrangement in writing and that the contract clearly specifies the responsibilities of both parties. Bottom line: If you have a chainsaw and own or can borrow a pickup truck or small utility trailer, you can harvest your own firewood, no matter where you live.

Chainsaws and Chainsaw Safety

If you're serious about TSI or cutting your own firewood, you'll need a serious chainsaw, one with enough muscle and bar length to slice through logs quickly and efficiently. My 30-year-old Husqvarna® 266SE has a powerful 66cc engine that delivers 4.7 HP to its 24-in. bar. This tool is basically an entry-level professional logger's saw. I use it for felling and for sawing logs into firewood, but, at $17^1/_2$ lb., it's a beast to handle. (The current generation of equivalent machines is much lighter, but that ol' thing keeps on going, and a replacement would set me back at least $800.) I don't have to be too long on the job before my sciatic nerve begins to shriek in protest, which is why, once the

tree is down, I switch over to my $12^1/_4$-lb. Husky 137 ("Husky" is the pet name for Husqvarna saws) for limbing. The lighter weight and 16-in. bar make it easy to maneuver between branches and are a mercy on my back and arms. Its 36cc motor can manage trees up to 8 in. in diameter, although the bar tends to wear out faster than normal when working the saw that way.

The chance of being maimed or killed by errant logs is probably of an order of magnitude less than the likelihood of being messed up or done in by your chainsaw. If you stop to think about it, a chainsaw is a truly scary machine. You're holding a powerful motor driving a very sharp set of teeth at high speed, completely unprotected by any guard, while you're standing on uneven, wet, slippery, or icy ground, often contorted into an uncomfortable or awkward position. Although the bulk of accidents can probably be charged to inexperience, experience itself is no guarantee against incident. In fact, I'd argue that the more familiar you are with a chainsaw, the more likely you are to let your guard down and make that really dumb mistake.

You can read about basic safety precautions (see p. 110), but learning to operate a chainsaw safely and skillfully only comes with hands-on experience, preferably under the tutelage of an accomplished mentor. Check around. The extension service or adult education program may offer a short course in chainsaw safety.

Twelve Tips for Chainsaw Safety

1. Wear protective equipment—at a minimum, ear protectors and safety glasses; a hard hat with attached earmuffs and protective face screen if you're working in the woods. Cut-resistant Kevlar®-lined gloves, shin guards, or chaps complete the outfit.

2. Don't work alone if you can help it. Carry a cell phone—or if you don't have a phone or service, carry a walkie-talkie.

3. Start your saw on the ground, with your foot firmly on the back handle—do not "drop start" from waist level.

4. Shut off the saw—or, at least, apply the chain brake—while carrying or not using the saw.

5. Make sure you have firm footing and a clear work area. Do not overreach when working from a ladder or cut above shoulder height. Wear steel-toed, high-top work boots for protection and ankle support.

6. Don't smoke while fueling the saw. (Duh.)

7. Keep your saw sharp and well maintained. A dull saw is a dangerous saw. A sharp chainsaw will almost pull itself through the log without any effort on your part, producing a shower of long curly chips. As the cutters dull, you'll notice that you have to bear down to push the saw through the log, and that it's spitting out sawdust instead of chips. A really dull saw will leave burn marks across the face of the cut. The saw may also cut to one side, no matter how hard you try to keep it straight. An unsharpened saw will work much harder than it should. The tip of the bar will overheat and wear thin, until the chain-drive links stick in the groove.

8. Let the weight of the saw do the work. Pushing on it increases pressure on your wrists and hands. Keep the blade out of mud, dirt, and gravel. Watch out for remnants of barbed wire when cutting brush along former fence lines.

9. Learn how to sharpen a dull chainsaw blade in the field. (There are several excellent online articles about sharpening, use, and maintenance, among them Stihl's® *Sharp Advice for Chain Saw Owners* (www.stihllibrary.com/pdf/sharpadvice061301final.pdf). Take your saw into the shop for machine sharpening after you've made a half-dozen or so field or bench-top touch-ups of your own.

10. Don't overdo it. Running a saw for extended periods can lead to carpal tunnel syndrome or hand-arm vibration syndrome (HAVS), which can result in permanent nerve damage. Vary your routine to avoid fatigue, which increases the risk of mishap. After an hour of cutting, switch to an hour of piling brush or stacking wood. Stop and rest occasionally.

11. Pay attention at all times! Always know where the saw is relative to your body.

12. Protect the environment. Use a funnel and take care not to spill chain oil or gasoline on the ground when refilling the saw. Keep containers and accessories in a carry tote, not strewn on the ground. Chains throw lubricating oil off the bar while running, so use biodegradable canola-based bar and chain oils.

Learning from your mistakes is not recommended! A hands-on blunder can all too easily become a hands-off accident. Leg and arm injuries together account for about 80 percent of all chainsaw mishaps (and for 100 percent of mine, fortunately none more serious than a nip, but a wake-up call from the universe, as it were). Unfortunately, when limbing, it's all too easy to swing the saw in an arc that ends against your thigh or to reach across the blade while it's idling but still moving.

A common error, which has potentially fearsome consequences, is kickback. Kickback occurs when the upper edge of the tip of the bar contacts the wood or when the bar is pinched, causing the saw to kick back violently in an upward arc toward the operator—a good reason to never cut while straddling the saw or with the saw directly in front of you. Modern saws have automatic chain brakes that will stop the chain instantly when the saw starts to kick back, but they're not foolproof. Cutting with the saw held to your side will allow it to kick back past you instead of into you.

Buying firewood   Buying firewood at "log length" is a reasonable compromise between the extremes of do-it-all-yourself and pay-for-split-and-delivered. Loggers are also usually in the firewood business, and some will cut the tops, limb wood, and cull logs from trees they've removed into firewood for sale and delivery at the landing. Others will sell you a truckload's worth (often called a "pulp cord") of cull logs, which they will unload right in your dooryard. In our part of the world, dry firewood, cut to length, split, and deliv-

ered, costs the most per cord; "green" fire-wood runs a little less; and a load of log length is the least expensive per cord. "Blocked" firewood, sections of logs that have been cut (or "bucked") to firewood length, runs somewhere between green and log length, but eliminates the need for you to own a chainsaw, so the price might be worth it.

Considering that the hardest and most dangerous part of the work has already been done for you, buying log lengths or block wood seems like a pretty good deal, especially if you don't have access to a woodlot—and saves time that you can more profitably devote to other projects. If you buy a load of log-length firewood every few years (logging is winter work, so you can have next year's firewood delivered midwinter), then whenever you feel like indulging in some wholesome exercise you can spend a few hours bucking logs. By spring the bolts will be ready for splitting, and by fall your firewood will be dry and stacked in the woodshed.

Splitting   A round bolt of wood takes a long time to dry out because only the log ends are exposed to air. Splitting hastens drying. It also makes it possible to fit the wood into your wood-burning appliance. If you don't buy your firewood already split, you have two options for splitting it yourself: hand and hydraulics. It's not quite the no-brainer choice that it seems at first. If you live in a region with a short heating season, or only intend to supplement your fossil-fuel heat by burning wood occasionally, splitting a cord or two of firewood (as long as you don't try to

What Is a Cord and What Does It Get You?

A cord is a legal measure of volume equivalent to 128 cu. ft. (CF), or a stack of wood 4 ft. high, 4 ft. wide, and 8 ft. long. A face cord (also called a "rick" or "run") is a portion of a cord, 4 ft. high, 8 ft. long, and whatever width the wood is cut to (typically, 16 in. or 24 in.). So, a face cord of 16-in. wood is one-third of a full cord; a face cord of 24-in. wood is one-half of a full cord.

Despite these apparently straightforward distinctions, there is an ongoing difference of opinion between people who buy wood and people who sell it to them as to just how many cords that pile of firewood that's been freshly dumped in the dooryard actually contains (especially when the buyer is one of those "damn fool flatlanders," just begging to be taken advantage of).

It's really a packaging problem. A neatly stacked cord will contain a lot more pieces than a pile of wood randomly tossed into a container of equivalent volume (like the bed of a pickup truck). Ideally, your firewood supplier will load wood onto the truck from neatly stacked, measured rows. More often than not, a supplier will "calibrate" the truck by filling it with a measured load and then assume future loads will occupy roughly the same volume. When the delivery from a conscientious supplier is stacked in the shed, that "guestimate" will be, if anything, slightly more than a true cord. The stack from a less scrupulous supplier will be significantly short.

Besides shorting the load—the equivalent of the butcher's thumb on the scale—

mendacious dealers have also been known to water the whiskey by slipping softwoods and inferior hardwoods, such as grey birch and poplar, into a load proffered as prime hardwoods. Given that BTU content is proportional to density, sneaking "weed wood" into a load is like siphoning gas out of your fuel tank. If you're buying from an unfamiliar supplier, check the load upon delivery. It behooves anyone buying firewood to become adept at identifying their local firewood species by sight and heft. In northern New England, where there are relatively few species of common hardwoods, that's not hard to do. Southward and westward, however, hardwood species proliferate into bewildering variety. Your wood-burning neighbors will have plenty of advice as to the most-choice options.

do it all in one marathon session) can be both good aerobic exercise and a pleasant meditation of the "chop wood, carry water" variety.

Many types of muscle-powered wood-splitting tools are touted as "the fastest gun in the West." Some may live up to their claims, and maybe someday I'll get around to trying them out, but in 35 years I've yet to find too many bolts that could withstand my splitting maul and a pair of iron wedges. I did have a load of American elm, wood so tough and stringy it would swallow as many wedges as I could pound into it without distress, and an occasional cross-grained beech or yellow birch, with a grain structure dense and chaotic enough to challenge even a hydraulic splitter. Those pieces ended up with the burl wood and other oddities in my "crazy wood" storage bin, stock for some future woodcarving project.

I prefer a splitting maul to a sledgehammer because it can do double duty. It's hefty enough to split a goodly portion of your bolts directly, and the hammer side of its head will drive steel wedges well enough to split the more recalcitrant pieces. I prefer the maul to the lighter splitting axe, which, while useful for straight-grained, easily split woods, is stumped by a more-squirrelly chunk. When splitting a large bolt, it's easier and faster to work from the outside edges in, splitting off slabs with the maul rather than driving wedges into the center to split the bolt in half.

Green wood splits more easily than dry wood, but frozen green wood is another story altogether. A gnarly block of frozen beech taught me a lesson I'll never forget during my first winter as a wood burner. The maul simply ricocheted off of the face of that rock-solid block, chipping my front tooth and splitting my lip. Still smarting from that demonstration of why cross-grained beech is the wood of choice for making nearly indestructible mallets, I tallied the remaining beech blocks in that pile, decided self-sufficiency be damned, and rented a wood splitter. Now when I put up my firewood, I do the bucking in winter and the splitting in spring.

Another good reason to wait until spring to split your firewood is that you won't be standing in line to rent a hydraulic splitter. In the fall, when everyone is rushing to get their wood in, there's a waiting list for splitter rentals. Splitters do make short work of it. With one person operating the hydraulic control lever and another lifting and clearing bolts, two people can split 5 cords of 2-ft.-dia. wood in an easy day and 10 cords in a long, hard one. The only drawback to renting a wood splitter is that the per diem cost may pressure you into marathon sessions.

I used to share long-weekend rentals and labor with family and neighbors. Finally, we bought our own machine, sharing the cost and use in a four-way split with our son and sons-in-law. We still help each other split our firewood, but we do it at a more leisurely and convenient pace. The high price of a good hydraulic wood splitter ($2,000–$3,000) is hard for the average homesteader or casual wood burner to justify, but the tool is an excellent investment in labor-saving convenience for a community group or small farmer's network.

Storage and seasoning If you have firewood, you should have a place to store it. If you intend to heat with wood full-time, where and how you store it is a particularly important part of the plan. Ideally, you'd have a shed or simple roofed structure that protects the wood from the elements, allows good ventilation, is close to or attached to your house, and is capacious enough to hold at least a winter's worth of wood. Most often, people store firewood in a random pile next to the cellar bulkhead, under a blue tarp, or (better but still less than optimal) neatly stacked and covered by sheets of old steel roofing. As long as the bottommost logs are above ground (resting on salvaged wood pallets, ideally) and the top is protected against rain and snow, the wood will certainly dry. Rain and snow will still blow sideways into the nooks and crannies, however.

If you store wood outdoors, a freestanding, three-sided shed (basically a roof with sideboards and pallets set on a gravel or crushed-stone base) will keep your wood dry and accessible. A hoop house, which has a clear greenhouse-fabric covering, offers the advantages of economy and solar-assisted drying. (Roll up the sides to encourage ventilation.) Finally, a woodshed on the north side of a house (where, if you have observed energy-efficient design principles, there should be few or no windows) is ideal both for convenience and as a buffer against the winter cold. You might even consider building a tilting hopper into the wall that can be filled from inside the woodshed and emptied into the living room where the woodstove is located.

Do not store firewood in your basement. Not only do you risk infesting the house with insects, but, given the likelihood that the ambient moisture level of your basement is lower than that outdoors, stored firewood will exude moisture, encouraging the growth of mold and mildew, excessive condensation, and generally unhealthy indoor conditions.

Finally, be sure to include some sort of bin or containment area for kindling.

Top: Son-in-law and granddaughter make short work of their firewood with our jointly owned splitter. Bottom left: My trusty old "Husky." Bottom right: The homemade wood bed on our pickup is handy for hauling firewood from the logpile to the woodshed.

During the fall and spring, when the days are warm enough to let the fire die out, you'll use a surprising amount of kindling to start the evening fires. We're always building something around our place, so there's no shortage of softwood lumber scraps to fill my kindling bin. Ask workers on a construction site if they would let you haul away the scrap trimmings that they would otherwise pay to dispose of. Softwood slabs and edgings from a local sawmill are another good source of kindling.

Heating with Wood

There are solid monetary reasons to heat with wood (either as a primary or backup fuel) where it's locally available, to say nothing of the advantages of sustainability and self-sufficiency that it offers. The decision is ultimately a matter of personal preference. It's a "lifestyle" choice. Until someone invents a mindlessly fully automatic woodstove that can be filled once or twice a season and forgotten about (like the typical oil or gas heating appliance), heating with wood will continue to demand what many would regard as an uncomfortable level of involvement, the very thing that led people to embrace the convenience of oil- and gas-fueled heating in the first place. Self-sufficiency is predi-

cated upon responsibility. It will never be fully automatic.

There are a lot more options available for burning wood today than there were back in the 1970s, when the double-walled, sheet-metal, Ashley woodstove—the first rudimentary "airtight" stove—was the apex of wood-heat technology. Although it didn't seem so at the time, they were inexpensive. They could almost hold a fire overnight, and boy, could they throw out the heat. I remember many an evening, sitting in our unlit living room, the darkness broken only by the dull red glow of the stove, a pillow of warmth radiating security against the cold night. The design was simplicity itself, nothing more than a barrel within a barrel, capped with a lidded cast-iron top. Its only embellishment was a chromed, bell-shaped, adjustable, round air-intake on the front loading door. There were fancier models, of course, wrapped in a boxy-grilled, brown-enameled-metal, heat-circulating jacket driven by a small electric fan, but that level of sophistication seemed pointless. In those days, "funky" was desirable.

During the oil embargo of 1973, the sudden spike in the price of heating oil and gasoline sparked interest in what were called alternative energy sources (solar and wind power) and in heating with wood, a traditional fuel in rural areas that, up until that time, had been considered outmoded and uncouth. By the 1980s, some 10 million households were heated entirely or in part with wood.

With the increase in wood burning came an increasing awareness of the po-tentially adverse effects of wood burning on health and the environment. In addition to producing polluting microparticles (PM2.5, which can lodge in lungs or bloodstreams along with the toxic molecules adhering to them), wood burning can also produce carcinogenic polycyclic aromatic hydrocarbons (PAHs), a group of tarring, intensely smelly molecules that give wood smoke its characteristic odor. Organizations such as Clear Air Revival, claiming that the 10 percent of the population that burns wood in stoves, fireplaces, and outdoor firepots is responsible for 50 percent of the total particulate pollution (the other half coming from auto and truck emissions and wood-burning power plants), are actively seeking to ban wood-burning heating appliances. Their eventual, stated goal is to make wood burning as socially unacceptable as "smoking a cigar in an elevator."

Some critics also worry that burning wood adds to greenhouse gases, but burning wood is actually carbon neutral, as the carbon dioxide that is released back into the atmosphere is the same that was sequestered from it by the tree. Whether that CO_2 is released slowly as the tree dies and rots on the forest floor or is released in a rush of oxidizing carbohydrates makes no difference.

The EPA reacted to the problem of particulate pollution by imposing strict emission standards for all woodstoves sold after 1990. These regulated woodstoves create 90 percent less pollution than unregulated stoves. EPA-certified stoves also employ a catalytic converter in the smoke outlet to physically trap particulates and pollutants or have some means of introducing extra air to create a zone of "secondary combustion" hot enough to burn off the bulk of them. Granted, even some EPA-certified stoves can still produce as much as 97 lb. of PM2.5 annually (versus the 244 lb. produced by older stoves), while oil and gas burners emit only 0.25 lb. and 0.16 lb., respectively.

Burning green Does all of this mean that we should stop wood burning and switch back to fossil fuels? As the Wood Heat Organization points out on its website (www.woodheat.org), "For most of us, wood smoke is rarely seen as an issue because the particular topographical and climatological features that trap smoke don't exist everywhere. Wood smoke tends to blow away before it annoys anybody." And those horrible PAHs? They're heavy

molecules and soon fall back to earth, where they biodegrade in the soil, helping to build humus.

Woodstove pollution, at least with the current crop of improved stoves, has more to do with how the stove is operated than with wood burning itself. As with most steps along the green pathway, clean wood burning requires heightened awareness. Properly operated, you can get the particulate emission of an EPA-certified stove down to almost oil-burner levels. Of course, as you might expect, there's a tradeoff. Most people who burn wood don't do it the "right" way for good reason.

If you maintain a hot, turbulent fire, the volatile PAHs, which are produced when wood first ignites, will burn in the extreme heat and break down into carbon monoxide, carbon dioxide, water vapor, and some unburned particles before they can exit

Fuel Equivalencies

1 cord of seasoned hardwood is equal to:	150 gal. of No. 2 fuel oil
	230 gal. of liquid petroleum gas
	21,000 CF of natural gas
	6,158 kilowatts of electricity

Do the math. If you know the cost per cord of wood and the cost per unit of energy from other sources—and also know how much fuel you will require for a heating season—the cost comparisons are straightforward to calculate. For example:

800 gallons of oil @ $2.50 per gallon	$2,000
5.33 cords of firewood @ $200 per cord	$1,066
Amount of savings from heating with wood	$934 per heating season

the firebox. When you load up the stove and damp it down to smolder through the night, those PAHs don't burn. A portion of the gooey compounds are deposited on the inside walls of the chimney as creosote. The rest, along with a great deal of particulates, emerges from the chimney as a thick pall of blue-grey smoke. The situation is exacerbated when you burn unseasoned and/or highly resinous wood (like pine). Running the fire hot reduces pollution, but it also overheats the house. Letting the fire idle or smolder, especially through the night, mitigates uncomfortable indoor temperature swings but increases levels of creosote and pollution.

The best response to the pollution issue is to reduce the amount of wood it takes to heat your house. First, downsize. How large a house do you really need? Since 1960, the average size of the American house has doubled, whereas family size has shrunk by half. Smaller houses are easier to heat. Passive solar tempering and thermal mass can also contribute to the heat load. A superinsulated house often requires no additional heat source other than the waste heat from normal household activities. Second, weatherize. Install or retrofit insulation weatherstrips and caulk and replace leaky windows with energy-efficient ones. The less wood you burn, the less pollution you produce. Consider the alternatives: more wars fought for diminishing reserves of oil and gas, the enormous

....

Top: A load of 8-ft. log-length firewood delivered to the farm.   Bottom: Our chickens investigate the woodpile.

carbon footprint of the current centralized system of refining and distribution, and the vulnerability to disruptions in supply and price fluctuations beyond anyone's control. Pick your poison.

Choosing the right stove size Manufacturers and dealers will tell you that such-and-such-model woodstove has a heat output of so-many thousands of BTUs. The idea is that, as for any heating system, you would calculate the heat load for your house and then install a heating appliance that can deliver the requisite BTUs per hour, with a bit of excess capacity thrown in for good measure.

Woodstove-BTU-output figures are mostly meaningless. How much heat a stove will produce under optimal laboratory conditions has no relationship to heat output in the real world. The kind of wood, its moisture content, the quantity of wood in the stove, whether the stove is damped down or burned wide open—all of these variables affect the stove's performance.

The rule of thumb regarding stove size is, if you have a big house, get a big stove. If you only want to heat a single room, get a small stove. The most important factor that determines how long a stove will burn is the size of the firebox. A firebox that can hold a good-size load of wood will easily burn all night and put out plenty of heat while doing so. A small firebox can't and won't. The commodious firebox of our Hearthstone® stove gulps down more than 3 cu. ft. of 2-ft. logs per serving and will reliably greet us at breakfast with plenty of glowing coals, eager to fire up a new batch of fresh wood.

Backup heat If you have an oil- or gas-fired hot-air furnace, you can use the existing ductwork to add on a wood furnace to serve as the primary heat source. You can then configure the original unit to provide backup heat, cycling on whenever the wood fire burns down and the thermostat calls for heat. This setup would allow you to burn hotter fires or leave for a few days during the heating season. After the nighttime fire has burned down to embers, a mobile-home-size wall- or closet-mounted gas furnace can take the edge off the chill that would otherwise greet you upon rising in the morning.

Our 1,750-sq.-ft., two-story house is heated (quite comfortably) by our Hearthstone woodstove. We have an LP gas furnace in a central utility closet that will keep the house from freezing on those rare occasions when we leave for a few days during the winter. More often, we use it to take the morning chill off those spring and autumn days that are otherwise too warm for a fire.

If you're buying an existing house or building a new house, be aware that your mortgage lender may require you to have some kind of "conventional" heat (especially if they repackage their loans for the secondary market). When we bought our house, the woodstove was allowed as a backup, for "occasional use." Wink wink, nudge nudge.

Installation and location Although it's not especially difficult to install a woodstove, in many parts of the country your installation must pass inspection by the local fire marshal or other official, and you may have to document that inspection to qualify for homeowner's insurance. The National Fire Protection Association (NFPA) promotes standards for the safe installation of woodstoves (NFPA-211). Basically, these standards boil down to maintaining recommended clearances between the sides of the stove and combustible surfaces and routing the smoke pipe to the chimney by the shortest and most direct route. For new NFPA-listed stoves, follow the manufacturer's installation instructions. Be wary of secondhand stoves. Although NFPA-211 supplies the approved clearances, in many jurisdictions unlisted and non-EPA certified stoves are no longer legal because of pollution concerns.

The location of your woodstove can have a significant effect on the comfort of the rooms it heats. A stove works best when placed in the center of an open room—providing true "central heat." Every additional wall interferes with efficient convective-heat circulation.

In most cases, the reality must fall short of the ideal. Except for a small house in which the heat can circulate up and down the stairwell, heat flow to the second floor is best accomplished via floor registers. Provide two for each room, one at the front and another at the rear. The efficacy of natural convection is limited, which is why forced-hot-air systems were commonly preferred. It's also why rooms in rambling old farmhouses often had individual fireplaces or woodstoves. Comfortable heat distribution is always problematic when a loft opens onto a living area that has a vaulted ceiling. Whether it's a "great room" or a small room, the stove should be placed well under the loft to keep the loft from becoming unbearably hot and main floor living areas uncomfortably cool. A ceiling fan will also help to break up undesirable heat stratification.

Consider the Humble Pellet

Pellet stoves are about as close to automatic as wood burning gets, and there are a lot of environmental, economic, and practical reasons to consider heating with them.

First, consider the fuel itself. Pellets, which look like rabbit or chicken feed, are manufactured from compressed sawdust, corn, or peanut shells, basically by-products that would otherwise end up in landfills. Manufactured by compression, they contain no polluting glues or binders. Because the compression force actually squeezes water out of the material, pellets burn extremely hot and efficiently, producing virtually no smoke and very little ash to clean up. Compared to handling firewood, pellets are a delight. Sold in 40-lb. bags, these days a 1-ton pallet retails for $190 to $250 at big-box discounters and local hardware stores. There is no bark, dirt, or dust. Pellets also require less storage space than an equivalent amount of firewood (and, unlike wood, they can be stored in the basement or in a trash can).

You dump the pellets into a hopper, which can hold anywhere from one to three bags at a time. An auger feeds the pellets into a firepot at a predetermined rate, which you can set manually or control electronically to automatically adjust to the setting of an optional wall-mounted thermostat. The intensity of the fire is determined by the rate of feed. Combustion air (ideally from outside the house) is blown into the firepot to supercharge the burn. At the same time, a fan draws room air across a heat exchanger, whose surface is about 250°F. The heated air warms the living space by convection, not, as with an ordinary woodstove, by radiation. The entire process is so efficient at extracting heat that you can substitute a 3-in.-diameter double-wall pipe for a masonry chimney. The stove is also cool enough to touch, which makes it safe in homes with little children. Finally, because the stove is power vented, the flue pipe can exit horizontally through a convenient wall, and the stove can be installed in any room.

Depending on the level of sophistication, pellet stoves are available with automatic ignition. Some stoves are large enough to hold a week's worth of pellets at a time and can be used in tandem with central heating systems. The typical stove will operate from one to two days per load. Because pellets burn so efficiently—producing only 1 gram of particulate matter per hour, compared to the 5 gram per hour standard of EPA-certified woodstoves—and considering the ease of venting, the flexibility of placement, and the ease of handling, a pellet stove would be ideal for heating an urban apartment. Pellet stoves are priced at $1,200 to $3,000 (in 2011), according to the number of bells and whistles and the hopper capacity, which makes them comparable in price to standard woodstoves.

Pellet stoves do share one drawback with conventional wood boilers—their dependence on the umbilical cord of the electrical grid. If there's no power, you've got no heat. There are battery backups available that will keep the auger and fans turning, but if the outage lasts for more than 18 hours, you are out of heat. The battery backup also depends on grid power to charge. Pellet stoves are also more finicky than other types of wood burners, and there is a learning curve to adjusting the setting for your particular conditions. Minor quibbles notwithstanding, however, pellet stoves offer a matchless combination of convenience and conscience—except for one big problem, which, in my mind at least, makes the whole enterprise questionable. If you are buying pellets, you aren't buying local. You are at the mercy of the same market forces that drive up the price of conventional fuels. There have already been shortages and price fluctuations in pellet supply. As more people switch to pellet stoves, the market for suitable by-products will overheat. Firewood is not without price gouging and shortages, but at least you can cut your own if you have a woodlot.

There are also concerns about the net carbon neutrality of pellet fuel. How does the embodied energy of pellet manufacture and packaging and transportation compare with that of backyard or local firewood? Granted, compared to oil and gas, there's no contest—better a renewable fuel any day, even if it's not perfect. For myself, the feeling of satisfaction I get when I look at a winter's worth of firewood filling the shed far exceeds the feeling I have when I see plastic sacks of pellets stacked at the back of the garage.

The Wood Boiler Alternative

Like any conventional boiler, a wood-fired boiler heats water that circulates through baseboard heaters, cast-iron radiators, or radiant in-floor tubing. The main advantage of a wood boiler is its considerably higher heat output and the fact that it can be integrated with conventional hot-water or radiant systems to deliver even heat throughout the entire house.

Unlike the heat from a woodstove, hot-water heat is thermostatically zoned. Boilers can also efficiently supply hot water for household use. They're located in the basements—not in the living area—so you're spared the mess that results from carrying and stacking wood by the woodstove.

The disadvantage of a boiler is the significantly higher cost, both for the boiler and its associated plumbing. Also, because the circulation pumps and controls run on electricity, if you lose your power, you lose your heat. Finally, if you decide to install a backup system, there is the added expense of a conventional boiler and its appurtenant plumbing. Combination wood/oil or other multifuel boilers were all the rage for a few years back in the 1970s and '80s, but these systems proved inefficient and troublesome.

Indoors or out? If you've driven down a country road and happened to notice, alongside or out back of someone's house, what looks like a small prefabricated garden shed with a stub of a smoke pipe sticking up through its roof, belching a thick cloud of ground-hugging white or grey smoke, you're looking at an outdoor wood-burning boiler. When the EPA first regulated wood-burning stoves in 1988, the rules specifically exempted wood-fired central-heating appliances—and, voilà, the outdoor boiler appeared. It can, and often does, burn almost anything, such as green wood, sawdust, household trash, wood chips, and even (by some astoundingly inconsiderate individuals) old tires, in order to heat the house, outbuildings, barn, and/or greenhouse, at a much lower cost than any other system.

The technology is primitive. A wood boiler is basically a firebox that's surrounded by a water jacket. Its simplicity makes the unit both inexpensive and inefficient. (Older outdoor wood boilers run at 28 to 50 percent efficiency—or, more graphically, for every two logs you put in the firebox, one log's worth of heat goes up the smokestack.) The hot water from the boiler runs into the house through buried insulated supply and return pipes to heat radiators and potable water. No wood or dirt gets inside the house. The huge firebox needs to be charged only once or twice every 24 hours, especially if the fire is damped down.

From their first appearance in the late 1990s, outdoor boilers have been controversial. Some models produced more pollution than the old-fashioned noncertified woodstoves they replaced. Neighbors complained about the noxious, stinking, irritating smoke that infiltrated their homes and made life outdoors unbearable when the wind was blowing the wrong way. Furthermore, unless there is some way to store (or "dump") the excess heat, burning a boiler hot and clean will overheat the house.

The latest generation of indoor wood boilers is typically more efficient and cleaner burning than outdoor boilers. Unlike outdoor boilers, they are designed to work with closed-loop hot-water systems, which are long lasting, require less maintenance, and are less troubled by corrosion. Indoor boilers are convenient in that you don't have to venture out into the cold to tend them, and freezing is not a concern. Because the smoke will exit from a rooftop chimney, there is less chance that concentrated ground-level smoke will drift into a neighbor's yard.

On the other hand, you do have to lug wood from the shed down into the cellar. There is a solution, however. Although you can't put an outdoor boiler inside, you can definitely put an inside boiler outside. Consider building an insulated boiler room as part of a woodshed attached to the house. Even better, make the boiler room accessible from inside the house. (Check with your building inspector; you'll probably need a fire-rated door and fire-rated wall construction.) Or consider putting the boiler in the woodshed—it's more convenient and tidier than tossing wood down a cellar hatchway.

Wood gasification boilers Indoors or outside, folks tend to starve their boilers of air to make the fire last and to keep the heat nice and steady rather than rich and hot, which limits smoke pollution. There is a way out of this conundrum, but it doesn't come cheap (once again reinforcing the stereotype of environmentalism as an annoying affectation of wealthy elitists).

There are new wood-burning boilers (outdoor and indoor) called wood gasification boilers that can burn wood at efficiencies approaching the theoretical maximum of 90 percent while producing almost no emissions. Gasification boilers circumvent the pollution/heat-output dilemma by addressing wood burning and heat storage separately. The wood is burned hot and quick in a well-insulated firebox. The heat is transferred to a large storage reservoir for use between boiler firings. (Water jackets for smoky boilers typically hold from 140 to 400 gallons; a Garn® reservoir, made by Dectra Corporation, holds from 1,400 to 3,200 gallons.)

Stored heat is ideal for radiant heating systems, which operate at lower temperatures than standard hot-water systems. The drawback to wood gasification is the high cost (about double the cost of low-end boilers, excluding the cost of the foundation pad, plumbing, and controls). It's the usual case of perverse incentives: Even with tax credits and subsidies, it costs a lot more than it should *not* to pollute.

The masonry stove There is a traditional low-tech alternative that maximizes the storage of heat produced by a hot, clean-burning fire. The masonry stove, sometimes referred to as a *kachelofen* or "Russian fireplace," has been around for at least 1,000 years. Masonry heaters are similar to wood-fired bake ovens. A series of internal baffles stores the heat from

an intensely hot fire in the masonry mass of the surrounding structure, where it is gradually and comfortably released after the fire dies out. Unlike a woodstove or boiler, the firebox can be charged with sticks, twigs, kindling, scrap lumber, straw, or any other dry biomass waste capable of producing a hot, quick fire. The fire needs to be kindled only once or twice a day during the heating season, so masonry heaters consume far less fuel than other types of heaters. Their heat output is steady and even, so overheating is not a problem.

The advantage of a masonry heater is that no fluids, plumbing, wiring, controls, pumps, or blowers are involved. It's just simple thermal-mass, radiant-heat-transfer physics. With professionally prepared plans, a reasonably skilled homeowner could build one, and if you include the traditional warming benches and baking ovens in the design, the heater could truly become the center of the home.

On the con side of the ledger, masonry heaters can take from one to five days to warm up to temperature. They are also huge and heavy, commandeering a sizable area in the center of the home. If the house has a basement, the heater foundation will extend upward from there. Besides the firebox and smoke baffle, the masonry also includes a chimney. Doing all the bricklaying yourself, calculating the cost of 3,000 to 5,000 standard bricks at upward of 50¢ apiece and several hundred more-expensive firebricks, mortar, flue tiles, and other accessories, the price can easily surpass that of a top-of-the line soapstone woodstove. It is possible

> "Solar tempering is simply sensible building. In the current time of rising energy costs and fossil fuel depletion, it's not an option. It's an imperative."

to buy prefabricated firebox/flue cores that greatly simplify the work, however. Hiring a skilled mason who specializes in masonry heaters will put you in the same price bracket as installing a state-of-the-art wood-burning gasification boiler.

Solar Solutions

Although Vermont is one of the coldest and cloudiest places in the continental United States, the solar panels mounted on the roof of our house still supply better than half of our yearly household hot water. The heat loop and storage tank plumbed into our woodstove provide much of the rest.

During the years we lived in Arizona, I remember driving past the luxury housing developments breaking out in the desert like a skin disease and being struck by what was missing from their Mission-style tile rooftops. How was it that there, I thought, in one of the sunniest parts of the country, solar collectors were as uncommon as sunstroke in Seattle? It could only make sense to a developer—if you're not the one paying the utility bill, 500 electric water heaters are a lot cheaper to install than 500 solar panels.

Everyone has an opinion about solar energy. I have a hunch that it runs something like this: "Sure, I think solar is great,

but it's not very practical, is it? I mean, at least not for the average homeowner. Who can afford it?" Part of the problem is that our culture thinks gizmos and gadgets are sexy. LED readouts, fans, switches, and digital monitors are fashionable, even, like the latest cell phone/computer, a status symbol. As a result, active solar space heating systems get all the press.

Solar space heating An active solar space-heating system involves some method of powered heat collection, transfer, storage, and extraction, relying on fluids, such as air or water. Basically, an active system collects heat in one place and stores it in another for distribution. Most active systems fulfill their design expectations and deliver some fraction of the heat load, but depending on where you live and the amount of available sunshine, the solar savings on your energy bill might never pay back the cost of hardware and installation. The decision to install solar space heating, then, becomes a moral choice rather than a strictly economic one. There's nothing wrong with spending money to do the right thing—but not everyone can afford to put their money where their heart is.

On the other hand, *passive* solar technology (the storage and transfer of heat without any mechanical assistance) has worked for as long as Planet Earth (an

appropriately sized thermal mass fitted with
an insulating thermal blanket called the
atmosphere) has been hurtling through
space. For example, sunlight that enters
through south-facing windows is absorbed
by the material it falls upon (the thermal
mass) and stored as heat. The amount of
heat this target area later releases depends
on its density, color, and composition and
on the ambient temperature.

That's about all there is to it—no high-
tech thermostats, electronic sensors,
whir-ring fans and pumps, or computer-
ized controllers. Concrete-slab floors and
vertical, decorative stone or brick walls
are typical examples of built-in thermal
masses.So would be a wall of 55-gallon,
black-painted, water-filled drums stacked
behinda curtain wall of glass. There are
no moving parts, although hybrid systems
employ simple fans or pumps to boost the
efficiency of heat transfer into a passive-
storage mass.

*Left: The sunspace that wraps around our house from
the southeast to southwest captures solar heat (and is
a pleasant room to sit in and enjoy a winter morning.) Right: A rooftop photovoltaic (PV) array.*

It doesn't cost any more to build a house
that faces south than to build one that
faces north. Simply by optimizing your
house's solar orientation, you can reduce
your heating costs and, depending on
prevailing breezes, maybe even lower
cooling costs, too. Furthermore, every
house needs windows. Changing their
orientation, distribution, and size can
make a big difference in the warmth and
comfort of your home. Likewise, placing
walls in direct sunlight and building them
in such a way to increase their ability to
store heat isn't difficult or expensive.
These are just a few examples of the
principle of solar tempering, which
involves nothing more complicated than

using site conditions and low-cost structural elements to lower fossil-fuel energy use by harvesting and storing some portion of the available solar energy.

You don't need to build a conspicuously solar house to take advantage of the sun. The traditional New England farmhouse had most of its windows on the south side and buffered the north wall with attached woodsheds and barns. Your solar strategies can be as simple as minimizing undesirable exposures and orienting the long wall of the house to the south. Controlling infiltration of outside cold air and adding extra-deep insulation are beneficial practices, too. Solar tempering is simply sensible building. In the current time of rising energy costs and fossil fuel depletion, it's not an option. It's an imperative.

Getting into hot water The constraints that limit the cost-effectiveness of active solar space heating don't apply to solar water heating. Solar water heating requires less energy and, therefore, a smaller collector area and storage tank than needed for the active solar space heating of even a small house. The heat storage and transfer efficiency of air is so inferior to that of water that it cannot heat water at all. The forced circulation of an active solar water-heating system transfers heat from the collector to the water much more efficiently than passive circulation.

Anyone who's picked up a garden hose that's been out in the sun will easily understand how solar water heating works. Water circulates through a collector, which is basically a pipe looped inside an insulated black-painted box with a glass cover.

The collector traps the sun's heat (the so-called greenhouse effect) so that the heat is transferred to the water, which then flows into an insulated storage tank. From there, it flows into an ordinary backup water heater or directly into the household plumbing system. That's pretty much all there is to it, at least in regions where it doesn't freeze (systems are more complicated when freezing is an issue).

Heating water for domestic use typically accounts for about 40 percent of residential energy use. That's a serious bill. A solar hot-water system can offset as much as 65 percent of the cost of natural gas, propane, oil, or electric water heating. Add the federal tax credits, state rebates, and electric-utility incentives (which can save up to 50 percent on installation costs), and the idea to take advantage of solar water heating is a no-brainer—and a big step toward sustainability—no matter where you live. I can't think of any reason why solar water heating shouldn't be an integral part of any new or retrofitted home.

The simplest setup is a batch heater, also known as an Integrated Collector System (ICS). The collector also serves as the storage tank. Cold water is piped into the bottom of one or more black-painted tanks that sit inside an insulated box with a glass cover that is mounted on the roof. The heat generated by the black surface warms the water inside the tank. When someone opens a hot-water tap inside the house, hot water flows from the top of the tank, drawing more cold water into the bottom.

A batch heater is the prototypical passive solar water-heating system. It's also what

Energy Conservation 101

Tax credits and rebates notwithstanding, the cost of solar electric systems—and to some lesser extent, solar hot-water systems—is still steep enough to discourage their widespread adoption. At the very least, it behooves us all to employ some basic conservation strategies to reduce our energy consumption and live more-sustainable lives.

• Choose compact fluorescent lights (CFLs) or light-emitting diodes (LEDs) instead of incandescent bulbs.

• Install tankless, on-demand water heaters instead of storage tank heaters.

• Install radiant in-floor heat instead of forced-air or standard hydronic heating.

• Use geothermal (groundwater) heat pumps, wherever practical.

• Replace old appliances with highly efficient ENERGY STAR–rated appliances (research carefully before buying).

• Replace top-loading clothes washers with more efficient front loaders.

• Wash clothes in cold water.

• Dry clothes outdoors, whenever feasible.

• Install double- or, better yet, triple-pane, argon-filled insulated windows.

• Insulate entry doors.

• Superinsulate with a minimum of R-19 wall and R-38 ceiling insulation.

• Opt for SEER-rated air-conditioning units (and locate the compressor on the shady side of the house).

• Use an evaporative cooler (where possible) instead of air conditioner.

• Whenever possible, use a whole-house attic fan instead of an air conditioner.

• Rely on an EPA-certified wood-burning stove or wood gasification boiler as primary heat source and use fossil fuel for backup only.

• Buffer mudroom or air-lock entryway.

• Build attached greenhouse or sunspace.

• Install insulated movable shades to minimize nighttime heat loss.

• Build with native or natural (minimally processed) materials or green and recycled materials whenever possible (avoid aluminum siding and vinyl anything).

• Xeriscape with drought-tolerant native plants in arid regions, rather than creating water-guzzling lawns; use drip-irrigation systems, and water plants early in the morning to reduce water loss through evaporation.

heating engineers call an open-loop or direct system, meaning that the house's potable water system supplies water to the collector. Batch water heaters are inexpensive and fairly easy to build from scratch. They have no moving parts or sensors that can fail, but they must be drained when there is danger of frost, so they're best suited to warm climates or seasonal use. The other big drawback to an ICS water heater is its weight. The water-filled tanks require strong support, both in the collector frame and the roof framing.

Active solar water-heating systems use small pumps to circulate either water or a heat-transfer fluid between the collector and the storage tank. Active systems can be either open-loop or closed-loop (indirect). In a closed-loop arrangement, separate piping circulates a heat-transfer fluid that is similar to antifreeze (usually, propylene glycol, called glycol for short) between the collector and a heat-exchanger coil inside the water-storage tank. The heat from the sun-warmed fluid is transferred to the water in the tank.

Like batch heaters, open-loop active systems are best suited to warm climates, but an open-loop system can work in winter. The system can be designed so that when a sensor indicates that the temperature at the collector is high enough, a solenoid-controlled valve would open, allowing the pump to circulate water. When the temperature drops to the lower limit, the pump would turn off and a drain valve would open, emptying the collector and pipes. The sacrifice of a few gallons of heated water during the emptying process is a small price to pay for the efficiency of an open-loop system (as long as the system is designed to automatically drain down in the event of a wintertime power failure). The question of whether to go with an open- or closed-loop system may already have been decided for you, however. In most states, plumbing codes no longer allow you to mix potable water with water in an open heating loop.

Improvements in heat exchangers and system controls have enabled glycol-based closed-loop systems to achieve efficiencies almost as high as those of open-loop systems. This fact, coupled with the elimination of the risk of freezing, is the reason why these systems are the most widely used throughout North America. They can supply water year-round regardless of outside temperatures. In most cases, the solar-storage tank (which can be a standard electric water-heater tank with its heating elements removed) is plumbed to the cold inlet of a gas or electric water heater. That heater serves as a backup during long stretches of cloudy weather. The water in a large (80 to 120 gallon) and well-insulated solar-storage tank will retain its heat for several days.

Some systems rely on a dual-purpose tank, which is oversized to maximize storage and contains both a heat exchanger and a single electric heating element for the rare occasions when backup is needed. In cold climates, the solar fraction of a household's hot-water supply can be augmented by water heated by a coil in the firebox of a woodstove. This two-pronged strategy nearly eliminates the need for conventional backup heating during those months when the woodstove is running full-tilt.

An even more efficient and, therefore, more sustainable option is to plumb one or more solar-storage tanks (with or without supplemental input from the woodstove) to a gas-fired, tankless, on-demand heater. One welcome problem with these systems is that, on a cold, sunny day, when both the collector and the woodstove are at maximum output, they can produce considerably more hot water than you can use.

Burning Wood

You don't have to live out in the country or own a woodlot to harvest your own firewood or even saw logs. According to estimates, almost 3 to 4 billion board ft. of otherwise marketable saw logs end up as "green waste" in the municipal solid-waste stream instead of in a sawmill. This lumber comes from trees that have to be cut down because of disease, age, public hazard, interference with roadways and sidewalks, road building, or real-estate development. Some municipalities convert these trees into lumber rather than mulch. Others simply sell or give away the logs for firewood. Efforts are underway to convince tree service companies to turn felled trees into salable logs.

Depending on where you live, it may be possible to obtain firewood (and even valuable hardwood saw logs for lumber) at a very reasonable cost. Of course, hauling a 1,200-lb. log to the nearest sawmill could present a challenge. Fortunately, it's often possible to find someone who will bring the sawmill to your logs instead. Portable sawmill operators are often found just outside many metropolitan areas.

Urban Homesteading

If you live in an urban environment where opportunities to acquire firewood are limited, or if you don't find the thought of cutting, splitting, hauling, piling, and stacking 20 tons of wood particularly enticing, having a load of dry firewood delivered to your home may be worth the extra cost, especially considering the time and effort (and not inconsiderable hazard) required to harvest your own. Burning firewood is a real commitment. There's the $700 chainsaw you'll need to fell the trees and buck up the logs. You have to rent a wood splitter and beg, borrow, rent, or buy a pickup truck or utility trailer to haul the splitter and the wood. You'll also need to have enough room somewhere on your property to stack and store your wood—which can be an issue if you're homesteading in an apartment or condominium complex.

Limited storage area is one good reason to opt for a pellet stove instead of a conventional wood burner. If you live where winters are relatively mild, however, a single cord may be all the wood you need to take the edge off of those chilly evenings.

This vintage furnace (the "Acme Hummer") appeared in the Sears, Roebuck and Company's catalog 1911.

Some urban homesteaders harvest all the firewood they need from construction-site dumpsters. Others cart off discarded wood pallets from local businesses. With a circular saw or inexpensive electric chainsaw, you can cut your salvaged wood to length—no splitting required, except to make kindling.

Suburban Homesteading

Burning wood produces microparticles, and, under the right conditions, temperature inversions can trap wood smoke at ground level, resulting in very irritating and unhealthy air when too many woodstoves are puffing away. Some communities, most notably Telluride, Colorado, have actually gone so far as to ban woodstoves entirely in any new house or house being sold. Others have sought to regulate wood burning and the installation of woodstoves in other ways.

Most prohibitions against burning wood apply to outdoor boilers, but your local zoning board may take a dim view of burning wood of any sort. Most communities prohibit the installation of wood-burning appliances that do not meet the most recent EPA standards, but some states have adopted even more stringent certification requirements. Keep this in mind as you browse the want ads for a secondhand woodstove. Some homeowners install outdoor wood boilers only to find that they have to remove or modify them because of new prohibitions. Check local regulations carefully before you commit to the idea of burning wood full-time.

The Mini-Farm

Until very recently, the conventional way to heat a greenhouse, poultry house, or livestock barn was with propane (LPG). In addition to the considerable expense, the main drawback of heating with LPG is that, for every gallon burned, 6.8 lb. of water vapor is emitted. Molds and pathogens flourish in the resulting high humidity, fostering disease and generally unhealthy conditions.

A wood-burning stove or boiler is a greener alternative to heating with propane, oil, or electricity (and creates no humidity problem), but the care and feeding of a woodstove is time-consuming. The self-feeding, multiple-day capability of a large pellet stove has advantages, but considering that farms produce all sorts of organic waste, a biomass boiler or furnace might be an even better way to heat your barn, workshop, and home.

Biomass is any organic matter—corncobs and kernels, wood pellets and chips, log wood, waste wood, and agricultural by-products (cherry pits, walnuts shells, and herbaceous materials, for example). Some biomass stoves burn only dry corn kernels; others burn almost any organic material, including pea coal. Like high-end pellet stoves, biomass units feature large hoppers, adjustable auger-feed rates, and programmable control of fuel and air ratios for optimal combustion.

PART II

Garden & Orchard

*"When tillage begins, other arts follow.
The farmers, therefore, are the founders
of human civilization."* —DANIEL WEBSTER

chapter vi

Choosing a Gardening System

We used to say, "There are more cows in Vermont than there are people." The demographics have changed, so now we say, "There are more cow T-shirts in Vermont than there are cows or people." The situation is similar for gardening books: There seem to be more how-to-garden books than there are gardens. So, with that in mind, we don't intend to write another. There are already too many books that list plant names and hardiness zones and specify how many inches apart to plant each seed. Most how-to books give readers a laundry list of methods and techniques: "Add X, Y, and Z to the compost pile and stir." Of course, every gardener needs such books— even two or three of them—but we're headed in a different direction. We believe it's far better to understand the reasons why a certain technique is better than another than it is to simply follow directions. Knowing the basics also helps you avoid stupid fads and rip-offs. Botany and soil science are the basics of agriculture in general and of organic gardening specifically. The more you know about these

sciences, the better farmer or gardener you will be. (And if someone tells you to put Windex® in your window boxes, you'll know not to do it and why.)

This section is, in no way, intended as the final word on the subject of gardening. Instead, we'd like to focus on subject matter that is rarely discussed in other gardening books and that can only be acquired through experience. For starters, we don't assume that everything always goes smoothly. Everyone gets behind schedule, and the weeds sometimes get the best of you. We know from years in the trenches that no one can do it all. So we'll discuss how to prioritize what must be done and what you can let slide while still getting a decent yield. We'll also clarify some topics that might be confusing—such as the difference between modern hybrid and heritage (or heirloom) vegetables and how to save their seeds.

Unlike other garden writers, we won't try to list every known vegetable along with

···

Our bountiful organic garden, farmed on the same plot of land for more than 30 years.

every conceivable factoid, relevant or not. Instead, we'll divide garden crops into their natural botanical families and then outline the characteristics and culture of each family, which is how botanists categorize plants—and for good reason. When you understand the families, you can apply that information to every vegetable in the garden. We'll also discuss other aspects of gardening, from planning to harvest. We hope that when you finish reading this section, you'll feel as if you've just spent the afternoon talking with your grandmother, who has shared her gardening secrets with you. But first we'll climb up on our soapbox and debunk some myths and straighten out some misinformation. We can't resist. It's too much fun—and you need to know the truth.

The "Farmers Feed the World" Myth

We chose to be organic growers because growing organically just makes sense. We believe that organic gardening is better for the environment and for the gardener—even if everyone else isn't yet convinced. Michelle Obama planted an organic garden at the White House during the first spring of her husband's administration. Upon hearing the news, some spokespeople for the agrichemical industry grumbled that raising vegetables organically was setting a bad example for the nation's gardeners. Can you imagine our First Lady discovering a potato beetle on her potato plant and yelling to one of the White House gardeners, "Betty, quick! Get me my Phospho kills-everything

sprayer!" I think she would be much more likely to bend over and squish the little sucker between her fingers. She may be a city girl, but she ain't stupid.

Of course, Big Farma (kind of like Big Pharma) doesn't really think a backyard garden plot needs heavy-duty pesticides. They just don't want organic gardening to get any good press, especially if that garden is in the First Backyard. So far, the industry has done a very good job convincing most people, including Mr. Obama, that, although organic gardening is fine for fuddy-duddies who wear funny hats, the only way that farmers can feed the whole world is with huge fields of monocultured, genetically modified crops. (What they don't say is that those crops must be kept in precarious health with regular doses of synthetic fertilizers, nerve toxins, and endocrine analogs.)

We simply don't know whether small diversified farms that rotate cattle, pigs, and chickens through fields of native grasses can feed billions of people. It may be that we need a whole lot more farms and farmers and a lot fewer housing developments and shopping centers. Three things, however, are undeniably true:

Truth #1: Agribusiness is not feeding the world. Invoking images of millions of acres of golden corn fluttering in the fields like ruffles on a party dress, corn tortilla mountains, ziggurats of boxed corn flakes, and semis hauling loads of corn bread to market, agribusiness behemoths boast about all the cheap food they help grow for the world to eat. They may be

Herbicide Wars

Presently, there are more than 100 different weeds that are resistant to Roundup®, the most widely used herbicide in the world since 1980. In the United States alone, there are between 7 and 10 million acres of crops infested with resistant weeds. One of the most noxious is pigweed (*Amaranthus hybridus,* et al.), which can grow up to 7 ft. tall and is so large and woody that it can damage equipment. The company that holds the patent on Roundup denies that herbicide resistance is a serious problem, but has devoted an entire division exclusively to the problem—just in case. This emerging problem is serious enough that a new international committee, the International Survey of Herbicide Resistant Weeds, is tracking and studying it.

Ninety percent of all soybeans and 70 percent of the corn grown worldwide are now "Roundup Ready" (in other words, their DNA has been modified to make the plants resistant to Roundup). This feature allows farmers to spray Roundup by airplane and kill only the weeds and not the crops. Before the existence of Roundup-Ready crops, farmers sprayed far less of the compound and far less often.

They had to spray using a tractor and had to take care not to overspray the herbicide onto the corn or soybeans. Because so many weeds are now resistant to Roundup, a lot of farmers have stopped buying the producer's expensive, patented, genetically modified seed. In response, the company, ever vigilant about maintaining its market share, is trying to develop crops that are resistant to an even stronger herbicide—our old friend 2, 4-D (2, 4-Dichlorophenoxyacetic Acid), of Agent Orange and Vietnam War fame.

---

growing a lot of corn, but very little of it is being made into real food.

Granted, some small part of that corn does actually end up on your plate as food, but the vast majority of it is transmogrified into high-fructose corn syrup (HFCS), a "stealth food" ingredient in almost all of the processed "food products" lining the middle aisles of America's supermarkets. HFCS is in ketchup, tomato sauce, salad dressing, and most low-fat foods. Most of it, however, goes into the millions of gallons of soda that Americans swill every year. HFCS is a major player in the worldwide epidemic of obesity.

Malnutrition (either too much bad food or too little food of any kind) is the number-one cause of preventable deaths in the world. All those pesticides, artificial fertilizers, and genetically modified monocrops that deplete our soil and pollute our waters aren't growing food. They're growing soda. Far from feeding us nourishing food, agribusinesses are

> *"The farmer works the soil. The agriculturist works the farmer."*
> —Eugene Fitch Ware

killing us with diabetes. Every penny, and then some, that we save on "cheap" food, we eventually pay in medical costs.

Truth #2: Fertilizer runoff and pesticides are harming our soil and water. Studies clearly show that factory-farmed food is impregnated with pesticide residues, as is almost every region of the planet. We do not yet know if those residues can affect human growth and development, but we do know that they cause abnormalities in the reproductive systems of laboratory animals and animals in the wild.

Potential health affects aside, who will pay for the loss of fertile soil, the erosion, and the ocean "dead zones" that are the true legacy of decades of abusive farming practices? Food and the soil in which it grows are a single living system, which resists our efforts to make it conform to the agronomist's notion of market efficiency. Planting a single crop on the same large acreage year after year seems efficient in the short run, but over time it creates two major problems:

1. It depletes the soil of nutrients and microbes. Monocropping and artificial fertilizers destroy the microorganisms that build soil structure. When soil structure breaks down, it erodes.

2. It intensifies pest problems. Spread the table with 500 acres of corn, and every corn borer within miles will show up for dinner.

Agribusiness's answer to the corn borer and other unwanted insects and weeds is always the same: new and improved pesticides (both insecticides and herbicides are pesticides). It doesn't take long, however—often less than 10 years—for the pests, be they insects or weeds, to become resistant to the remedies. Eventually, breeds of superbugs and monster weeds evolve that are immune to every chemical weapon in the arsenal. *This cycle occurs over and over for every single major pesticide or antibiotic that has ever been developed.* In fact, the more that a pesticide or antibiotic is used, the quicker the organisms develop resistance to it.

For example, antibiotic sulfanomide (aka sulfa) drugs, invented during World War II, were very effective up until the 1990s. Then poultry farmers started to feed them to chickens prophylactically. Fewer than 10 years later, most of the bacteria against which sulfas had been effective had become resistant, and the drug was practically useless for both humans and chickens. Farmers switched to Ciprofloxacin, a stronger (and much more expensive) miracle drug to fight the sulfa-resistant microbes, until Cipro, too, lost its punch. Everyone from the casual observer to the researchers who develop the latest drugs knows that this is how it goes, yet the brilliant and talented biochemists at the agribusinesses respond

Squashing the Squash Beetle

Winters are really cold here in northern Vermont, so we haven't been plagued by a lot of the pests that are common just a few hundred miles south of us. That may, however, be changing. The winters aren't as cold any more.

Until a few years ago, we had never seen striped cucumber beetles, which are also called squash beetles (cucumbers and squash are in the same family, so share many pests). We also saw Japanese beetles for the first time that year. The year before, there had been a scattering of the yellow-and-black-striped monsters, but only enough to qualify as a curiosity. The next spring, however, they were so numerous that they annihilated the squash sprouts before they could fully emerge. At first, I went out and picked them off several times a day. I sprinkled the squash hills with diatomaceous earth—a naturally occurring mineral used to control beetles and other insects—but the bugs were always a step ahead of me.

As a last resort, I dusted them with pyrethrum, a nominally organic compound of questionable repute. Pyrethrum is a nervous-system poison with a very short half-life (it breaks down quickly). It's good for the environment, but not so effective at killing bugs. It worked for a while, but almost as soon as I turned my back, the beetles were back with a vengeance.

Apparently, I was not the only gardener in the state who had been vanquished by the Squash Beetle Ambush, because one Sunday, the National Public Radio garden guy was talking about ways to save the cucurbit (squash) family. As he explained, it turns out that even the really nasty pesticides are no more effective than pyrethrum. His suggestion was to cover the plantings until the sprouts grew big enough and strong enough to withstand the cucumber beetles.

Inspired, we replanted our squash hills and protected every grouping with shields that we fashioned from plastic 1-gallon milk jugs. It worked! The hatchling plants flourished despite the squash bugs, but we knew the bugs were still there, hanging around in larval form in the soil. So, that fall and the following spring, we put about 35 chickens into the garden. They scratched, scoured, and scarfed down grubs, bugs, and larvae of all kinds, and, as a result, we had far fewer pests in the garden. That same year, with my help, our guinea fowl discovered the Japanese beetles on the *Rosa rugosa*. To guinea fowl, Japanese beetles are raspberry mousse with chocolate sauce—so no more Japanese beetles. This year, we didn't find a single squash beetle.

The lesson here is this: For all garden problems, there is an organic solution that does not require harmful pesticides—although the solution might take a little time to figure out, a little more time to implement, and a little more time to work. Educate yourself not only about the soil and the plants, but also about the uninvited insects, viruses, and fungi that want to share your bounty. The more you know, the more you'll grow.

Top: Periodic weeding keeps any weeds that emerge through hay mulch from becoming established. Bottom left: Mulching. Bottom right: Rhubarb gone to seed.

....

by developing even stronger pesticides. What do they think is going to happen in the next cycle?

Truth #3: Subsistence farming is sustainable. You *can* feed yourself (and your family and even a few friends or the entire neighborhood) with a fairly small organic operation. There have been some recent studies that conclude that, in the face of climate change, the only way to feed the world with nutrient-dense foods is to change our farming and eating practices to more-sustainable methods.

Corporate farming suffers from the same bias toward short-term profits as the rest of corporate culture. Proponents of "conventional" farming defend their methods by declaring that they produce more food per acre than traditional organic farmers. That's true in the short run but not in the long run. Growing monoculture acres of annual crops entails an inescapable commitment to chemical fertilizers and pesticides, progressing in a predictable downward spiral toward the same familiar dismal outcome. At first, there are huge increases in yields with relatively small chemical input, followed in a few years by smaller and smaller yields requiring larger and larger inputs, until the entire enterprise becomes economically unsustainable—which explains why the same fields in China that managed

to maintain their fertility for 4,000 years, have, only now, with the large-scale shift toward "modern" methods, begun to lose it.

This paradigm, at the heart of the Green Revolution that began in the mid-20th century, is also the counter to the lie that organic farming practices cannot feed the world. If you graphed the input/output of factory farming against organic farming, the two curves would begin as an exact inverse of each other. That is the yield of organic farms is initially low, but it builds over time as inputs diminish.

Sustainability starts with the small farms and homesteads that are raising diversified crops and livestock. Monoculture farming is not merely unsustainable, it is toxic to living systems. We are constantly boasting that a very small number of farmers feed very large numbers of people—as if this were a good thing. It's not. As long as this idea persists, we will have more pesticides and pests that are resistant to those pesticides. We will have more artificial fertilizers and fewer soil microbes and more dead soil. Even if dangerous pesticides are barred, it simply takes more and more synthetic fertilizer to keep dying soil on life support.

Dirt versus Soil

A local Vermont compost company has issued a bumper sticker that reads, "Don't Treat Your Soil Like Dirt." Every organic gardener gets the joke. We spend our time turning dirt into soil. The soil is everything. Without good soil, there is no garden and no farm.

The difference between organic farmers and factory farmers is that organic farmers turn dirt into soil and factory farmers turn soil into dirt. All over the world, Big Farma is turning soil into dirt, and the dirt is blowing away. This destruction is happening because Big Farma disregards the soil and focuses on the plant. To him, per se. What they do is supply the humus and micronutrients that are vital not just to plants but also to the microbes and fungi that are the building blocks of healthy soil. Think of them as enablers or potentiators of the soil's innate fertility. Meanwhile, far from the farm, down at the Concentrated Animal Feeding Operations

> *"The difference between organic farmers and factory farmers is that organic farmers turn dirt into soil and factory farmers turn soil into dirt."*

the soil is merely the medium that puts plant roots in contact with fertilizer. Add more fertilizer, he assumes, and you get more plant. It's as simple as that.

Mainstream farmers are fond of saying that nitrogen, phosphorus, and potassium (NPK)—the three essential macronutrients—are the same to a plant whether they come out of a bag or a compost pile. They're right, but they and others who argue that organic methods don't matter miss the point. Continued applications of synthetic fertilizers, although initially very beneficial to the plant, are harmful to the microbial life of the soil, which is even more essential to healthy plants. You need manure and compost to nourish that microbial community. Although these substances do indeed contain some amount of NPK, the percentages are far less than those found in chemical fertilizers. It's really a misconception to think of manure and compost as fertilizers

(CAFO) feed lot, manure—this supremely beneficial resource—has been debased into a pollutant. The runoff from too much manure concentrated in too small an area has become a huge problem.

Commercial farming techniques eventually kill the microbial life that manure, compost, and organic techniques foster. Soil that is farmed exclusively with artificial fertilizer becomes thinner and thinner until it virtually disappears. Adding a small amount of manure only slows the deterioration process a bit. Once soil has been eroded, it takes a very long time and a lot of work to restore it. Agribusiness doesn't care about the soil, however. It only cares about the end product: More soybeans! More wheat! More hamburgers! If there were a way to grow soybeans on concrete, factory farmers would jump right on it.

Organic farmers, on the other hand, are in love with the soil. George and I have gardened on the same plot of land for more than 30 years. Our soil is light, fluffy, and deep. I can't remember when we last checked the pH or mineral content. Peruse a periodical on eco-farming or sustainable agriculture, and you'll see that most of the articles and advertisements are about soil improvement and amendments. We organic farmers read about the latest recommendations for improving the soil's ability to hold moisture or its ability to drain. We debate which are the best trace mineral amendments and organic fertilizers. We talk about indigenous microorganisms (IMOs) and compost-tea inoculants. And we just enjoy digging in the stuff.

The Many Schools and Churches of Gardening

As with every passionate pursuit, there are numerous schools of thought on the best way to garden. Some of these "philosophies" border on religious beliefs. You may ask, "Can't you just grow stuff?"Apparently not. In addition to the (capital O) Organic Method, you can follow biodynamic, French intensive, and permaculture systems—to name a few of the better-known methods that fall under the organic heading.

Humans have a tendency to make up religions whenever and wherever they can, and gardeners are no exception. In fact, gardeners can grow dogmas at least as well as they grow lettuce. There are numerous spin-offs and splinters from what might be regarded as mainstream organic philosophy. Some promote complicated

rituals intended to bring every organism and molecule into holistic balance with the cosmos (for example, by burying a cow's horn and a sprig of yarrow in the east pasture at the new moon)—you might call this "faith-based farming." Unbiased research proves the phases of the moon have no bearing on plant growth, and there's no reason to think that basil makes tomatoes taste better, as some claim, except in a sauce. (That said, it might be a fun spring ritual to plant the first lettuce seed on the full moon in May. Add some dancing around the fire and chanting, and you've got yourself a pagan spring festival.)

If you spend any time reading about the various gardening philosophies that fall under the rubric of "organic," you'll soon discover that a principle of one sect may directly contradict that of another. The biointensive folks, for example, want to "double dig" everything. The permaculture camp thinks that disturbing the soil is the last thing you should do. Some true believers embrace all the tenets of their chosen path; others pick and choose to believe in whatever has worked for them. Fortunately, Mother Earth and the plants she grows are hardier than we think. They can survive the various and changing whims of the human race fairly well. When examining the tenets of the various gardening doctrines, remember, there is a difference between opinion and fact, even if the opinion comes from a very cool person. The bottom line is, use common sense. If a claim doesn't seem reasonable to you, it probably isn't.

Good old-fashioned organic farming

When I was a kid, plenty of farmers and gardeners grew food without resorting to pesticides and incorporated organic wastes (rotted manure and compost) into their soil, but they didn't call themselves organic farmers or gardeners. They were just growing food. My father, a dairy farmer, was one of these. He had a small herd States, and others began writing and lecturing about the evils of modern farming and its monoculture crops of hybrid seeds, which were made possible by ammonium nitrate fertilizer and the internal combustion engine. In 1942, J. I. Rodale first published the magazine *Organic Farming and Gardening*, which later morphed into *Organic Gardening*.

"Cultivators of the earth are the most valuable citizens. They are the most vigorous, the most independent, the most virtuous and they are tied to their country and wedded to its liberty and interests by the most lasting bands." —Thomas Jefferson

of about 30 to 40 milkers and as many replacement heifers. He never "got big." He was just trying to feed his rather large family. He had no more of a gardening philosophy than he had an eating philosophy. He grew food and ate it. He never read a gardening book until he was well into his seventies, when we bought him a subscription to *Organic Gardening* magazine. He was surprised to find out he had been "organic gardening" his whole life.

Until the early 20th century, "organic farming" was just simply farming. It was the way people had worked the land for thousands of years. What we have come to think of as the organic method was a revolt against the new agriculture that was then less than 50 years old. More or less simultaneously, Sir Albert Howard and Rudolf Steiner in Europe, Rebecca Kidd in Japan, F. H. King in the United

Until very recently, "organic" was the generic name for any type of gardening or farming that utilized "natural" rather than chemical methods. Most people who compost and avoid pesticides consider themselves organic gardeners—as well they should. Until 2002, when the U.S. Department of Agriculture (USDA) published the National Organic Program Standards (www.ams.usda.gov/nop), there was no real definition of organic agriculture. These standards do not apply to home gardeners, so there is no legal definition of "organic gardening." In short, if you think you're an organic gardener, you're an organic gardener. But are you a biodynamic gardener, a biointensive gardener, or a permaculture gardener?

....

Top: Loading up the hay. Bottom: We use hay mulch to control weeds and conserve moisture.

Do you practice year-round gardening, extreme gardening, or companion planting? Like my father, you might be one or all of the above and not even know it.

Biodynamic gardening It's unlikely that you would be a biodynamic gardener and not know it—that would be like being a devout Roman Catholic or an Orthodox Jew and not noticing. Biodynamic gardening sprang, full blown, from the fervid imagination of Rudolf Steiner, of the Waldorf School and learning-to-read-based-on-your-dental-development fame. Biodynamic theory agrees with every other organic method in that it rejects the use of synthetic fertilizers and pesticides. Likewise, biodynamic adherents believe in respecting the soil and its microbial life. The reasons why, however, seem to be based more on witchcraft than soil science.

For example, Steiner describes nine "preparations" that are concocted from various medicinal herbs mixed in precise proportions at certain critical phases of the moon. He claims that each concoction imparts certain "spiritual traits" and taps into "cosmic forces." Steiner is not channeling ancient tribal lore or even "old wives' tales" handed down through generations. No, Steiner invented these remedies more or less on the spot when he was asked how to counteract chemically depleted soil. In 1924, he gave eight lectures on the subject, and biodynamic "research" on his concoctions was conducted some time later. Several independent studies showed that these preparations, when paired with standard organic methods, worked as well as the organic methods did alone—which is hardly surprising, given the similarities between the two methodologies.

Despite its quirky mysticism, biodynamic farmers mostly worship at the same altar as everyday organic farmers. They share the same creed: fertilize with manure, compost, and green manure and don't use synthetic pesticides. The evidence confirmed that Steiner's biodynamic/organic methods help build soil that is alive with humus and microorganisms. If you believe that a homeopathic dilution of a concoction fermented in a buried cow's horn will improve your yield, more power to you.

Biointensive and square-foot gardening Biointensive (previously known as French intensive) gardeners would shudder to think that their elegant, spiritual, holistic gardening system could be equated with something as plebeian as square-foot gardening. Although biointensive gardening is not fraught with the superstitions found in biodynamics, the rationale for its very precise techniques does have something to do with cosmic harmonies—call it Aquarian (as in "Age of Aquarius") Agriculture. Biointensive practitioners do not simply grow vegetables very close together, in raised beds, in very fertile soil, which is what those lowly square-foot gardeners do. Biointensive gardeners have an exact system for digging beds and determining the correct proportions of what to plant, which is based on the calories provided by the crop and other complicated and confusing criteria.

Square-foot gardening (based on the eponymous PBS television show and book by Mel Bartholomew) is basically the same methodology, but stripped of the fancy neologisms, theory, and attributions of Universal Oneness. Bartholomew came up with the idea for square-foot gardening after managing community gardens for a describes in minute detail how to turn bad soil, poor drainage, and way too many rocks into an amazingly productive small garden. If you have never gardened before, it's a good idea to start small, and Bartholomew's method is a great way to begin.

"If every U.S. citizen ate just one meal a week (any meal) composed of locally and organically raised meats and produce, we would reduce our country's oil consumption by over 1.1 million barrels of oil every week. That's not gallons, but barrels."

—*Barbara Kingsolver,* Animal, Vegetable, Miracle

number of years. He noticed that people's enthusiasm tended to fade long before their gardens did and he wanted to devise a system that would help forestall the inevitable. Using his common-sense methods, you can get a surprisingly large yield from a surprisingly small area. Bartholomew suggests dividing the garden into 4-ft. squares and then further dividing those squares into four 1-ft. squares. The 4-ft. squares are delineated by paths made of scrap lumber. The 1-ft. squares are marked off with string. With this method, you plant the seeds one at a time, thus eliminating the arduous task of thinning. The overall garden could be in raised beds, if desired.

The one thing that both biointensive gardening and square-foot gardening have in common is that they require soil rich in organic matter and other nutrients. Bartholomew's book, *All New Square Foot Gardening* (Cool Springs Press, 2006),

Companion planting For most people, companion planting is just a natural part of organic and permaculture gardening. It is the antithesis of monoculture and so, in that regard, it mimics nature. For some people, however, the matching of certain plants with other plants is imbued with mystical qualities. There is no evidence that arranging plants in the manner prescribed by this philosophy has any particular benefit, but, hey, it does no harm either, so if the idea appeals to you or has worked for you in the past, go for it.

The companion planting theory goes something like this: Certain plants have specific attributes that complement or encumber other plants. This theory isn't referring to the tried-and-true lore that you should plant beans with corn because the beans will fix the nitrogen that corn plants need to thrive or the recommendation to plant winter squash with corn to keep away raccoons (who, although they love corn, can't stand the prickly squash vines that will bar their way). This theory is also not related to polycropping, another commonsensical approach to interplanting, based on the notion that insects are less likely to attack your plants if they can't find them (for example, if some of your cabbages are growing in rows but others are at the end of the garden with the beans). This version of companion planting is more of a superstition than a science, asserting that beet roots "like" French beans but not runner beans, and beet greens, which also like French beans, haven't yet decided how they feel about the runners. (I'm not sure why beet roots and beet greens are considered separately, as it would be very difficult to grow beet greens without the roots and vice versa.)

While researching companion planting, I was struck by the degree to which the certainty of its proponents corresponded to the lack of evidence for their claims. There is little or no logic to support the extensive lists of friends and foes ascribed to various plants, let alone any supporting research or empirical evidence. There is, however, a grain of truth to the companion planter's claim that marigolds deter nematodes. According to the University of Louisiana, one particular nematode, endemic to Louisiana, that causes root knot in tomatoes can be held at bay by marigolds. You cannot, however, just plant a few marigolds next to a tomato and get the desired results. Nematodes are ubiquitous, microscopic, wormlike creatures that can only be identified by someone who is familiar with the thousands of nematode varieties. Only the Louisiana branch of the family is affected by marigolds.

Furthermore, to deter tomato root knot, the area must be heavily planted with French marigolds (the only effective variety of marigold) months before the tomato crop goes in. After the marigolds have flowered, the gardener must turn them under. The anti-nematode effect is good for only one season, so the process must be repeated year after year. To further complicate matters, another study confirms that marigolds attract spider mites, sometimes in large numbers, leading to your basic out-of-the-frying pan-and-into-the-fire scenario.

Another widely held companion planter's belief is that basil and tomatoes make good companions. Some claim that basil makes tomatoes grow better and even taste better; others don't offer any reason

"Permaculture is anti-political. There is no room for politicians or administrators or priests. And there are no laws either. The only ethics we obey are: care of the earth, care of people, and reinvestment in those ends." —Bill Mollison

We grow certain plants in our garden just because they are beautiful. Left: Dill florets. Right: Scarlet flowers of runner beans.

why the two plants should share space. I could not find a single scholarly article about either claim, but I did find a source that said there were no such studies. I also came across a post on a gardening blog maintained by a blogger in the Southeast about problems with white flies on tomatoes. There were many responses to the post, and about three-quarters of the responders claimed to have read or heard that interplanting basil was the solution to the white-fly problem. There was, however, not one (not one!) poster who had actually tried planting basil with tomatoes and had any success. One respondent went so far as to say that basil had no effect whatsoever on her tomatoes, so she was convinced that she must have done

something wrong. No one suggested that the basil-tomato solution might just be a myth. (Why let reality get in the way of a good theory?)

Planting a specific plant next to another specific plant imparts no advantage to either. Intercropping—placing plants in groupings of different families rather than in neat rows—does, however, have merit, as it forces insects to work a little harder to find their dinner. Once an insect spies a plant it wants to visit, it makes a few stops to scope out the area. If it misses the target

Utility is not the only reason to plant a garden. Flower beds impart serenity and beauty to the grounds adjoining our house.

....

a few times, even if it has had one success, it will move on. The only criteria for the intercropping is that the other plants should be a similar green color, so don't mix green and grey-green plants in the same area.

Permaculture Proponents of permaculture-based farming techniques agree that there are benefits to growing several species of both flora and fauna, together. They also strive to promote a healthy energy balance and wax philosophical about the "interrelated whole," but do not confuse permaculture with the fuzzy gardening theories of biodynamics and companion planting. Although permaculture was not rigorously studied before it was presented to the world, it was not pulled out of thin air. Permaculture—now synonymous with sustainable agriculture and organic farming and gardening—arose in the 1970s, out of the premises and observations of the then-new science of ecology.

Bill Mollison and David Holmgren, two Australian students of environmental science and forestry, were troubled about the poor state of agriculture, its disregard for the health of the soil, and its lack of concern for the destruction of ecosystems by agribusiness. Both men realized that current agricultural practices were antithetical—even hostile—to sustainability and were threatening virtually every ecosystem on Earth. In response, Mollison bought a 5-acre spread and set out to build a homestead based on their new eco-savvy design for "permaculture" (from the words "permanent" and "agriculture"). In an interview with *Seeds of Change*, a publication dedicated to organic gardening and related issues, Mollison explained that the design relied on the principles of environmental science (a relatively new discipline at the time) and credited Kenneth Watt (of the University of California-Davis) for outlining those principles. Mollison later took his show on the road with workshops and wrote two books on permaculture.

Permaculture—a system of sustainable land use that integrates biology, agriculture, horticulture, architecture, and ecology—is the latest phase of organic agriculture, based on research that is coming out of major universities and the USDA. In short, it is *the* eco-agriculture of the 21st century. Thousands of studies have confirmed that the core principles pass scientific muster. Farmers and researchers continue to expand the knowledge base of sustainable practices.

From its inception, permaculture was not just about agriculture and the environment; the ideas are intentionally applicable to economic and social systems, too. Sustainable permaculture is at the heart of my life's work. That said, its proponents can be as opinionated and dogmatic as any of the "true believers," so never lose your critical eye.

chapter vii
....

Soil & Garden Basics

The soil comes first. Build good soil, and everything else falls into place. The soil is more than a medium into which you put fertilizer—even if it is the best organic fertilizer. Soil is alive, complex, and equal to more than the sum of its parts. It also adjusts and changes as it matures. Each year builds on the previous year, until, eventually, your garden soil seems to live a life of its own.

Most new gardens don't have perfect or even good soil. I have seen glorious gardens built on soil that was little more than a gravel pit the first year they were planted. With enough compost and mulch, almost any spot, short of a toxic-waste dump, can be developed into a garden. It just takes a little hard work and a good source of manure and compost. There are three things you need to grow a garden: sun, rain, and soil. You can't force the sun to shine or

make the rain fall, but you can definitely build your soil.

If you garden organically (and we're assuming you do or will), eventually you will ask these questions: "What the heck *is* soil anyway? What's it made of? Why does the texture and even the smell of it change as I add nutrients and compost?" We can't put our finger on an actual definition of soil, but we know it when we see it or smell it or feel it in our hands.

It turns out that the actual difference between soil and dirt is very simple. Unlike dirt, soil is full of fungi—but not just any fungi. Soil contains a particular group of fungi known as arbuscular mycorrhizal fungi (aka AMF) or vesicular arbuscular mycorrhizae (aka VAM). These mycorrhizal fungi develop symbiotic relationships with plants through interactions with their roots. Ectomorphic mycorrhizals encase the plant's rootlets; endomorphic forms grow in between the cells of the rootlets and extend outward.

Both forms collect nutrients and distribute them among various local groups. The mycorrhizal hyphea (a web

Top: Garlic is one of the first crops to mature in our garden. Bottom left: You can allow chickens to free-range everywhere—except in your garden. Bottom right: Late-summer bounty: We can hardly wait for the tomatoes to ripen.

153

of microscopic fungal filaments) increase the surface area of the plant's roots by a factor of thousands. In the forest, AMF take nutrients from trees in sunny areas and distribute them to trees in shade. This particular group of fungi makes a substance known as glomalin, which is a sticky protein that gives soil its ability to be worked and to hold water and nutrients. Glomalin also gives soil its characteristic texture, determining whether it can easily be formed into a ball or crumbles into pieces. Glomalin is the reason that soil smells sweet and not dusty like dirt.

Soil Building 101

We used to think the partnership between plants and fungi was like a marriage. Sure, it was a good thing, both parties benefited, but optional. Now we know that the relationship between plants and AMF is more like the relationship between you and your arm. At the heart of building good soil is building the relationship between plants and AMF.

In healthy ground, it's impossible to tell where the root stops and the fungus begins. Most gardeners know that rhizomes (from beans and peas) fix nitrogen, but all types of vegetables form symbiotic relationships with fungi, although not all of these relationships are visible. If you go into the woods and gently lift up the forest-floor litter, you'll see an endless network of fine white fibers—the mychorrhizal hyphea. You'll find a similar pattern under logs or old boards.

We gardeners talk about soil as light and sandy or heavy with clay. We check the pH to determine if the soil is acidic or alkaline. These qualities are important, but what is actually essential to making soil something more than just dirt are the microbes, the billions of them, from fungi to bacteria to single-celled amoeba and protozoa, within the soil. A farmer's first crop should be the soil microbes. Take care of these microbes, and they will see to it that your other, visible crops and your animals both will flourish.

Okay, so how, exactly, do you farm microbes? It's really very simple. Consider the four basic elements of soil composition:

1. Structure and texture (the physical properties)

2. pH level (the degree to which the soil is acidic or alkaline)

3. Nutrients (macronutrients and micronutrients)

4. Organic matter (living microbes and humus)

As with most things in the natural world, these four categories are not tidy—one spills over into the next, while another merges into the third—but, if your garden is not doing well, look to one of these four as both the cause and remedy.

If you're just starting a garden, your soil will need work in at least one if not all of these areas. Fortunately, adding manure and compost yields wholesale improvements in texture, nutrient levels, and pH. If you do nothing but turn over the ground, sift out the quack-grass rhizomes, and add a few inches of rotted manure and/or compost, you'll have a decent garden in the first year. Add more manure and/or compost the next year, and the

Soil Structure

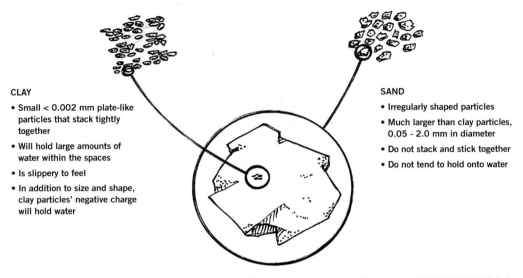

CLAY
- Small < 0.002 mm plate-like particles that stack tightly together
- Will hold large amounts of water within the spaces
- Is slippery to feel
- In addition to size and shape, clay particles' negative charge will hold water

SAND
- Irregularly shaped particles
- Much larger than clay particles, 0.05 - 2.0 mm in diameter
- Do not stack and stick together
- Do not tend to hold onto water

garden will improve still more (especially if you mulch your crops every year).

If you're a bottom-line gardener, that's about all there is to it. If you'd feel better with a more detailed plan, send a soil sample to your local extension service. When you get the test results, follow the recommendations for additional lime and mineral supplements while continuing to add manure and mulch. My guess is most gardeners eschew the soil test and still end up with plenty of thick, juicy tomato slices for their burgers, but humor me. Let's talk about the details anyway.

Structure and Texture

Soil contains minerals that are ground and worn into fine particles, organic matter, microbes, air, water, and even small animals. The ideal ratio for soil is 50 percent voids (between the particles) and 50 percent solids. The voids are ideally filled with a 50/50 mixture of the air and water that microbes thrive upon. The solids consist of 10 percent organic matter and 90 percent inorganic matter. As a result, organic matter makes up 5 percent of the entire soil mixture. Some of the organic matter is alive, and the rest is in varying stages of decomposition.

The mineral component is comprised of infinitesimal clay or sandy particles and silt (particles that range somewhere between clay and sand in size). In the best of all possible worlds, your garden soil would be composed of equal amounts of clay and sand, a mixture known as loam. A slight preponderance of sand (sandy loam) is the acme of perfection. Most of us, though, are blessed with something less than this perfect mix and must work with science to grow vegetables. Just observe the quality of your soil. Sandy soils are lighter and easy to work with, but do not hold moisture very well or contain much organic matter. Clay soils are heavy and pack

 *"If a healthy soil is full of death, it is also full of life: worms, fungi, microorganisms of all kinds . . . Given only the health of the soil, nothing that dies is dead for very long."*
—Wendell Berry, The Unsettling of America

soil that is either too heavy with clay or too light with sand.

To work with a less-than-perfect soil, it helps to understand a little about the properties of clay and sand. Clay particles are flat and stack on top of each other. They are electrically charged and, therefore, attract water, which holds the particles together, binds minerals and organic matter, and explains why clay is sticky and tends to clump together. In contrast, sand particles are crystalline, with a cuboidal shape. Sand particles have no electrical charge, so they do not attract other particles or water and do not tend to aggregate. Clay and sand complement each other perfectly. The clay attracts the water and nutrients; the sand keeps the mixture from turning into a gloppy mess.

Of course, soil is much more complicated than you might think from this simple explanation. Soil scientists spend their whole lives studying the stuff. Just as you don't have to be a mechanic to drive a car, you fortunately don't need a PhD in soil

together easily. Pinch a small amount of wet soil between your fingers and thumb. Clay soil will feel slippery and slightly slick. Sandy soil will feel gritty and dry.

As discussed in Chapter 2, soil scientists have mapped out the entire country and labeled all the soils, including yours, with colorful and occasionally intriguing names, like Peacham Stony Muck. (From the name alone, you can tell that Stony Muck is not a very desirable type of soil.) If you're lucky enough to have a good sandy loam, be thankful, but if the soil that came with your land doesn't have good texture, you can improve it—without need of a soil test or any fancy additives. Good soil holds water well, but also drains easily (think cellulose sponge). Your goal is a light, fluffy soil that has a pH of just slightly lower than neutral (about 6.5 to 6).

Compost, manure, and mulch Growing plants is one of the best ways to improve the soil. Even if the soil is not perfect, you can still get a decent crop of vegetables in the first few years. Mulch those vegetables, and you'll see an improvement very quickly. There is hardly a soil problem that cannot be cured with compost or manure and a thick layer of mulch.

A soil that lacks sufficient organic material will be heavy and compact. By adding organic matter in the form of well-rotted manure, compost, or decomposed mulch, you can lighten a heavy soil in two to three years. A 1-in.-thick layer of organic matter will give you a soil whose first foot is made up of 6 to 8 percent organic matter. A 2-in. layer will yield a first foot of soil that is 16 percent organic matter. Each additional inch thereafter doubles the percentage of organic matter in the first foot of soil. Practically speaking, you can't add too much organic matter, as long as you add it at the right time and in the right proportions (see p. 165 for guidelines).

After you've spread the organic matter, till the soil down to the subsoil—or at least 1 ft. deep—with a power tiller or by hand. If you're working a small plot, lift and turn the sod with a garden fork. Knock the clumps that you removed with the back of the fork to break up any clods. Never, ever, work soil when it is too wet or too dry. If the soil is too wet, the resulting clods will turn rock hard and will be very difficult to break up after they dry. Working soil that is too dry can pulverize the structure, which is

Managing Mulch

Although we are great believers in the benefits of heavy mulching for weed control, moisture retention, and soil improvement, there are times when any mulch at all can be too much of a good thing. In a very wet year, mulch can provide a nursery for an exploding slug population and serve as incubator for a plethora of nasty fungal, bacterial, or viral diseases.

Some gardeners believe that you should always till mulch under in the fall to prevent insect pests from overwintering. According to permacultural principles, however, bare soil should never be left exposed, so you would then need to plant a green-manure cover crop (like winter rye), which you'll till under in the spring. (This added chore is why other overworked gardeners just wait until spring to till under the mulch. If you decide to do the same, pull back any overwintered mulch as soon as the snow melts to hasten soil warming and drying.)

Over the years, we've experimented with all these approaches to mulching, albeit not always intentionally—there were years when we weren't able to put the garden to bed before winter did it for us. So, we have good evidence that ranging pigs on mulch in the fall and ranging chickens on it in the spring is a great way to nourish the soil, improve its tilth, and extirpate any grubs and pests that had the temerity to overwinter there.

equally detrimental. To test for the correct water content, grab a handful of soil and squeeze it into a ball. The ball should hold together for only 10 or 15 seconds, then readily fall apart with a light shake. If the soil is too wet, the ball stays well formed and does not shake apart. If the soil is too dry, it won't form a ball at all.

After you turn under the compost, cover the bare ground with mulch or sow it with a cover crop and leave it to mellow until you're ready to plant. If it's already planting time, lay down a heavy layer of mulch on the pathways between the rows (assuming they aren't paved) to discourage weeds. Rather than mulching, some gardeners prefer to control weeds by lightly tilling their pathways through-out the season. Our garden rows run parallel with a slope, so we find that mulching the paths helps restrain runoff and improve moisture retention. In any case, if you have young plants, you'll need to hoe and hand-weed the planting beds until the plants are established enough for you to mulch.

Cover crops Deep-rooted cover crops and plants with extensive root systems help to break up the soil and encourage fungal growth. Grasses are known to develop a stronger relationship with mycorrhizals than any other plant, so mulching with hay or straw will provide plenty of fungi to inoculate your soil. Turning under the crop along with the mulch in the fall, after the garden is done, or after each vegetable is harvested, adds nutrients to the soil just as effectively as tilling in a "green manure" cover crop. (A "green manure" crop is a crop that grows quickly—often a nitrogen-fixing annual—and is tilled into the soil before the final crops are planted. Green manures add beneficial microbes and nutrients to the soil.) Deep mulching with organic matter (like hay or straw) and then adding a layer of black plastic on top of the mulch also invites microbes and hastens the decomposition of organic matter.

pH Level

Many of the measures intended to improve the tilth or texture of your soil will also improve the soil's pH level. The pH scale is the chemical shorthand for measuring the acidity and alkalinity of a given substance (in solution). Water, which has a pH of 7, is considered neutral. A pH level of less than 7 indicates acidity; a level of more than 7 is considered alkaline (or basic).

Most living things hover around a pH of 7, the pH of water. Animals prefer a pH of 7.4. Most plants are more versatile, tolerating pH levels that range from 6.5 to almost 7. Whether or not a particular mineral or nutrient is available to a plant depends on the pH level of the soil. When you add compost and mulch to soil, you are also adding microbes that assist their partner plants by realigning the pH level of the soil to near neutral. We have not added lime to our soil for many years, but we use compost and mulch every year. We haven't bothered with soil tests either, because the lamb's-quarters (*Chenopodium album,* an edible weed that only grows in fertile soil with a pH of 6 to 7) that grows abundantly along our garden's margins tells us that our soil has the right pH level.

There are still some out-of-the-way spots, however, where the presence of sorrel and horsetail signal an acidic soil that is starved of organic matter.

Once the tilth is corrected, it tends to stay corrected as long as the organic matter

> "Your goal is a light, fluffy soil that has a pH of just slightly lower than neutral (about 6.5 to 6)."

ratio stays between 5 and 10 percent. The pH balance will sometimes drift toward its original levels for the first few years, however, particularly if you have sandy, alkaline soil. Heavy soils that tend to be acidic will stay neutral longer without the aid of additives (excluding organic matter). For an immediate correction with long-lasting results, apply fast-acting wood ash that's mixed with slow-acting dolomite lime (five 13-oz. coffee cans of wood ashes and three coffee cans of lime for every 100 sq. ft. of area). Eventually, when your soil has built up plenty of humus and microorganisms, it will autocorrect the pH level to suit the plants.

If your soil is too alkaline, you probably live in the Southwest, have a lot of juniper trees around (if you have any trees at all), and have a sandy soil. Correcting an alkaline (or "sweet") soil is only one of many problems you will have when gardening. Adding (acidic) sulfur in various forms will quickly bring down the pH of an alkaline soil to an optimal level, but you'll also need to incorporate a lot of humus

to maintain it there, especially with desert soil, which is high in calcium. (Gardening in the Southwest is challenging—you must battle insects, extremes of weather, *and* thin soil with a high pH—but that's a topic for another book.)

You should certainly correct the overall pH level of your garden, but you may also want to customize the soil in one particular area of the garden or even customize the soil for a single plant. For example, depending on the exact cultivars, blueberries and rhododendrons like an acidic soil (around pH 4 to 5.5). Blueberries are usually planted in groups or in long rows, and rhododendrons are usually planted singly or in groupings of two or three. It makes sense to group together plants that like the same pH. You can manage the pH levels by adding sulfur before planting. If you're only acidifying a small area, however, you can simply incorporate your morning coffee grounds into the soil around the plant. Mulching under the plants with pine needles is another way to raise the acidity level (lower the pH).

Nutrients

When organic gardeners think of nutrients, we think manure, green manure, and compost. When conventional farmers think of nutrients, they think NPK (nitrogen, phosphorus, and potassium)—the three main macronutrients that plants need to grow, thrive, and reproduce. You can provide these nutrients to your plants with artificially formulated NPK from a bag, or you can feed your soil with compost and manure and let your soil then feed your plants. Nitrogen, phosphorus, and potassium are present in every living thing, so they are present in compost and manure. To flourish, plants also need carbon, oxygen, carbon dioxide, and several trace minerals, and these are also present in compost and manure.

Nitrogen Having healthy soil means that, most of the time, you don't need to concern yourself with any one particular nutrient, but there are times when you may need more of one nutrient than another. For example, nitrogen, which is a component of chlorophyll, is vital to leaf growth, so it is a good nutrient for lettuces and other leafy vegetables. Plants that are grown for their fruits—tomatoes, peppers, berries—should not have extra nitrogen because the plant's leaf growth increases at the expense of the number and size of the fruit. Nitrogen is also highly soluble in water and washes away rapidly, so if you apply it to the soil in the fall, it will probably be gone by spring. It also will trigger a leafy growth spurt that may be nipped back by an early frost.

Nitrogen is a major component of proteins, so any material that is rich in protein contains nitrogen. Dried blood, fish meal and fish emulsion, kelp, grass clippings, and any green vegetable matter are all good sources of organic nitrogen. (Some portion of the nitrogen contained in green vegetable matter is consumed by the bacteria that break down the vegetable matter, leaving more or less available as a nutrient, which is why you should let organic materials rot before incorporating them into the soil.) The most readily available and practical source of nitrogen, however, is animal manure—specifically, chicken manure. Another important, although often overlooked, source of nitrogen are the soil bacteria that take atmospheric nitrogen and "fix it" in a bio-available form. The nodules on the roots of legumes such as peas, beans, and clover are home to colonies of nitrogen-fixing bacteria, so these plants are sometimes used as cover crops or companion plantings to increase the soil's nitrogen level.

Intercropping is a practical way to take advantage of nitrogen fixation. For example, corn is a "heavy feeder" (meaning it requires a lot of nitrogen). Plant the corn as usual, but broadcast white clover seed between the rows. The clover grows quickly but won't grow very high (less than 6 in.). The added benefit to this method is that the clover also acts as a weed suppressant and as a green-manure or cover crop when you plow it under in the fall.

Phosphorus Phosphorus promotes root and fruit development. Plants such as tomatoes and peppers and root crops such as carrots and rutabagas may benefit from extra phosphorus. Be careful when applying phosphorus, however. Too much of it can compromise a plant's utilization of vital zinc and iron. Among the organic sources of phosphorus is rock phosphate, mined from naturally occurring deposits and available in either the slow form (preferable) or quick form. Bone meal is another good source.

Green Manure on a Small Scale

You don't need a big field to utilize green manure. You can plant a small patch of a cover crop in your garden between the plantings of other crops. For example, let's say that your spring spinach has gone by, and there's a five- to six-week hiatus before you can plant fall peas on the same bed. After you harvest the spinach, plant white clover or buckwheat. A week or two before you plant your fall crop of peas, turn over the cover crop so it has a chance to decompose. If you pasture your chickens on the same ground during winter, you'll add brown manure to the green to further enrich the soil for the next planting season.

Potassium Potassium is fundamental for the overall strength of a plant. Potatoes respond especially well to potassium. One good source is wood ash, but don't apply the ash before planting your potatoes, or the tubers will develop scabs, which—although not harmful—are ugly enough to be. You can purchase greensand, another naturally occurring mineral rich in potassium, at garden supply stores that carry organic supplies. Greensand is expensive, but a little goes a long way.

Trace minerals There are many trace mineral micronutrients—such as iron, magnesium, zinc, selenium, and copper—that, alongside NPK, are vital to the growth and development of a healthy plant. Plants need only very small quantities of these trace minerals, however, so, in most cases you don't have to keep track of them all. Often a deficiency problem is not so much caused by a lack of the minerals in the soil as by the fact that the minerals aren't bioavailable—in other words, they are present in a chemical form that the plants cannot absorb. Fortunately, soil bacteria and fungi are able to convert these minerals into bioavailable forms. At the risk of sounding like a broken record (now there's an obsolete metaphor), compost and manure promote the development of those converting microbes.

Plants that are suffering from trace-mineral deficiencies are characterized by pale and often deformed or stunted new growth. Unlike plant diseases, whose symptoms are specific to a species or family, problems that are caused by trace-nutrient deficiencies affect all plants in the same way. If you suspect a trace-mineral deficiency, don't simply add one or more minerals willy-nilly to the soil; if you do, you could cause chemical reactions that make other minerals unavailable to the plants.

If the affected area is a new plot, your first response should be to add more compost or bacterial or fungal inoculants. Planting deep-rooted green manures will bring trace minerals up from the subsoil.

Compost Pioneers

The first person to compost and live to write about it was Sir Albert Howard. He named his composting method the Indore Method, after the region in India in which he was working from 1905 to 1934. Essentially, Sir Howard alternated 2-in.-deep layers of manure with 6-in.-deep layers of plant materials and sprinklings of chalk and earth. Occasionally, he added layers of sticks and brush to facilitate aeration. The heaps were about 5 ft. high and as wide as need be.

Most composting methods are just variations on Howard's ideas. Harold Gotaas designed a composting method for the World Health Organization in 1935. Clarence G. Golueke designed and built a famous composting system for the University of California in 1952.

During the 1970s, every hippy gardener learned the Ruth Stout method. If you have access to hay and a relatively small garden, her method—a fusion of mulch, compost pile, and garden—is ideal. Stout, a Maine gardener who was in her nineties when her fame peaked, developed a method of composting/mulching that worked well for me and many fellow novice gardeners. Instead of building the compost piles apart from her garden, she combined the two. After Stout mulched her garden the first time, she left the mulch in place year after year. In the spring, she pulled the mulch aside to let the ground warm up and dry out. Then she planted her seeds. When the plants got big enough, she put the mulch back in place. All year long, she slipped kitchen scraps and other waste materials between the layers of hay to decompose in situ.

Diagnosing and correcting trace-mineral problems can be complicated if you are dealing with an established garden. If the affected area is an old plot, it may be time for a soil test. If the test shows a lack or excess of a particular mineral, hit the books and the Internet to learn all you can about that mineral and how to correct the problem under your specific conditions.

....

Top left: Daniel among the squash. Top right: A heavy mulch keeps our garlic patch healthy and weed free. Bottom: Antique tractors on parade at the county fair.

In reality, because of their diversified plantings, home gardens experience trace-mineral deficiencies only in the first year or two of gardening, before the microbial population is fully established. Once there are plenty of microbes and organic material in the soil, the trace minerals become readily available to the plants. Soil is a better chemist than most farmers, so don't get bogged down trying to figure out which nutrient goes where. Just continue to feed your soil with compost and green and brown manures and let nature and her microbes do the rest.

Organic Matter

For the purposes of gardening, organic matter is any substance that was once alive. All living structures are built with carbon, hydrogen, oxygen, nitrogen, a few major minerals (for plants, phosphorus and potassium), and several minor ones. The elements in organic matter are not in a chemical form that plants can use, however. When organic matter is composted, the matter is converted into humus.

post. Basically, to make compost, you mix together organic materials containing carbon and nitrogen in the ratio of 10 to 25 parts carbon to 1 part nitrogen. Then, you inoculate the mixture with microbe-rich soil and allow it to ferment in the presence of oxygen until microbes digest the pile of raw compost and transform it into a much smaller pile of humus. The nutrients originally present in the raw organic matter remain in the humus, but

"If I wanted to have a happy garden, I must ally myself with my soil; study and help it to the utmost, untiringly . . . Always, the soil must come first."

—*Marion Cran,* If I Were Beginning Again

Composting is, essentially, controlled rotting. In the process, bacteria and fungi alter the organic material to make it bio-available. For example, plants can't utilize nitrogen when it is attached to a protein, as it is in raw organic matter. The bacteria and fungi in the compost pile, however, release some of the nitrogen from the proteins and oxidize it into soluble nitrites and nitrates that can be absorbed and utilized by plants. Plants cannot absorb phosphorous in its mineral state either, so it must be converted to phosphoric acid through composting, and potassium and the trace minerals must be converted to salts or acids through the same process.

Organic gardening is inseparable from composting. Whether you have 50 acres or a container garden on your fire escape, you need to make some kind of com-

in a form that can be utilized by plants. Humus is the visible manifestation of a largely invisible complex ecosystem inhabited by myriad microorganisms, bacteria, fungi, protozoa, nematodes, and tiny invertebrates that together make the soil loose and friable. They also impart a certain sweet smell and characteristic texture that anyone, even someone who has never seen garden soil before, will recognize as fertile.

There are a lot of different approaches to composting—some folks like to be precise; others are more laissez-faire—but the basic concept is still the same, whether you're making small bottles of compost tea (to use as a spray or soil drench) or 100-ft. windrows of sheet compost (piled on top of garden beds). The most important thing is just to make sure there is enough nitrogen to go with the carbon so

The First-Year Garden: Two Methods

How do you start a garden from scratch? There are two methods—one takes time, and the other takes effort.

I've Got Plenty of Time

1. Start small. If you live in a temperate climate, pick an area that gets good sun all day. If you live in the South, pick an area that gets morning sun and afternoon shade.

2. Spread at least 6 in. of manure over the garden to be. You can add any type of compost or vegetable matter you can find (dry leaves, weeds, wood shavings, hay). If you live in an area of the country that tends to be acidic (which applies to most of it), spread limestone (not quick lime) over the area at a rate of 50 lb. per 1,000 sq. ft. If you live in the Southwest, spread sulfate the same way instead.

3. In late summer or early fall, cover the area with material that is impervious to light and heavy enough to hold all the additives close to the earth: unopened hay bales (in the spring, remove bales to use as mulch throughout summer; they will be loaded with earthworms and mycelium); black plastic, anchored with rocks; metal roofing, anchored with rocks.

Leave the covering in place until the organic matter and soil have "melted" together and all sod has been killed. Uncover the area in spring—the longer you leave the covering on, the better. The finished soil will be loose and loaded with microbes and will need little further preparation other than a bit of rototilling.

No Time but a Strong Back

1. Pick your spot, following the guidelines in Step 1 above.

2. Rototilling alone does not make a good garden; you need to turn over the soil to get rid of sod. With a flat shovel, cut through the sod to make 6-in. to 12-in. squares. With a sharp spade shovel, dig out each square and put it in a wheelbarrow or garden cart.

3. When you've removed all the sod, add several inches (or as much as you can) of well-rotted manure and/or compost and lime at a rate of 50 lb. per 1,000 sq. ft.

4. Incorporate compost with the help of a tiller or dig it in by hand. If the area is small enough, you can double-dig. Double-digging produces a compost-enriched top layer and loosened subsoil. Remove the top 6 in. to 12 in. of soil from a small portion of the garden and put it aside. Then loosen the next 6 in. to 12 in. with a shovel or fork. Repeat in the next section of the garden, but rather than putting aside the top layer, enrich it with compost and put it back into the first dug-out section. Continue the process until you've dug the whole area.

5. Regardless of which digging technique you use, plant a cover crop such as clover, forage beets, alfalfa, or other taprooted crops to break up the subsoil and pull deep minerals up into the root zone. Unlike the first method, described above, this method does little for adding microbes, but after two or three years the two gardens will be of equal quality.

the pile will "cook." Manure is the best source of nitrogen, and green vegetable matter is the second best. The best source of carbon is dry plant matter, such as the hay, straw, sawdust, or wood shavings you would use for animal bedding. The easiest way to build garden soil is to either till the manure and bedding directly into the soil (this works best if you have an abundance of manure) or allow the materials to accumulate and ferment in a compost pile for a while before incorporating it into your garden. Add your household scrap and garden weeds. In the fall, rake up the fallen leaves and add them, too.

Beyond the basics, here's the real down and dirty on composting: How the compost piles are constructed and turned is not as important as what goes into the pile and how regularly it is turned. You don't have to measure everything that goes into your pile. Just make sure you have a lot of dry, bulky, dead matter (high in carbon) in relation to green matter or manure (high in nitrogen). The carbon-to-nitrogen ratio ideally should be about 25 to 1, which is approximately the ratio obtained when manure is mixed in deep straw or hay bedding. With shavings from deep-litter bedding—like that from a chicken house— the ratio is more like 10 to 1. These figures are purely an estimate, based on how well those mixtures decompose.

The point is the bacteria and fungi need to have enough carbohydrates and proteins to eat, just like other living creatures. If they have the right amount of each, they will grow well. Without these microbes, the whole story ends before it gets started.

Top: Canada thistle is an unfairly beautiful plant for such a noxious weed. Bottom left: Dill. Bottom right: Borage.

The easiest way to get them into your pile is to add soil layers to the compost every now and then. Once the pile really gets "cooking" and is quite hot, you no longer need to add soil layers. Or you could buy compost inoculants, which are very useful, especially if they include mycorrhizals. Mycorrhizals are everywhere, so, with a little effort, you can find them locally for free. A few shovels of soil dug from the base of a large tree will have plenty of active fungi (especially if the soil is near tiny rootlets). Throw a few bean plants into the pile, too; the nodules on the roots have bacterium that fix nitrogen. Wet and moldy hay is also loaded with fungi and bacteria of all sorts—especially mycorrhizals.

Of equal importance to good compost is the moisture content of the pile, which should be about 45 to 50 percent. In the dry part of the year, you should water your pile. Finally, remember to turn the pile now and then to be sure it continues to heat up. If the pile is hot, it is still working. When it cools down, it is ready to use.

As with most other homesteading activities, there are a variety of ways to make compost—whether by adding organic matter directly to the garden, just throwing some stuff in a pile and turning it over whenever you happen to remember, or painstakingly building proportioned piles that are monitored for internal temperature and turned on a regular schedule.

You can learn all you need to know on the subject of composting from *The Rodale Book of Composting: Easy Methods for Every Gardener* (Rodale Books, 1992), the revised edition of their 1979 bible. Certainly, any organic gardening book you pick up will include at least a chapter on the subject. As long as your pile gets air and moisture, some starter bacteria (the "yeast" for the "dough"), and is of an adequate size, it will do its work. If you already have a composting system that is working well for you, great. Don't change anything if you don't want to. Whatever method you use must fit into the context of the whole farm or homestead. Ultimately, how you make and use your compost is as much a matter of personality and style as it is of depth of knowledge.

Here at Gopher Broke Farm, we combine a few methods. As I clean the hay bedding from our duck and goose shelters (an almost daily chore), I put the spent hay directly on the garden. Even though waterfowl manure is not as hot as chicken manure, it can still burn plants if you aren't careful, so I use this spent hay only on paths and near the edges of beds. Some nitrogen is probably lost as the manure rots in the garden—technically, we should put the mixture in the compost first, but then we would not be able to use the bedding hay as mulch. We have a lot of bedding (carbon) and a lot of manure (nitrogen), so the slight loss of nitrogen is the trade-off.

We also use hay as a ground covering around the chicken yards and turn it under in place. It usually has already started to decompose when we spread it or use it to mulch berries. We mix chicken manure with wood shavings and spread the mixture on the fields or in the berry patch. Sometimes it stays in place for a while until we decide what to do with it, during which time the chickens add more richness to the pile and spread it around even more. In short, most of our mulch gets run through the birds before we use it in the garden. In the fall, the pigs and chickens do the work of turning. We have too much to do to be fussing with finicky compost piles. Maybe we could get more nitrogen from our manure if we composted everything before we applied the material to the fields and garden but if our garden were any more prolific, I wouldn't know what to do with all the food.

Buying Seeds

Deciding which seeds to buy and who from can be a daunting task whether you are planning your 1st garden or your 31st. Even if your goal is to eventually grow only heirloom vegetables from seed you save yourself, you'll still likely be buying seeds for a while. When selecting seeds, you can choose between hybrid and heirloom (also known as heritage) varieties.

If seed saving isn't an important part of your gardening, there's no compelling reason to rule out the hybrid cultivars of any fruit or vegetable. Hybrid vegetables are the products of pairings between two different kinds of plants, but there is some argument about what exactly constitutes an heirloom vegetable. The dispute is mostly over how old a variety must be before it qualifies as heirloom. Some people draw the line at 1945, the year World War II ended; others set the date at 1951, the year that hybrids first emerged on the scene in a big way. A few people even include some old hybrids under the heading. Many of these old hybrids are easy to find and good for the homestead garden—and do

if you buy at the feed store or other local vender rather than by mail order— if you wait too long, you may find 5,000 packets of Brussel sprout seeds left on the rack, but no more corn or green beans. Find out when the seeds go on sale and be there on that day or soon afterward. Large garden stores are also good

"Gardening is not a rational act. What matters is the immersion of the hands in the earth . . . In the spring, at the end of the day, you should smell like dirt." —Margaret Atwood

much to promote diversity in the gene pool—but, because the plants are not open pollinated, the seed can't be saved, so you'll have to buy seed every year.

Hybrid seeds aren't cheap. You can save one-third to one-half on your seed costs by buying heirloom seeds instead. There are some very real drawbacks to growing heirloom seeds, however. (After all, if open-pollinated varieties were perfect, no one would have ever tried to produce hybrids.) For example, you might lose an heirloom crop to a disease a hybrid might survive. Hybrid seeds have been bred for increased productivity and resistance to disease and insect pests. Bear in mind, however, that few hybrids have been bred for better taste. If you have the space, there is no reason you can't grow hybrids and heirlooms together or even grow an heirloom and a hybrid of the same vegetable.

If you live in Zones 1–6, order your seeds by January or by February at the latest. Buying early is particularly important

places to buy seeds, as they often stock seeds from a wide variety of suppliers, which makes it easy to compare prices. The best garden stores have knowledgeable staff that can help you make informed decisions.

We typically buy the bulk of our seeds from a trusted mail-order source (what better way to spend a long winter evening than browsing a stack of seed catalogs, which are always stuffed with valuable information?). We buy from Johnny's Selected Seeds (www.johnnyseeds.com) or any other supplier who meets our criteria for good seed, extensive and interesting varieties, and, most important, location in the same hardiness zone as ours. We're willing to pay for the extra quality. One can be picky or one can be cheap, but one can't be both. You'll invest a lot of labor, love, and, yes, money, in your garden. It would be a shame to allow less than high-quality seeds to compromise the results. Take note, however. The most expensive seeds aren't always the best seeds. Some

Cold Frames

Planting seeds directly in cold frames is easier and
less messy than starting plants indoors.

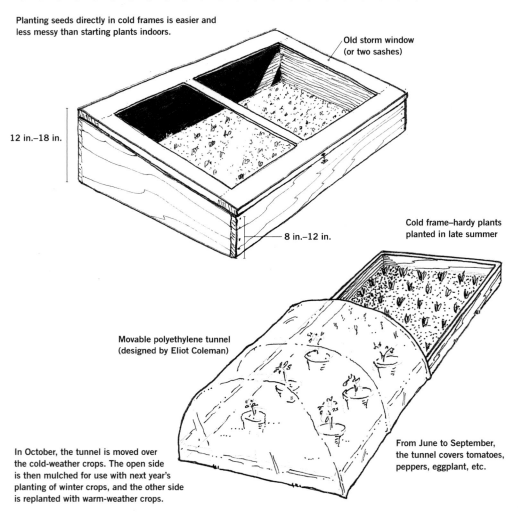

Old storm window
(or two sashes)

12 in.–18 in.

8 in.–12 in.

Cold frame–hardy plants
planted in late summer

Movable polyethylene tunnel
(designed by Eliot Coleman)

In October, the tunnel is moved over
the cold-weather crops. The open side
is then mulched for use with next year's
planting of winter crops, and the other side
is replanted with warm-weather crops.

From June to September,
the tunnel covers tomatoes,
peppers, eggplant, etc.

fancy and expensive seed companies charge a lot for heirloom seeds that have poor germination rates. In particular, watch out for unfamiliar companies selling heritage seeds (all the rage right now) in elaborate packaging at stratospheric prices. They may be fly-by-night outfits, attempting to cash in on the latest gardening fad. Do your homework. I am a big fan of supporting small companies, but be careful and check everything out. In a pinch, go with the large, well-known companies. Many of them have very good hybrid and heirloom seeds.

One way to buy good seeds inexpensively is to buy large quantities. Perhaps go in on a seed order with one or two other families. Not all of you are going to want all the same seeds, but there will be enough overlap to make the effort worthwhile. In the last few years, gardening and farming collectives have sprung up like mushrooms after a three-day rain. These groups do many things together, including owning equipment in common, organizing workshops on topics of interest to the group, and buying seeds in bulk. If there isn't a group in your area, consider starting one. Many of these collectives got their start buying seeds at a discount and then went on to other shared projects.

Another way to benefit from bulk pricing is to buy enough seeds to last a couple of years. During the first few years, the decline in germination rate is relatively small as long as you store the seeds correctly, but after that, the rate drops precipitously. Store your bought seeds just as you would your saved seeds (see p. 201).

As you might expect, some seeds store better than others. In 2005, a Chinese lotus that was carbon-dated as 1,300 years old was planted and developed into a viable plant. So your lettuce seeds will probably do all right after two years in the jar.

Starting Plants and Planting

If you're planting your first garden, I recommend buying transplants rather than growing your plants from seed. After you've had some experience tending a garden, indoor planting will make more sense. Starting your own transplants can be messy and can take up a lot of time and space, but it's not brain surgery and no one is going to die if you screw it up. The worst that will happen is that you will lose some money and maybe get discouraged—but don't get discouraged. Just wait until you've gained a little experience.

Starting plants indoors Planting indoors in preparation for the summer garden is a pleasant promise of what's to come. I like starting plants in the greenhouse in early spring, just to get some dirt under my fingernails. For most plants, the best time to start seeds is six weeks before the set-out date, which is the last average frost date on the hardiness map (in Vermont, that's May 30). Plants started too early develop weak, spindly stems that fall over easily. If you don't have a greenhouse or other warm and sunny indoor space, you can usually find started plants locally. (Offer to give farmers a hand with their transplants in exchange for a few flats for yourself—this way, you'll get some experience and some plants, while also helping a local grower.)

One of the reasons to start your own plants is because of the increased choices. The varieties available in seedling six-packs are quite limited, and you'll only find varieties that are in vogue. Not long ago, heirloom varieties were rare, but now that

"The rule of thumb is to plant the seed as deep as the seed is long."

heirlooms are in style, you'll find Brandywine tomato starts everywhere. Another reason is cost. The varieties I want, if I can find them, are usually expensive. I don't begrudge the premium price, but if I can do it myself, I want to do it myself—then I can spend my money on things I can't do myself, like grow coffee.

Not all plants need to be started indoors, but if they do, there are two reasons to do it: to get a jump on the season and to prolong it. Unless they are about eight weeks old when they hit the ground, tomatoes, peppers, and other long-season crops won't survive long enough to mature in cooler climates. Take note of the "days to maturity" indicated on the back of the seed pack or in the catalog. If that number is greater than the number of frost-free days in your hardiness zone, then you need to start the plant indoors.

The first step is to mix up a batch of potting soil in a tub or contractor-size wheelbarrow. You can buy premixed

potting soil, but I prefer to mix my own, combining dehydrated organic cow manure with peat moss, perlite (those little white beads of volcanic fluff), and a bit of garden soil (see sidebar on p. 176).

After I fill all my pots and flats, I set them out on planting benches in our attached greenhouse/sunspace. Check on the seedlings each day and water them frequently. Keep in mind that, if your sunspace is confined to a south-facing windowsill and the dining room table, those up-and-coming transplants will take over your living space. If your response is, "Why else have a dining room table if you can't cover it with projects of one kind or another," then, by all means, proceed. You are a true homesteader.

Planting outdoors Planting seeds directly into your cold frames is easier and less messy than starting plants indoors. Use one of the potting mix recipes on p. 176. Spread the mix, a couple of inches deep, right over the garden soil in the cold frame—or you can lay down a layer of peat moss instead of the mix (the seedlings will find the soil soon enough).

Divide the areas into a 3-in. grid and plant a seed or two in each block. Sprinkle a little dirt or peat moss over the seeds. Pat the whole area firmly with your hand or a trowel, in order to make good contact between the soil and the seed. The rule of thumb is to plant the seed as deep as the seed is long. The seed packages will tell you how deep to plant each seed and how to space them. When you've finished planting, water the area gently, but thoroughly.

Controlling Pests Our Way

Well-managed permaculture-based organic gardens tend to be relatively free of serious pests (at least, the six-legged variety). Healthy plants grown in healthy soil develop strong immune systems that resist predators, but no natural garden will ever be entirely free of pests or disease. The losses can be kept to a tolerable minimum, however, through good management, prophylactic measures, and diligent observation, as discussed in every gardening magazine, online forum, and magazine. One of the best preventative strategies we've employed has been our chicken army.

We turn 20 to 30 chickens loose in the garden and its surrounds for a few weeks before planting and after harvest each year. Chickens are relentless and voracious predators of just about every insect and small critter they encounter. Since we began letting the chickens into the garden, the level of our pest problems has plummeted.

The ducks are in charge of the slug-eradication program. We don't let them rummage through the garden because they like lettuce and other tender greens almost as much as they do slugs. Instead, we lift up the mulch mat early in the morning, collect the slimy little boogers, and serve them up to the ducks on a platter.

We've had mixed results with keeping some pests (geese, turkeys, dogs, and raccoons) out of the garden. Two strands of electrified twine or tape have been effective against most small- to medium-size four-legged animals. (The pasture apples surrounding our garden areas seem to distract the deer during the late summer when they would otherwise be inclined to sample our garden buffet.) The company Premier One Supplies (www.premier 1supplies.com) has recently introduced 2-ft.-tall electrified netting that is intended to repel both bird and mammalian invaders. Ultimately, we plan to enclose the garden with a permanent 4-ft.-high fence made of sawmill slab pickets—not only because it will be more effective than electrified netting or tapes, but also because it will look better.

Don't start your seeds or put out transplants for winter-keeping vegetables too early. Some crops (like tomatoes, squash, and corn) don't like soil that hasn't yet warmed up to 60°F to 65°F; they'll be stunted all season. If you wait until the soil is good and warm, you'll also have a chance to till the soil one more time before you plant, which helps fight the weeds. Till the ground once as soon as it is dry enough to work. Then till under the next generation of weeds while they're still small.

You also don't want to plant cool-weather crops too early. For example, if your cabbage matures before your cold room is cold enough to store it, the heads will crack and rot, and you will lose most

> *"A garden should make you feel you've entered privileged space—a place not just set apart but reverberant—and it seems to me that, to achieve this, the gardener must put some kind of twist on the existing landscape, turn its prose into something nearer poetry."*
> —*Michael Pollan,* Second Nature: A Gardener's Education

of the crop. Carrots, turnips, and rutabagas turn tough and split open when they get too big too early. So, don't be in a rush to get started when you're planting your main or storage crop. Count backward from your expected harvest date and plan to sow your seeds on that day. Do, however, set out fresh-eating crops—like onions and peas (both the edible-pod and shelled kind)—as early as you can. Support peas with a trellis, and they are among the easiest vegetables to grow. It's the processing that requires all the work—but if you really love peas, don't let that stop you.

Weeding

The results of good weeding carry over from year to year. In an ideal world, you would never allow the weeds to get ahead of you. You would have dispatched them with your hand hoe and/or a Mantis® mini tiller as soon as they emerged (which is the only time hoeing and other shallow-weeding techniques are effective). The key is to kill or uproot your annuals before they go to seed and to grub out all the roots of the perennials before they get established.

The best time to pull weeds by hand is the day after a steady rain, when the soil is soft. You can easily extricate the entire plant, leaving no broken roots behind to sneak back up when you're not looking. To dislodge weeds with long and tenacious taproots (dandelions, docks, thistles, and burdock) or wide-ranging adventitious roots (quack grass), you'll require mechanical assistance from a weeding fork or some other device. There are as many kinds of hand hoes, cultivators, and other weeding tools as there are species of weed. The Wonder Bar® pry bar, a carpentry tool, is excellent for the task. We've found that the narrow blade of an onion hoe is also quite effective; if kept sharp, the tool is easy to maneuver around the vegetables. Cut the juvenile weeds off from their roots just beneath or at the surface, stirring the soil slightly so that the exposed plants shrivel and die in the hot sun.

To control weeds, some people lay plastic sheeting over their beds and set their transplants in holes punched in the plastic. We're not believers in plastic sheeting for full-time weed control, as it does not contribute any organic material as it degrades. We do, however, use black plastic sheeting as an organic alternative to herbicides in order to kill sod and weeds

Recipe for Potting Soil

I'm not fond of the soil-less potting mixtures some people use. I like dirt—or, to be more precise, good garden soil lightened with nutritious organic material and inert mineral matter. My basic recipe calls for:

1 part garden soil

1 part organic material (your choice of compost, peat moss, or leaf mold)

1 part drainage material (perlite, vermiculite, etc.)

This recipe is the starting point for any potting soil mix. If you're starting seeds that will be transplanted into pots when established, use peat moss (excellent for holding water and aerating the nascent seedlings). To avoid the risk of fungal disease (damping off) in the seedlings, sterilize the soil by heating it in the oven long enough for the entire batch to reach 200°F for at least 15 minutes. (If you need more than a small batch or two, it's probably more practical to buy a bag of sterilized soil or add your sterilized dirt to a bag of commercial potting soil.)

If you plan to keep the seedlings in pots until you transplant them into the garden or if you are repotting container plants, you'll need to boost the nutrient content of the mix to provide long-term sustenance. You don't need to sterilize this soil as the plants are beyond the stage where they are vulnerable to soil-borne pathogens. Mix this "long-term" mix in the fall for use in the spring. I use:

3 buckets peat moss

2 cups of fertilizer mix (organic fish meal or Miracle-Gro)

3 buckets of compost (sifted, if need be)

1 bucket of perlite

---

in preparation for planting new ground or when reclaiming overgrown areas.

All your weed-and-disease control efforts will come to naught if you don't clean up the garden after harvest. All those dried stalks, leaves, roots, and stems left behind provide a refuge for overwintering insect pests and viral, fungal, and bacterial diseases. We used to try to till the garden residue under before the freeze-up. Some years we'd manage it; most years we wouldn't. Around here, when the weather turns cold, it also turns wet. You cannot till or rotovate wet ground.

Now we employ a walking, all-weather rotovator that not only turns under the garden leftovers, but also removes weeds and picks stone and fertilizes the ground, too. This wonderful device is called a pig. We drag the portable shelter into the garden, enclose with an electric fence those areas that we want to turn under (blocking off access to our asparagus and other perennial beds), and let the pigs do their work. The animals can either spend the entire winter in the garden or move to the barn when the snow gets too deep.

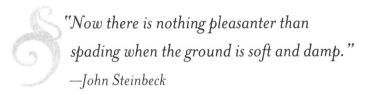

*"Now there is nothing pleasanter than
spading when the ground is soft and damp."*
—John Steinbeck

Never compost or turn under any infected or blighted plants. The plant matter will decompose, but the virus or fungus that killed them will survive in the soil, infecting a new generation of plants the next year. Remove any blighted plant as soon as it shows signs of infection. Don't wait to see if it will survive long enough to bear fruit, because it will bear poisoned fruit. Always burn—never bury—all infected plant materials.

Watering

In a normal summer, a thick hay or straw mulch is one of the most effective ways to maintain a comfortable level of soil moisture. The mulch blanket slows evaporation and retains runoff so that the water is available to the roots of your plants and keeps the soil from overheating (so refrain from mulching in a cool and damp summer). A deep, healthy, organic clay loam with plenty of humus will naturally hold enough water in reserve so that you may be able to get by with little or no need to irrigate. Even if your well can deliver enough water to run a sprinkler day and night, groundwater is a precious and dwindling resource, and it behooves all of us to conserve it.

Planting vegetables in slightly raised rows that run parallel with the slope slows wasteful runoff. A soaker hose or some form of drip irrigation that allows water to percolate directly into the root zone of the plants is less wasteful than sprinklers. If you do irrigate with sprinklers, do so early in the morning. In the heat of the sun, the beads of water on the leaves act like tiny lenses to concentrate the sunlight and scald the foliage. Also, much of the applied water will evaporate before it can reach the roots. On the other hand (much to the delight of nocturnal slugs), water applied during the cool night won't evaporate at all, but can promote the growth or spread of fungal diseases.

The general rule (for unmulched soil) is to irrigate whenever there is less than 1 in. of rainfall within a week. When you do water, water deeply or not at all. Barely moistening the top of the soil does not benefit the plants in any way. The water must seep down to the roots, which takes hours. Regular, deep watering is probably the single most important thing you can do to help your transplants become established. Certain vegetables require extra water at certain times. Tomatoes, for example, will crack if not given supplemental water when the fruit is ripening. Lettuces and other cool-loving greens appreciate a cooling shower on a hot afternoon.

Planning Your Garden

Planning your garden and ordering your seeds go hand-in-hand. You can't plan the whole garden until you have assembled your seed list, and you can't order your seeds until you've drawn up your garden plan. Although you don't necessarily need a detailed drawing or diagram, you do need to have a basic idea of what you wish to grow where. That being said, many a wonderful gardener has no idea what they are going to plant or where until they are standing on the edge of the garden with a few packets of seeds purchased that morning. We're not necessarily advocating this approach, but don't give up gardening just because you can't plan or won't plan ahead.

The big questions will answer themselves. How large? The answer is obvious if you live on the Upper West Side of Manhattan and share a fire escape. If you have some land, your garden dimensions may still be a foregone conclusion if most of it is covered with trees, too steep, too wet, or too dry. But if you're blessed (or cursed) with options, your first decision is, How big and how much?

Summer in the garden is a time of intense and competing demands and activities. When the beans are coming in, the spinach is bolting, and the cilantro is going to seed. It's frustrating to watch the fruits of all your labors go by—spoiling on the vine or going to seed unpicked—just because you are stretched too thin to get to them. For this reason, start out with a small, manageable-size garden.

Decide which vegetables you want to grow and about how much of each. We grow food for several families, friends, and animals, and we put up all of our vegetables—so, obviously, if you are growing a container garden on the patio, your plan will be nothing like ours.

How much is enough? Let's say your plan is to fill the freezer, the root cellar, and the canning shelves. Where do you start and how do you decide how much of each vegetable to grow? When the kids were growing up, there were six of us for dinner every night. We figured we needed 50 units of each food item. (A unit is the quantity of food needed to feed your family one meal. Fifty units provide at least one meal of that item per week for nearly the entire year.) Think about how much of what you will really need. Adjust our calculation so that it fits your family's needs. Then refer to the chart on p. 210 to determine how much of each vegetable you should plant. Your garden will always be much more rewarding if it provides your family with enough of the vegetables they really enjoy eating throughout the winter and into the next season.

Urban Homesteading

From lettuce to potatoes, almost anything you can raise in a small garden plot you can raise in a container garden. Choosing the plants that produce the most bang for the buck is what makes all the difference. For example, you need only a couple of parsley plants in a single pot to have that herb at hand to upgrade any meal. You can plant vegetables in pots of various sizes or in rectangular planters or flats. Plastic containers may not look as attractive as natural materials such as terra cotta, but impervious plastic holds moisture better than porous terra cotta does and is also easier to keep clean.

You can also plant in plastic tote bags, plastic woven bags (like those reusable shopping bags), or even in stiff-sided plastic kiddy wading pools. Just remember to punch or drill holes in the bottom of any container to provide good drainage. If you set the containers outdoors, the runoff can seep into the ground. If they are indoors or on a tiled patio or balcony, use catch trays to contain the runoff water.

Maintaining adequate moisture levels is always a concern with container gardening. Mulch works just as well in containers as it does on the ground. The soil also needs to be especially fertile and so, therefore, constantly refurbished. For this reason, container gardening and vermiculture (worm composting) are natural soulmates.

The site location is just as important for a stationary garden—with one big advantage. You can arrange your containers on one or more wheeled platforms and move them to follow the sun (or the shade) daily, avoiding frost at the start and end of the cold season.

Pocket microgarden

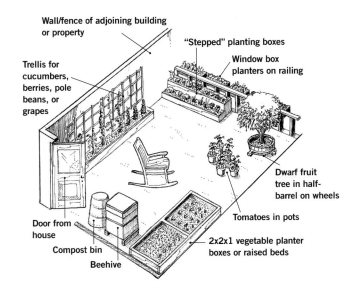

Wall/fence of adjoining building or property

"Stepped" planting boxes

Window box planters on railing

Trellis for cucumbers, berries, pole beans, or grapes

Dwarf fruit tree in half-barrel on wheels

Tomatoes in pots

Door from house

Compost bin

Beehive

2x2x1 vegetable planter boxes or raised beds

For raised beds, you need to import the soil or build it up (about 1 ft.) in an enclosed area. Be sure that the enclosed area is not so wide, however, that you cannot comfortably reach the middle from either side, or you will have difficulty weeding and harvesting—3 ft. to 4 ft. is ideal.

Suburban Homesteading

Most new gardeners are amazed to discover how much food they can grow in a very small area. For example, a 3-ft. row of Swiss chard will provide four people with all of the fresh greens they could want all summer long, and chard regrows after it's cut, so there's always plenty to freeze for winter. A garden is a lot of work and very time-consuming, however—even if you love weeding—and most of us have other things we also have to do every day. The number-one mistake new gardeners make is they make the garden too big (we know because we did it ourselves).

Think hard about how much time you can devote to your garden. There is no moral or legal imperative to grow all of your own food in your first year. Pare down your expectations as far as you can, and then cut that in half. If your garden is too much to handle the first year, the gardening work not only overwhelms you, but it also commandeers time you've allotted for other projects. If you start slowly, you're more likely to succeed. With one good year under your belt, you can jack up the scale fast. The worst conse-quence of planting too small a garden is that it will be completely weed free, your compost pile will be neat and well aerated because you have time to turn it often, your lawn and flower gardens will look well tended and beautiful, and you will have time to read a good book. If you get bored, you can always build a really cool henhouse.

Plant only a few of each of your favorite vegetables. Everyone likes tomatoes—plant no more than six your first year. Cucumbers? Two plants. Lettuces and greens? Plant very small amounts of a good variety in succession. Three 1-sq.-ft. patches of mesclun will keep two to four people in salads all summer if they're planted in 10-day successions. You can plant various greens for stir-frying or steaming the same way. Two mini-plots will keep you in greens from early spring to late fall. (For those of you who might be turning part of your lawn into a garden, leave the grass between the rows. Established sod suppresses weeds and helps control soil erosion.)

The Mini-Farm

As discussed in Chapter 2, the ideal spot for both a house and garden (if you live in a temperate four-season climate) is on a slightly sloping south-to-southeast-facing hillside. The next best location is on level ground with a good southern exposure. On a slightly sloping site, when there are mild patchy frosts at the beginning and end of the growing season, the frigid air will drain down the slope, sparing your garden from frost for the longest possible time. Sloping sites also allow surface water to drain. The worst spot for a garden is at the bottom of a gully, where frost strikes first. If you're making plans far enough in the future, notice which areas on your property stay frost free the longest—these are your ideal garden locations. Consider developing several small plots instead of one large one. Not all of your garden space has to be contiguous, so you might maximize your growing season by capitalizing on your microclimates.

There are an endless number of ways you can arrange your garden. You can adopt the permaculture paradigm, eschewing straight rows of single-variety plantings and interplanting perennials with annuals, fruits, and flowers—the chaos is intended to mimic the homeostatic balance of natural ecosystems. The traditional, orderly row garden, on the other hand, is easy to cultivate and harvest and can be deeply satisfying. Planting your garden in blocks rather than rows allows intensive interplanting, as do raised beds. Experiment with any combination that suits

Large permaculture garden with double fence

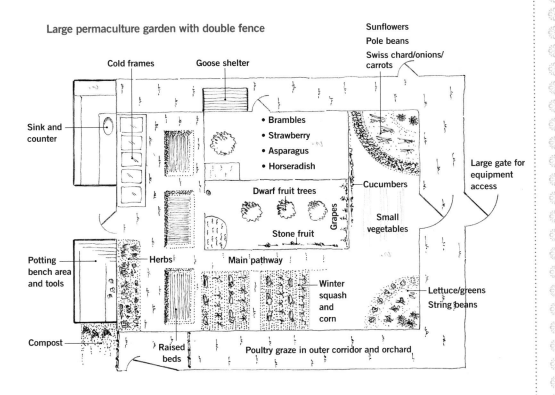

Cold frames

Goose shelter

Sunflowers
Pole beans
Swiss chard/onions/carrots

Sink and counter

- Brambles
- Strawberry
- Asparagus
- Horseradish

Dwarf fruit trees

Cucumbers

Grapes

Stone fruit

Small vegetables

Large gate for equipment access

Potting bench area and tools

Herbs

Main pathway

Winter squash and corn

Lettuce/greens
String beans

Compost

Raised beds

Poultry graze in outer corridor and orchard

Our garden plan

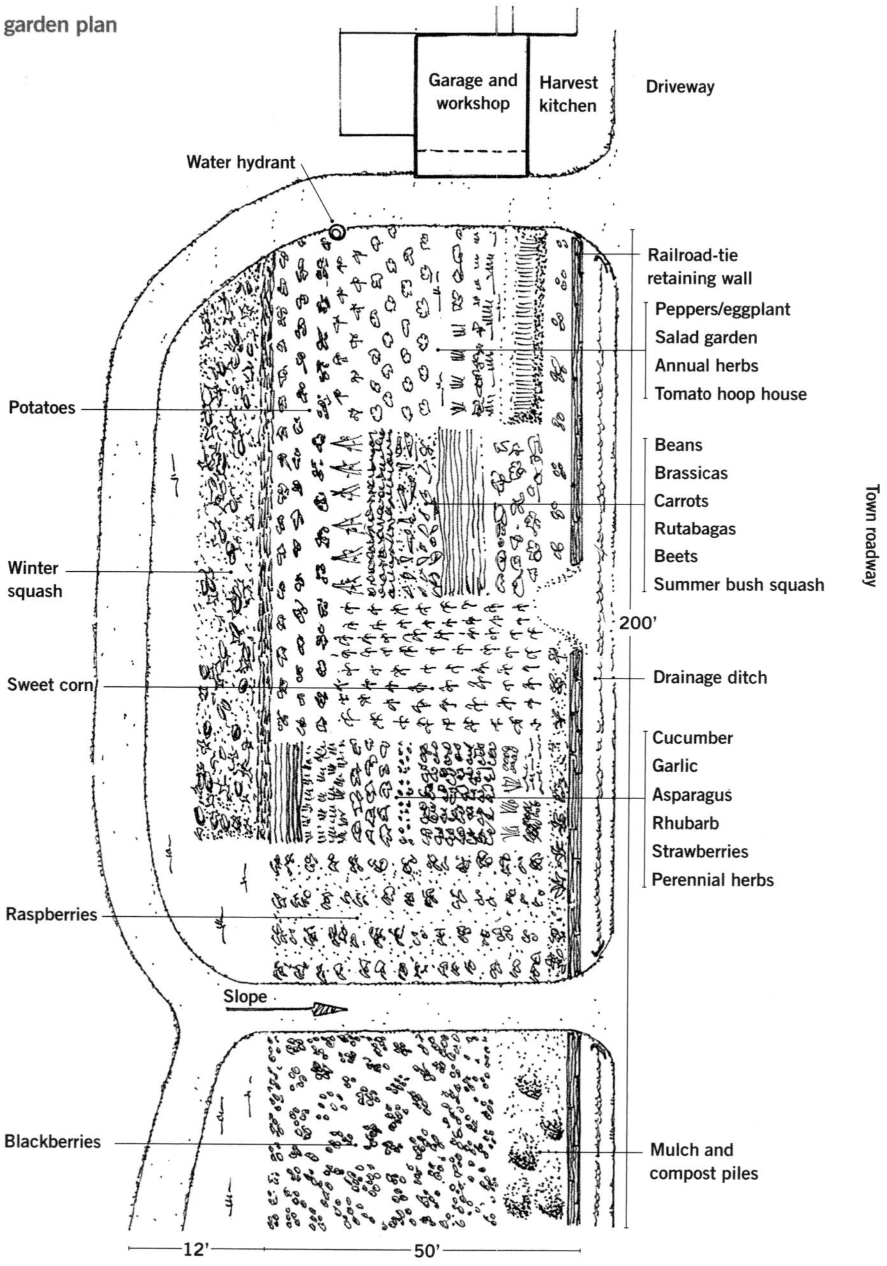

Garage and workshop

Harvest kitchen

Driveway

Water hydrant

Railroad-tie retaining wall

Peppers/eggplant
Salad garden
Annual herbs
Tomato hoop house

Potatoes

Beans
Brassicas
Carrots
Rutabagas
Beets
Summer bush squash

Winter squash

200'

Town roadway

Sweet corn

Drainage ditch

Cucumber
Garlic
Asparagus
Rhubarb
Strawberries
Perennial herbs

Raspberries

Slope

Blackberries

Mulch and compost piles

12'

50'

your fancy. Any gardening layout will work so long as you follow a few common-sense rules.

1. Beware of erosion. Build pathways and rows parallel with the slope contour, or part of your garden will wash away every year. Mulch or pave permanent pathways.

2. Plan the pathways. Be sure to make pathways wide enough to accommodate garden carts or tractors.

3. Consider fencing. Do you need or want fencing? Is the ground level enough for it? Keep in mind that free-ranging poultry can be very destructive in your garden. Dogs can disturb freshly planted seeds and transplants. A fence also allows you to fence livestock into the garden when you want to—for example, to let chickens forage for grubs and larvae before planting or let pigs hog down the stubble and weeds postharvest.

4. Site thoughtfully. Site for the optimum amount of sun. Be aware of shadows cast by adjacent structures, fences, and trees that will create cold or shady pockets. Site near outbuildings or a dedicated shed for convenient tool and supply storage.

5. Interplant as much as possible. Let plants share the same space. Interplanting is almost as effective as a tall electric fence and less expensive as a way to repel raccoons and other pests. Be careful not to

grow members of the same family together, however, as they usually share the same pests and will only attract more of them.

6. Utilize succession planting. Crops like lettuce, greens, and early carrots will mature in less than a season, so after you harvest them, you can plant a second crop to utilize the same space.

7. Rotate crops. If you avoid planting the same crop on the same ground in successive years, you will reduce the buildup of pathogens and pests in the soil and on the plants. Some say that tomatoes don't like to be moved, but we had tomato blight one year and moved our tomatoes to a new home, where they did great (although it might have been because of the drier weather that year).

Fall garden: Potatoes are dug and left to "cure" for several days before storing them in the root cellar.

chapter viii

Vegetables & Grains

You don't need to know a lot of botany to grow a very nice garden. Plant a seed, give it water, and it will grow. If your soil is alive and healthy, your vegetables will be, too—but gardening is much more fun and rewarding when you know a little plant science. The solution to most, if not all, problems is more likely to emerge when you understand the basics. The winter before you start gardening, curl up by the fire with an accessible and readable book on basic botany for nonscientists (for example, *Botany for Gardeners* by Brian Capon [Timber Press, 2010]). If you make the effort to learn the basics of classification, nomenclature, plant anatomy, and (don't be scared) a little biochemistry, you'll be rewarded with a solid theoretical foundation on which to build your practical knowledge.

The classification system for plants, known as botanical taxonomy, is not random. It's based on the plants' precise characteristics—such as whether or not the plant has flowers (gymnosperms do not) or whether one or two leaves emerge as a seed germinates. Nowhere, however, in this seemingly endless list of classification characteristics is the term "vegetable" mentioned. There is no such distinction in botany. Vegetables are a hodge-podge mixture of plants and plant parts that have been domesticated by humans for the purpose of feeding us. Some vegetables (tomatoes and squash) are fruits; others (broccoli and cauliflower) are flowers; and others (lettuce) are leaves. Rhubarb and celery are stems, and potatoes are tubers, which are modified stems. Onions, garlic, and leeks are bulbs; carrots and beets are roots. Most of our vegetables are flowering plants, which are characterized as angiosperms. Mushrooms, however, aren't plants at all—they are fungi—but the ones that we eat we call vegetables. Basically, if we eat a plant and call it a vegetable, it is a vegetable.

Vegetable Families

Plants belong to families. All members of a particular family share unique characteristics and requirements for good growth

Your basic healthy vegetable diet: corn, squash, and cabbage. Beans would complete the nutrient profile.

and yield. There are fewer families than individual plants, so rather than consider each vegetable plant individually, consider its family. Once you understand the family, you'll understand the needs of all

All members of this family tolerate and adapt well to cold-frame, low-tunnel, and unheated-greenhouse winter gardening techniques, so you can eat brassicas either fresh or out of the cold room all winter

"The greatest delight the fields and woods minister is the suggestion of an occult relation between man and the vegetable. I am not alone and unacknowledged. They nod to me and I to them." —Ralph Waldo Emerson

its members. Not all members of a given family come from the same locale, but they usually come from similar climates. A family may have annual plants (one-year life cycle), biennial plants (two-year cycle), and perennial plants (continuous cycle). The flowers of all these plants will be similar, however, as plant families are classified by their reproduction methods.

Brassicaceae (brassica or mustard)

This family is made up of cabbages, broccoli, cauliflowers, kohlrabi, mustard, kale, collards, and rape (canola or rapeseed). It was formerly known as Cruciferae, meaning "cross bearing," because of the crosslike shape of its four-petaled flower. All the brassicas thrive in cool, rainy climates, which is why cabbages have always been a staple storage crop for folks in northern regions. Here in Vermont, a head of cabbage will keep in the cold room through February, even if you just pick it and toss it on the shelf. If you are careful to pick only the best heads and wrap them in newspaper, they will last even longer.

long. In fact, most leafy vegetables, except lettuce, actually taste better if they've been exposed to a slight frost (also true for chard and beet greens, although they're in another family). In the South, brassicas will grow nearly throughout the winter with zero-to-minimal frost protection. Every southern garden has a crop of collards—the region's signature green— even in January and February. If you have never had collards stewed with bacon or fatback, you've never eaten real greens (and this coming from a Yankee girl).

In the Northeast, the brassicas' major nemesis is the slug. This slimiest of slimy creatures is not particularly picky. Slugs will eat just about any kind of plant, fruit, and mushroom (except nightshades), but they do like certain plants more than others. Brassicas are at the top of their list. Slugs prefer to remain in the shade while they indulge their appetite, which is why they thrive in deeply mulched gardens. We're big fans of mulching, but if the slugs get out of hand, you'll have to pull the mulch away from your brassicas, lettuce, and anything else that they may be feasting upon.

The one thing that slugs like better than brassicas is beer—hence, the renowned beer trap, the hands-down best method for eliminating slugs. Dig a small hole in the garden close to the at-risk plants. Just before nightfall, place a shallow bowl in the hole and then fill it almost to the rim with beer (fresh or flat, it doesn't matter). In the morning, you'll have a nice bowl of slugs marinated in beer. To ensure that the trap will work, make sure that the bowl is easy for the slugs to climb into but hard to get back out of. The best preventative for slugs and all other insects, however, are chickens, guineas, turkeys, and ducks. Let these birds into your garden at various times throughout the year (see Part 3 starting on p. 262 for the garden-management pros and cons for each species).

Flea beetles, another brassica pest, are very tiny beetles that jump, just like their namesake. They emerge in the early spring to punch miniscule holes in almost every plant in the garden. They do little real harm to the plant other than to ruin its appearance, which isn't so bad if you are eating the greens yourself, but chewed and punctured greens are not salable. So, if you're planning to sell your greens, you should plant them under a row cover, even when the weather is perfect.

At the time of this writing, we had our first encounter with a brassica disease called root knot. Although not exclusive to the brassicas, this virus is definitely partial to them. The roots of an afflicted plant turn into grotesquely deformed knuckles,

devoid of almost all of their tiny nutrient-gathering root hairs. Wilting is the first sign of trouble. If your plants appear wilted despite being well watered, examine the root. If it looks gnarled, pull up the plant and burn it. Unfortunately, there is no cure. Once infected, the plant is a goner. If some portion of the plant looks okay, there's no harm in eating it or feeding it to animals. The virus is not harmful to you or anything else except the cabbage. Root knot dislikes a sweet soil, so topdressing with a little lime or wood ash may help (brassicas can tolerate a little alkalinity). In any case, if you discover root knot, don't plant any brassicas in the infected area for at least three years.

Cabbage is a biennial, so the roots must be held over the winter and replanted in the spring. The brassicas are cross-pollinators, which means they reproduce when fertilized by the pollen of another plant. Saving brassica seeds requires some fancy footwork, so start with something simpler.

Amaranthacea (amaranth) The Amaranth family, sometimes known as chenopods, includes spinach, chard, beets, quinoa (grain), and the ubiquitous pest pigweed. Other than occasionally bolting when they aren't supposed to, this family is trouble free. The only bothersome insects are flea beetles, which bother every plant in early spring. When the weather settles, the beetles go away. You can protect your plants with a row cover, or you can just live with the peppering of tiny little holes that the bugs leave. Most of the plants in this family like cool

weather and do best on either side of the summer.

I plant chards and beets in the spring because they are among the first things we're able to eat. I plant them again in mid-August. Flea beetles and hot weather don't bother the bigger plants harvested in the fall. These plants look and taste better, and their leaves go in the freezer. Swiss chard and beets are both biennial and are cross-pollinated by the wind.

To save seed, overwinter the roots of your best plants in damp sand (as you do the beets) and replant the roots close together in the spring. Close plantings will enhance cross-pollination. Chard and beets that are going to seed can reach 5 ft. to 6 ft. in height, so they will require staking. Because these two vegetables are really subspecies of the same species (*Beta vulgaris*), they will cross-pollinate, so it's best to gather seed from only one subspecies in a given year. The good news is that the seed lasts for six years.

Asteraceae (sunflower) The sunflower family includes lettuces, endive, and chicory. It is sometimes still called by its older name, Compositae. This family is named for the inflorescences, which are the clusters of tiny flowers that they produce. A sunflower may look like one giant flower, but it's actually composed of hundreds of small flowers arranged in spirals in the center of a disk that is surrounded by petals. When lettuce flowers, it has the

....

Still life with garden. Top: Sunflowers Bottom left: Red Norlands and Yukon Gold potatoes Bottom right: Cabbage leaf.

same kind of arrangement, although its inflorescence is organized vertically.

There are many wonderful lettuce cultivars (cultivated varieties), from micromixes, mescluns, and baby leafs to loose heads and tight heads. The recent lettuce craze started with mesclun, that gourmet mix of tiny baby lettuces and assorted leafy plants with exotic names and piquant tastes. Over the past decade or so, good ol' all-American iceberg lettuce, and even its Mediterranean cousins— escarole, endive, cos, and others—had to make room in the salad bowl for the ever-increasing horde of new arrivals. Now there are literally dozens of "new" greens for salads. Most of them are not new, however. They are actually either immigrants from Asia, where they have been cultivated for thousands of years, or they have always been here, languishing in obscurity until their new celebrity status launched them onto the pages of mainstream seed catalogs. Many of the Asian greens are in the brassica family and have the same culture as the rest of the family and make great choices for early spring and fall plantings and cold-frame use. There are also many heirloom lettuce varieties, including loose leafed, miniature heads, and red leafed.

Lettuce is not difficult to grow, as long as you can keep the soil moist and cool. In the North, the spring, early summer, and fall seasons are cool, especially at night, even when the days are hot. Including what we grow in our greenhouse, we have lettuce or some kind of greens in the ground most of the year.

Also within this family are the salad greens endive, escarole, and radicchio. These vegetables are very hardy and, unlike lettuces, do equally well in cool or warm weather. They take from 50 to 60 days to become edible (although you can nibble at the leaf edges fairly early on) and, best of all, they stay crisp and rarely bolt until after frost. Start some in the cold frame in late July for use well into winter.

If you live in a warm climate, it will be difficult to impossible to grow lettuce in the summer. Rather than confronting the challenge, grow more heat-tolerant crops, like mustard greens, and wait for the cooler months to plant your lettuce. Or you could try some of the new heat-tolerant lettuces with pelleted seeds. Pelleted seeds germinate better because a priming process reduces their tendency to go dormant. (Lettuce seeds are dormant at temperatures above 60° F to 65°F.)

Lettuce can be started outside as soon as the soil can be worked—or even earlier in a cold frame (see p. 170). Continue to plant a new row every 7 to 14 days to keep the crops coming. Heat and drought will stress members of the Asteraceae family. As summer progresses, switch to pelleted seed for heat-tolerant varieties. Mulch also helps conserve soil moisture and keep the plants cooler. Asteraceae also dislike excessively damp weather. If you have this problem, set the plants farther apart to increase air circulation. In low-humidity situations, lettuce does very well planted close enough together to crowd out weeds and shade the ground. The perfection of lettuce—like that of nearly every other crop—is marred by flea beetles in the spring, so plant it under a row cover or in a cold frame until the pests have gone. Fall crops tend to look better (because the insects are gone) and taste better (because of cooler temperatures).

All lettuce seed keeps fairly well, so buy more seed than you will use in one year to save money the following year. (The larger the packet, the cheaper the unit price.) Pelleted seeds, lose their vigor rapidly, so buy only the amount you will plant that year. Lettuce is self-pollinating, so saving seed is relatively simple. Pick the best plants that are the last to bolt and let them reach maturity and flower. Put the seed heads in a paper bag and let them dry thoroughly for about one month. Then clean the seed heads (a messy and tedious job). You get a lot of seed from just a few heads, and the seeds will keep for three to five years.

If insects get to the flowers, cross-pollination will take place, so separate the varieties from which you wish to save seed from other varieties by at least 20 ft. Alternate the varieties that you save from year to year. Even when plants are separated, some cross-pollination will happen, and volunteers will pop up here and there, along with freelance tomatoes and vagabond squashes. The quality of all volunteers is usually poor, but every now and then you might discover a gem. Some people collect knick-knacks. I collect lettuces.

Cucurbitaceae (cucurbits) It is hard to imagine a vegetable garden without some member of the Cucurbitaceae family. Squash, pumpkins, melons, and cucumbers belong to this family. Many species are native to the Americas, especially the southeastern United States, as the family is at home in the tropics and subtropics. Aboriginal Americans introduced the cucurbit family to European arrivals to the New World. Cucurbits are among the easiest plants to grow. They like rich soil that has a lot of moisture and thrive over a fairly wide-ranging pH level. Many gardeners plant their squash seeds in small hills that they've enriched with a few shovels of composted manure—a tradition that likely started when gardeners noted how well the volunteer squash plants growing on the manure or compost piles were doing. Cucurbits do like rich soil, but don't overdo it, or you will end up with a lot of lush foliage and very few fruits.

Squash bugs and squash borers are the two major predators of the cucurbits. Squash borers are fat white caterpillars with brown heads. In their moth stage, they have dark front wings and transparent rear ones. The moth, as its name implies, bores into stems, causing the plant to wilt. Picking individual caterpillars off of the stems has been the traditional—and not very effective—defense. To control squash borers and other types of caterpillars, experts recommend applying the bacterium *Bacillus thuringiensis* (BT) directly on the invader and then on the entire garden. Personally, I've never had much luck with BT and have yet to hear another gardener sing its praises either. We've never been attacked by borers, but we have waged war against the squash beetles and won (see p. 139).

(see p. 139).

Bottom line, prevention is far better than counterattack. The two most effective defenses against the beetles and, I suspect, against the borers, too, is, first, protect the young plants with a row cover from the time the seeds are planted until the flowers appear. The cover will prevent flying adults from laying their nasty little eggs. Second, let the chickens forage in the garden in the spring and fall every year. We've found that, after the chickens have policed the garden for a couple of years, there aren't many pests of any kind to worry about. A small platoon of special-force ducks and guineas serve as reinforcements.

Cucumbers and summer squash are ready to pick much sooner than winter squash, both because they mature faster and because they are harvested before the fruit matures. Even if you've never set foot in a garden, you've likely heard the legends of monster zucchinis and wheelbarrows that are full of cucumbers too big to eat, let alone pickle. One bush-type summer squash plant and no more than three or four cucumber vines will provide plenty of fruit for all but the largest families. At our place, two zucchini plants produce too much even for 10 people—happily, our pigs take up the slack.

Once winter squash plants are planted and mulched, you can forget about them for the rest of the summer until harvest. Mulching keeps the weeds at bay and the soil moist. All other things being equal, you'll get a better yield if you use mulch than you will if you weed and frequently water. Rotten hay, straw, and other organic matter (even old newspaper) work

Shelly Beans

I had never heard of shelly beans until I moved from New Hampshire to Vermont when I was in my early twenties. Our newly purchased 60 acres came with a neighbor, Marilyn. She was a few years older than I was and had a Vermont accent that was so thick I could barely understand a word she spoke, but we had one thing in common—gardening. I grew many things that she did not, such as lettuce, herbs, and Swiss chard. She grew only potatoes, peas, tomatoes, corn, and what she called "shelly beans." (Her husband had refused all other vegetables, declaring that they were "hippie food.") Marilyn showed me how to cook and eat shelly beans (which include any of several bean varieties that can be eaten soft). I freed the plump pink-and-white beans, which are slightly bigger than kidney beans, from their stiff pods. I cooked them for about 20 minutes after the boil started and served them with plenty of butter. As we all know, God only made vegetables so we would have something that could hold our melted butter.

as mulching materials. Squash and other heavy-feeding plants also benefit from living mulches, especially nitrogen-fixing low- and densely-growing legumes like clover. As soon as the squash plants show their first true leaves, give the whole area a good weeding, either by hand or with a Mantis cultivator, and then thickly broadcast white clover. The clover will provide extra nitrogen and crowd out the weeds.

Harvest winter squash just before a heavy frost or after a very light one. The timing can be tricky. Your goal is to leave the plants in the ground, growing, for as long as possible without exposing them to frostbite. When you pick your squash, leave the stems attached to help protect the fruit from invasion by microbes that promote rotting. Don't try to eat freshly picked winter squash; it has no flavor until it has cured. Leave the picked fruits in loose piles in the field for a few days, but cover them if a heavy frost threatens. The fruits (which are, technically, modified berries) will withstand a light frost. After field curing, bring the harvest into an open, unheated building, like your garage or barn. Spread the squash on the floor and leave them there for about a week. Before you store them (see p. 251), wipe around the base of the stem with a cloth that's just barely dampened with a bleach-and-water solution to kill the bacteria that cause rot. Exact proportions are not critical as long as there is plenty of bleach.

Most of the Cucurbitaceae are annual vines. They have unisex flowers on the same plants (monoecious) and are pollinated by insects. Squashes have large yellow flowers, which, incidentally, taste great when battered and deep-fried. The flowers are designed to attract insects, which flit from one flower to the next carrying pollen. Because members of this family are not self-pollinators, saving squash seed is more complicated than saving beans or peas. Again, if cross-pollination occurs between two varieties of the same species, the seeds will not produce offspring that closely resemble their mother.

Luckily for gardeners, there are four subspecies of garden-variety squashes that don't cross-pollinate, which makes it possible to grow a good variety of squash and still save seed. *Cucurbitaceae pepo* includes the summer squashes and delicata, spaghetti, and acorn winter types. The varieties of *C. maxima* are buttercup, kobocha, and Hubbard. The two last subspecies, *C. mixta* and *C. moschata,* include less well-known varieties, such as the Cushaw pumpkin. *C. moschata* varieties are also known as crookneck squash (not of the summer squash ilk). Butternut squash belongs to this group, too. Originally cultivated by Native Americans and reputed to have medicinal properties, these plants are also resistant to squash borers.

Fabacea or leguminosae (legumes)

The legume family is the family of peas and beans. Legumes are famous as high-protein vegetables (often replacing meat in the diets of vegetarians and others), but they are also well known as green manures. The nodules on the roots of legumes house the soil bacterium *Rhizobium,* which has the ability to draw nitrogen from the air in the soil, convert it into ammonium ions (a nitrogen form usable by all plants), and then share the nutrient with the host plant. Not only do the legumes benefit from this symbiotic relationship, any plants nearby can partake of a nitrogen meal, too, because the ions are diffused into the surrounding soil.

Many legumes are also capable of hydraulic redistribution. Water moves through plants from the soil to the topmost leaves because of osmotic pressure. In other words, water moves from where there is a lot of it to where there is less, like liquid moving up a dry wick. The long taproot of many legumes takes up water from deep in the soil and disperses it closer to the surface through a network of shallow lateral roots. As a result, legumes both fertilize and water their neighbors.

The term *legume* actually refers to the fruit characteristic of this family. What is commonly called a pod is actually a "dry" fruit, edible in all stages of its development. Green beans, pole beans, and edible podded peas are plants in the early stage, when the pods are fleshy, tender, and sweet. Peas, edamame, and "shelly beans" are legumes in the intermediate stage, when the seeds are still green and tender but the pods have thinned and are too tough to eat. The third stage of the legume is the dry stage, which leads to Boston baked beans, burritos, and split pea soup. Many heirloom varieties are suitable for eating at all three stages. I've never tried any of them, but most are reported to excel at one stage more than another. For example, Blue Coco Bean, a French bean dating from around 1775, is said to be pretty good as a green bean but excellent as a dry bean. I can't wait to try it.

Because of their proficiency in nitrogen fixing and hydraulic redistribution, beans and peas are just about the easiest vegetable to grow. A bean plant can practically grow in a gravel pit and has very few serious pests. (Cover crops—like clovers, alfalfa, and vetches—are fussier; alfalfa only grows in Zones 1–5 and can't tolerate heavy soils.) As an extra bonus, all legumes are well suited for intercropping. Planting them between or alongside heavy feeders helps maintain soil fertility. Beans really don't like wet or cold soil, so wait until the soil is good and warm before planting your seeds. With only 50 to 60 days to wait before you are eating green beans, there's no rush to get them in the ground. Try succession planting. Sow a short double row (about 3 ft.) every 7 to 10 days for the first four or five weeks. You'll have tender beans to eat throughout the summer without being overwhelmed by the volume of beans you need to pick and process. If you are overwhelmed, however, take heart. You're not alone. Everyone plants too many beans. I fight the bean battle every year. One reason we keep pigs is so I never have to feel guilty about the vegetables I never get around to picking or putting by.

Saving bean and pea seeds is very easy. Along with tomato seeds, they are one of the best choices for novice seed savers. Just remember, all legumes are self-pollinating, and, as with almost all self-pollinating plants, insects will disrupt your seed-saving plans if they are allowed to cross-pollinate your legumes. To minimize the chances of this unhappy outcome, plant several different varieties of beans at least 20 ft.

apart from each other and surround them with plantings of brightly colored flowers to divert the bees away from the less-conspicuous bean flower. Don't plant beans that are the same color next to one another. If beans of different colors cross, the event shows up in the bean itself. To harvest for seed, let the pods dry on the vine. Save the best-looking seed from the best-looking bush or vine. If properly stored, bean seeds will remain viable for four to five years.

Lilaceae (lily) The lily family is very diverse, and its membership roll has been edited and rearranged many times, particularly in the last few years. Here, we'll consider just the genus *Allium,* which includes garlic, leeks, chives, shallots, and all kinds of onions. Life without garlic and onions would be weary, stale, and flat indeed, at least for anyone who enjoys cooking or eating. Alliums prefer a sweet soil that has a lot of organic matter. They have only one major pest—the onion maggot—although I've never seen one (now I'm jinxed!). Nowadays, crop rotation is de rigueur for everything, but when onions were first grown commercially in Connecticut in the mid-19th century, they were planted on the same fields year after year. One farmer even boasted that his family had been growing onions on the same plot for 80 years. Onion farmers claimed that, as long as the soil was rich in organic matter, onion maggots stayed away. On those occasions when the pests did make a foray into the onion field, they were rerouted by the application of a strong burdock-leaf tea to the bulbs.

Plants in this genus are bulbous perennials that form new bulbs each year from the base of the old. Garlic is planted in the fall—one clove per desired plant. The plants overwinter and produce a multi-cloved bulb the following summer. Onions also produce cloves (called sets),

> *"Life on a farm is a school of patience;*
> *you can't hurry the crops or make an ox*
> *in two days." — Henri Alain*

but only a few, and they're much smaller than the mother plant. Onions develop the second year, the same as garlic. Sets of the most common onion varieties are sold everywhere in spring. You can also grow onions from seed or simply buy bunches of field-grown plants started from seed.

Each method has its pros and cons. Bulbs grown from seed or started plants tend to be of all-around higher quality than those started from sets. They are reputed to keep better, too. Growing from seed offers the largest and least expensive selection of varieties, but the cost is in the amount of work and commitment required. Starting onions from seed is a little like growing a lawn one blade at a time, setting out the transplants you start indoors. Some people have the patience and fortitude to enjoy the challenge, and I'm lucky my son-in-law is one of them. He grows enough beautiful onions from seed to last our extended family all year. (He also grows our potatoes and corn.)

Because sets are inexpensive and easy to plant, most gardeners grow their onions from sets, and we've had good luck with them. The downside is that there are only a few varieties of yellow, white, or red onion sets to choose from. If you are interested in growing, say, Ails Craig Exhibition Globe Onions from sets, you're out of luck.

Starting with plants is the most expensive method. A bunch of 60 to 70 onion plants typically costs four times more than a pack of 300-plus seeds and several times more than an equal number of sets. There are enough advantages to growing onions from plants to justify the premium price, however. Although there are fewer varieties of onions available as plants than as seeds, there are still more plants available than there are sets, especially if you buy from farmers that grow nothing but onions or alliums.

However you decide to start your onions, be careful about the varieties you choose. They are not all equal. Bulb development is dependent on the length of daylight exposure (the photoperiod). Some subspecies require long days to produce bulbs, some need short days, and others require day lengths somewhere in between. Not surprisingly, the various types are known as long-day, short-day, and intermediate-day varieties. The zone for short-days extends from southern California eastward to the North Carolina-Virginia line. The long-day zone is anywhere north of North Carolina and the California-Oregon border. The intermediate zone overlaps the remaining two areas, from Pennsylvania to Georgia and across the country through Colorado and Utah, but intermediate-day onions are flexible and will do reasonably well in all regions. Reputable companies that sell onions designate the zones to which their varieties are best suited. If they don't offer that information, don't buy their onions.

Beyond onions and garlic, the garden branch of the Lily family also includes bunching onions, Egyptian onions, chives, and scallions. Bunching onions, one of my favorites, are very easy to grow. Simply sow the seeds directly into the ground in early spring. You can make a second or even third planting if you have a cold frame to keep them going into fall and early winter. You can eat bunching onions at any size, from thinning until after the cold gets the last plant. If your winters are mild, you'll have them all winter—and, if the snow covers them before they freeze, your onions may be waiting for you in the spring.

The species of *Allium* we commonly refer to as garlic is *Allium sativum,* and there are two subspecies, known colloquially as soft-neck garlic (*A. sativum, subsp. Sativum*) and hard-neck garlic (*A. sativum, subsp. Ophioscorodon*). Soft-neck garlic is the most common and is hardier than the hard-neck varieties. You'll find soft-neck garlic at the supermarket or hanging in braided stalks at farmers' markets. Hard-neck garlic requires more labor to grow and won't keep as long as soft neck. These varieties produce tall woody stalks (scapes), which develop large capsulelike structures that have small bulbs (bulbils) inside. When planted, the bulbils will grow into garlic plants, but they take much longer to do so than garlic cloves would. Garlic aficionados believe these varieties are the most flavorful, so are willing to put up with the inconvenience.

There is a lot more to successfully growing garlic than you can glean from a brief overview or the paragraph or two in your basic gardening book or Wikipedia entry. I'd recommend the book *Growing Great Garlic: The Definitive Guide for Organic Gardeners and Small Farmers* by Ron L. Engeland (Filaree Farm, 1991), which celebrates deep garlic culture. I avoided growing garlic for years because, after hearing experts expound on the minutiae of culture and subspecies, I was convinced it was just too hard. Then, one year, I helped my son-in-law Dan with his crop and found that the hardest thing about garlic (like most other crops) was keeping the weeds at bay. A heavy mulch solved that problem, and the next fall we had more of the best garlic we've ever eaten than we could use. Dan had obtained the cloves, which were hard neck, from a garlic-growing friend, so our bulbs didn't keep as well as we had hoped. We gave a lot away—no one left the farm without a bag of garlic—but still a lot went bad before we could eat it. We resolved then to experiment with several varieties of both hard- and soft-neck types until we find our favorites. The jury is still out on that question, and we look forward to a long trial.

New gardeners often think that leeks are hard to grow. The only seemingly tricky part about leeks is that you need to blanch the stalks as they grow to make that nice, long, white portion—but it isn't really tricky at all. Set your transplants (if you live in Zones 4 or 5) or seeds (if you live farther south) in shallow trenches and push dirt up against the stalks a little at a time as the plants grow. Leeks are very hardy. Early varieties can be planted in the spring, and late varieties will grow into the fall and even into early winter in a cold frame.

Saving seeds from *Alliums* and other biennials is not as straightforward as saving seeds from self-pollinating annuals. The bulbs must be stored over the winter and then replanted in the spring. With onions, you can plant seeds in August, grow the plants until they form sets, and overwinter the sets for planting in the spring. If you're really lucky, you'll get both flowers and seeds from your sets. Because onions are entomophilous cross-pollinators (pollinated by insects), let only a single variety go to seed each year.

Apiaceae or Umbellefeae The distinguishing characteristic of this family is a large, flat flower that looks like an umbrella. Its most public face is Queen Anne's lace, whose close cousins include carrots, parsnips, and dill. Her slightly more distant relations are celery, parsley, and cilantro. All garden vegetables in this family are biennial and entomophilous. Most of the common garden species prefer cool growing conditions and, except for the root crops, are not very picky

about anything. However, they will bolt if stressed or if the weather is too warm. Hybrids of this family are rare, as most improvements have been accomplished through open-pollination breeding strategies.

Carrots, the main vegetable in this family, are an important winter vegetable for most Northern gardeners. Only absolutely impeccable roots will last throughout the winter in the root cellar. There are five keys to achieving perfect carrots:

1. Light, deep, stone-free soil. It often takes a few years of gardening on the same spot to develop the fine, sandy loam that will produce perfect, long carrots.

2. The right combination of variety and soil. Essentially, the only real difference between carrot varieties is shape. The differences in taste are determined mostly by the soil, the amount of water available to the plant, and the weather in a given year. Some carrots are short and stout; others are long and thin. As you might guess, shorter carrots mature faster, so they're good for spring and summer salads. (You can also eat longer varieties when they're young during these seasons.) The main objective when growing carrots is to match the shape of the carrot to your soil. A new garden needs a carrot with a shorter root to minimize the chance that, as it grows, it encounters stones that deform the shape. When you've worked your soil for a few years, you can plant any carrot you like. The year that my crop of Danver's Half Long grew straight and true was the first year I felt like a real gardener.

3. Proper spacing. Plant your seeds at least 2 in. to 3 in. apart. If you crowd them, the roots will twist around each other or curve to get out of their neighbors' way. The conventional wisdom is to sow carrot seeds thickly and thin the plants as they grow. Then, theoretically, you'll eat the thinnings as baby carrots.

I believe it's better and less wasteful to plant the seeds where you want the plants to grow. If you'd like some small early carrots (who wouldn't?), sow a small patch more thickly than your winter rows.

4. Weeding. Keep your plants free of weeds. Too many weeds will also cause deformed roots.

5. Good timing. Don't plant too early. If carrots mature while there is still a lot of summer left, they'll split or develop dark, tough shoulders. Split carrots are poor keepers. You can deal with the tough shoulders by covering the exposed heads of the roots with soil or sand.

If you have a root cellar—and, eventually, you will—you want to put up a good supply of carrots (although carrots grown in cold frames are so wonderfully sweet and tender they're almost a different vegetable). There's no reason not to treat yourself to both.

Saving carrot seed is not difficult, except that all carrot species will cross-pollinate, so pick only one to save. The seeds will keep for 3 to 5 years. Carrots are biennial, so you'll need to keep the roots in good shape and replant them the next year, just as you would beets and chard. Grow at least six or seven plants of the same species. When the flower head dies back, collect the seed head and let it dry for a week or two before storing.

Poaceae (grass) The grass family includes corn, wheat, oats, rye, millet, your lawn, and our pasture. There are 600 genera and 10,000 species, and at least one of them will grow in virtually every climate zone on Earth. In the United States, the king of the grasses is corn. At one time, hundreds of varieties of field and sweet corn grew across the country. Some farmers would raise several varieties on their farms, each for a particular purpose or market—but that was then, this is now. In corn country today, farmers plant either a variety intended for stock feed and/or the variety that yields high-fructose corn syrup; most farmers grow the latter. (If there ever was a reason to promote saving heritage seed, the story of what's happened to corn is just that.)

Many of the multitudinous sweet corn varieties are adapted to particular regions or climate zones, so here's yet another reason to call your extension agent for advice. When it comes to choosing which kind of sweet corn to plant, there are four basic choices:

1. Traditional open-pollinated corn. This variety will grow true to type if you plant kernels from the ears (the kernels, of course, must be fully matured and dried).

2. Older hybrids. The hybrids are also called "normal sugar" or SU (a term denoting the sugar gene). Technically, the open-pollinated and heirloom corns are also SU, but they are usually not included in this category.

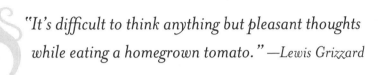

"It's difficult to think anything but pleasant thoughts while eating a homegrown tomato." —Lewis Grizzard

3. Sugar-enhanced varieties. These recently developed supersweet hybrids are known as SE, SE+, and SH2. They are not only sweeter than older hybrids, but they also hold their sweetness longer. This category also includes the "synergetic" varieties that are both sweeter and more tender. The problem with these tasty new varieties is that you cannot grow other varieties anywhere near them—when they cross-pollinate, you end up with a tough and starchy result.

4. Heirloom varieties. Happily, there are quite a few seed collectors who are dedicated to saving heirloom corn. Buying their seeds will help support the endeavor—and it's easier than saving your own heirloom seed. In Vermont, you would need to grow and save at least 200 ears to get 200 plants—an awful lot of ears to set aside before you even get to eat any. Of course, those 200 ears contain a lot more kernels than you'd ever use, but you want the redundant kernels to help preserve the gene pool. To add to the complexity, the seed is only viable for three years, so you would have to collect it almost every other year.

Solanaceae (nightshade) Tomatoes, peppers, eggplants, potatoes, and tobacco belong to this family. All the common garden species of these plants, save the potato, love the heat and need long, hot days to reach their potential. Almost every backyard and patio garden, even in the North, has at least one tomato plant (some gardens have nothing but). Although California can lay claim to growing the greatest quantity of tomatoes— 90 percent of the U.S. and 35 percent of the world market share—New Englanders, with our cool nights and long summer days (or perhaps our sour soil), *know* that we grow the best-tasting tomatoes in the world. A few people in Minnesota may disagree and, because I've never, to my knowledge, tasted a tomato grown in Minnesota, I won't open that particular can of sauce.

For now, let's just say that, although it is considerably more challenging to grow tomatoes in the northern states than in the southern states, it's worth the effort. Northern-grown tomatoes (that would include those grown in Minnesota, of course) are much tastier than any you could grow in the South, East, or West. Indeed, the same magical quality that infuses a northern-grown tomato also applies to sweet corn. Whether my observations are the result of typical Yankee chauvinism or are perfectly reasonable statements of fact may require further study, but there is no argument that store-bought tomatoes can't, in any way, compare to tomatoes from your own garden, no matter where you live.

Given people's passion for tomatoes today, it's hard to believe that in Colonial America home gardeners and commercial growers grew only a handful of tomato varieties. Tomatoes were native to Central and South America, but our ancestors were dubious about the wisdom of eating this seductively brilliant fruit from the "deadly nightshade" family, the same bota-

types in their time to maturity. All of my tomatoes seem to ripen within a few days or, at most, a week of each other, no matter what date the seed catalog gives.

Tomatoes can also be classified by leaf shape as either "potato leaved" or "regular leaved." The Brandywine tomato is an example of a potato-leaved type. Much is made of these distinctions in seed catalogs,

"Seeds have the power to preserve species, to enhance cultural as well as genetic diversity, to counter economic monopoly, and to check the advance of conformity on all its many fronts."
—*Michael Pollan,* Second Nature: A Gardener's Education

nical family as the poisonous belladonna (*Atropa belladonna*)—indeed, the leaves of tomatoes and the rest of the cultivated Solanaceae are toxic to greater or lesser degrees. By the 1830s, this attitude changed as gardeners worldwide began to follow the lead of Italy and Spain, which were growing and, more important, eating tomatoes in earnest. The change was so rapid that, within only two decades, no garden in the United States was considered complete without at least a few tomato plants.

Tomato varieties can be classified according to several traits. One of the most practical is the length of time it takes for the plant to reach maturity and produce ripe fruit. The three classifications are early, midseason, and late season. In many northern climates, only early and midseason types will ripen without season-extending protection. I've found little difference between early and midseason

but I don't understand why, as the plants and their habits seem to be exactly the same in every other respect. The third classification indicates plants as indeterminate or determinant. Indeterminate plants will keep growing indefinitely; determinant varieties will grow to be only so large and then stop. The difference between these two types is more theoretical than practical. When you prune a tomato plant for optimum production of large, ripe fruit, you cut off the growing tip, which makes the plant, de facto, determinant.

The fourth classification is heirloom versus hybrid. Heirloom plants are fertilized by naturally occurring, or "open," pollination. These plants will yield another plant that is the same as the mother plant, or "true to type." Hybrids are the product of pairings between different kinds of plants, usually subspecies. This pairing yields an offspring that is

Saving Seeds

People save their own seeds for a multitude of reasons, but probably the major reason gardeners save seed is because the process is enjoyable and interesting. It seems almost magical when the seeds you collected the year before, stored in little jars, and then planted pop out of the ground to start the cycle all over again. After a few years, those plants are truly yours. They have a history, and you are part of it.

We save seed for the same reasons we raise heritage animals—to increase and preserve genetic diversity on the farm and to be part of our farm's history. Seed saving can also save you a pile of money. Even with a small garden, it's not hard to spend hundreds of dollars on seeds every year. Although it's difficult to save seeds for every variety of vegetable you might want to grow, every bit helps.

If you want to try your hand at saving seeds, self-pollinators are the place to start. Start with beans or peas and then branch out to tomatoes. Once you get established with your own seeds, you can trade with your neighbors or even start trading seeds on Seed Savers Exchange (www.seedsavers.org).

Most of the time, pollination takes place in the morning, before the flower opens up, but, on occasion, insects spread pollen from one blossom to another, thereby cross-pollinating. If the nearby plants are of the same variety, there's no problem. In fact, if all the neighbors are the same open-pollinated variety, cross-pollination strengthens the gene pool. (If they are different varieties, the offspring produced by the seed won't be true to type.) All you have to do is keep all other plants away from the variety whose seeds you are saving.

Saving seeds is easy. In most cases, you just remove the seeds from ripe fruit and dry them for a week or so. (Eggplant seeds must be ripened in the fruit, so let the eggplant wither on the plant. Scrape the seeds into a bowl of water and save the ones that float.) Then put the seeds in labeled, airtight, insect-proof jars and store them in a cool, dry place. Seed savers should also keep journals that record how, where, when, and why every variety was grown and how it turned out. Keep a hard copy, an actual, old-fashioned, handwritten journal—or at least a printout of your computer entries. Include some photographs or prints of digital images. This document is important not just for you but also for your children and grandchildren. Someday, a young man or woman you'll never meet will be thrilled to discover their grandfather's or great-great-grandmother's farm journal. Wouldn't you be?

"All gardeners should have the number for their local extension service's master gardener on speed dial."

generally better than either of the two parents because of "hybrid vigor," but the plant won't look like the parents or have the same attributes. Hybrid pairings are, at best, unpredictable, and some hybrids can even be sterile. The USDA has a library of 5,000 seed varieties, and heirloom and hybrid seed producers offer thousands more.

The one distinguishing characteristic that is most important to a tomato fancier is taste. If you are blessed with a particular variety that tastes like the Platonic ideal of tomato, you will put up with any and all trials and tribulations to grow it, even if you have to feed it olive oil by the teaspoon three times a day. Such is the power of the perfect-tasting tomato. No one seems to agree just what that perfect taste is, however, or which variety possesses it. Presently, Brandywine is the leading contender for the title, but I prefer a tomato with a little more acidic tang. Like signposts on the road to Nirvana, no one can tell you what the perfect tomato is. As Mr. Gump's mama says, "You're gonna have to figure that out for yerself, Forrest."

Begin by choosing the best varieties, all the while remembering that there is no one "best" variety. Selection depends on where you live and what you like. Explore the

offerings from the catalogs of some of the mainstream seed companies located in your region or in locales with a similar climate and photoperiod. Before large seed companies and industrial farming dominated the field, farmers and gardeners developed tomato varieties to meet their local challenges. Some varieties thrive near the ocean, others in the desert, still others can withstand the weather in Siberia. Look for those that are adapted to your region or even your microclimate.

Seed Savers is a good place to begin your quest for the best. Your county extension agent may also have some helpful advice to offer (all gardeners should have the number for their local extension service's master gardener on speed dial). Johnny's Selected Seeds (www.johnnyseeds.com) is a good source for both heritage and hybrid varieties. W. Atlee Burpee, founder of the seed and plant company that bears his name (www.burpee.com), was one of the early developers of hybrid tomatoes like Big Boy and Early Girl, both of which are very good and have been around so long they're practically heirlooms.

Don't be satisfied with growing only one kind of tomato. Even if you have room for only two plants, make sure they're two plants of different varieties. Heirloom types are all about taste, so try at least one of those, especially if it was developed for your region. Keep in mind, however, that there's a reason hybrids replaced heir-

Top left: A tomato vine, staked and pruned for maximum yield. Top right: "Supersweet" hybrid corn. Bottom: Some of our heirloom tomatoes.

looms. In general, hybrids are more resistant to insects and disease and have more uniform and predictable ripening periods. If seed saving isn't an important part of your gardening, there's no compelling reason to rule out the hybrid cultivars of any fruit or vegetable.

There really aren't any bad varieties, but some are better than others. Mostly, only individual preferences separate the cultivars. To find the right varieties for you, do your homework and then experiment. Grow a few different types and compare fruit and notes with other gardeners. Don't be surprised if everyone chooses a different tomato as the favorite.

Growing Tomatoes

If competitive gardening were an Olympic sport, tomato growing would be the main event. The most luscious rows of lettuce, basil, and cabbage matter not a whit without at least 10 heavily fruit-laden tomato vines of almost as many varieties. The appearance of the foliage is not a consideration. What matters is that the fruit is beautiful, delicious, and abundant—and with our cold and often damp weather in Vermont, achieving that result is no small feat. Tomatoes need to be started indoors, but you can get a sizable crop without end-of-season protection.

Like every serious gardener, I have a system for growing tomatoes, which has taken me 35 years to develop. (I'll let you know when I have the kinks worked out.) If your grandmother has a better method, use hers. Eventually you'll have one of your own. You'll know you've got it when you

harvest more tomatoes than you can freeze, can, dry, or give away.

Starting plants Every gardener in the North knows that you must start tomatoes indoors. The Vermont tradition is to start your tomato plants on the first Tuesday in March, which is Town Meeting Day. Another Vermont tradition is to think for yourself, and I think that the first week of March is too early to start tomatoes. By the time you put them out, the transplants are so tall that they have become weak and leggy. If you use grow lights, be sure the fixture hanger is adjustable so that the bulb is always less than 6 in. above the growing plant. If the plant doesn't have to "stretch" as it grows toward the light, the stem tends to be stouter. I prefer to wait six or, at most, eight weeks before the expected last frost date before starting my seedlings.

Don't be in a rush to get your plants outside. Tomatoes flourish in hot weather, but the cold and damp days of spring and early summer can stress them enough to stunt their growth. Tomatoes simply refuse to grow when the soil temperature is below 60°F. The same goes for peppers, eggplants, and the cucurbits. After a disastrous two weeks of cold, rainy, damp weather in mid-May one year, we now play it safe and wait until June 10 to set out our transplants, no matter how tempting the balmy breeze and blue sky. Of course, you can safely get a jump on the season if you set your plants out under the protection of a hoop house or high tunnel, which is exactly what we plan to do in the future.

Some gardeners start their plants in tiny peat pots or seedling trays, but I prefer to

Planting Tomatoes

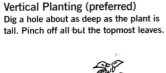

Vertical Planting (preferred)
Dig a hole about as deep as the plant is
tall. Pinch off all but the topmost leaves.

Water/
Compost tea

Pinched-off leaves

Two weeks later, a
healthy, well-rooted
plant

Horizontal Planting
Set large transplants sideways in small trench

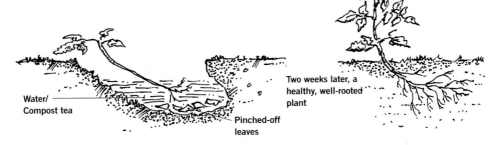

Water/
Compost tea

Pinched-off
leaves

Two weeks later, a
healthy, well-rooted
plant

Shallow Planting
(Not Recommended)

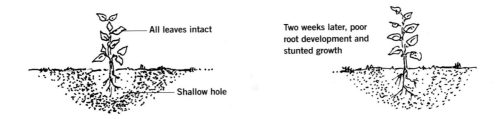

All leaves intact

Shallow hole

Two weeks later, poor
root development and
stunted growth

start all my warm-weather Solanaceae in 4-in. or 6-in. pots. My tomatoes and peppers will be in these pots for a long time, so I want to give them enough room to promote good root development without becoming root bound and avoid having to transplant them to larger pots as they grow. I fill each pot only three-quarters full with soil. As the plant grows, I add more soil, burying the stem, which makes the plant send out new roots, encouraging robust root growth and helping to prevent "legginess." (Of course, if you live in a mild climate, you can sow the seed directly into the ground or set out tender seedlings, so pot size won't be as important.) My transplants are small enough to fit comfortably under my inverted-milk-jug makeshift hot caps, which nurse them along, protecting them from cold and flea beetles until they are strong enough to brave the elements on their own.

Planting When it's finally safe to plant your tomatoes outdoors, dig a hole about as deep as the plant is tall. Fill the hole at least halfway with water or compost tea. Allow the slurry to seep into the surrounding soil. Pinch off all but the topmost two to four leaves, set the transplant into the hole, and backfill up to the leaves with garden soil. Pat the soil firmly but carefully around the plant and water gently and thoroughly to remove any air pockets.

If your tomatoes are so large that a vertical hole would extend below the topsoil layer, dig a small trench instead and lay the plant on its side, gently bending it upward so the top leaves are exposed, as shown in

the drawing on p. 205. Many gardeners have a hard time with this concept. It may seem criminal to bury up to their noses those nice big plants you have worked so hard to grow, but I'm convinced that this method provides the best way to build a strong root system that will promote growth for the whole life of the plant. In about two weeks, deeply planted trans-plants will catch up with shallow-rooted tomatoes that are set out at normal depth. They'll surpass them in a few weeks more.

Tomatoes are heavy feeders of both nitrogen and phosphorus, but if you have healthy soil, your tomatoes won't require any special soil amendments. Many gardeners—myself included—believe that there are at least three good reasons to grow your tomatoes and their warm-weather relatives in permanent raised beds. First, the soil in a raised bed warms up faster and stays warmer day and night. Second, the soil dries out faster after a downpour. Third, a timber-or masonry-bordered raised bed makes a level foundation for the fabric-covered growing tunnel you'll eventually want to build to extend your tomato season (and grow greens into early winter). (For more about movable tunnels on raised beds, see Eliot Coleman's book, *Four-Season Harvest: Organic Vegetables from Your Home Garden All Year Long* [Chelsea Green, 1999].)

Training and pruning I train my tomatoes by tying them to 6-ft.-tall, No. 4 ($\frac{1}{2}$ in. dia.) steel "rebar" (concrete reinforcing) stakes with strips torn from rags. (Over the years, I've tried every type of tie doohickey sold or homemade, and I still

Training and Pruning Tomatoes

Tie the tomato stem to a pole or rebar support.

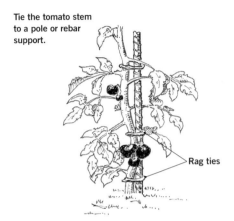

Rag ties

After three clusters have set, pinch or cut off the growing tip. Remove suckers or they will grow into new vines.

Tomato cages

Wood stakes and wire

Factory-made or homemade from #9 concrete reinforcement wire mesh.

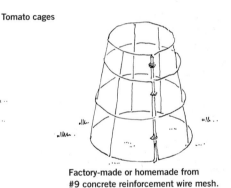

prefer rags. They do the job perfectly and add visual interest, especially if brightly colored.) Some people secure their tomatoes to trellises; others to fences or wood poles. The type of support isn't important, as long as it permits you easy access to the plants to prune and tie them, allows plenty of air circulation to prevent the blight and wilt that is endemic to crowded plants surrounded by stagnant air, and is strong enough to bear up under the weight of a bounty of heavy fruit on stout vines. These requirements pretty much rule out all the wire tomato support towers and commercial cages, which are fine as supports for cherry and grape tomatoes.

Left to its natural design, a "free range" tomato grows up to become a perennial vine, reaching a height and spread of about 20 ft. Tomatoes grown in the North must be treated as annuals, in other words, they must flower and produce fruit and ripe seeds (if you want to save the seeds) before the end of the growing season. A strong and healthy Northern tomato—transplanted into good soil, provided with a supporting scaffold, and well watered but otherwise left to follow its own inclinations—will put out lots of strong leafy vines festooned with hundreds of marble-size green tomatoes that will never mature enough before the first killing frost. If you want big fruit that ripens in less than 100 days, you must prune the vines—true also for tomatoes grown in the frost-free Southwest or in the Deep South, with its extended growing season.

Think of a tomato plant's energy as a zero-sum game: There is only so much to go around. It can go into either the leaves and stems or into the fruit, but not into both. Pruning directs the growth toward the fruit instead of the greenery and also promotes a beneficial balance of sun and shade on the tomatoes as they grow. Depending on where they live, gardeners may have different styles of pruning, but they all share the same goal: Increase the ratio of red to green fruit and provide just enough sun to ripen the fruit but not so much as to scald it. We believe in "precision pruning," although some gardeners hack away the leaves and stems indiscriminately until the tomatoes peek through. My father taught me the Waterman Method when I was quite young, but I doubt it's original or especially unique.

I've even seen it elsewhere referred to as the Anderson Method.

Pruning techniques depend, in part, on your hardiness zone. The shorter the growing season, the fewer the tomatoes that will ripen on the vine. Tomatoes form clusters, much like grape clusters, but less dense. Depending on the variety, there can be as few as three or as many as nine fruits per cluster. Fruits ripen from the bottom up. Here in Zones 4 and 5, we usually can harvest only three, or sometimes, four ripe clusters before the first frosts of September or early October. Of course, you can lengthen the growing season with row covers or tunnels, but, at best, you'll only get one more cluster. In regions with longer or year-round seasons, you'll get more, but pruning will increase the fruit's size.

The principle behind pruning is to remove any superfluous growth that does not support the clusters that are most likely to ripen. (Around here that means allowing only a single main vine, supporting three clusters, to grow. After that third cluster has set, I pinch or cut off the growing tip.) Pruning causes an increase in the number of suckers, and you need to be extra-vigilant about removing them. Suckers are the little, quick-growing shoots that pop up in the crotches between the main leaves and the stem. If left alone, they'll grow to form more foliage and also entirely new vines and fruit clusters. Each sucker will produce several clusters of tomatoes as if it were a whole plant unto itself. Pinch these shoots off as soon as they emerge. Be persistent, because as soon as you pinch one off, another appears. Scrutinize your plants a couple of times a week. If you get behind, remove them with pruning shears or a sharp knife. You could break or tear the main vine if you try to pull off a sucker that's already grown too strong.

As you survey your plants, prune off any extra fruit, too. Three to five fruits per cluster is a good target goal. I find that the plants usually prune themselves to some degree, as lower-quality fruit tends to drop off on its own. As you prune, tie the tomato stem to your support. If you have a single main stem, you could use a sturdy sapling pole or rebar. We prefer rebar because it's rigid, doesn't rot, and is easily driven into the ground. If you have two main stems, you can still use one or two bars; for three or more stems, a cage might work better. With a cage, however, it's difficult to discern which stalk is which and what branch is what, which makes it harder to work. Some people simply place the cage over a young plant and then let the plant grow as it will within the confines of the cage, pruning leaves and stalks as needed to keep the plant in check.

Whatever method you choose, strive to limit the number of immature fruits so as to concentrate the plant's energy into ripening the rest of the fruit. The end result will be several pounds of red tomatoes rather than a handful of small reds and some number of green marbles. Your second goal is to remove enough of the large compound leaves to expose the tomatoes to the ripening sun while still keeping them from scalding and leaving enough leaves to continue the process of photosynthesis. Start with the bottom leaves, removing all that grow between the ground and the lowest cluster. After you've picked the first cluster of ripe tomatoes, remove the next layer of leaves, up to the second cluster. A pruned tomato plant is not very pretty. It looks rather naked and scarred, but the fruit will be its best.

Growing Warm-Weather Vegetables in a Cold Climate

In general, gardening in the desert is much more challenging than gardening as far north as Zones 3 and 4, with the notable and enviable exception of such warm-weather-loving fruits and vegetables as peppers, eggplant, okra, and tomatoes (although, as I've said, desert tomatoes are not the best tasting). While gardening in Arizona, I missed the lettuce but was thrilled to have so many peppers with so little effort. Back in Vermont now, I'm lucky to get a handful of stunted jalapeños. As for bell peppers and eggplant, forget it. Getting even a small crop (if you can call three eggplants a crop) is as likely as picking the winning lotto number. Nonetheless, true gardeners delight in testing their mettle, accepting the gauntlet thrown down by Mother Nature—optimistic in February when ordering the seeds, hopeful in June when setting out the transplants, worried in September while observing the single larval fruit, and triumphant in October when carrying into the greenhouse the one pathetic plant that grew in a large pot all summer.

As far as garden culture goes, peppers and eggplant are the same plant. What works for one, works for the other. Both

Planting and Yield Guide
(For every 10 ft. of row)

Vegetable type	Number of seeds/plants	Yield (in lb.)	Pints (frozen or canned)
Beet greens	100	4	3–4
Broccoli	17	7.5	7–8
Brussel sprouts	20	6	6
Cabbage	20	15	n/a
Carrots	300	10	n/a
Cauliflower	20	9	7–8
Corn	20	1 dozen ears	2 (as kernels)
Cucumbers	60	12	n/a
Eggplant	5	7.5	7
Kale	45	7.5	6–7
Leeks	60	20	n/a
Onions	200	10	n/a
Peas	260	2	1
Peppers	5	5-7	8
Pole beans	40	15	15-20
Pumpkins/Winter Squash	10	30	10
Rutabaga/Turnips	120	15	10
Spinach/Greens	125	5–10	8–10
String beans	80	8	8-10
Tomatoes	3-4	15	10
Watermelon	20	7	n/a

vegetables like warm, almost hot, sandy soil. Raised beds fit the bill, if you mix sand with your native loamy clay. You can warm the soil by placing a polyethylene tunnel over the bed. For a family garden, it works best to build a movable structure over the raised beds. Basically, you erect a movable tunnel over one-half of a raised bed (that's, let's say, 12 ft. by 20 ft.). In summer, plant the bed within the tunnel with tomatoes, peppers, eggplant, and other heat-loving species. Stake the tomatoes to rebar or support them on a trellis that's hung from the center purlin of the tunnel. The tunnel creates warm days and nights, especially if the plants are mulched with stones to hold the heat, and it will also extend the season.

In July and August, plant your greens and winter crops in the other half of the raised bed. When the tomatoes and their friends are spent, move the tunnel over the winter crops and keep it there until spring. If you live in Zone 5 or colder, you can grow a very good crop of tomatoes by starting them indoors and then putting them out under the tunnel. Without the aid of at least some sort of season-extending structure, however, you'll end up with a lot more green tomatoes than red, no matter how diligent your pruning techniques. We've also brought our tomatoes to fruition with a simple protective tent of plastic sheeting. We lay the sheeting over wood battens that are lashed to our rebar support stakes and secured at the bottom edges with bricks and stones.

If you are satisfied to have only a few hot peppers now and then, try planting your seeds in a pot at least 6 in. in diameter. Use a potting mixture that is poor in nitrogen so you don't grow a plant that's all glorious leaf and no fruit. Plant your seeds about 8 to 10 weeks before the last frost, as peppers take longer than most other vegetables to germinate and get started. When the weather is reliably warm, especially at night, place your pots outdoors and surround them with rocks, which store heat. Keep the pots well watered, as they dry out faster than garden soil does. A light bark mulch will help reduce evaporation. You can also cover the plants with plastic sheeting at night. (Bell peppers won't respond all that well to this extra attention, but hot peppers certainly appreciate it.)

In the fall, bring a few pots inside. If you're really committed, put them under grow lights to maintain an 8- to 10-hour photoperiod. Eventually, the plants will succumb to the stress, but, in the meantime, each one may reward you with a few to half-dozen ripe peppers. Including your time and effort, they will be the most expensive peppers you have ever eaten, but we don't garden for love of money, do we?

Growing Sweet Corn

Corn is a hungry plant, but beyond satisfying its appetite for nitrogen, it isn't difficult to grow. The main problem most beginners have is premature planting. Corn will not germinate at soil temperatures below 65°F. If you aren't sure of the soil temperature, check it with a soil thermometer or wait until the last frost has passed before sowing. There's nothing to gain by planting too early and plenty to lose if your seeds rot in the cold damp ground.

You can plant corn either in rows or in hills. I prefer rows because they're easier to mulch, weed, and pick—although people who plant in hills swear there's no better way. There are a variety of ways to weed a corn patch. My father used to hoe our kitchen garden corn until it was about 6 in. to 10 in. high (he managed the sweet corn he raised for market much differently). Then he would forget it. The weeds would come back, but with less enthusiasm, and by then the corn had a head start that it would maintain for the rest of the season.

We alternate between two methods, depending on how much room and how much mulch hay is available in a given year.

Sometimes we use my father's method, but we apply mulch at the point where he stopped hoeing. We don't like to let weeds set up housekeeping. It just encourages them to come back next year. Usually we use moldy hay as mulch, but in wet years, hay mulch can attract slugs and slow the growth of plants. In those years, we sow white clover between and in the rows after the corn is 6 in. high or so. The difficulty is prognosticating what type of weather that summer will bring.

If you want to actually eat your sweet corn, you'll have to secure the patch. You might not ever see a raccoon, but somehow they know just when the corn is about to reach its peak of perfection. The night before you plan your big harvest, an entire platoon of local raccoons and all their relatives show up for their annual Sweet-corn Gala. You get the leftovers and seconds. We've found that a double strand of 1/2-in.-wide electrified plastic tape is an effective deterrent. Set the top strand about 18 in. to 2 ft. off of the ground, and the bottom strand at about 6 in.

We're also great believers in the Native American tradition of interplanting corn with winter squash as an effective defense against both raccoons and weeds. You have to control the weeds by cultivating or tilling until the corn and squash establish themselves, however. Then mulch between the corn rows and squash hills. Once the squash vines start creeping, they'll crowd out the bulk of the weeds. For the best protection against critters and weeds, combine all of the methods: Plant the squash and corn together, hoe the small plants, and mulch when they get bigger. When the corn is developing its "silk" tassels, put up the electric fence.

Without the benefit of a raccoon's prescience, deciding when to harvest your corn can be tricky. Picking too early isn't much of a disaster if you are just getting a dozen ears for dinner, but if you are harvesting the bulk of the crop for putting by, it is. Around two to three weeks before the corn is ready to pick, you'll start to see the ears develop their tassels. When half the ears have tassels, you're about 18 to 24 days before harvest (this date is known as half-silk). Pull the husks off a few ears and look inside. To be entirely sure they're ready, you have to pick a few ears and taste them.

One advantage to planting regular corn rather than the supersweet varieties is that you can extend the harvest of fresh corn over a longer season by planting a few varieties of early, midseason, and late-season types. Plant the earliest varieties for fresh eating. Plant less of the early and more of the late corn for putting by. In general, in Zone 4 or colder, vegetables tend to ripen over a short period of time, so planting more than one variety in order to extend harvest time doesn't work as well as it does in warmer, long-season zones. Corn is an exception to the rule, however, if you plant as early a variety and as late a variety as you safely can.

One advantage to the supersweets is that the ears remain sweet on the stalks for a long time. In fact, you don't want to pick these varieties too early, or they'll be watery. The supersweets also hold their sweetness long after they are picked, which is why they are popular—and why even some supermarket corn can still taste almost as good as backyard corn.

Growing Field Corn

As long as you take care not to let it cross-pollinate your sweet corn, you can certainly grow a few hundred feet of field corn to mill for flour and cornmeal. Keeping the corn varieties separate is especially critical if your sweet corn is one of the supersweet hybrids. Plant the field corn at least 100 ft. upwind of your garden. Both crops will be ruined if they cross-pollinate. There are two basic strains of field corn, Flint and Dent. Flint corn is the hardier and harder of the two and has less starch. Dent corn is softer and is the variety that is usually grown for flour.

If you raise field corn organically, by hand, you can expect to get about 100 bushels an acre, although yields can vary quite a bit depending on soil fertility, weather, and weed management. It takes one person with a double-row planter two days to plant that acre and a laid-back, happy-go-lucky gang of family and friends a couple of weekends to pick all of that corn, husking as they go.

If you want to just grow a bushel or two, figure 1 bushel per 100 ft. to 150 ft. of row. It takes 350 seeds (about 4½ oz.) to sow 100 ft. Therefore, 1 lb. of seed (about 1,250 seeds) will plant about 350 ft. of row and yield about 3 bushels of grain. That's a lot of handwork, no matter how you husk it. Start off small—you don't necessarily need to supply all your livestock with grain right from the start. If you want to grow a

bit more for your animals, just add a few extra rows. A chicken will eat 1 bushel of corn a year. A feeder pig will grow to market weight on 15 bushels.

Basically, you grow field corn the same way you grow sweet corn. As with every other crop, weeding is key to success. In addition to interplanting winter squash with your corn, you can also let pole beans and cucumbers climb up the cornstalks. You might try alternating a double row of corn with rows of beans on either side, with swaths of clover in between. If you simply broadcast clover between the corn plants after your first weeding, you'll provide extra nitrogen for the heavy-feeding corn, crowd out the weeds, and, in the fall, after the ears are harvested, you'll have some great fodder and forage for your livestock. A beef cow or pig would finish very well on such a rich repast.

The only equipment you'll need for harvesting field corn is a knife (even better, a machete or that big old Bowie knife you never use for anything), a husking peg (a small, metal finger guard), some bags or buckets, your two hands, and a liberal supply of Corn Husker's® Lotion. Store your picked corn in 5-gallon plastic pails (½ bushel per pail) with tight-fitting lids in the root cellar or in an extra refrigerator. You can grind cornmeal in a blender or a small, home-size electric grain mill.

Growing Grains

Excluding corn, the rest of the edible grasses in the Poaceae family are what we call grains. Not all that long ago, the average gardener—ourselves included—would

What about Wheat?

There are six basic types of wheat: hard red winter, hard red spring, soft red winter, hard white, soft white, and durum. Hard red winter wheat is grown in the western states and is the most common high-protein bread wheat. Protein is what makes gluten, and artisan bakers rely on high-gluten flour to make their hard-crust, chewy artisan bread (see pp. 258–261). Soft red winter is grown in the East and has less protein, which is ideal for pastry flour. Durum wheat is reserved for pasta flour. Winter wheat is grown in most of the country except the far North, where spring wheat reigns. It's best to grow the type of wheat that is already grown in your area, rather than experiment with unsuitable types.

Commercial wheat seed is broadcast (spread evenly over the whole field). For small patches, sow at a rate of 2 bushels per acre, which translates to about one seed per square inch. Seeding with a small handheld broadcaster makes the process easier—it takes some practice to broadcast evenly by hand. After a winter wheat crop is established, let a few chickens graze it down before snow cover.

Weeds are hard to keep down when crops are broadcast, even if you plant on ground that has been managed for weeds. So it's best to plant your wheat in rows. You can then cultivate or hoe to control the weeds and even mulch between the rows. Harvesting will be easier, too.

Winter wheat ripens in June in the South and into August in the North. To test its readiness, remove a few kernels from their sheaths and chew them—they should be crunchy and hard when ripe, like wheat berries. Start the harvest just before the kernels are completely dry. Harvesting grains is one of those combined work-fun farm activities that's best done as a family-friends affair. We can usually get our friends to do things by offering them beer and a barbeque.

not have thought of growing wheat, barley, or oats. The conventional wisdom was that it is simply too hard to grow them (or, to be more precise, to harvest and process them) on a small scale, but that notion has changed. We have yet to try, but with all the chickens and other poultry we have and with the amount of bread we bake, it's just a matter of time before we get started. Vermont was renowned as the breadbasket of New England until sometime after the Civil War. These days, young, adventurous, and very smart new farmers have taken up the challenge to resurrect that part of our agricultural tradition. We're looking forward to launching our grain-growing venture with some rehabilitated old varieties bred for our region. Do a little research to find the same for where you live.

All cereal grains (except corn) are harvested in basically the same way. After cutting the ripe stalks with a sickle, scythe, or tractor-powered (or horse-drawn) sickle-bar mower, you gather them by the armfuls and tie them into sheaves. (Watching someone with even a small amount of proficiency cutting wheat or hay with a scythe is mesmerizing; being that someone is exhausting.) Then stack the sheaves together to make a shock (also known as a stook) and leave it in the field to cure and dry for about three to four weeks.

Once the last trace of green is gone, lay the sheaves on a tarp or an old sheet spread out on a hard surface. With a hardwood tool designed for this purpose or, alternately, with a broom or pickax handle, beat the seed heads to knock the seeds loose. Winnow the threshed grain by tossing it into the air on a breezy day (or in front of a fan) to separate the grain from the chaff (the husks and other detritus). Not only will you now have your own grain, but you'll also have some nice straw for bedding or mulch. As an added bonus, the bedding will include little wheat snacks, as some of the wheat berries will still be attached. Store the cleaned grain in a metal trash can in a cool dry place to protect it from insects, rodents, and mold.

There's a pretty big difference between raising a small patch of wheat or corn to grind into flour for your own use and growing enough grain to feed all the critters on a small, diversified farm, too. During peak production, our egg layers go through $1^{1/2}$ bushels of grain a day. We'd need to dedicate at least 10 acres to fill their annual grain order, a lot more grain than would be feasible to grow and harvest by hand and too little to justify the cost of mechanical harvesting. Depending where you live, there are contractors who do custom combining for smaller grain operations. Even so, finding someone willing to harvest a mere 10 acres with a machine designed for hundreds of acres could be difficult.

A family farm that has a handful of critters, bakes its own bread, and eats lots of other grain products (like porridge and pies) might need a plot of about 6,000 sq. ft. ($^{1/7}$ acre). A plot this size is still small enough to work with hand tools and manual labor and can produce at least 1 bushel of wheat, $^{1/2}$ bushel each of corn and oats, and a peck ($^{1/4}$ bushel) of rye. Increase that plot size to include an acre of field corn or some oats and barley, and you'd be well on your way to eliminating your entire feed-store account. We know it's possible to grow all of a family's meat, vegetables, and grain because it's been less than 100 years since most people stopped doing it. Nowadays, the prospect of doing anything that can't be done on an iPad® seems overwhelming. Nonetheless, there are people out there who have small farms and raise all the food they and their animals can eat—including the grains.

chapter ix

Brambles, Berries & Apples

When we lived in Arizona and California, we had grapefruit, lemon, avocado, fig, cherimoya, papaya, and pomegranate trees in the backyard. The only thing we know about these tree fruits is how good they taste. In this chapter, we'll stick to the brambles, berries, and tree fruits that we do know something about—raspberries, blackberries, strawberries, blueberries, and apples—which grow in our New England backyard.

Keep in mind that growing berries and tree fruits is a long-term project. Brambles take two to three years before they bear any significant fruit, and tree fruits take anywhere from three to seven years to reach bearing age. It's worth doing the research before planting these perennials —and given the relatively high cost of tree fruits, choosing the wrong tree variety hurts. You don't want to put in all that work only to discover, two years later, that you planted a Northern variety although you live in Georgia. For berries, we suggest you conduct a trial run with a few each of several different types to see which

does best on your soil and site and which impresses you most with yield, hardiness, and taste.

Because there are so many choices, choosing the variety of cane fruit or fruit tree that's best for you can be challenging. Do your homework. Ask other farmers and gardeners in your area and consult your county extension service. Consult books that provide in-depth information about growing fruits—a couple of paragraphs in an all-purpose gardening book won't cut it. Here, we'll just provide an overview, based on our own experiences.

Bramble Fruits

Raspberries and blackberries are bramble fruits, aka cane fruits. They are in the genus *Rubrus* and members of the Rosaceae (rose) family. The thorny, upright canes propagate readily from underground runners. If not kept in check, blackberries and raspberries will run wild, forming an expanding and encroaching tangled

George picks apples from a tree that Jane grafted their first year as a couple.

thicket. Containing them is a lot of work—but you'll forget all your trials and tribulations as you are filling your bucket and pop one in your mouth. The only way you can really eat fresh raspberries is to grow them yourself. That teensy $\frac{1}{2}$-pint carton sold at farm stands or the produce aisle won't even feed one person, and it costs about a dollar a berry. When I eat raspberries, I want a bowl full, drowned in fresh cream, but I don't want to take out a home-equity loan to have it.

Brambles in general, and red raspberries in particular, are very hardy perennials. Red raspberries are one of the few fruit types that will grow reliably as far north as Zone 3. Black raspberries, however, only thrive up to Zones 5 or 6. Raspberries are very forgiving. Even if you plant them in the wrong location and never fertilize, mulch, water, or weed them, you'll still get berries. On the other hand, if you put just a little effort into your crop, you'll get a respectable yield; if you do everything you should (especially keep the weeds at bay), the plants will reward you with all the berries you could possibly want, to eat out of hand, cook, freeze, or jelly.

Raspberries are highly responsive to weather conditions. They need plenty of water and lots of sun. If there are too

Our raspberry patch.

many gloomy or rainy days, not only will the damp increase the risk of viral and fungal infection, but it will also hinder bee pollination. (Proper care can help counteract most of the detrimental

These berries were legendary for their size and sweet taste. We planted them, with no preparation, on a very steep bank just behind our vegetable garden, and we're still struggling with them. We've moved

 *"A fruit is a vegetable with looks and money. Plus, if you let fruit rot, it turns into wine, something Brussels sprouts never do."*
—P. J. O'Rourke, The Bachelor Home Companion

effects of poor weather, but pollination is not within human control.) Brambles are susceptible to viruses and fungi, but the symptoms of infection may not be visible, especially if the plants are robust and growing—which is why experts advise against accepting plants offered to you by friends or neighbors. A long-standing infection that remained almost dormant in your neighbor's berry patch could spring to virulent life in yours, triggered by the stress of relocation or some other unknown factor. Once viruses and fungi are invited in, they do not leave. It's always safer and wiser to purchase only certified virus-free canes from reputable growers.

We agree with that general proposition, at least now, in the wisdom of our senior years. If we had heeded the experts' advice the weekend we met, 34 years ago, we would not have planted those half-dozen canes of heirloom blackberries of unknown provenance. They were transplants from the ancestral homestead of an old family from Stowe, Vermont, and had been planted just after the Civil War.

some to the real patch, but there are still a considerable number of plants on that impossible bank.

Sometimes, however, you just have to take a walk on the wild side. In truth, a fairly large percentage of our landscaping and fruiting gardens trace their origins to cuttings that friends have given us or plants dug at the cellar holes of long-gone farmhouses. I would not advise ignoring biosecurity protocols for just any plant or animal, but if you feel the gain is worth the risk, quarantine the specimen from the rest of your plants (perhaps in a far corner of your property) for at least a season.

Choosing plants Raspberry types include red, yellow, and black. These plants bear fruit either in the summer or fall. The summer-bearing types produce fruit on the second year's cane (floricanes). The fall-bearing types produce fruit on the top of the first year's cane (primocanes). Red and yellow raspberries are either summer or fall bearers, but the black varieties are summer bearers.

Raspberry Bed Layouts

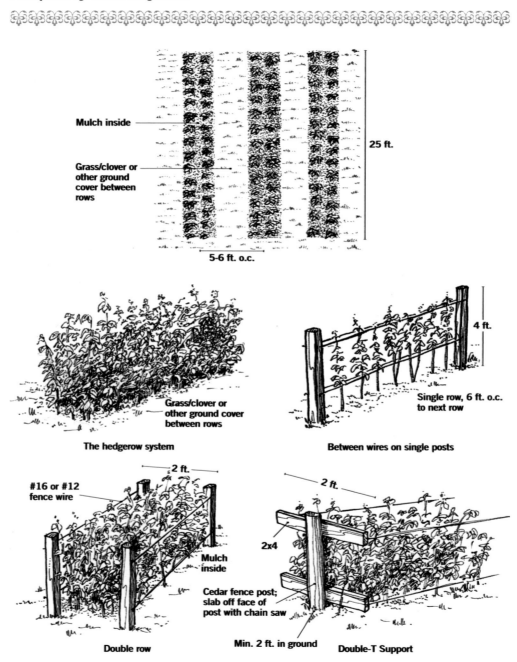

Mulch inside

Grass/clover or other ground cover between rows

25 ft.

5-6 ft. o.c.

Grass/clover or other ground cover between rows

The hedgerow system

4 ft.

Single row, 6 ft. o.c. to next row

Between wires on single posts

2 ft.

#16 or #12 fence wire

Mulch inside

Cedar fence post; slab off face of post with chain saw

Double row

2 ft.

2x4

Min. 2 ft. in ground

Double-T Support

The Raspberry Grower's Keys to Success

You can always judge how together the homestead is by how together the berry patch looks. So here are a few tips to keep the raspberries in good order and your homestead in top form:

• Do it right the first time. Site and prepare the patch carefully. Remember, if you don't have time to plant all the canes you've purchased, just give the plants away to someone who does. No harm done.

• Make the patch a manageable size. You'll get a better yield from a well-managed small patch than you will from a sprawling disaster area. (In case you haven't figured it out yet, this is really the take-home message for all of the gardening chapters.

• Plant all of your berry patches in an area that is conveniently located. Berries might seem like a good thing to put out on the back forty or in a distant corner, but you'll typically be too far away to tend the patch on a regular basis—unless there are berries to pick, of course. If the patch is nearby, you're much more likely to make a pass between the rows while you're mowing the lawn.

• Give your berries plenty of space and air circulation to prevent viruses and fungi attacks. Don't work in the area when the ground is wet.

• Mulch deeply, around and close to the plants. Plant clover and grass between the double rows. Make the areas between rows wide enough to accommodate your lawn mower, in order to deter weeds. Avoid edging or fencing that could interfere with the movement of the mower.

• Enlist the troops. In early spring, before all of the other projects get ahead of you, get together with a few friends, your kids, grandchildren, or farm apprentices to weed, prune, and mulch the entire patch in one long day. This intensive session will keep Mother Nature (just barely) from reclaiming the patch for another season.

Yellow raspberries are the sweetest of all. Their high sugar content makes them short-lived on the vine, and, increasing their overall fragility, once picked, they neither ship well nor last long on the shelf. These otherwise detrimental traits make yellow raspberries good candidates for local markets. Black raspberries are not quite as fragile as the yellow varieties and not as hardy as the red ones. There are also so-called purple raspberries, which are a hybrid between red and black. The fruits are tasty, and the plants are quite productive but also very thorny.

The Latham raspberry (*Rubus idaeus*) is the standard, tried-and-true, summer-bearing red, but there are lots of other good varieties that ripen early through late in the season. In theory, if you plant a few canes of each type, you'll be picking berries throughout the summer. Some people might be thrilled to have ripe raspberries all summer up to frost, but others might discover that it's a burden to pick berries every day or else lose them. Raspberries do not hold well on the cane. They must be picked the day they ripen. In fact, at the height of the season, you should pick twice a day. If you really do want fresh berries all summer, plant a main crop variety that ripens in July, which you can harvest to freeze and make preserves. For fresh eating, plant a few canes that ripen before or after the main crop. Then it won't be a disaster if some berries go by—you'll still have plenty for every purpose.

Raspberries are prolific. In about three years, a mere dozen canes planted 3 ft. apart will yield up to 5 or 6 quarts per foot of row. Even if you have a large family to feed, you should plant no more than 10 to 20 canes. If you do, all too soon you'll find yourself aggressively thinning out your patch.

Although people often confuse them, blackberries and black raspberries are two entirely different plants. Black raspberries (*Rubus occidentalis*) are a raspberry variety. Like most raspberries, they are well adapted to cold climates, prefer heavy moist soils, and fruit in midsummer. Blackberries (*Rubus fruticosus*) fruit later, signaling the advent of autumn. If you cultivate them, space the plants and train them to wires to avoid getting snagged on the nasty thorns and wood canes. Blackberries also grow wild in dense thickets. Removing dead and dying canes will significantly increase the yield and extend the life of the patch. Many folks feel that domesticated blackberries, although larger and more prolific, aren't as tasty as their wild cousins.

Is there a "right" amount of raspberries to grow? Is it even possible to have too many raspberries (or too many strawberries, blueberries, or apples, for that matter)? I don't think so. If you have time to make them, pies and other pastries freeze almost as well as plain berries do. (Don't freeze the berries plain, however. They hold their color and taste much better if you sprinkle on a little sugar.) Think how wonderful it would be, some gloomy February day, to take a raspberry pie from the freezer and pop it into the oven. The memory of summer invoked by that tart and sweet treat could bring one to tears of bittersweet joy.

Location and preparation In northern regions, cane fruits need lots of sun; in the South, they need partial shade in the afternoon, good drainage, and soil that is rich in organic matter. Avoid low-lying gullies that become frost pockets. Pick a location that has enough room for the plant's future expansion and convenient access to water. Your plants will thrive if you can set up a drip or soaker irrigation system. You don't need anything fancy— just lay a soaker hose down along the berry rows and leave it there.

....

Top left: Heritage Wolf River apples, from a cutting grafted onto native rootstock. Top right: red raspberries. Bottom: a cluster of black raspberries in three stages of ripening.

Don't rush the preparation of your berry patch. If you have to, it's better to give away the berries that you purchased but don't have time to plant than it is to rush the planting. Take your time and do it right the first time. (Trust me, we've been there. If there was an exactly wrong way to do it, we've done it that way.) Ideally, you should prepare the soil in the fall and plant your canes in the spring, although the whole job can be done in the spring. Brambles prefer a slightly acidic soil and lots of organic matter, particularly rotted wood, supplemented with a bit of bone meal or rock phosphate. These preferences explain why wild brambles are often found growing on a pile of old boards, logs, or in the cellar hole of a long-collapsed house.

There's no one best way to prepare a bramble patch, but we have a system that has worked for us. In the fall, spread a thick (6 in. or more) layer of organic matter—for example, a combination of compost or rotted manure, bone meal or rock phosphate, and sawdust. Be sure the sawdust either sits at the top of the layer or is mixed in well so as not to form a crust on the ground. You can till this organic layer into the soil in the fall or wait until spring. Moisten the area well. Sprinkle a compost starter or mycelium inoculant over the whole of it and cover the area with either black plastic sheeting or sheaves of hay. If you use hay bales, be sure not to leave any gaps between them where weeds may grow. Come spring, remove the plastic or hay covering. The soil will be friable, filled with earthworms, and ready to go.

Planting First, set up your support system. We prefer the double-T support shown on p. 220. Build the supports about 6 ft. on center, so you have about 3 ft. between rows. Cane fruits need a lot of air circulation around them to help prevent viruses and fungi.

Dig a trench under each wire support and plant the canes 1 ft. to 2 ft. apart. Blackberries sucker even more than raspberries, so space them at least 1 ft. farther apart. Spread the roots laterally along the trench and set the crowns a bit deeper than they were planted when you bought them. Prune the canes to about 6 in. in height. Liberally cover the plantings with soil and water and then pack firmly to remove any air bubbles.

The next step is mulching the canes. When we clean the deep litter out of our chicken coops early in the spring, we cart it over to the berry patch where we use it for mulch. Because the litter has already undergone some decomposition in the coops, we can place the mulch directly over the dormant canes. (In the summer, we clean out the coops and spread the litter out onto the chicken yard so it can mellow before we use it for fall mulching.) Mulch only the area directly next to the canes and a few inches beyond. Plant the paths between the supports with white clover or a clover–grass mix. Keep these paths mowed to discourage any suckers that sprout up between the rows from taking hold. Mow as often as necessary until frost.

Harvesting Picking the berries is the fun part. Gently remove the berry, leaving the stem and the hull on the cane. Pick often to get the best quality—and to beat the birds to the prize. As with all plants, to prevent the spread of disease, do not work in the canes when they are wet. Collect the berries in small buckets or bowls to keep them from squishing, which they do easily. Berries do not keep well, so you'll just have to eat them right away if you can't cook or freeze them quickly.

Summer-bearing raspberries and blackberries produce fruit on the second year's cane, so you will not get any berries for at least two years. Immediately after the harvest is over, cut the floricanes back to the ground. Early next spring, cut back all the remaining canes and prune the new floricanes to a height of 4 ft. to 5 ft. Thin the canes so that there are no more than three or four strong canes per foot of row. Then secure these canes to the support wires (we use 4-in. plastic cable ties). Weed and mulch the rows and prune any misshapen or diseased canes. If any further care is needed, this is the time.

Fall-bearing species are much easier to care for. In the fall, after harvest, simply mow the entire row down to the ground. Otherwise treat these plants in the same way as you would summer-bearing species. Blackberries are treated the same way as summer-bearing raspberries, except that they tend to have more lateral branches and so must be pruned more aggressively.

Care and maintenance There are three major problems with brambles: weeds, weeds, and weeds. There are so many things to do on a homestead that, if one of them is not screaming at you the minute you wake up, it gets put off in favor of the projects that are. By the time the berry patch starts screaming, it's so far gone that it doesn't seem worth the trouble. After all, there will still be some berries to pick even if you have to climb through a jungle of thorns to get there, right? We've spent a tremendous amount of backbreaking work rehabilitating our once hopelessly overgrown and neglected raspberry patch.

There are a few viruses and fungi that are inclined to take up housekeeping in a bramble patch, but if you keep the weeds under control, the other pests will remain in check, too. If disease does take hold, there is no choice but to destroy the infected canes. Prevention is the key. Keep the patch well cared for and weeded and promptly remove any sickly looking canes. Black raspberries are considerably more susceptible to viral infection. Plant them in their own patch, at least 1,000 ft. downwind of the main berry patch. Be sure to keep out aphids—they spread disease.

Left: Blueberries ripening Right: Apple harvest

Yes, berries are more trouble to grow than annual vegetables, but—with no disrespect to buttercrunch lettuce intended—will you ever be as satisfied by a bowl of lettuce as you are by a bowl of fresh raspberries and cream? Start small and add more plants and varieties as you go. The worst-case scenario is that you will start off with great plans and end up with an overgrown patch that can only be left in the hands of God— and everyone knows how She runs a farm. Some years later, when you are much older and more settled, you can reclaim the patch and that will feel great, particularly if you undertake the project with an enthusiastic granddaughter like ours.

Strawberries

Many people claim that strawberries are their favorite fruit—or at least their favorite type of berry. Little compares to homemade strawberry ice cream, particularly if it's made with your own strawberries and your own fresh cream. There is a downside to strawberries, however. They require a lot of work to grow, and there's a fairly steep learning curve. In my humble opinion, you have to really love strawberries to grow them. I only *like* strawberries, whereas I *love* raspberries, which are much easier to manage—so much so that I eventually gave up strawberries and expanded my raspberry patch. Just because I can grow something doesn't mean I have to. You, however, might be one of those strawberry lovers, so here's the skinny.

As always, the first step to success is choosing the right variety. Don't just wander into the local Agway and buy whatever they have on sale. There are certain varieties that do better in certain climates—and who, might you think, knows the exactly right variety for your state and county? Why, once again, your friendly neighborhood extension agent.

The strawberry, which is also a member of the Rosaceae family, is from the genus *Fragaria*. The most common varieties are from the hybrid *Fragaria ananassa*. There are four basic type of strawberries: June-bearers, ever-bearers, day neutral, and alpine.

June-bearers taste the best but require the most work. As the name implies, June-bearers all ripen within a few weeks in June (earlier in warm zones), so you can have your own summer strawberry festival and then freeze and jam the left-overs. If you're not completely on top of the patch during the height of the plant-ing season, however, the yield can be less than you hoped for. Maintaining a good strawberry patch requires you to control all the runners (or "daughters") that the mother plants put out. June-bearers have a lot of daughters and granddaughters. You can control the chaos with the "mat-ted row" system. After the picking season ends, mow down a wide bed of plants to clear a path, cut out any unruly runners,

and then heavily mulch the path. This system doesn't address the overcrowd-ing problem, however. You still must go through and thin the plants frequently, even between fruiting periods. With our diverse farm and even more diverse life, it's hard for us to maintain such an inten-sive maintenance schedule. Our beds are often unruly.

Ever-bearers are a bit easier to take care of than June-bearers are. The plants are larger and have fewer runners. Simply plant them far enough apart to encourage air movement around the plants and also mulch heavily. The "ever-bearer" desig-nation is something of a misnomer—the plant doesn't actually bear all season. It produces a crop in early summer (after the June-bearers, but before raspber-ries) and repeats the performance again in late summer, when no other fruits are ripening. Ever-bearers put out large ber-ries that, in my opinion, lack the intense strawberry taste that characterizes the June-bearers.

You manage day-neutral strawberries as you do the ever-bearers. The day-neutrals bear light crops throughout the summer. Alpine strawberries, aka *fraises des boise*, bear tiny fruits all season. They don't spread by runners, so are easier to manage than the others.

Blueberries

Blueberries are a shrub plant from the genus *Vaccinium* and a relative of cranber-ries and bilberries. Three common species are lowbush blueberries (*V. angusti-folium*, Zones 2 to 6), highbush blueberries

Carpe Diem

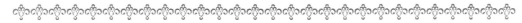

When George and I met, I knew a little about apples because I had spent about a year working in a large apple orchard in southern New Hampshire. The weather and terrain there are perfect for apple growing. Organic orchards were rare at that time. As a ploy to keep me in his clutches, George hired me to prune his old trees. I managed to get one done.

You might think our affinity and affection for apple trees would have encouraged us to plant a lot of trees on our farm, but we did just the opposite. We kept thinking that as soon as we learned more about growing apples, we would choose some varieties and plant a small orchard. Today, 35 years later, we still have only one domestic apple tree on our property. I eventually got around to grafting a Wolf River variety onto a sapling, and that tree is fruiting regularly every other year—with no help from us except the occasional pruning.

Our mistake was thinking we needed to know everything to get started. When I think back now, I realize I knew a lot more than I thought I did. Granted, there is a pretty steep learning curve when you start out, but don't wait to plant your fruit trees. Do it this year, right now, and climb the curve as you learn. Before you know it, 35 years will be behind you.

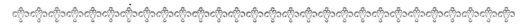

(*V. corymbosum,* Zones 3 to 8), and rabbit-eye blueberries (*V. ashei,* Zones 7 to 9). All of these species are native to the United States and grow from Florida to Maine and across the northern tier.

Lowbush blueberries, the state fruit of Maine, are often referred to as wild Maine blueberries and are responsible for some of the most beautiful scenery in that state. They grow in otherwise barren rocky fields just back of the Atlantic Coast. In springtime, the plants are covered with tiny white flowers and honeybees. In summer, the field is bathed in a blue glow, and in fall, it blazes brilliant red. Connoisseurs claim that these small blueberries have the finest flavor, and we agree. We also agree that picking those tiny morsels is tedious at best and can be achingly debilitating at worst. If you intend to grow any number of lowbush berries, you'll need a blueberry rake, which is a basketlike device that speeds up the harvesting considerably. If you already have wild berries that you can improve, it's worthwhile to do so. Planting them is another story. A few in the rock or woodland garden might be nice, but we've never known anyone who has had a good stand of transplanted lowbush berries.

Highbush berries have much larger fruits than the wild berries. They grow in larger clusters and so are much easier to pick, too. A 4- to 5-year-old bush will yield a gallon or more of berries. Their flavor is but a faint whiff of wild berries, but, fortunately, that's still pretty good. Prune annually to remove dead or weak wood or excessive growth. Mulching helps to preserve moisture. The rabbit-eye variety does not require winter dormancy and so does well in the South, including Florida.

Luckily, all types of blueberries are easy to grow and maintain. The most important consideration when starting your patch is choosing the site. Blueberries need plenty of sunlight, lots of elbow room around the plants, and a pH below 5 (4.5 is ideal). Although most garden plants will tolerate a wide range of levels on either side of their preferred pH, blueberries won't, so have your soil tested. If possible, start with soil that is already on the acidic side. You'll still most likely have to work to drop the pH low enough and to keep it there, as all soils tend to return to their initial pH. Till in acidic organic material, such as pine cones, coniferous bark mulch, peat moss, rotted leaves, and coffee grounds. Don't be tempted by the recommended quick-and-dirty fix sulfur or aluminum sulfates; they destroy the mycorrhizae on which blueberries are so dependent.

Blueberries must cross-pollinate to bear fruit. The more crossing that takes place, the higher your yield, so plant at least three varieties as close together as you can while still allowing air circulation. Mix up the varieties. Keep a record of what variety was planted where so that,

if the plant dies, you'll be able to analyze the result and also know what plant to replace.

Plant bare-rooted blueberry plants about 4 ft. to 6 ft. apart on all sides when they are dormant. Don't add compost or fertilizer to the hole, but do enrich and acidify the area. Pinch off the largest fruit buds the first year to give the plants a chance to get settled and establish themselves. Mulch heavily (bark mulch works well) and cultivate by hand.

Blueberries ripen for almost two to three weeks longer if you plant two or more varieties that fruit at different times. Leave the berries on the bush for about a week after they turn blue. If the fruit doesn't almost fall off the bush with the slightest disturbance, the berries aren't ripe. Taste them first to be sure. Not many diseases effect blueberries, but the birds will fight you tooth and nail for some or all of the crop. You'll need nets if you expect to keep any of the crop for yourself. If the birds don't find your berries during the first year, they surely will the second. Blueberries freeze like a dream. They also make great syrups, good jams and jellies, and, of course, excellent pies.

Apples

Whenever I see the four or five paragraphs about growing apples in all those "complete guide to homesteading" books, I have to laugh. It's just as likely that someone could write a page or two about performing surgery or installing a plumbing system and expect the reader

"Almost all wild apples are handsome. They cannot be too gnarly and crabbed and rusty to look at. The gnarliest will have some redeeming traits even to the eye." —Henry David Thoreau, "Wild Apples"

to have enough information to perform an appendectomy or plumb their kitchen and bath. The skill of growing apples organically—or even conventionally—takes years to learn. Although it's no major feat to plant an apple tree and keep it alive, to actually produce a good crop of apples that are clean enough to store over the winter or sell at a farm stand is a big deal, indeed. (The same is true of learning to grow other fruit trees, such as peaches and plums.)

For starters, consider this: There are more than 60 insect pests that regularly infest apples—and I don't mean they make just a quick visit. They set up housekeeping. The infamous apple maggot alone is enough to ruin your whole crop for storage. In time, with some serious study, you can learn how to grow at least some "perfect" apples that will store in the root cellar and maybe even be salable. Fortunately, in the meantime, you can still make very nice cider or applesauce with the shabby apples from your trees.

Planting Get at least one full-size apple tree (or another fruit tree that grows well in your area). Dwarf trees don't last long, and it's good to leave something for posterity. As so often advised, don't go overboard. Buy no more than a total of four to six trees (if you're also includ-ing pear trees, peaches, or one or two others)—but be advised, six trees is a lot of work. You'll get more fruit from a small number of properly cared for trees than you will from a lot of neglected ones.

Apples like sunshine, so a southern location is best. One of the major reasons a crop will fail is that a late frost has hit the flower blossoms. To reduce the likelihood, pick varieties that do not blossom too early and plant trees on a slope, so that cold air drains off into the valley below. Visit a good local nursery and see what kind of locally adapted varieties are available. Chances are good that anyone running a small operation in a small town is a true apple aficionado and will be fairly knowledgeable. Often, these types of nurseries offer warranties and will take the tree back if it fails to grow. Be sure to get a second opinion about the best varieties for your region before you buy. There's that county extension agent again (have you made her godmother to your children yet?).

Although it's tricky to get perfect fruit, planting and growing the apple tree itself is easy. Just pick the right spot, dig a big hole, and stick the tree in the hole. Make sure the grafting site is above ground level. The grafting site is that small swelling above the roots, which marks where the cultivated variety was grafted onto a hardy native rootstock at the nursery.

Saving pasture runs All across New England (and probably in other Northern dairy states and in surprising places like high up on an Aztec Mountain in central Arizona), you'll find old, abandoned pastures that are reverting to forest. Many of these pastures are dotted with feral apple trees. These trees are known as "pasture run" trees, from the old term for apples that have sprung from seeds planted by grazing cows and deer.

Unlike their more civilized cousins, pasture-run trees are typically 25 ft. tall or taller and very unruly in their growth habit. They'll often bear apples of surprisingly good taste—and pasture-run apples will make some of the best cider you've ever had—although, to be fair, most of them are not much better than crab apples.

To restore the trees that are worth saving, you'll need to thin out the suckers, open up the middles, and, most important, clear away brush and other trees that block the sun. Do the pruning over the course of a couple of years so the tree will not be shocked. Although a little shock can increase fruit production, too much will have the opposite effect.

Bad Apples Make Good Cider

Growing apples for cider is much easier than growing apples for eating. Test the apples first to make sure that you aren't working with too many sour varieties. If you mix in about 10 percent sour, dry,

wild apples with sweeter, more civilized fruit, you'll have a cider with intriguing complexity and zing. Much more than that percentage of sour apples can ruin the cider, although you can always add a batch of sweet fruit to correct the taste. The good thing about cider is that it's not done until you say it's done.

The cider press The cider-making apparatus is called a press but actually it's a composite of two machines—the pomace mill and the press. The mill portion is a hand-cranked or electric-motor-driven drum that is fitted with blades to chop the apples into small pieces. The chopped apples then go into a slatted oaken bucket that is set on a sturdy shelf under an iron frame that holds the pressing screw. You turn a lever to rotate the screw downward, and the flat pressing plate at the screw's base squeezes the apples until the juice runs out. The squeezed pomace makes great pig feed—and your pigs will appreciate it even more if it's left to ferment for a few days. A cider press is one of those items that is used so infrequently that it might be best to buy and share it with a group. Many a homesteading alliance has started with the purchase of a cider press or some other seasonal equipment. If you have enough apples to make it worthwhile, a homestead-scale cider mill (accommodating about 3 gallons of chopped apples per pressing) is not prohibitively expensive.

In a good year, you can squeeze out 50 to 100 gallons of cider from just 25 trees. Undoubtedly, you will have more fresh cider than you and your friends can drink. You can freeze or can the surplus or make jelly or apple juice—but, even then, you'll likely still have plenty left over. There's only so much jelly you need, and you probably won't need more than two gallons of cider to make it. Another option is to make some hard cider.

Hard cider Hard cider is a lot easier to make than wine or beer is. All you need are a few essentials: a glass or plastic "carboy" (a large jug with a narrow mouth, similar to the 5-gallon jugs used to stock water coolers with bottled water), the carboy stopper, an air lock (to keep the air out while allowing the gas from the fermenting cider to escape), and some fresh-pressed cider. The carboy and air lock are available from any company that sells home-brewing supplies.

Just as in chili cook-offs, everyone has their own version of the absolute best hard cider recipe. Some folks add special gourmet yeasts. Some add sugar; others don't; and some even advocate for raisins or molasses. Feel free to experiment with your own recipe. Although straight cider contains enough natural sugar to produce a modest alcohol level, if you prefer cider that's a bit more on the hard side, you can add 1/2 lb. of sugar for each gallon. Stir in the sugar and cap the carboy with a rubber stopper that's fitted with the air lock.

Set the carboy in a cool, dark place (like a basement or root cellar) and let the naturally occurring yeasts that live on the apple skins ferment. Fermentation should be an unhurried process. The best results are obtained at temperatures

Making cider. Top: Turning the press screw is a two-person job. Bottom left: Wash the apples before milling them. Bottom right: Fresh apple cider flows from our press bucket. Wild apples add a superbly tangy taste to the mix.

between 40°F to 50°F. When there are no more bubbles percolating through the air lock, the primary fermentation process is finished. As the concentration of alcohol reaches the toxic level that we humans recognize as a pleasant alcohol "buzz," the yeasts that had been busily turning sugar into alcohol are killed off.

At this point, you can let the finished "still" cider sit in the carboy, drawing it off at your leisure to drink as it is. Or, you could decant the cider into clean, sterile, wine bottles. Add 1/3 to 1/2 teaspoon of sugar, cork the bottle, and let the cider sit for a few months more, until it carbonates and turns into a fine, dry, sparkling apple wine. Another option is to set out a few gallons of hard cider on the coldest night of the year, allowing it to freeze solid around a liquid core of high-proof, applejack liquor.

(Jane's note: George likes making up traditions, so he puts up his cider in late September or early October, after the first frost has sweetened the apples, and broaches the carboy on New Year's Eve.)

chapter x

The Gardener's Kitchen

What good is a basket full of bleeding ripe tomatoes and large flawless leaves of basil if no one makes them into a fresh pasta sauce? What use is the nest box stuffed with white and brown eggs if no one scrambles them for breakfast or makes after-school cookies for the kids? What about the squash in the pantry that the farmers leave to rot while they write their book on gardening? That high-omega-3 grass-fed beef does no one any good if it lies entombed in the freezer.

Homesteading is all about eating the good food you worked so hard to grow. What's the point of growing your own vegetables and meat if you don't know how to cook them—or can't find time to prepare and eat them? For most folks, modern life is still about fast cooking and fast food. We work so hard and so long that we don't have time to make home-cooked meals from scratch or even to sit down to enjoy eating them. It's not just urban apartmentniks or suburban commuters who get stuck on the treadmill. Farmers and homesteaders do, too. We've been guilty of focusing so intently on the growing that we've forgotten about the eating. Or, after a long day spent weeding and mulching, I've been just too damn tired to prepare any of our wonderful vegetables. (After talking with many other farmers and homesteaders, I've learned I'm not the only sinner in the choir.)

To the inexperienced cook, preparing a meal from scratch—using fresh vegetables and pastured meat—can seem like a daunting challenge. Get a few basic cookbooks and just dive in. The Cook's Illustrated and America's Test Kitchen series are a good place to start. Be fearless and keep it simple. Usually the simplest techniques are the best ones. With only minutes from the garden to the plate, your ingredients are so fresh and perfect that, often, the less you do with them the better. For example, it would be a sacrilege to do anything more with an ear of sweet corn picked at

Top: Preparing sweet corn for freezing in our harvest kitchen. Bottom left: Home-made corn salsa and relish. Bottom right: Butter 'n sugar sweet corn—from field to table in 20 minutes.

the pinnacle of perfection than dunk it in boiling water or grill it in its own husk. Fresh vegetables are usually best either steamed or lightly sautéed and served with plenty of butter (preferably freshly churned).

Whether you get your food from your own farm or garden or from a Community Supported Agriculture farm (CSA), eating seasonally and locally requires a different

Here is an overview of some methods for processing, preparing, cooking, and storing your fresh foods—and the space and equipment you'll need to do it.

Kitchen Essentials

Successful homesteading—at every level—is all about the infrastructure. Each of the many operations and routines that fill the hours of the homesteader's days requires

"Our mothers were sans mixes, sans foil, sans freezer, sans blender, sans monosodium glutamate, but their ingredients were as fresh as the day; and they knew how to bake bread."

—*Eudora Welty,* The Jackson Cookbook

sensibility. Instead of browsing through the cookbook, deciding upon a recipe, and then shopping for the ingredients, you need to make your recipe according to what foods are in season and available. Winter squash and fresh peas, for example, won't likely share the same platter, as peas are a spring crop and squash ripens in the fall. If you know how to freeze those spring peas, however, they'll pair nicely with your winter squash at table.

Our goal is to process and store our fresh foods in whichever manner requires the least amount of energy (either ours or the environment's) and still guarantees a tasty product. We rely on minimal processing, because, as we've said, the less you do to your vegetables, the better they taste, and—possibly even more important—the less work involved in processing those veggies, the more likely you are to do it.

dedicated tools and equipment and facilities. Food raising, harvesting, storage, and preparation are no different.

When it comes to dealing with the bounty of the garden harvest, a lavish gourmet kitchen with state-of-the-art stainless-steel appliances, high-style cabinets, and granite countertops is about as useful as high heels in the barnyard. The kitchen of a self-sufficient homestead is a workshop, not a showroom. People spend insane amounts of money on designer kitchens, sometimes more than the cost of a modest small home. Many of the folks with these gourmet kitchens are so busy working to support their lifestyle that they arrive home too late and too exhausted to cook anything more demanding than warmed-over takeout food. I'm not saying that a working kitchen shouldn't or couldn't look good. Just as the handle of a humble kitchen knife, polished by long use, has its own unique beauty, a simple, well-organized, and well-used kitchen can be beautiful, too.

Design criteria When you work in your kitchen several times a day, every day, having your tools at hand saves both time and labor. The following essentials are relevant to almost any kitchen, but are especially applicable to the needs of an efficient homestead kitchen:

- Opt for plenty of open shelving to allow you easy access to your tools when needed.
- A U-shaped or walk-through galley, with fixed or movable island layouts, will maximize the usefulness of the space in your floor plan.
- There's no such thing as too much countertop area. Extra-deep countertops create enough room to keep canisters and small appliances that are frequently used within reach, without encroaching on work areas. The standard depth is 24 in.; 30 in. is better.
- Make counters and other structures out of materials that are appropriate for their intended use. Concrete countertops are durable, yet "softer" and much less costly than granite. Wood slab or butcher block are more vulnerable to wear, but kinder and gentler to dropped dishware. Recycled bowling alley flooring (which you can sometimes find at architectural-salvage warehouses in widths up to 4 ft. and lengths up to 16 ft.) makes an excellent butcher-block-style counter-top. Periodically renew the sealant on both materials to prevent staining.

- Two sinks are better than one (if you have the room). In any case, the sink should be large and deep enough to accommodate a tall stockpot. Likewise, the faucet spout should be tall enough to clear items you're likely to be washing or setting in the sink. If you can find one, an antique, slate "farmhouse" sink is the perfect size and depth.
- Include multiple work stations to accommodate more than one cook and more than one activity in the kitchen at the same time. Arrange work areas so that the tools and utensils appropriate to the activity will be close at hand. For example, keep the standing mixer, measuring cups, etc., stored in the baking area; keep the cutting board and knives in the food-preparation area.
- Every farmhouse needs a mudroom— a transition space from outdoors to indoors, where muddy boots can be sloughed off so less of their cargo is tracked into the home proper. The mudroom can be a vestibule or an extension of the kitchen. Mudrooms can vary in size from nothing more than an enclosed back porch to an entire "backhouse," complete with storage cabinets, lockers, shelving, a wash sink, or even a washroom or shower stall (a good place to wash the family dog). It can function as a storage space for seasonal items that otherwise clutter up the garage. It's also a good place to keep emergency supplies (kerosene lamps, flashlights, extra batteries, and drinking water). The mudroom can also multitask as a pantry and/or harvest kitchen. A laundry-tub-style utility sink

The Outdoor Harvest Kitchen

What with the wheelbarrow-loads of vegetables for canning, freezing, or pickling; the simmering stockpots of applesauce; and the hindquarter of grass-fed beef sprawled across the countertop, even the most capacious country kitchen can be overwhelmed by the seasonal surge of farm and garden produce. Although we were willing to put up with the inconvenience of cluttered counters and muddy floors in exchange for the incomparable satisfaction of a cellar and freezer filled with homegrown healthy food, we didn't look forward to the annual ritual of disassembling the sink trap and snaking out the drain line to remove all the garden dirt brought in with those vegetables. The promise of an unclogged drain was just one of the many reasons we decided to build an outdoor harvest kitchen.

The south-facing sidewall of our two-story garage/workshop was ideally situated between our garden and the main house. The frost-proof hydrant that served the garden was a conve-nient water source. A layer of crushed rock screenings (Sta-Mat, a quarry by-product that packs down readily) furnished a dry floor. I adapted a garden hose from the hydrant to poly pipe and plumbed the sink supply. An electric 2½-gal. miniheater provided hot water at the taps.

In our harvest kitchen—with its large, easy-to-clean coun-tertop and two double-basin sinks equipped with spray heads for washing, soaking, or rinsing—preparing bushels of fruits and vegetables for freez-ing or canning is a pleasure. The trimmings go directly into pails for the compost pile or to the pig trough and chicken yard. Often, we can skip the pail. The geese, chickens, and even our two goats patrol the perimeter, waiting for us to toss them the scraps. There's no floor to mop up.

We took advantage of the high heat output and the large capacity of a turkey fryer to bring water to a quick boil for blanching corn, string beans, and other vegetables for freez-ing. The same rig, on its lowest setting, further damped down with a heat diffuser to prevent scorching, will boil down toma-toes and apples for sauces and meat scraps and bones for dog food (and we won't stink up the house when rendering lard). You could also use the fryer to scald chickens to loosen feath-ers for plucking. (Because we raise broilers for market, we set up one end of the kitchen for poultry processing.)

Another great feature of our outdoor harvest kitchen is that, if we need to leave off the task at hand to start dinner, we don't have to put everything away and clean up first or work around a mess. But the truly best thing about it is that it is outdoors. We can enjoy a beautiful day, working next to or even in the garden, while keeping an eye on things, instead of being stuck inside the house. Eventually we'd like to add a concrete floor with a drain. Screen panels would be nice—and maybe even a gas cooktop or recycled apartment-size stove. There's always room for improvement.

is handy for washing off freshly harvested vegetables, and for scrubbing a really dirty, really big stockpot.

- The pantry is premium space. Bulk foods require much more storage area than is typically incorporated into the typical home or kitchen design. A walk-in pantry (10 ft. by 10 ft. or +/- 100 sq. ft., if possible) is preferable to a storage-closet type. The pantry should be thermally isolated from the rest of the house (an insulated door will help) so that it can be kept relatively cool.

Provide strong shelving for glass gallon jars in which you can store flours, dry beans, and grains. You can also store bulk flours and grain in 5- to 10-gallon galvanized steel or food-grade plastic "garbage" pails.

If you have a big family or have eggs to sell, consider adding a dedicated refrigerator in the pantry, both for the additional storage capacity and to prevent confusing the cache of eggs intended for sale and those intended for your household. A compact freezer in the pantry will also come in handy. Stock it with your most frequently used frozen items to save you the trouble of rooting through densely packed layers in your full-size bulk-storage freezer in search of ingredients for that evening's dinner. (*Jane's note: We've talked about making a "map" of our storage freezer's contents, but it's easier to send George out for whatever I need. Although he often can't remember a thing I said just the day before, along with his truly weird ability to remember every gas station we ever stopped at during our years of cross-country wanderings, he also*

retains a clear mental map of the freezer's contents. I suppose I should count my blessings.)

Be sure you have a storage space for equipment and supplies when they're not in use. Seasonal equipment—such as large stockpots, canning jars, kettles, utensils, and drying and freezing supplies—take up too much space to be stored in the kitchen. Reserve kitchen storage only for those items that you need daily. If space in the pantry is likewise at a premium, store seasonal items in a mudroom or basement.

You'll also need an outside root cellar or basement "cold room" if you intend to grow and "put by" all your family's meat, veggies, condiments, and alcoholic beverages.

The cooking range If you're serious about homesteading, you're going to be serious about cooking, so I recommend that you buy the very best kitchen range that you can. If you can swing it, at some point in your life, consider buying a professional-style home range. What's the difference between a $600 and a $6,000 kitchen range? Just as a carpenter can build perfectly fine cabinets with a $250 light-duty tablesaw, a cook can prepare a lot of great meals on a standard range. In both cases, however, high-quality equipment will provide a much higher degree of accuracy, safety, convenience, and control.

Serious cooks (assuming no chemical sensitivities) prefer gas ranges to electric and six burners to four. Gas heat permits the cook to have finer control over cooking temperatures. The additional burners allow more cooking surface; on a four-burner stove, there simply isn't enough space between burners to allow each to accommodate a pot or pan at the same time—especially if one is a stockpot or Dutch oven.

At least one of the range burners should be capable of very high heat (12,000 to 15,000 BTUs). Another should be able to operate at very low heat for simmering. Even at the burner's lowest setting, you'll still need a stovetop heat diffuser to prevent scorching when making sauces, jellies, jams, and chili, and, especially, when rendering lard. This cast-iron or steel disk is inserted between the burner and the underside of the pot to distribute heat evenly across the bottom of the pan, preventing the hot spots that cause scorching. Professional-grade heavy-bottomed stainless-steel stockpots can set you back hundreds of dollars, so an inexpensive heat diffuser that you can use with your light-gauge department-store stockpots is a good investment.

Be certain that the range burners are operable during a power outage—the burners of gas stoves are, but the burners of electronic-ignition stoves must be lit with a match, and some ovens will not function without electrical power. Also, make sure that the range's hood ventilator is correctly matched to the range so that it properly exhausts the irritating and potentially unhealthy combustion by-products to the outside. Most high-end stoves will accept only same-brand range hoods. Because they rely solely on charcoal filters to trap cooking odors, unvented range hoods should only be used with electric burners.

Two ovens are nice to have, too. Many is the time we've wished we could bake bread and a ham at the same time. Even if the range oven is large enough, you usually can't cook two different items in the same oven at the same time. The presence of a second item can disrupt heat circulation and cooking temperature, leading to unpredictable results.

Before professional-style home ranges became ubiquitous, many serious homestead cooks and amateur gourmet chefs outfitted their kitchens with new or second-hand commercial restaurant stoves. Even though you can buy a restaurant range for a lot less than a professional-style home range, it's not a good idea or a wise economy to do so. If you've ever spent any time in a restaurant kitchen, you'll notice that it's hot in there. The sidewalls, rear wall, and oven door of a commercial stove are not insulated, so the surfaces are (as the warning label on some woodstoves helpfully reminds us) "hot when in use." By law, the surfaces of ranges intended for home use cannot be more than 75°F hotter than the ambient room temperature, which makes them safe around toddlers and pets and also accommodates situations in which there is zero clearance between the stove and any of the various combustible surfaces found in the standard kitchen. Commercial ranges require a minimum of 6 in. to 12 in. of clearance to combustibles. Given that these ranges are usually 32 in. deep and the standard home countertop is only 24 in. deep, the range will project well beyond the cabinets, interfering with traffic flow within the kitchen.

The top burners, rated at 24,000 to 32,000 BTUs, are fine for the demands of high-volume high-speed restaurant cooking but are overkill for home cooking. Not only do they burn a lot more gas (their continuously burning pilot lights use gas round the clock), but their high heat output requires much more powerful ventilation to keep the air healthy and the kitchen from overheating. In most cases, a building inspector would never permit the installation of a commercial range in a domestic kitchen; it's also likely that your homeowner's insurance would not cover the damages from a fire caused by such a range. Finally, commercial ranges lack many of the features that most home cooks have come to depend on—such as an oven-door window and oven light, an in-oven broiler, simmer burners, and a charbroiler option. The control knobs are not child-safe, either.

Wood cookstoves People who cook on wood-fired kitchen ranges tend to be passionate about them, almost to the point of religious fervor. Cooking on a wood-fired range establishes a personal relationship between the cook and the stove. Every stove is unique; each has its peculiarities of temperament and action. You simply must get to know your stove if you are to have any success cooking on it. This familiarity only comes with experience. Once you've invested the time and effort it takes to become comfortable with your wood range, you will naturally become devoted to it and brook no criticism or any rumored shortcomings.

Back in the early 1970s, no homesteaders worth their sea salt would consider their cabin complete without a big, black, nickel-and-chrome-trimmed or pastel-enameled Home Comfort wood cookstove in the kitchen. Fortunately, in those days, working cookstoves in very good condition were easy to find, often for a few hundred dollars or less. Like the formerly free-for-the-hauling claw-foot bathtub, these quotidian appliances have become precious antiques. Nowadays, a fully restored specimen can set you back hundreds, if not thousands. If you can find one with solid grates and almost all of its parts present and accounted for, most likely in need of rechroming, expect to pay one-fifth of the price. If you're really lucky, you may even find a stove that still has its copper hot-water reservoir.

Although woodstoves are unmatched for producing the steady slow heat needed for braising and other tasks that would otherwise necessitate a heat diffuser, they are not as good for high-heat cooking. It takes a long time for the stove to reach really hot temperatures and, once attained, they're difficult to maintain. Baking can be especially challenging, as the location of the firebox tends to create uneven temperature distributions. Soot and ash deposits on top of the oven and underneath the cooktop also interfere with heating. Woodstoves generate ash and dust during normal operation and during cleaning, more than enough of which ends up distributed throughout the living area. This type of stove also takes up a lot more floor area than a conventional kitchen range, and, unless you fire it up in the cool of predawn hours, cooking on your woodstove is not something you will want to do in the summer. Old timers traditionally moved their cookstoves out into the "summer kitchen" for the season.

Although one could argue against wood cookstoves on the grounds of practicality and utility, if you have the space to accommodate one, even if you use it only occasionally, it can be a welcome addition to the house. Wood-fired kitchen ranges are undeniably handy for taking the chill off of early spring and fall mornings or evenings, when a fire in the heating stove would overheat the house. Although they can't serve as a primary heat source, as they won't hold a fire overnight, when plumbed to a "sidearm" heater a wood-fired range can supplement your hot-water supply. Further, your wood cookstove will be a true comfort to you in the days after Fossil Fuel Armageddon, when there is neither electricity nor propane to feed your professional restaurant-style dual-oven gourmet range.

The Kitchen Toolbox

As is true in any type of workshop, the kitchen is all about the tools. You need good tools to do good work, and you need a goodly amount of them if you're going to accomplish much. If you are just designing or in the initial stages of renovating or building your kitchen and the money is tight, hold back on the fancy finishes and spend what you need to acquire your tools. Delayed gratification isn't a habit that comes easy to most modern Ameri-

cans—especially when it means postponing the realization of your dream kitchen—but if you can tolerate indefinite delay, you could free up the funds to buy a good meat grinder, a professional-grade standing mixer, and a good range and double oven. In other words, if you are going to go over budget, spend the dollars you don't have on the appliances, cookware, bakeware, and other equipment that will make your kitchen functional. Think practical, not pretty. Whatever those glamorous people are doing in their glamorous kitchens, it ain't homesteading.

Knives Buy the best you can afford, but not necessarily the most expensive. The brand you choose is a matter of personal preference.

Knife sharpener Even the best knife is no good if you can't keep it sharp—and you can't cook efficiently with a dull knife. Invest in a good knife sharpener and use it regularly. Electric sharpeners produce more consistent results than manual sharpeners, which may make them worth the expense.

Pots and pans Cookware sets are like home-entertainment systems. You can spend hundreds or even thousands of dollars on increasingly more rarified and subtle options. Whatever floats your boat, but you shouldn't have to spend more than $500 for a complete set of serviceable pots and pans that will last a lifetime. Beyond the usual items, the well-equipped homestead kitchen should include the following:

• **Cast-iron fry pans** You'll need at least two. One should be 8 in. to 10 in. in diameter and the other 12 in. or larger (for those Sunday morning pancake breakfasts).

- **Cast-iron Dutch oven** You'll need both a round and an oval Dutch oven. This pot is the best one for braising and is a necessity when cooking lean, grass-fed meats. Buy pots with an enamel finish, which is easier to clean.
- **Stainless-steel stockpots** These lidded pots range in size from 8 to 20 quarts. Larger sizes (up to 40 quarts) are useful for rendering lard, making head cheese, and cooking up batches of dog food and stock (among other things). Unless you are as wealthy as Martha Stewart, light-gauge stainless-steel stockpots are your only affordable option. Consider splurging on a single heavy-bottomed professional-grade 12- or 20-quart pot, however, to minimize the risk of scorched jellies and sauces.
- **Half-sheets** You'll want to have at least two of these heavy-duty restaurant/bakery-size "cookie sheets." They have many uses and are just as handy for roasting meats and making pastries and breads as for sorting eggs.
- **Baking pans** Stock up on bread pans in several sizes, especially the standard 2-lb. loaf pan. Loaf pans can also be used to mold head cheese, scrapple, and lard. You'll also need cake pans and baking sheets. Pyrex® or dark-colored pans are best, as they produce richly colored crusts; aluminum pans produce pale, anemic-looking bottoms. You should also have several casserole dishes.
- **Bowls** The homestead kitchen can never have too many bowls. Sizes should run the gamut from Toy Poodle to Great Dane. Stainless-steel bowls are relatively cheap and lightweight, and, most important, more or less unbreakable. Unlike plastic bowls, stainless-steel bowls won't leach toxins into your food. They're available in every size imaginable and, although not very pretty, they do the job for which they were intended. Of course, it's also nice to have a collection of antique or new stoneware bowls to grace those open shelves on the kitchen walls.
- **Terra cotta pots** Spanish, French, and Mexican clay pots, although not absolutely necessary, are inexpensive enough that you should have at least one unglazed covered pot for roasting meat and one uncovered dish, glazed on the interior, for making specialty treats, like paella. Our Römertopf® covered clay roaster has been a kitchen stalwart for decades. (If you love roasted garlic as much as we do, you might also get yourself a terra cotta garlic roaster. After baking in the oven, the garlic is soft and sweet—amazing when smeared on fresh bread with olive oil.)

Pressure cooker Beans take a very long time to cook and sometimes aren't tender even after hours of simmering. All beans except split peas, lentils, and soybeans are much better when cooked under pressure. If you have a pressure cooker, you can cook some dishes (like risotto) that once were so time-consuming that you tackled them only rarely. Stainless steel is prefer-

Top: Our kitchen has open shelving and lots of work surfaces. Bottom left: Canning is a lot more practical than many folks think. Bottom right: A Vitorio strainer quickly makes tomato (and apple) sauce.

....

able to aluminum, which can react with acidic foods.

Water-bath and pressure canners Fruit, including tomatoes, can be canned in a standard water bath. Water-bath canners are big black-and-white-speckled enameled pots. They are inexpensive and readily available. Nonacidic foods—like greens, pumpkin, squash, and stock—must be pressure-canned (see pp. 256–257). You'll need to special-order a pressure canner or buy one online—and they're not cheap. We prefer to freeze our meat and most of our vegetables (other than those that keep in the root cellar and pantry), so we got by for years without a pressure canner. After I splurged on one, however, I wondered why I had waited so long. If your homestead is off the grid or if having a freezer is not an option, pressure-canning meat and veggies is the safest and most practical storage option.

Containers You can never have too many plastic pails with lids around the farm and garden. You need 1-gallon to 5-gallon sizes. You can recycle from other sources, but if you intend to store food in them, buy new buckets or recycle only those formerly used for food. Bakeries and restaurants are a good source.

Stoneware crocks We amassed a great collection of antique crocks, but at some point during our sojourn out West, they

disappeared. They have since become seriously collectible, and the prices have risen accordingly. You can buy new stoneware pickling crocks imported from Germany or Poland or a new vintage-style 5-gallon stoneware crock from Lehman's℠ (www.lehmans.com). There's nothing better for making pickles, salt pork, or sauerkraut or for the primary fermentation and steeping of beer and wine.

Plastic milk crates However you come across any of these, hang onto them. (Somehow, despite the dire warning of fine and imprisonment for misappropriation that they clearly display, an awful lot of them end up a long way from home.) They are great for transporting and storing large vegetables and also serve as step stools, shelving units, market crates for egg flats, and instant storage drawers. Likewise, hold onto any sturdy boxes you come across, especially wooden ones.

Standing mixer If you are a serious bread baker, a standing mixer is a must. KitchenAid® (www.kitchenaid.com) is the most popular brand for good reason. I have the Artisan model, which is adequate, but if I were buying one today I would buy the next-largest size. These machines are fairly expensive, but they are worth every penny if you bake a lot. If you don't, you can probably manage to get by with a small handheld mixer and a whisk and knead your bread by hand.

Food strainer/food mill If you make apple and tomato sauces or authentic chili (from chili peppers, not powders), you'll find that this tool saves a huge amount of effort and time. Our Vitorio strainer is

> *"There is no chiropractic treatment, no Yoga exercise, no hour of meditation in a music-throbbing chapel, that will leave you emptier of bad thoughts than this homely ceremony of making bread."*
> —M. F. K. Fisher, The Art of Eating

consistently rated the best on the market. Its oversized hopper and simple hand-cranked auger easily separate the skins and seeds from the juice and pulp of soft fruits and vegetables and expel them through a separate opening. Hard foods like apples must first be steamed until soft. The standard screen will make sauces, mashed potatoes, baby food, and refried beans. Optional screens will process grapes, berries, squash, and veggies for pies, jams, and salsa.

Meat grinder Unless you are seriously into home butchering, a tabletop electric meat grinder or a hand-cranked machine will make easy work of turning your meat scraps into hamburger or sausage. Most grinders come with a sausage-stuffing attachment. The so-called "industrial" model sold by Harbor Freight Tools® (www.harborfreight.com) is a good choice for the homestead kitchen.

Sausage stuffer The action of the auger in the sausage-stuffing attachments of electric home meat grinders tends to turn the mix to a mush, which makes for mealy textured sausage. An inexpensive, horn-style hand-lever sausage stuffer preserves the meat's texture, but you need to exert some serious force to push the mix through the horn. A cast-iron hand-

cranked sausage/lard press stuffs sausage smoothly and effortlessly, without affecting the texture of the mix. It also does double duty as a lard press, separating and squeezing the last drops of lard from the rendered cracklings. They're expensive, but if you're lucky, you may find one at an antique shop, or like us, have one passed on to you from your daughter-in-law's grandmother.

Electric meat slicer Home-smoked meat is smoked as a slab. If you have a commercial smokehouse do the job, you have the choice of getting the smoked meat back either as a slab or sliced to your desired thickness. How thick I want my bacon depends on what I'm going to do with it. I like thick chunks to put in beans or soups, but I like thin slices for breakfast or in my BLT. With an electric slicer, we can have our bacon anyway we like. A slicer is also great for slicing cheese and other types of meat for sandwiches.

Food dehydrator Electric and solar-powered food dehydrators provide another way to put up food. You can also dry fruit slices to make healthful sweet snacks.

Smoker You can chose from among a huge assortment of commercial smokers, but if you are smoking meat in quantity to preserve it—rather than just to enjoy a meal's worth—it makes a lot more sense to build your own smoker, unless you've got money to burn (or smolder). You can improvise with a 55-gallon steel drum, an old refrigerator, or a wooden box—basically any container large enough to hold a pair of hams, shoulder roasts, and some slabs of bacon on hooks or racks.

Grain mill Freshness is just one of the many good reasons to consider milling your own flour. The texture and flavor, to say nothing of the nutritional value, of bread baked with freshly ground flour is noticeably superior. Hand-operated mills that can actually produce a fair amount of flour in a reasonable time are available. Although expensive, the Diamant Grain Mill, imported from Poland, is reputed to be the finest in the world for milling everything from fine pastry flour to coarse animal feed. This and many other large hand mills can be adapted for electric or pedal power.

Cider press You can buy home-scale cider presses that can yield a few gallons or larger, farm-size presses that can easily produce 50 gallons in an afternoon. The hardware for these presses (chiefly the cast-iron press screw and heavy cast-iron yoke) are roughly two-thirds of the total cost. If you have access to hardwood, you can easily build your own press. Alternatively, you can build a press that utilizes a hydraulic bottle jack instead of the pricey hand-screw hardware. (For plans and construction information, check out one of the many online sites for cider-making aficionados.)

Putting Food By

Late summer until snowfall is a very busy time for the homesteader in the North country. All those veggies, meat, grains, and beans must be appropriately stored to keep all winter. Some food keeps best frozen, and some is better canned. Other produce can be stored in cool places without being altered in any substantial way.

Some produce prefers its cool storage damp (95 percent to 98 percent humidity), as in a cold room or root cellar. Others like to hibernate at 60 percent humidity, in the proverbial "cool, dry place." A couple of hundred years ago, that cool, dry, place was the attic, which was not well insulated and so stayed fairly cool and was "naturally" ventilated and fairly dry. Few modern houses have such a space, so you may have to build the equivalent by insulating the interior walls of a closet to make a pantry.

A cool basement could house both your cold room (cool and damp) and a storage room (cool and dry). If you live in the North, your basement is likely to be damp, so you might need to find another room, equipped with a dehumidifier, to store squash and friends. In milder climes, a root cellar may not be necessary at all. Roots can be safely wintered over in outdoor clamps—a variation on the root cellar—which are, basically, straw-lined pits into which the roots are laid, covered over with more straw, and then mounded over with a thick layer of protective dirt.

The key to successful storage of unaltered produce (sometimes called live storage) is to store only *absolutely perfect produce.* Start sorting in the field. Pick only specimens that are without blemish and perfectly shaped. The little crevices formed by legs, twists, or appendages create a hospitable environment for the molds and bacteria that cause spoilage. Sort through each root and meticulously cull for any and all imperfections. "One rotten apple spoils the barrel" is a cliché because it's absolutely true. Even if you are conscientious about culling, it's likely that only half your crop will be in good enough shape for long-term storage. You don't have to throw out all the rejects—you just can't put them in live storage. You can still freeze or can them after trimming off the imperfections.

The root cellar (cool and damp storage) At its most elemental, a root cellar is just a covered pit. For optimum storage, it must be able to maintain a temperature that is between 33°F and 40°F at around 95 percent humidity (it's helpful to have a humidistat to measure and control the level). An earth floor is best—because it tends to maintain a fairly even temperature throughout the year—but a concrete floor covered with a layer of gravel or pea stone that can be wet down to keep the humidity up will work almost as well. A root cellar provides the ideal conditions for storing root vegetables (carrots, beets, rutabagas, turnips), tubers (potatoes, Jerusalem artichokes), and apples, cabbages, endive, celery, and others. A root cellar is also the best place to store canned foods, condiments, and crocks of fermenting vegetables (such as sauerkraut and kim chee) and home-brewed beer, wine, and cider.

Before you invest in building a root cellar, you should know as much as you can about it. Consult an in-depth book on the subject. We believe that anyone who is serious about growing most of their own food should have one of these ingenious, low-tech wonders. A properly functioning root cellar will be one of the most useful and well-used additions to your homestead.

Store your roots in bins. You can build bins with wooden boards or salvaged pallet lumber or adapt recycled wooden crates. Wood has a natural ability to ward off some bacteria and molds. Plastic shipping crates, milk crates, or storage totes provide more options—and plastic is light, stackable, impervious to rot and moisture, and easy to clean and disinfect with hot water and bleach between harvests.

Packing the roots in dampened sand, peat moss, sawdust, and the like helps maintain the optimal 95 percent humidity level. Besides keeping the roots from drying out, the sand also serves to isolate the roots from each other. Then, if one root goes bad, the infection won't spread to the others. Dump some clean, washed "sandbox" sand (available in bags at hardware and building supply stores) into a clean container, such as a wheelbarrow or garbage can, or spread it out onto a clean plastic tarp. Sprinkle water on top of the sand to moisten it. It will be the right consistency for packing when you can form a ball that falls apart very easily with a little shake of the hand.

Clean hay, straw, dry sawdust, or peat moss also make good packing materials, and they're a lot lighter to lift. If you opt for hay or straw, take care that they are completely free of mold (do not use mulch hay). Be sure not to use sawdust from aromatic woods like cedar or redwood (their resins are toxic, which is why they are naturally rot resistant) or poisonous pressure-treated lumber.

Put a few inches of the sand (or other packing material) in the bottom of the bin and then add a layer of root vegetables,

debris from the bin. Don't leave even a trace of old vegetable matter. When the bin and its surroundings are clean, wipe it down with a clean cloth or sponge that has been moistened with a weak bleach solution ($\frac{1}{2}$ cup of bleach to 2 or 3 gallons of water). Let the container dry and the bleach evaporate.

Some people don't bother with bins. They just wrap their veggies in newspaper

"There is no love sincerer than the love of food."
—*George Bernard Shaw,* Man and Superman

leaving at least $\frac{1}{2}$ in. of sand between each individual root. Continue alternating sand and vegetables until the bin is full. If you are filling portable bins, put them in place before they get too heavy to lift and move. Packing roots in sand is worth the trouble. We've pulled carrots out of the bins in May, and they were just as crisp and tasty as when they were put up in October.

It's important to thoroughly clean all your storage bins and containers every year before use. Remove the sand and spread it to dry in a suitably hot place, such as the empty greenhouse in summer, or in an open building. Alternatively, spent sand can be used as litter for brooding chicks during their first week or tilled into the garden to lighten a heavy clay soil. Buying new sand each fall is easier than reusing old sand and is also a surefire protection against the spread of rot-causing bacteria and mold spores. Use a shop vacuum cleaner and stiff brush to remove any

and lay them out on shelves. Others pack everything in whatever more-or-less clean containers they have lying around, stash them in the cellar, and call it done.

Fruits like apples and vegetables like cabbage are usually wrapped in paper and laid out on shelves. Vegetables like kohlrabi and celery can also be kept for up to several months in a root cellar. They are stored in buckets, with roots attached, in dampened soil. Endive and swiss chard are also fairly good keepers.

Clamps (root cellar variation) For centuries, European gardeners have stored their vegetables in clamps (as they are called in England) or silos (France). Clamps are either shallow pits dug in the ground or mounds built on top of it, covered with a protective layer of straw and packed earth. They are well suited to regions that have relatively mild winters and little snow cover. Clamps won't work well, however, in climates where the aver-

Clamps

Clamps are a European variation of the root cellar. Mine are two types: dug into the ground or mounded on top of it.

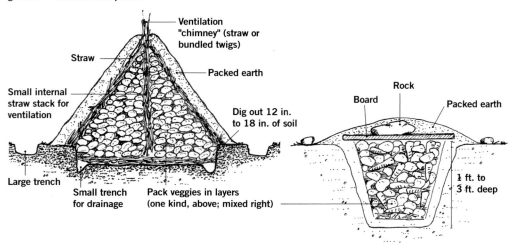

Ventilation "chimney" (straw or bundled twigs)

Straw

Packed earth

Small internal straw stack for ventilation

Dig out 12 in. to 18 in. of soil

Large trench

Small trench for drainage

Pack veggies in layers (one kind, above; mixed right)

Rock

Board

Packed earth

1 ft. to 3 ft. deep

age winter temperature is above 40°F. The vegetables will spoil. In such regions, many plants can overwinter right in the garden.

To make a clamp, dig a trench or pit in the garden. It should be 1 ft. to 3 ft. deep and as wide and long as needed to contain the sorts of vegetables that you would ideally store in the root cellar you don't yet have. Pack the vegetables loosely in layers separated by straw, sawdust, or dried leaves. You can add a central "chimney" of straw or bundled twigs to ensure good ventilation.

You can either pack a single large pit with different kinds of vegetables or make several smaller clamps, each containing a single variety. If you opt for the all-in-one clamp, mix different vegetables in each layer so that you can pull out the ones you want without tearing apart the whole pile. Fill a small clamp with a cabbage, some parsnips, carrots, potatoes, and turnips, and when you open it, you've got your fixings for a great winter soup, stew, or boiled dinner. When the pit is full, cover it with a layer of straw and then with a layer of packed earth, as shown in the drawing above. Don't use plastic sheeting; it will block air circulation and cause the vegetables to overheat and spoil. If you need to protect the clamp from rain and critters, cover it with boards or stones.

The pantry (cool and dry storage)

There are, of course, many bulk foodstuffs that should be stored in a cool, dry place. Flour, for example, would definitely not keep well stored in a root cellar. Squash, onions, and garlic also keep best in a cool, dry room—for example, the pantry. Again, be very picky when selecting candidates for long-term storage. Keep only the best blemish-free specimens.

Squash is usually picked just before the first frost. (We often find ourselves pulling up the vines and covering over piles of gathered fruits with tarps as the evening of the first predicted frost is falling.) Usually, you can just twist the squash off the vine. Sometimes, it takes a sharp knife. Either way, be sure to leave at least 2 in. of stem. If the stem has broken off but the amputation site is clean and dry with no sign of contamination, put that squash on the top of the pile and use it within a week. Keep an eye out for any bloom end rot.

Squash should be "field cured" before it is stored away. After picking, spread the fruits out in a sunny place for as little as 3 to 4 days or as long as a couple of weeks, until the rind hardens in the sunlight. Cover them as needed to protect them from rain or frost. When you bring in the squash, wipe off any dirt with a clean, dry rag, then gently wipe again with a clean cloth dipped in vegetable oil. The oil will help deter mold growth. Most books recommend that squash be stored spread out on shelves so that the fruits don't touch each other—this is probably ideal, but that approach would require more shelf space than we have. We put ours in open plastic totes or stackable milk crates. We can count on about 10 percent of the squash spoiling—sometimes more in bad years (but a bad year for us is a good year for the chickens).

Onions and garlic also do well in a cool, dry place. Although our pantry is cooler than the rest of the house when the door is kept shut, it's still warmer than these vegetables would prefer. Onions, especially, keep best just above freezing. The root cellar is cool enough but too damp. A walk-in cooler would do the trick, but that's not something most homesteaders can justify adding to their pantries. We've found that onions will tolerate higher temperatures more readily than they will tolerate excess moisture, so we keep them with the squash. The onions do, however, tend to get soft and grow green shoots as soon as the days begin to lengthen. Clearly our storage method could use some improvement. The right spot can be hard to find (if only we had an attic!), but the sprouts are good to eat as garnish and in salads and stir-fries.

If you want to store onions, it's important to pick varieties that are bred for storage (good keepers include Copra, Cortland, and Gunnison). You can also buy started plants. Garlic bulbs store more easily than onions. Soft-neck varieties of garlic won't last nearly as long as the hard-neck varieties. Hanging works well for both onions and garlic if you don't have too many bulbs to store—otherwise it takes a lot of time, as we learned as were clipping the dried stems of many onions and garlic to strung wires with clothespins. (We later learned you could stuff them into old pantyhose and hang that instead. You just cut the tube to empty it and then retie it.)

Throughout winter, make it a habit to inspect your stored vegetables every week or so. Clean any vegetables that need it and move them around to expose them to circulating air. Apply more oil to squash as needed and immediately cull any vegetables that are beginning to spoil. Timely culling increases the survival rate of the remaining vegetables—one day's pea-size mold can spread throughout the entire bin in a week. The bottom line with storing food unaltered in root cellars or pantries is that the more picky you are about which vegetables stay and which don't, the better your vegetables will keep.

Freezing Facts and Fancy

For vegetables, freezing is our preserving method of choice because it conserves the taste, texture, and color better than canning or other methods. If properly frozen and packaged, vegetables will be crisp yet tender, hold their color, and taste almost freshly picked. The downside of freezing is energy dependency—specifically, a dependency on electricity. If your goal is to shrink your carbon footprint, a freezer's energy consumption can be troubling.

In cold climates, a freezer that is kept in an unheated garage or shed uses a lot less electricity than a freezer that sits in a warm house. In our early days as homesteaders, we had no electricity. We dried or canned all our vegetables in our solar greenhouse and on our wood-burning stove. The reward for keeping a low carbon profile

(albeit not voluntarily) was the traditional, exquisite exhaustion of long hours spent slaving over a hot stove. Dependency is more of an immediate problem when there is a power outage, as is all too frequently the case when you live out in the boonies. As long as the freezer lid remains closed, the contents should remain below freezing for at least 24 hours. Keeping a small generator handy is good insurance against catastrophic loss in case of an extended outage.

Without a freezer, we couldn't raise and keep all of the meat that we grow for ourselves and our family. We think the energy consumption is a reasonable trade-off (or necessary evil, if you prefer), for which we compensate by trying to conserve energy elsewhere around the homestead. Although the prospect of saving hundreds of dollars by buying a used freezer is tempting, unless that used unit is almost new it will not be anywhere as energy efficient as the current generation of ENERGY-STAR-rated appliances. You'll spend more for electricity in a few years than you saved by buying that old freezer.

Chest freezers are more energy efficient than upright freezers, but a packed chest freezer is also very good at hiding your food from you. Enhanced accessibility is one reason why some cooks prefer upright freezers—if you can see what is on the shelves, you might be more likely to use it. Pack your chest freezer from top to bottom in columns of a single item. When storing food, whether from the garden or bulk purchases, think about how soon or frequently you'll need to retrieve the items rather than how efficiently they can be packed into the available storage space. Keep items you use often easily accessible, even if that arrangement appears to "waste" more space.

Timing Whenever possible, pick your vegetables in the morning when both the air and the vegetables are still cool. Select only specimens in peak condition—a day or two past prime makes a big difference in the quality of the end product—and don't worry that you're wasting food by being fussy. Any preservation method is a step down from just-picked status. If you start at peak, the next step down will still be close to peak. Tough old string beans will be even tougher after they're frozen and thawed. Even after all the work of processing, you'll still have to toss them to the pigs—or you may inadvertently inculcate a lifelong aversion to string beans in small children.

Vacuum sealing Perfect freezing technique demands excruciating attention to detail—and a vacuum-sealing system. When we first started putting food up, no one paid very much attention to packaging. We just put chilled vegetables into plastic bags or containers and then tossed them into the freezer. After decades spent freezing tons of meat and vegetables, one thing we've learned is that the less air in the package, the better the food keeps. Vacuum packaging greatly improves the quality of the end result. Freezer burn can undo all the care and devotion you've put into growing and harvesting your food. The only surefire way to prevent it is with a good vacuum sealer.

Inexpensive vacuum-sealing machines of the kind you'll find at the big-box stores are basically worthless. I've found that inserting the nozzle of a household vacuum cleaner into the bag works just as well and often better than any of the discount El Cheapos. A good-quality external bag sealer costs a few hundred bucks. One way to lessen the sting is to share the cost with a few friends or relatives. A vacuum sealer is also just the sort of useful equipment that a local small farmer's organization or church group might want to make available to its members.

Freezing Fruits and Vegetables

The common supposition that freezing is much easier than canning is only half-true. Freezing is quicker, but it's actually much trickier. If not done exactly right, the end product can be tough and rubbery. Some vegetables, particularly greens and string beans, are very demanding. Their palatability depends on exact timing, precise blanching and chilling, and careful bagging. Others vegetables—such as tomatoes, peppers, and onions—are much less fussy. Most fruits and certain herbs can be frozen raw.

Although the skill of freezing vegetables comes with practice, the following instructions should help you put up a good product. Here's a bit of what we've learned after many years of trial and error:

Freezing before bagging The problem with freezing an entire bag of fruits or vegetables is that the contents tend to form a solid mass. After the bag is thawed, you have no choice but to use the entire contents—

which sometimes means that some portion ends up in the compost bin or as piggy hors d'oeuvres. The problem disappears if you freeze the food before you bag it.

Simply allow the fruit or vegetable pieces to dry. Then spread them out on cookie sheets or half-sheets. Individual pieces should not touch each other. Place the sheets in the freezer until the pieces are completely frozen. (Don't let them sit for more than two days.) Pour the pieces into large freezer bags. Work quickly—you don't want the pieces to thaw while repackaging, or they'll freeze together inside the bag. When you need them, simply scoop out the desired amount and reseal the bag.

Tomatoes Freezing tomatoes is a last-resort time-saving option. Frozen tomatoes are watery and less flavorful than canned tomatoes. They are much better if you peel them first because the skins are tough. Cut out any blemishes, too. Pack the tomatoes in freezer containers or freezer bags. Either way, gently press the container to free up enough juice to cover the fruit. Be sure all the fruit is covered and all the air bubbles released. Add a little salt to each container and freeze without further ado.

Peppers and onions Peppers and onions are easy to freeze. Wash peppers and cut them into desired shapes or size. Scatter them on cookie sheets and freeze overnight. Put the pieces into large freezer bags, press out the air, seal, and store.

With onions, you have options:

1. Peel small onions and freeze them whole in individual freezer containers.

2. Chop peeled onions into $1/2$-in. to $1/4$-in. squares and treat just as you would peppers.

3. Grate or chop the onions in the food processor and pack them in small freezer bags, pressing out the air by hand, and seal and store. You can also freeze grated onions in ice-cube trays and store the frozen cubes in a large bag to use as needed.

Brussels sprouts, broccoli flowerets, potato cubes, and peas are some other vegetables that are good to freeze before packing. Simply blanch and cool vegetables, then spread them on sheets, as described above. The bags will keep better if vacuum sealed. Once opened they can be resealed or you can reseal with a twist tie. To avoid freezer burn, use the remainder within a month or two.

Fruits and berries Stone fruits and berries are very easy to freeze. Apples and pears tend to turn brown, so before freezing toss them with a little lemon juice or a solution of ascorbic acid and water (about $1/4$ tsp. of ascorbic acid to 1 cup of water). We prefer to freeze our berries and other peeled fruits individually. Remove any leaves, twigs, or unripe fruit. Wash the fruit gently in cold water. Allow the fruit to dry on clean cloth or paper towels and then spread them out on cookie sheets.

Sliced or chunked pieces of other fruits are also amenable to freezing. Peaches, cantaloupe, and other melons (except watermelon) are good candidates. Experiment by freezing just a small batch before you go in on a case-lot wholesale order.

Blanching Many vegetables must be blanched to prepare them for freezing.

Herbs Year-Round

Among the trials and tribulations we routinely endure over the course of our endless winters, the absence of fresh herbs is only another small but grating privation, nourishing the seeds of the peculiar madness we call "cabin fever." A small bundle of aromatic green leaves in the midst of an endless white landscape is as much a balm to the spirit as a blessing to the pot it grows in—and there's nothing like cooking with fresh herbs. So we always keep a few herb plants in the greenhouse or in a sunny window. If your winters are mild, many herbs will survive outdoors year-round. Some, like oregano and rosemary, actually fare better in cool (but not frigid) weather.

Just before the first frost, start preparing pots. Different herbs are treated differently. Herbaceous plants like basil, parsley, and cilantro are best planted from seed. About a month before the first frost, plant some seeds in appropriately sized pots. Leave the pots outside to get the plants started. Then bring them indoors. Keep in mind that they probably won't grow as fast as they did in the spring. If you don't have grow lights, consider buying one or two.

For woody herbs—like oregano, sage, and rosemary—dig up two of the best whole small plants in your garden or two halves of big plants. Plant in pots and bring indoors. Leave one dug-up plant as is. Cut the second one back to just about 1 in. above soil level, leaving only a few, if any, leaves. Harvest leaves from the first one and let the second rest for a while, watering it just enough to keep it alive. In late January, start to water the second plant again in earnest and keep the grow lights on. Soon you will have new growth and fresh herbs. When the first plant starts looking tired, cut it back, give it a short rest, and then jump-start it with some compost and plenty of water.

---

1. Wash and prepare each vegetable as needed. Cut into pieces of desired size and remove any stems or damaged leaves.

2. Fill a graniteware double-boiler or steamer with enough water to cover the vegetables. Heat the water to boil.

3. While waiting for the water to boil, clean your kitchen sink thoroughly and plug the drain (if you can't stopper the drain, place a large shallow bowl in the sink). Fill the sink or bowl with cold water and add ice. The water should be literally ice-cold, that is, 32°F to 30°F—so cold that it is painful to immerse your hand for more than a few seconds.

4. When the water is briskly boiling, place 1 to 1½ large handfuls of vegetables in the steamer basket and submerge the basket into the water. Start the timer immediately, setting it for the proper blanching time for the type of vegetable (consult a comprehensive book on pre-

serving). Don't leave the kitchen while your vegetables are blanching—you don't want to leave them in the water for even a second too long.

5. The instant the timer goes off, remove the basket from the hot water and dump the vegetables into the cold-water bath. Swirl the vegetables around with a spoon or with your hands to cool them as quickly as possible and stop the cooking process. Timing is critical to the outcome. Overcooked or undercooled vegetables will be tough or rubbery.

6. While the first batch of vegetables is cooling, start the second.

7. As the second batch is blanching, scoop the first batch out of the cold water and into a colander to drain. Add fresh ice. (It's helpful to have a partner in this frantic kitchen tarantella.)

8. Continue until all the batches have been blanched and cooled. You can blanch two or more kinds of vegetables without changing water or equipment.

Packing When you have blanched and cooled all your vegetables, take a deep breath before the next step.

1. Gather your freezer bags and begin to pack the vegetables into them. Don't fill the bags with more vegetables than you will need for a single meal—the bags shouldn't be filled to bursting. If you don't have a vacuum sealer, try to press as much air out of each bag before sealing it.

2. Loosely distribute the filled bags on top of the food already stored in the freezer. If you pile a lot of freshly packed, room-temperature bags into the freezer, they won't freeze fast enough, which diminishes the quality. The bags might also freeze together as a solid clump.

3. The next day, go back into the freezer and arrange the bags of frozen vegetables for long-term storage.

Canning

Canning is labor-intensive, but it can be a lot of fun if you share the work with friends, in-laws, or your grown children (but forget about the willing participation of any child older than 12). Canning takes more time than freezing, but good results are almost always assured. No store-bought tomato, especially in the winter, compares in any way to the ones you can grow at home. Tomatoes are worth every second it takes to can as many as you can.

Some vegetables, tomatoes in particular, are at their best simply packed raw in a glass jar with some salt and a fresh basil leaf. Other vegetables that are well suited to canning are creamed corn, sliced beets, winter squash, and, of course—in a category all their own—pickles. Many fruits, including apples, are better canned than frozen. Freezing can cause the fruit's pulp and juice to separate, and the thawed fruit tastes flat and watery. As a rule of thumb, any fruit or vegetable that is good after it's been cooked for a long time will be good canned.

To some extent, the decision also depends on your taste. For example, Southeasterners traditionally boil their greens, green beans, and fatback forever. Canning doesn't even come close to their preferred texture. On the other hand, Yankees (like us) and the coastal elite are reputed to prefer their greens lightly steamed or sautéed. This group will likely find canned greens too mushy.

Food safety There are two types of canning processes: water-bath and pressure canning. Both involve pretty much the same simple steps: Put prepared vegetables into a very clean canning jar. Put on the two-part lid and raise the temperature of the whole apparatus until any actual or potential bacteria are destroyed.

Fruit and acidic vegetables (which have a pH of less than 4.6) are suitable for water-bath canning. The acidic nature of fruit and acidic vegetables (tomatoes, for example) creates an environment that is inhospitable to the lethal *Clostridium botulinum* bacterium, which causes botulism. Alkaline vegetables, however, must be heated to temperatures above the boiling point of water to ensure destruction of *C. botulinum.* Pressure canning, which increases the pressure to levels above atmospheric pressure, accomplishes just that.

If done properly—and it is not hard to do properly—canning your own food is very safe, but it is not something to fool around with. If you reuse lids, take shortcuts, or can low-acid foods in water baths, you can turn good food into deadly poison. Simple steps and a little care will yield very rewarding results.

Equipment The canning equipment for both water-bath and pressure canning is simple and, except for the canning pots, identical for both processes. You'll need canning jars, screw tops, and flat lids that sit on top of the jars and under the screw tops. You can use the screw tops more than once, but *never* reuse the lids (the

seal is a one-shot proposition). Canning jars (aka Mason jars) are sold in cases of 12. Buy only top-quality name-brand jars (like Ball®); avoid the less-expensive Chinese knockoffs. Wide-mouth jars are best because they are easier to fill and clean.

Be sure to buy a good pressure canner. The Presto® brand has been around for a long time. It's middle-of-the-road in price but more than adequate in performance, and parts are easy to find. Mirro® and Sears® also make a good product. Most pressure canners are cast aluminum. The expensive models are stainless steel. You can often find used pressure canners for sale. Pressure canners are sort of like exercise equipment—people decide that they're going to be virtuous and can all their vegetables and meats instead of freezing them and, after a few halfhearted attempts, that fancy new canner languishes in the nethermost corner of a closet waiting for the yard sale. Before you buy a used canner, make sure that parts are still available for that particular make and model. Gaskets and seals become brittle and cracked with age. When you order replacements, buy two of each.

Canning isn't something you should improvise or try to improve upon. Rely on tried-and-true instructions and follow them to the letter. The Ball guidebooks and USDA publications are the oldest and best home-canning guides. As an added bonus, the newest edition of the *Ball Complete Book of Home Preserving* by Judi Kingry and Lauren Devine (Robert Rose, 2006) features a lot of very good, updated relish, ketchup, and condiment recipes.

Baking Bread: An Improvisation

When I first started baking bread, I was barely 20 years old. Like everyone else, I went to the cookbooks. I tried many, many recipes. None of them produced the kind of bread I wanted: thick and chewy, with a crisp crust and moist substantial crumb (the inside). I'm sure there has to be a good recipe out there—maybe even more than one—I've just never found it. Finally, I gave up on other people's recipes and developed my own.

My recipe is not really a recipe in the traditional sense. It's more like notes for an improvisation. Bread ingredients change as the weather changes. Even small changes in the relative humidity can make a significant difference in the ratio of flour to water—but I don't measure or weigh anything, so the quantities I suggest in the steps below are approximate. I'm more comfortable changing the ratio by feel, kind of like playing music by ear.

I bake bread almost every day. Mostly, I make a rustic white bread with a thick chewy crust. Some days, I make sandwich bread; other days, whole-wheat raisin bread. They taste and feel different, but basically they are all the same bread as far as technique is concerned. When I veer off course and make some another kind of bread, I rarely veer off in the same direction twice. There are a few key concepts in making

bread, and once you have them down, you can make any bread you want simply by changing a few ingredients, the temperature of the oven, and the pan you bake in—without ever needing to knead or follow a recipe.

Good bread begins with good bread flour. Bread flour has more protein (gluten) than all-purpose flour. Gluten is what makes bread chewy and breadlike rather than "cakey." Flours are differentiated by their protein percentage: bread, all-purpose, cake, and pastry flour (from highest protein content to lowest). For a chewy, artisan-style bread, you must develop the gluten in your dough by mixing it with water—notice I said mixing, not kneading.

A basic rustic bread is made with four ingredients: flour, water, salt, and yeast. If you add more ingredients, you change the texture of the bread. You also increase the shelf life. For example, ascorbic acid or vitamin C powder (also called sour salt) in very small quantities (pinches) will improve the texture, make a very nice crust, and add a touch of tanginess.

Time is a critical factor. The longer the process, the more flavorful the end product. You can make some types of bread in a short time. Dinner rolls, for example, which owe their flavor to additives like butter, aren't mixed for long in order to keep them light, not chewy. Pizza dough, bread sticks, ciabatta bread, and whole-grain raisin bread can also be made rather quickly (in less than an entire day). Even the fastest-rising yeast bread takes 3 to 5 hours, although most of that time is spent waiting.

The water should be as pure as possible. If you need to filter your tap water for cooking or drinking, filter it for baking. Most bread recipes call for warm water. Except for proofing (dissolving) the yeast, the water should be cold. The optimum temperature for bread dough is 75°F. If the dough is too warm, it will rise too fast, and the flavor of the wheat will not develop. When you add warm flour to the cold water, and then mix, which provides additional heat, the temperature of the dough will average out about right.

The ratio (by weight) of water to flour is the single most important aspect of bread making. Novice bread bakers often add too much flour. The key is to keep your dough moist—

Some of our artisan breads.

much wetter and stickier than you will think it should be if you have been reading baking books. The dough will be very difficult to handle at first, and you'll be tempted to dust it with too much flour to make the job easier. Don't. Anything more than the lightest dusting will make the dough too dry, and don't knead in the flour. It takes practice, both to find the right consistency and to handle the proto-loaf (aka "sponge") with finesse instead of extra flour.

Oven temperature is almost as important as dough consistency. It takes a hot oven (425°F to 450°F) to produce a good crust. A slower oven (375°F) makes a softer crust for dinner rolls and sandwich bread. A loaf is not done until its interior temp is 200°F to 210°F (use a thermometer to be sure).

Step 1. Pour about 2 to 2½ cups of cold water (to make two fair-size loaves) in the bowl of your standing mixer. If desired, add about 1 tsp. to 2 tsp. of sweetener (sugar, malt, maple syrup, or honey). Add 1 tsp. to 3 tsp. of yeast (you can dissolve the yeast in warm water first or just mix in instant yeast directly). When the mixture is creamy and bubbly, it's ready.

Step 2. Add 3 to 3½ cups of bread flour. Attach the wire whisk to the mixer and beat at a low setting (#2 on the KitchenAid Artisan mixer) for 5 minutes or so, until all the ingredients are well mixed. Scrape the sides of the bowl to incorporate all of the flour. The mixture should be the consistency of a thick cake batter. Beat at a medium set-ting (#3 or #4) for about 5 minutes. Let the dough rest for 20 to 30 minutes.

Step 3. After the rest period, beat the dough for about 30 minutes at a medium speed setting (#4). You should see a distinct change in the structure of the dough, which will look and feel elastic. The strands of dough should be difficult to break and should be very sticky and gluey.

Step 4. Add 2 tsp. to 3 tsp. of salt. Replace the wire whisk with the bread hook and mix at a low setting (#2 or #3), slowly adding more flour, until the dough comes together but is still very wet. (The dough should just pull away from the sides of the bowl when the mixer is turning, but fall back when it stops.) Best to err on the too-little-flour side than the too-much side.

Step 5. Pour the mixture onto a floured countertop (or a granite or, better yet, marble slab). Ease the dough out of the bowl with a crescent-shaped scraper. Knead the dough slightly, shaping it into a ball and adding just enough flour (less than ½ cup) so that it holds its shape. If you knead too much flour into the dough to make it easier to handle, it will be too dry and you'll sacrifice the bread's texture.

Step 6. Cover the dough with a cloth and let it rest for 20 to 30 minutes. Most of the flour will be absorbed into the dough during this phase.

Step 7. There are two options for the next step. If you're in a rush (how likely is that?), shape the dough and transfer it to baking sheets or loaf pans to rise. Dust the dough and your hands with flour before shaping the loaves (you'll have enough for two large oval loaves or two skinny baguettes). To keep the bread from sticking, line the sheets or loaf pans with parchment paper or use silicone baking sheets. (If you are making sandwich bread, bake in oiled loaf pans.)

Slash the tops of the loaves to allow steam to vent in a controlled way (skip this step when making rolls or sandwich bread). Put the loaves into a hot oven, preheated to 425°F to 450°F, and you'll have fresh-baked bread in about 1 hour. (This method is Standard Operating Procedure when making pizza, focaccia, or ciabatta.)

Alternately, you can let the dough go through one or more risings, either in an oiled bowl or on the countertop, before you shape and bake it. The repeated risings (proofings) add flavor and body to the bread—and give the finished loaf some loft. (If you want to bake the bread the next day, place the dough in a covered container in the refrigerator. The next morning, punch it down, let it rise again if you'd like, then shape and bake it.)

The loaf is ready for the oven when the dough doesn't readily spring back when pressed lightly (err on the side of too springy rather than too laid back). If the dough rises for too long, the yeast are suffocated by the carbon dioxide they produce and the dough falls. When the loaf is put into the oven, it should be at almost, but not quite, the zenith of its rising potential. Then, when blasted by the heat of the oven, the yeast explodes in one last burst of gas to produce a full and flavorful loaf.

To make a thick, chewy crust, place a large baking stone on the bottom rack of the oven to replicate the heat-tempering effect of a stone or brick oven. After the crust has begun to develop, mist water toward the back of the oven with a spray bottle. Repeat the misting about three or four times during the course of the baking. Bake the bread until the crust is golden brown and fairly dark—usually about 20 minutes. (Don't take it out too soon; undercooking will ruin a good loaf.)

Step 8. Remove the finished loaves from the oven and stick an instant-read digital thermometer into their centers. Be discrete, so you don't ruin the appearance of the loaf. The bread is done when the internal temperature reads at least 200°F.

Allow the loaves to cool to almost room temperature before cutting into them. I accept that everyone (except me) loves hot bread, but cutting open a loaf that is still hot arrests the last stage of baking and makes the bread gooey inside.

PART III

Raising Animals

"Well, if you've seen my milk cow,
Please ride her on home.
I ain't had no milk or butter
Since that cow's been gone."

— GEORGE STRAIT, LYRICS FROM "MILK COW BLUES"

chapter xi

·················

Living with Animals

More than likely, if you're reading this book, you're a backyard farmer or a wannabe homesteader who's maybe sitting on something like an acre or two (or less) and who, for a number of admirable reasons, wants to raise your own meat or eggs. So we won't get into a lot of detail about raising big animals that require big spreads.

Although saving money might seem like a good reason to raise and grow your own food, if you consider time to be money, store-bought will always be cheaper than homegrown, at least for anyone with a full-time job that earns full-time pay. People raise their own food as a way of not only eating better but of getting closer to the very bottom line of what it means to be alive on the planet. If you have read this far, you're probably one of those people.

Up until the 1950s, most of our food was "natural." Vegetables and fruits had their seasons, and you enjoyed strawberries in June, apples in October, and special treats like oranges only in February. You bought your meat at the butcher's shop, where the dressed carcasses that hung from hooks served as a visceral reminder of the food's relationship to a once-living animal. Milk, with a thick layer of cream on top, and day-old eggs were delivered to your doorstep. The farms and dairies that raised the food you ate were within a day's drive of your kitchen, not halfway around the world.

Within less than two decades, however, food that had been grown on relatively small and local farms, food with dirt on its roots and blood on its feet, was on the way to extinction. The Victory Gardens that had sprung up in nearly every neighborhood during World War II disappeared, along with the backyard chicken flock. Unable to compete against the phenomenal output of the industrial-agricultural complex (the mutated spawn of the wartime military-industrial complex), small farmers got big or got out.

Emigrants from rural communities moved to the new suburbs that, fertil-

··

Geese can be noisy and aggressive, but these two appear to be enjoying an affectionate moment.

ized by the GI Bill, sprouted like weeds in abandoned fields at the edges of the cities. Unlike the "organically grown" neighborhoods of the past, which grew at the rate of one or two houses at a time, dozens of ticky-tacky boxes, all in neat rows, with clean square yards, were cloned overnight. Lest someone challenge that comforting symmetry, zoning ordinances proscribing "dirty" activities—like keeping chickens or (God forbid) pigs and, in some instances, even growing gardens—were put on the books.

For the most part, folks went along with the change. Why bother with planting, weeding, feeding, shoveling, killing, and curing, when, for almost nothing, you could buy anything you might want or imagine at the giant new supermarket that had replaced all those tiny, messy produce and butcher shops. There were endless aisles of shiny, bright, new packaged and processed foods. They were "clean and convenient," and this was "progress"—and under the postwar spell of the 1950s and early '60s, progress was good. The new foods would rescue housewives from the drudgery of cooking. Cake mixes and frozen carrot cubes saved time and labor. When soda (or tonic, as we called it in New England) was first mass-marketed, no one questioned whether it was good for you or not. We just drank it. Who would ever have thought that our modern, clean, safe, vitamin-enriched, and fortified-12-ways food might be unhealthy? No one had ever even heard of food preservatives or colorings, so how would we know enough to **worry about them?**

During the late 1960s, however, the kids who later grew up to become the Baby Boomers rejected that paradigm of progress as sterile and deadening to the soul. By the early 1970s, the back-to-the-land movement was in full swing. Young men and women, many of whom had never even set foot on a farm or touched a live cow—pilgrims in search of authenticity, community, and communion—set out in their Volkswagen microbuses for the backwoods and backward places between the cracks and beneath the radar, to "live off the land."

Each of these modern pioneers, no matter how much or how little they thought they knew about nutrition or growing food, had a philosophy (a religion really) about their rightful place in the food chain. There were the Vegetarians, who did not eat animals (the Vegan "higher beings" among them also eschewed eggs and dairy); the Macrobiotics, who lived on brown rice and not much else; devotees of the Raw Food Diet; consumers of only nuts, seeds, and berries; advocates of cleansing diets and colonic enemas; proponents of the benefits of spirulina and wheatgrass; and those extremists who believed that, once they attained the required level of spiritual development, they could photosynthesize and live on nothing but water and sunlight.

The common thread that bound all of these diverse views together was the belief that there was something wrong with the food that everybody else ate, and that eating right was one of the keys to living right. As these passionate advocates matured,

their views concerning dietary absolut-
ism mellowed. There may be slightly less
dogma these days, but there's still a lot of
fuss and fury over what one should eat.

Eating Native

There is a theory that posits people do
best when they eat a diet based on the
foods of their native land. The reasoning
is that different groups of people in different parts of the world evolved alongside
the foods of their region. Due to natural
selection, the most well-nourished groups
or tribes prospered, and their appetites
and dietary preferences passed on through
cultural evolution.

Following this logic, you could argue
that people of northern ancestry might be
healthier on a diet based on animal fats
(meat and dairy) and cold-adapted bland
vegetables like cabbage, potatoes, and
turnips, than they would be on a diet of
rice and fruits and small amounts of highly
spiced light meats or fish, a diet typical of
the tropics. There is some empirical evidence that supports this argument: When
the Pima Indians of southwestern Arizona
abandoned their traditional corn, squash,
and bean diet in favor of processed white
flour and sugar, they became morbidly
obese, with the highest rate of diabetes on
the planet.

Of course, things are more complicated than that. People have always moved
about—and in the age of air travel ex-
ponentially more than ever before—so
what diet should someone of Levantine
ancestral stock who grew up in Miami
favor if they're homesteading in Alaska?

We are northern people. Both of George's
grandparents were found under the cabbage leaves of the Polish countryside,
and Jane's father's ancestry was gloomy
Scotch-Irish and foggy New Brunswick
Micmac Indian. If there's a gene for meat
and potatoes, we have it.

Should Humans Eat Meat?

Let's ask Jane this one: I spent the summer and fall of my 18th year in the woods,
living in a canvas teepee that I made by
hand with a treadle sewing machine. (At
the time, I didn't realize that teepees were
designed for life on dry plains, not in
moist woods.) I hauled my own water
and, guided by Euell Gibbon's book
Stalking the Wild Asparagus (Alan C. Hood
and Company, 2005), ate only brown
rice, tamari, and whatever wild food I
could forage. I believed I was following
the fundamental macrobiotic rule, which
is to eat only those foods that are native to
your environment. Indeed, the wild leeks,
mushrooms, cattail shoots, and dandelion
greens I garnished on my brown rice were
native—but brown rice and tamari? Those
foods are cornerstones of a Japanese diet.
Rice was impossible to grow in New England, and soybeans nearly so.

It wasn't until I met George, who ate
the venison he shot on his own land and
the pork and lamb he had raised, killed,
and butchered with his own hands, that it
occurred to me that the concept of a truly
macrobiotic diet might be much broader
than I had imagined it to be. It may be
that for as long as people have been killing
and eating animals there have been veg-

etarians opposed to the practice on ethical and spiritual grounds. Today, in light of increasing awareness and concern about the evils of industrial meat farms, the toxic residues found in the most remote corners of the globe, peak oil, unchecked population growth, and impending water and food shortages, there may be more reasons than ever to question the morality, utility, and sustainability of eating meat.

Should humans eat meat? If so, what kind and how much? For many reasons, including health and environmental questions, many people seem to be turning against eating animal products. In certain politically correct circles, you have to justify why you are not at least a vegetarian, if not a total vegan. Everybody knows, it seems, that meat is full of artery-clogging cholesterol, nasty fats, and indigestible "toxins" that, even if they don't cause an immediate heart attack, will certainly retard your spiritual development. Corn-fed cattle are also high on the food chain, so eating beef contributes to world hunger by preempting land and water that could otherwise grow grain for human consumption. Now that we know that global warming threatens the continued existence of our species, we worry about the carbon footprint of all those herds of farting cows, pigs, and sheep. There's also the air and groundwater pollution caused by runoff from manure at feedlot operations. If those weren't reasons enough, there's also the immorality of the massive animal abuse that is endemic to CAFOs, the predominant method by which America raises its meat.

For the last 30 years, raising animals (and, therefore, eating lots of animal products) has been a central theme of our lives. If meat raised on a CAFO was the only meat we could get, I would still be the vegan that I was back in the 1970s. I don't believe I've succumbed to spiritual atavism or have abandoned my reasons for not eating meat back then. What's changed is that now I raise my own meat. Grass-fed beef is entirely different from agribusiness beef. It has far less fat, and the fat it does contain is biochemically different from the fat in grain-fed beef. Numerous studies support the hypothesis that CAFO meat may be a major factor in the current heart-disease epidemic.

Knowing how my meat was raised and slaughtered and how my vegetables were grown (whether it is food I grew myself or purchased locally) is more important to me than whether the food is organic or not. It is even more important than the issue of whether or not I eat meat. When you eat locally (how much more local can you get than your own yard or a step or two removed from the farmer next door or the village farmer's market?), you're supporting small farmers, butchers, bakers, your local feed store, and the restaurateurs who source local ingredients. You're supporting your neighbors and community, not some international conglomerate that is exploiting Third World farmland to sell you tomatoes in February. Your ethical footprint is lighter, and your carbon footprint is smaller, because you've eliminated the intermediaries. Because of your choices, there will be fewer refrigerated semis burning up miles of highways.

Balancing the Ecosystem

Raising meat and animal products in concert with garden vegetables, forage crops, and perhaps grains creates the balanced ecosystem known as a farm. A vegetable garden alone does not make a farm. You cannot grow vegetables on the same plot year after year unless the nutrients in the soil are replaced. Animal manure, for many reasons, is the best and most practical material for the job.

Animals add more than just fertilizer to the farm. If that was all there was to it, we wouldn't keep any animals of our own. We could simply haul in manure from someone else's farm (although this is getting harder to do cheaply, as more farmers realize the value of their "brown gold").

We feed our animals and keep them safe and warm through the winter. In return, we eat them or their offspring or drink their milk. Beyond just giving us food, animals give us clarity and relativity. When the wood shavings are fresh and deep, the chickens cackle and chuckle as they bury themselves in their new bedding. We see they are happy and we feel fulfilled.

On a bitter cold January morning, Number 9, our big Buff gander, dunks his head in the bucket of warm water we brought him. His beak knocks against the stainless-steel walls of the pail as he shakes his head from side to side (this is how waterfowl keep their nose and sinuses clean). He uses a lot of water and makes a huge, soggy, frozen mess. We don't eat

our geese, and although their eggs are four times the size of a hen egg, they lay too infrequently to sustain the kitchen. Instead, they earn their living by weeding the berries, keeping the lawns mowed, and intimidating strangers. The chickens, the geese, the goats, the pigs—together, these animals order our day. They are the axle on which the wheel of farm life turns. No matter what else is going on, no matter if you're happy or depressed, no matter if it's sunny or raining, the daily chores of caring for the animals must be done.

Animal chores are different from other farm tasks. Building a barn is done once. Planting the garden and getting in the firewood are seasonal tasks. Animal chores are done every day and at the same time every day. They set the rhythm of the homestead. No matter what else is going on, everything stops when it's time to do chores, whether there's been a birth or a death, on a lazy August afternoon or during a February blizzard. Then, when you are finished, and all of the animals are warm and fed, everything is as it should be—a good feeling.

One of the reasons that homesteading in general and raising animals in particular feel so deeply satisfying (despite the financial absurdity of the whole enterprise and the at-times-endless, mind-numbing, and back-breaking labor) is that farming connects you with cycles. It may be that the connection reaches us on some primordial level of consciousness, triggers a deeply felt need in the pituitary gland, the part of the brain that controls our biorhythmic clock. Farming is all about cycles: daily, monthly, and seasonal; animal, vegetable, water, carbon; birth and death. Because we ourselves are animals on the planet, we are part of the cycle. One living thing eats another. At one time, humans, like other carnivores and omnivores, were hunters.

vegan organic gardeners that, as an alternative to animal manure, promote heavy mulching, vegetal-based green manures, and compost that is free of all animal products. Theoretically, you could have a prolific garden without animal

 "Animals are such agreeable friends, they ask no questions, they pass no criticisms." —*George Eliot*

Ten thousand years later, we are farmers. We are still living within the same cycle—and if we destroy it, we destroy ourselves.

The Importance of Manure

A city dweller might wonder how anyone could rest against a cow's hairy flank in the barn, milking, or spend even a second longer than they had to in a chicken house. Aren't these places full of poop? Don't they smell? Well, yes, wherever there are animals, there is animal excrement, but farmers have a completely different attitude toward it than other people do. We don't think of manure as "excrement"—to a farmer, animal feces are a gift to be treasured, among the most valuable things on the farm, and a damn good reason to keep animals, even if you don't intend to eat the meat. Manure makes it possible to grow food, which requires fertile soil, which requires organic matter rich in nutrients. The best source of this organic matter is animal droppings.

Animal manure is the bridge between the animal and vegetable cycles that power the farm. There are organizations of

manure, but you have to be extremely attentive to your compost piles and leguminous green manure crops to succeed. Achieving the optimal carbon/nitrogen ratio for good compost, without the addition of animal manure, requires a highly sophisticated awareness of compost science.

Much of our land cannot produce anything but grass and weedy shrubs. In Vermont, pigs, chickens, and cows are easier to grow than soybeans. You might suppose we could cut the grass, compost it in large piles, and use that to fertilize our garden. It's a lot more efficient and easier to put animals on the grass, at the same time yielding healthy protein for us and fertilizer for the gardens and pastures. A single cow, contentedly chewing her cud over the course of the winter, will turn 200 bales of hay into nearly 12 tons of high-grade manure. That manure, mixed with sawdust or straw bedding and composted, is the key to improving and maintaining the fertile soil needed to grow healthy food for yourself and your animals—completing the cycle.

Having a steady supply of all the "free" manure you can use is definitely a good thing, but manure requires management. You need to collect it, store it properly to preserve its nutrients, aerate and turn it so it mellows, and then haul, spread, and till it into the soil. Even with a tractor, loader, and spreader, there's still an awful lot of wheelbarrow and fork work involved. Fortunately, for those of us who love keeping animals, a clean coop or barn is its own reward.

Can You Handle Commitment?

Animals need care several times (or at least twice) a day, and they prefer that you be on time about it. By nature, all animals want yesterday to be just like today and today to be exactly like tomorrow. In winter, our birds expect to be fed between 7 and 8 a.m., and in summer, much earlier. If we're late, two geese, three guineas, and two pet chickens are standing on the walkway at the door honking, screeching, clucking, and tapping their beaks on the greenhouse windows. They won't give up and go away—not because they're hungry (they have grain in their feeders), but because they want their morning treats (bread crusts, leftover rice, or, best of all, something green). Come summer, the routine changes. They have the whole farm to graze, so they're less interested in treats. Instead, at the first hint of daylight, they chorus, demanding to be let out of the barn. Of course, they're spoiled. Nevertheless, they have to be fed and watered at least twice, at more or less the same time, every day.

Most farm animals and, certainly, pets, will tolerate a bit of irregularity in their feeding schedule, although they may not like it. When you have animals that need milking, it's another story. Lackadaisical milking can cause mastitis and other serious problems for a milk cow or goat. Ultimately, all barnyard animals thrive when they have a predictable routine and feel stressed when they do not. Stressed animals are not happy animals, and unhappy animals will not thrive.

In some ways, animals tie you down even more than children do. They don't make car seats for geese or goats, so you can't just take them with you when you run errands in town (although we've been known to, upon occasion, take our pet rooster with us for a ride). Furthermore, it's much harder to find animal-sitters than it is to find babysitters. Just about any teenage girl loves to watch babies, but not quite as many want to clean out a chicken coop. Even if you are lucky enough to find a temporary farmhand who is willing and able to care for your birds, milk your goats, and feed the pig while stoking the woodstove, keeping the pipes from freezing, and watering the houseplants, there are consequences when someone else manages your livestock.

Animals become very attached to their people. New people make them nervous. A cow may not give even half of her regular amount of milk to a stranger. It's a given that your otherwise gentle rooster will attack the new guy. Hens, however, tend to be more forgiving. As long as their routine, especially the photoperiod, is unchanged, they'll keep laying eggs.

No matter how many details you include on the list you leave for your farm-sitter, it's guaranteed you'll forget to mention something important (like the fact that, if the trash is put out the night before it's picked up, the geese will spread it all over the yard before the garbage truck arrives). It helps to have your sitter do practice runs for morning and evening chores with you several times before leaving the sitter to handle things alone—but, keep in mind, it's unrealistic to expect anyone to take care of your animals as well as you do. It's hard enough to get a spouse to do the everyday chores the way you do them. Bottom line: If you find a good farm-sitter, hold onto him (or her).

Animals take over your life. If you like to travel, go out at night, or just laze about on weekends with little or nothing to do, *don't keep farm animals.* Keep a cat, or a guinea pig, maybe. You must want farm animals more than anything else, or you will be broke and unhappy, instead of just broke.

The Five Traits of Domestication

Domestication is not a condition that humans force upon animals. It's more like a partnership. Some animals have traits that naturally lead to domestication. There are 148 large terrestrial mammals on Planet Earth that could be considered candidates for domestication. Of these, there are only five major domesticated species: sheep, goats, pigs, cows, and horses. There are also nine minor species, which include water buffalos, camels (one-

and two-humped varieties), llamas and alpaca (which are actually two strains of the same species), donkeys, reindeer, and yaks. There are a very limited number of small animals, too—dogs, cats, guinea pigs, and rabbits. Of all the avian species on the planet, very few have been tamed: chickens, ducks, geese, guinea fowl, and turkeys (and parrots and a few other house pets).

The process started, probably with dogs, around 10,000 BCE. By 2,500 BCE, all of the animals that we keep today had been domesticated. No new species have been added since. After 7,500 years, there are still less than 20 species of animals living with humans. What makes these species unique? Why, for example, aren't there domesticated lions or penguins? There are five traits that successful candidates for domestication must share:

1. The animal must be an herbivore, or an omnivore that eats mainly plants supplemented with a side of insects or small rodents.

2. Their dietary preferences must be fairly catholic and nonselective. (Pandas and koala bears, for example, are herbivores, but they eat only bamboo shoots or eucalyptus leaves, respectively.)

3. The animal must be able to reproduce in captivity, grow, and mature quickly.

4. The species must live in herds, flocks, or packs and have a highly evolved pecking order.

5. The animal must be at ease with or at least tolerate humans. (There isn't a lot of physiological difference between a horse and a zebra, but zebras don't like people. They spit at us. They bite us. They would

rather die than let humans ride on their backs.)

Barnyard animals and garden plants are genetically programmed to live with humans, preferring the barn (or the garden) to the wilderness. They weren't forced into this partnership—it was a two-way street. There had to be mutual advantages if the arrangement was to succeed.

Some people want to "free" all animals—but how do they know that cows and horses want to be free? Domestic animals, with some notable exceptions (pigs come to mind) probably could not survive for long on their own. If we let all the cows free, most of them would not make it through the first winter. The ancestors of our big five domesticated species (and many of the lesser species) became extinct long ago, yet their domesticated progeny are thriving.

Goats, chickens, and cows do not pine for freedom. When they're left to roam, they never run away (unless they have been scared). They go to the garden or to some other animal's pen and try to squeeze in with them. Every farmer knows this. If your cow is not in her stanchion, don't look for her in the woods. Look in the goat pen or maybe the garden. If a goat gets loose and can't get back to the barn, it will stand at the kitchen window blatting until someone puts it back where it belongs. Barnyard animals don't want freedom. They want *comfort.* They want to eat hay and grain in a dry, clean barn. They want people to stroke them and talk to them. The closest thing to the type of freedom they yearn for can be found in a good, green pasture.

Many domestic animals even prefer people to their own species. Farm animals don't really know it, but they've made a bargain with us farmers. We eat their flesh and eggs and drink their milk and, in exchange, we agree to care for them, feed them, and protect them from harm. If we do it right, we give them a very pleasant life, with an all-you-can eat buffet, safety from predators and parasites, and shelter from cold. As Joel Salatin, a producer of meat chickens and author of *Pastured Poultry Profit$* (Polyface, 1996), says, his chickens only have "one bad day." If you're a chicken, that's not a bad deal, especially considering the fate of most breeding stock and egg layers.

Taking Care of Animals

If you keep animals, you need to take your half of the bargain seriously, which means learning as much as you can about the creatures in your care. Each species has its own specific needs, but the basics of animal husbandry are common to all species. All animals have five core needs: *food, water, security, comfort,* and *contentment.* These essentials are the same for every barnyard species—from day-old chicks to that old sow.

Most good farmers know that if you take good care of your animals they will take good care of you. You must develop a daily routine that helps you evaluate the status of your animals relative to those basic needs—all five, all the time. You can't ignore any of them. Come chore time, some you need to do immediately, others you can make a mental note to do later.

Chores are typically done twice a day. Our schedule more or less tracks with sunrise and sunset. Morning chores are later in winter, earlier in summer; afternoon chores, earlier in winter, later in summer. (Farmers really do work from dawn to dusk. Except for the 75 years or so since electric lighting broke the link between daylight and the workday, this arrangement was the only workable one for millennia, which is why it feels comfortable for animals and humans both.) When animals are in a vulnerable condition—very young, about to give birth, sick, or growing very fast—you may need to check on them three or more times a day. When I have day-old chicks or a sow about to farrow, I'll check them every hour or two.

In some cases, tending to an animal only once a day will suffice. For example, in spring and summer, beef cows set out to pasture with a good source of fresh water may just need a quick look in the evening before dinnertime. Once you get to know your animals, you'll instinctively know if their needs are being met. Without even really thinking, you'll be able to run down the list of five core essentials and know that all is well. If you think an animal is stressed and want to know why, just double-check the list. Does it have enough food and water? Is the temperature right? Does it have clean, dry bedding?

Food You should learn the specific nutritional requirements of each animal you keep and how they vary according to the season. You should also understand its growth and breeding stages. At every chore time, you must ask yourself, is there enough food of the right kind(s) to last until the next chore time? You must also check to see that the food is clean and accessible to the animal. If the same grain has been in the feeder for the last few days, you need to find out what's wrong. Has it spoiled or been contaminated with droppings? Is the animal unable to reach it or is sick and not eating? Healthy animals are almost always at least a bit hungry.

Water All animals need lots of clean, fresh water, served at the right temperature. Water buckets should be filled often and rinsed at least once a day and whenever you notice droppings in them. Buckets should be scrubbed clean with bleach at least once a week. Along with algae, bacteria and other pathogens multiply rapidly in dirty water buckets—especially those used for chickens and turkeys.

Security Most farm animals need shelter at least some of the time. Shelter offers both comfort and protection from predators. Sometimes they'll need housing, other times, a fence will do, but usually you need both. We have had very good luck with electric poultry netting and have lost very few hens to marauders since we started using it.

The concept of protecting your animals from prowlers is simple, but no matter how good the shed, the barn, or the fence, you still have to close the gate, shut the door, or plug in the fence charger. Losing a favorite chicken to a raccoon because you "forgot" is a horrible feeling. Double-check security as the last thing you do before you leave the area. If, one time, you do forget to close a hatch or turn on the electrical fence, if you've otherwise kept a tight ship, predators will have already learned that they'll have no luck at your place and will likely skulk off in search of better pickings—but they never really give up entirely. They'll return from time to time to probe your defenses, so don't get too complacent.

Locating shelters and outbuildings close to your house also tends to keep all but the boldest predators away. A cat or two will keep mice and rats at bay (although it's not a great idea to keep a cat if you also have baby birds around). You should also get a dog. The yapping of our toy poodles is enough to chase off any skunks or foxes that venture too close to the barn. (Of course, a coyote would be delighted to come upon such tasty little snacks.) Any raccoon unlucky enough to encounter Big Dog—aka Odie, our German shepherd— would not live to tell the tale, however. Only a very wily or very foolish coyote would dare trespass on the dog's territory or threaten his chickens. Owners of farms and larger homesteads often keep guard animals like border collies—and some even keep llamas for the same reason. Think twice about these options unless you have a sizable herd. (The temptation to bring home a new and interesting animal is hard to resist.) The problem is that working dogs are smart, and smart dogs get bored when they aren't working, and bored animals can cause a lot of trouble.

Comfort There's a big difference between surviving and thriving. If you want your animals to thrive, you must keep them comfortable. Conditions that are too hot, too cold, dirty, or just generally unpleasant create constant low-level stress, which causes the animal to produce relatively high concentrations of adrenaline, the stress hormone. Adrenaline has powerful effects on metabolism and the central nervous system. Numerous studies have shown that increased blood levels of adrenaline slow the growth rate in animals by decreasing the levels of growth hormone. In addition, if adrenaline levels are high at the time of slaughter, the meat is tough, because adrenaline decreases the production of the proteolytic enzymes that break down protein.

Stress also causes poor egg and milk production, low birth weight, and other reproductive problems. Adrenaline makes the mucus membranes of the intestines more permeable and less able to prevent bacteria from getting into the blood stream. It also interferes with the immune system's ability to fight infection. As a result, stressed animals are at a much higher risk of getting infections and less able to resist them.

Contentment Contented animals are a farmer's ultimate reward. There is good science to back up the benefits of keeping your animals happy and content, although if you are devoted to them, nothing feels better. We want to keep the animals on our farm content because we like animals, and we're happy when they're happy.

Animals are content when they are free of stress. You might wonder, "How can I eliminate or minimize stress for

my animals when I can barely do that for myself?" Fortunately, the effort to do one helps with the other. First, you must learn what animals like and don't like. Basically, the things that make you happy and comfortable are the same things that make your animals happy and comfortable. They like to eat on time, be reasonably clean, and have a stimulating environment. They want to be warm when it's cold and cool when it's hot. These are the physiological basics. If you want to excel at your endeavor (and have a lot more fun to boot), you have to bump it up to the next level—the neurological level, or, one might say, the emotional level.

Temple Grandin is an autistic woman who has made her living translating the needs of animals into English. She tells us humans what animals feel and fear and how to put them at ease. Her theory is that the main difference between the way animals and humans think lies in the relative size of the neocortex, the part of the brain responsible for generalized thought. Animals have very little neocortex—in other words, all they can see are the trees, never the forest. (There is some evidence that autism may be related to a deficit in the human neocortex, which is why, Grandin claims, she is able to understand animals. She thinks like them.) In short, for Grandin and the animals she observes, the devil is definitely in the details.

....

Top: Tiny leghorn hens lay huge white eggs.
Bottom left: Olive with Ophelia and Desdemona.
Bottom right: New born pigs suckling.

In her book *Animals Make Us Human* (Mariner, 2010), Grandin says that "all animals and people have the same core emotion systems in the brain." These core systems, as described by neuroscientist Dr. Jaak Pankseep, are "seeking, rage, fear, panic, lust, care, and play." The rules are simple: Don't stimulate rage, fear, or panic. For example, a small change in an animal's surroundings, which a person might not even notice, can trigger a sudden paroxysm of fear and rage in an otherwise placid animal. The systems you can stimulate are seeking and play. There's a world of difference between an animal that's confined to a sterile pen and one that receives daily attention from its caretaker or is allowed to forage and free-range with others of its kind. Care and lust take care of themselves.

Often, what we think is the root cause of an animal's problem behavior isn't, and this misunderstanding can make the problem much worse. Luckily, you don't need to be autistic to gain some insight into animal behavior. It's pretty easy to grasp the importance of satisfying the five basic needs, stimulating positive emotions, and attenuating negative ones. A keen eye is a good tool. Spend time every now and then just watching your animals—for maybe a half-hour; an hour is even better. You have to know how your animals act when they're happy and healthy before you can know when they're not.

Listening and watching animals is one of those Zen things, a meditation that you can't learn from any book. Granted, some people are naturally better at understanding animals than others. The more you practice, the better you get. In the process, you'll learn a lot more than just how to feed a goat.

Keeping Boredom at Bay

One of the biggest problems with farm animals is that they get bored, especially when they're shut in during winter in the North or in the heat of the summer in the South. They get bored for the same reasons people do. When animals are on pasture, where they have space to explore, they stay out of trouble. Like people, animals like to have a certain amount of challenge and novelty (just not too much and not too suddenly). Some animals—cows, for example—don't seem to mind standing in the same stall month after month; for others (birds and pigs), it's a big problem. Bored chickens will actually kill each other just to have something to do.

The smarter the animal, the more easily it gets bored. The best thing you can do to prevent boredom is to give your animals enough space to do the things they naturally do. Chickens typically walk around pecking the ground and occasionally fly up into trees and bushes. Pigs are very curious and like to explore and discover; they also like to root up the ground looking for interesting things to eat—and delight in finding the best way to flip over a water trough to make a mud wallow. Cows like to graze and hang out together under shade trees. Horses like to run and to roll around on fresh grass. Goats like to browse shrubs and brambles and climb on rocks, tree trunks, and the hood of your pickup truck.

Animal husbandry books of our grandfather's generation often offer good advice on reducing boredom and stress. F. W. Woll's book *Traditional Feeding of Farm Animals* (Lyons Press, 2004), originally published in 1915, suggests building flats for sprouting rye or wheat to be feed to the chickens. Some old-timers insist that animals that receive a bit of green throughout the cold months seem happier and more productive because of the added vitamins and minerals in the greens.

Here are just some of the strategies you can use to combat animal boredom:

- Don't keep just one animal. If you can, keep two (of the same species). Ruminants (grazing animals, such as sheep, goats, cows) are hardwired to live in herds; when apart from others of their kind, they are on edge. If you can't have two of a kind, at least get a companion of another species. Wether (castrated male) goats are good for this purpose. You have probably seen a horse and a goat together in a pasture, keeping each other company.

- The more space animals have, the less bored they will be. If your barn is small, allow the animals to go outside as much as possible. When too many chickens are crowded together, they will solve the overcrowding problem by engaging in cannibalism.

- Put animals near windows and doors so they can see the comings and goings of the farm. Geese and ducks are more active in the winter than many other

"What is man without the beasts? If all the beasts were gone, man would die from a great loneliness of spirit." —*Chief Seattle*

animals. They seem to enjoy the snow and want to be outside most of the time. Keep them where penned animals can watch the show.

- If bedding is deep and clean, chickens and pigs will spend hours burying themselves and playing in it.
- Tempt animals with healthy treats that they'll have to work to get. Chickens will spend hours pecking at cabbage or winter squash that's been suspended by a string. Later, they'll continue to find the bare string endlessly entertaining.
- Introduce a new item into the pen regularly. It doesn't need to be exotic. Fresh hay is a big treat for chickens and pigs. Pigs also enjoy toys or anything else they can push around with their snouts. (Avoid too much novelty, however. Don't move animals between pens or coops or casually introduce new animals into an established group, or there will be a fight.)

Feeding Animals

Barnyard animals are either vegetarians or omnivores. The vegetarians are further divided into ruminants (which have four stomachs and chew their cud, like cows, sheep, and goats) and nonruminants (like horses and donkeys).

Chickens, turkeys, and waterfowl are omnivores. Geese may consume some bugs when they forage, but they don't really go after meat like the other fowl; they prefer green stuff. Chickens, turkeys, guinea fowl, and ducks, on the other hand, love all kinds of insects, particularly fat, juicy ones. Chickens especially enjoy meat scraps (even remnants of Sunday's chicken dinner), kitchen trimmings, and table scraps. Pigs, dogs, and cats are also omnivores, although left to their own atavistic nature, the latter two would probably be pure carnivores.

Understanding the digestive system of your animals helps you decide how to feed them. Of course, you can simply go to the feed store and ask for pig food, but what fun is that? More to the point, to keep your animals at their best and to keep their production high, you should know something about their nutritional needs (although you can learn quite a bit by talking to workers at the feed store and by reading grain company pamphlets). Here are the basics.

Vegetarians Vegetarian farm animals eat pasture, hay, and silage (a fermented, high-moisture fodder). Ruminants' complicated digestive system allows them to digest poor-quality roughage, so they can squeeze every molecule of nutrition out of plain old grass. Nonruminants may also require concentrates (high-protein feeds made from grains and legumes).

When the livin' is easy, horses, although they are nonruminants, do well on grass alone, but if they're asked to work or if the weather turns very cold, they need the extra protein and/or carbohydrates from grain supplements.

The macronutrients that farm animals require are the same as those that human animals require: protein, carbohydrates, and fat. Grass and grass products (hay and silage) are high in carbohydrates. Concentrates are higher in proteins and fats. Proteins support growth; carbohydrates and fat supply energy. The nutritional needs of an animal are based on its age and rate of growth, the amount of work it performs, the amount of stress it is under, and, for an adult female, where she is in her breeding cycle. A growing, pregnant, or lactating animal needs more protein. Working animals—and, in winter, all animals—need more carbohydrates.

Omnivores Omnivores cannot digest grass as efficiently as vegetarians can, so they must be fed differently. You can't raise chickens and pigs on just grass and hay (or, to a lesser extent, waterfowl, although geese and ducks will eat almost nothing but grass all summer). These animals must have feed that has more concentrated nutrients—usually grain, but also certain plants or root crops.

Omnivores should still be pastured. They will eat quite a bit of grass and will also find other foods, like insects and roots. Even with pasturing, two-thirds of their diet should consist of concentrates. Think of the pasture as a diet supplement. Studies back up the anecdotal evidence that a pasture-based diet boosts the animal's immune system, reduces parasite loads, and produces superb-tasting meat (these ideas form the basis of the notion of *terroir*, the idea that food's flavor is greatly influenced by the microclimate and other idiosyncratic attributes of the region in which it was raised).

About Feed

Although we often use the terms interchangeably, animal feed (or ration) and animal grain are not really synonymous. Feed is a mixture of grains, vitamins, minerals, and meals (for example, cottonseed meal, soy meal, or blood meal). Animal feeds are formulated intentionally as a nutritionally complete diet. Grain is just that: oats, corn, barley, etc., with no additives.

Most farmers these days give their animals premixed feed. Some have their ration custom-mixed by the grain dealer, if they have the multiton order required to qualify. Others mix their own custom formulations. There are plenty of recipes available if you want to make your own, but, in most cases, the process isn't practical for the small farmer. Although you can buy all the grains and supplements individually, the powerful mill you'll need to grind several hundred pounds of grain in a reasonable amount of time is expensive. Less-costly motorized or hand-powered grain mills are just too small for anything but kitchen use. Small farmers also don't typically qualify for bulk-delivery discounts, but you can easily store all the feed that you can use before it

Going Organic

Should you buy organic feed? Organic feeds typically cost almost twice as much as non-organic feed, which might not be a consideration if you are raising just a few animals for your own freezer. Many folks who manage the rest of their homestead organically buy nonorganic feed to avoid the extra expense.

If you're raising a fair number of animals to sell, the premium you'll need to charge in order to return a worthwhile profit can definitely price you out of the most accessible markets. Before you decide to produce organic meat or not, study your market and calculate your production costs very carefully to see if the numbers work. You may discover a high-end niche that hasn't been already tapped. Or you may find there are a lot of customers who will buy a less costly product that's "all natural" and locally produced using sustainable practices. (We switched from growing organic to "all natural" pastured poultry for this very reason.) Whichever way you decide to go, you won't taste any difference between the two feeds in the finished product—but the taste of organic, moral superiority may be sweet enough for you to justify the cost.

goes stale in a few 55-gallon plastic drums or extra-large garbage cans.

In most cases, there are only two things you absolutely should know about a commercial feed: the percentage of protein and whether or not it contains antibiotics. The protein percentage is often closely associated with the product's name. (For example, in Vermont, Crunchy 16 is a popular dairy-cow feed, a bovine granola of grains, molasses, and other additives that contains 16 percent protein. When I ask for Game Bird 22 to feed my fast-growing chicks, the folks at the feed store know what I want.) Most "starter" rations, especially those intended for poultry, are prophylactically medicated. Medicated feeds have no place in sustainable, "all natural" farming.

Different parts of the country utilize different feeds and grains—and even different methods for feeding farm animals. In addition, different breeds of the same species may have differing nutritional requirements. Also to consider are the needs of the individual animal. Your local county extension agent would love to discuss your feeding program with you. Most animal enthusiasts are eager to talk about this subject, too, so learn more by finding a club, magazine, or blog devoted to the breed.

Animal Choices

You may think that having only a small piece of land limits you to raising small animals like chickens or rabbits—but there is only so much chicken and rabbit a person can eat (in Jane's case, the amount of rabbit is zero). With a plot as small as $\frac{1}{3}$ acre, you can raise a couple of pigs and even a veal calf if you so desire. Both types of animals can be raised quite easily in a small space. (Raising veal calves doesn't make much sense, either ecologically or economically, unless you live close to a dairy farm and can get culled milk for free or nearly so. The taste of homegrown veal is so matchless, however, that the project is worth considering—just think of it as a luxury indulgence.)

Urban Homesteading

Before you decide to keep a small flock of egg layers or meat birds, check your town or city ordinances (many municipalities post their laws online). Most zoning ordinances draw a distinction between domestic animals and household pets, prohibiting the former except in areas that are specifically zoned for agriculture. The laws vary widely. For example, in New York City, chickens are classed as household pets, so you can keep as many as you please, as long as the neighbors don't complain. The city considers the duck a domestic fowl, however, and therefore quacka non grata, one might say.

Quite a few municipalities allow a small flock of four to six hens, but most prohibit roosters. There are often setback requirements for the placement and design of coops, which—due to the small size of city lots—effectively rule them out. Some cities impose other specific and rather quirky restrictions. Miami, for example, abhors chicken droppings so much that it requires them to be collected and disposed of in plastic bags twice weekly.

The same patchwork quilt of regulations governs the keeping of other small domestic animals, such as rabbits, which are arguably a more manageable and productive source of meat than chickens. Some cities will permit you to keep a dairy goat or two; others will allow a combination of four or five domestic animals.

Suburban Homesteading

As with real estate, when it comes to backyard farming, it's all about location. My eldest son lives on a quiet street in a hillside neighborhood of nice homes on small lots in Santa Barbara, California. He keeps a small flock of chickens and a few turkeys in his backyard and could (should he be so inclined) also keep a pig. His neighbor on the next street is not allowed to keep any domestic animals at all. The reason? My son lives in the unincorporated county, whereas his neighbor's house is within the city limits.

If you live in a community that prohibits the keeping of domestic livestock, you could try to change the law, but be forewarned—it won't be easy. You'll be bucking 150 years of tradition. Zoning laws were originally enacted to clean up cities and suburbs that were overrun with noisome livestock and their excrement (not altogether unreasonable when you consider that in 1859 the population of Manhattan included some 50,000 hogs). Your best bet is to join or create a grassroots organization to lobby officials to change antilivestock ordinances. Many municipalities are already reconsidering existing prohibitions, due to the burgeoning backyard chicken movement, so it's a good time to start your campaign (www.madcitychickens.com provides a helpful guide for effective action).

The Mini-Farm

If you intend to produce meat, eggs, dairy products, and vegetables or other value-added products (such as jams, jellies, sauces, and baked goods) for sale—either wholesale to restaurants or other institutions or retail at a farm stand or farmer's market—check with your state's agricultural department first to find out what licenses you'll need. You'll also need to know the rules and regulations that apply to the handling, processing, and labeling of your product. Regulations vary considerably from state to state and from product to product. For example, in Vermont, we can sell to restaurants and farmer's markets up to 1,000 whole birds of any species that have been raised and processed on the farm, exempt from state inspection (but must state so on the label). All other meats must be processed by a state or federally inspected facility. Vegetables and eggs are usually subject to less-stringent regulations than meats and dairy products (raw milk, which is unpasteurized, is still illegal to sell in many states).

If you plan to market products that you make in your kitchen, you'll need an approved commercial-kitchen setup. If you plan to promote your farm products as organic, you'll need to be certified—a costly and time-consuming process. In most cases, labeling specifications are very exacting. You can't just claim that the meat you're selling is "all natural" or "pasture raised." You (or, actually, one of the several businesses that exist to provide this service) must submit to the USDA for approval an exhaustive affidavit detailing your feeding and pasture programs along with a sample of your proposed label.

You may find your state agricultural department to be extremely helpful and supportive of your attempt to market your products, but they won't take kindly to the willful disregard of regulations designed to protect the public. So do your homework.

chapter xii
....

Chickens:
The Gateway Critters

Grow vegetables and you're a gardener. Add a few chickens and—whether you live in the country or the city—you're a homesteader (or at least you're on your way). Chickens are my favorite farmyard critters. I can't imagine a satisfying life without them. Whether as pets or production animals, they reward you for your labor many times over. There's just something about them. They aren't very smart, but they know enough to return to their coop every night at exactly the same time. They don't have expressive eyes like Jersey calves do, but somehow they let you know when they are contented or flustered, hungry or satisfied.

Small in size but large in presence, chickens inhabit the heart of the farm. There's hardly a home or farmstead that does not have at least a few chickens strutting around like barnyard royalty. Even on a place with quite a few chickens,

....
Top left: Chickens have keen eyesight and don't miss much of what's going on around them. Top right: Chickens at play. Bottom: A red "production" layer.

you'll often find a couple of favorite "pet" chickens. Lucy and Eunice, my special hens, roam wherever they please. They sleep with the geese in the garage rather than in the coop with the other 200 or so working girls whose eggs we collect daily and sell. Then there's Newton, my White-Crested Black Polish Rooster, with his metallic green—black suit and foppish (and floppish) white top hat. Jealous of his finery, the other chickens peck relentlessly at his topknot until he's bald and bloody. Banished from the general population and too skinny to make a good soup, Newton has become our house chicken. He keeps me company when I'm working at my desk. He perches by the bookshelf, studying the titles, muttering to himself and, every now and then, crowing as if he's found something interesting.

We can't possibly tell you all there is to know about chickens within the pages of this book. Our goal is simply to get you started and then point you toward more information. Fortunately, you don't need to know a lot to begin. Many people who

Helpers in the Garden

Chickens not only provide food—eggs and meat—they also produce very "nutritious," high-nitrogen manure (on average, 95 lb. per bird per year). Properly managed, the manure and bedding from the coop have the ideal carbon/nitrogen ratio to make superb compost. Your chickens will be delighted to help you process it. Turn them loose on the compost pile, and they'll spend the day scratching, turning, and aerating every square inch, shredding coarse material into fine, adding a bit more manure as they search for insects, weed seeds, and other delicacies.

Don't let their usefulness seduce you into letting your chickens into the garden proper, however. True, they'll devour bugs and snails, but they'll also sample your tender young veggies and ripe tomatoes, uproot seedlings, and take dust baths in your carefully prepared seedbeds. On the other hand, if you give your flock the run of the garden *before* you plant, they'll clean out the weed seeds, grubs, and larvae of insect pests while also tilling under last year's rotted mulch. They'll be happy to provide the same valuable services after your harvest in the fall.

don't know much about chickens raise them quite happily. If you are the kind of person who just wants a few eggs and minimum fuss, you'll love chickens. They are very hardy and will probably survive all but the most egregious or irresponsible mistakes that you'll make as you learn.

To start, just get a few birds, house them where they'll be safe from predators and out of the rain and wind, and give them fresh water, some commercial feed, and all the table scraps they can eat. Let them out into the world as much as possible so they can eat bugs and green stuff. A small farm flock is susceptible to very few diseases, and most of them can be prevented by ensuring good hygiene and basic biosecurity protocols (such as avoiding contact with other people's flocks).

That's pretty much what you need to know to begin, but chickens are very amenable to finicky care, too. Many chicken people like to develop their own feeding mixtures and breeding programs, for example, and keep tight control over every aspect of their charges. Take your pick as to the best approach for you. If you want to learn more, you'll find lots of books and websites that provide helpful information. Reading books and magazines and surfing online sites and blogs are all good ways to learn. Finding a mentor or joining a chicken fanciers' club is even better.

All barnyard poultry are resilient and will survive while you learn. Just read up as much as you can, use your common sense, and take the time to enjoy watching your hens scratching and clucking in the yard.

Buying Chickens

The first question people who want to raise chickens ask is, "What kind of chickens should I get?" There's no easy answer. The decision, of course, depends on what you want and need—but that answer still only helps you narrow the choices. Picking the right chicken is like picking the right car. The breed you ultimately choose depends on what you like. There are significant differences in the basic traits of chickens: temperament, productivity, appearance, and egg color among specific laying breeds. There is no one best chicken for everyone, but a novice can't go too far wrong sticking with the most popular breeds—there are good reasons for their popularity.

If you've never kept chickens before, you might think you can compose a flock by simply browsing through the pages of a poultry catalog and ordering some interesting-looking birds. Some black ones, some red ones, or maybe one of those birds with the feathery legs. You could indeed do this, but if you base your selection on appearance alone, you might be very disappointed when those chicks grow up.

For example, Mediterranean breeds, like the Golden Campine or Blue Andalusian, are often strikingly beautiful, but they are rather skittish and will never really become completely tame. Convincing my six Campines to live in the chicken coop was a struggle. Unless there's a blizzard or driving rain, they prefer to sleep high up in a tall spruce and would rather forage than eat grain from the feeder. Supposedly, they lay white eggs, but I wouldn't know because I was never able to find where they laid them. These birds are exquisite creatures, however, and I enjoy the challenge of gaining their trust. At the other end of the spectrum, the English and American breeds (Araucanas and Speckled Sussex, to name two) love to be the center of attention. Eunice, my pet Araucana, lays her eggs in the mudroom and visits with me every day. (We and other chicken fanciers use the names *Araucana* and *Ameraucana* more or less interchangeably for just about any chicken that lays green or blue eggs. The actual pedigree of these two distinct breeds is complicated, but some strains of the modern Ameraucana may be distantly related to the South American Araucana, which doesn't have a tail.)

Not all chickens lay a lot of eggs, and not all chickens make a good Sunday dinner. Many chickens actually do neither. In fact, the fancier the bird, the less likely it is to produce food, as, historically, breeders were more interested in looks than productivity. The very fancy breeds, like the Phoenix and Cochins, aren't good layers or meat birds, and the miniature bantam breeds have one job—to be cute.

Still, many very attractive birds are productive. For example, Silver Laced Wyandottes and Araucanas are beautiful birds and also good layers. They are even passable meat birds. As in the realm of beauty pageants, raising chickens for show is a world unto itself, and one we have not been inclined to explore. So we will confine our remarks to the practicalities of meat and egg production. (Rest assured, however, should you become interested in

How Many Chickens Do I Need?

Chickens lay between 150 to 300 eggs a year. The production layers, of course, produce the most.

Figure about one egg every other day on average, if you provide extra daylight hours in the winter. If you just want enough eggs for your family, get one chicken for each person and then one more "for the pot," so to speak. If you want to raise your own replacements, get a rooster, too.

A 3½-lb. chicken will feed four people comfortably and leave nothing left over. So 50 chickens will give you almost one chicken a week. That's a good number for a family of four, if you don't plan on eating a lot of beef or pork.

an ornamental breed, there is sure to be a society or club or website devoted to it.)

Pure Breeds or Hybrids?

Once you decide what you want from your birds, the next step is to choose a breed or two. Sounds easy, but the process can be very confusing. To begin with, you have to choose between pure breeds (also known as heritage or standard) and hybrids. Think of purebred chickens as generalists, and hybrid chickens as specialists.

The differences between hybrids and pure breeds are more pronounced in the meat birds than in the egg layers. Both types are well suited to the home layer flock. Our 200 layers are evenly divided between hybrid "production" birds and pure breeds. We need the efficiency that the hybrids offer in order to make a profit, but we also like the hardiness and vigor of the purebreds.

Hybrids A hybrid is the by-product of the crossing of two different species—like a horse and a donkey to get a mule, for example. In the case of chickens, hybrids are the result of crossings of different varieties of the same species. Hybrid chickens are not as pretty as the pure breeds, and they lack the "cool" names and colorful pedigrees of their more aristocratic cousins.

Hybrids are bred either to lay a lot of eggs or to produce a lot of meat as soon, and on as little feed, as possible. Although they express desirable traits better than either one of their parents, they do not reproduce true to kind. In fact, much hybrid poultry cannot reproduce at all. Either they don't live long enough to breed (as is true of hybrid meat chickens) or they are too heavy to carry out the act of copulation (as are Giant White Turkeys).

So, if you raise hybrid chickens, you have to buy replacement birds from commercial hatcheries instead of raising them from your own eggs. Still, because hybrids lay so many more eggs and grow so much faster, it is difficult, if not impossible, to farm profitably without them. Factory poultry operations utilize hybrid birds exclusively. Given the conditions under which these hapless creatures are raised, it's not surprising that the resulting "product" is bland, tasteless, and unhealthy for you and the environment. When raised on pasture and unmedicated feed, however, these same hybrid birds yield meat and eggs that are just as tasty and considerably more tender than standard birds—and are incomparably better than commercial chicken.

A hybrid broiler (meat bird) grows to market weight in half the time of a purebred meat bird. More important, hybrids have a conversion ratio of two to one, which is much higher than that of any other breed. In other words, it takes only 2 lb. of feed to produce 1 lb. of live chicken weight. Hybrids grow fast because all they do is eat.

Unlike their purebred counterparts, these birds have no personality. They are incurious and barely scratch to search for bugs or seeds. They just want to eat grain, lie down for a while, and then eat more grain. Give them plenty of feed, and they'll grow incredibly fast (at the rate of about 1 oz. per day). Although you have to work at getting them to forage or eat greens and pasture, the upside is that their total lack of personality makes it easier to kill them when the time comes.

Pure breeds Pure breeds are categorized by place of origin and by size—light, heavy, and bantam. For all practical purposes, the terms *light* and *heavy* are synonymous with *small* and *large*—although these differentiations do not hold true 100 percent of the time. Light-breed hens weigh from 4 lb. to 5 lb., at most, whereas heavy hens generally weigh in at about 6 lb.

Pure breed are also categorized by class, according to their geographic origins: American, English, Continental, Asiatic, and Mediterranean. Generally, the breeds from England and America are heavy, and the breeds from Asia and the Mediterranean are light.

Purebred chickens are further identified by the color of their eggs (brown, white,

Approximate Growth Rate of Hybrid Broilers (in lb.)		
Week	Male	Female
1	0.31	0.23
2	0.89	0.67
3	1.80	1.35
4	3.08	2.31
5	4.51	3.38
6	5.91	4.43
7	6.70	5.03
8	7.50	5.62

or tinted), their type of comb (pea, rose, single), and their intended purpose (meat, eggs, dual). Knowing the basics of classifications will help you decide which kind of chickens to raise.

If you just want eggs for yourself and a few loyal customers, the pure breeds are a better choice than hybrids. They are more self-sufficient and can reproduce true to kind. Once you understand basic breeding principles, in three or four years you can develop your own strain to uniquely fit the microenvironment of your farm.

Light pure breeds The light breeds are, generally speaking, either show birds or egg layers. Most layers come from the Mediterranean and Continental classes; the light Asiatic breeds are usually show birds. Many Continental breeds are also ornamental breeds; Oriental breeds began as and remain ornamental breeds. All Mediterranean chickens (and most Continental) have white earlobes and lay white eggs. They are slender, quick-moving birds that are excellent foragers.

Heavy pure breeds By definition, all heavy breeds are meat or dual-purpose chickens. The heavy breeds mostly originated in England and America. Most of today's dual-purpose birds are descendants of the old-fashioned barnyard chickens of the 19th and early-20th centuries. Some heavy breeds were originally bred as table birds, but hybrid meat birds are so much more efficient that very few people still raise heavy breeds for that purpose. All of the chickens from this class have red earlobes and lay brown eggs. (Some, like the Speckled Sussex, lay light

brown eggs; others, like the Maran and Welsummer strains, lay deep chocolate brown eggs.)

Heavy breeds tend to lay fewer eggs than either the Mediterranean or hybrid production varieties, but they lay for a longer period of time. Although not quite as prolific as the hybrid types, which were bred for industrial egg production, they're ideal for a family flock. A good New Hampshire Red hen, for example, can be as fruitful a layer as a mediocre hybrid. Most heavy breeds are very docile and tame, which means they're easy to work with. They also winter well—especially the strains with tiny "rose" combs, which tend not to freeze.

Dual-purpose chickens are, by definition, big birds. They weigh more than 8 lb. at maturity and have deep, meaty breasts. Because a heavy purebred chicken takes at least 12 weeks to reach the same size as a hybrid does in 6 weeks—and because it's then older and closer to sexual maturity—the meat won't be as tender. What these birds lack in tenderness is made up for in fine taste if cooked with moist heat. You can cook (or pressure-cook) any tough old bird long enough to tenderize it, but there is nothing you can do to fix stringiness. We'll stew an old hen slowly with vegetables to make stock. (A skinny old Leghorn makes excellent stock.) We freeze or can the strained liquid and feed the solids to my animals. Everyone—from the dogs to other chickens—loves cooked chicken.

....

Top left: "George," our Cuckoo Maran rooster.
Top right: A Lakenvelder. Bottom left: A Lacewing
Wyandotte. Bottom right: A Welsummer pullet.

If you're raising meat birds for home rather than for market, heavy, dual-purpose chickens are a good choice. They don't lay as many eggs as the light or production breeds, but they lay enough and will continue laying for a longer period. A hybrid white-egg layer might lay 250 to 280 eggs during her first year, but she is likely to drop off sharply in her second year and even more so in her third year. As a result, many farmers, even with small operations like ours, replace their hybrid birds every year. On the other hand, although a heavy purebred chicken may lay only 180 to 240 eggs a year, she may very well keep up that pace for two or three years if supplied with good food, constant fresh water, and a large forage area.

Birds within a given hybrid strain have uniform habits. In other words, all the hens will lay about the same number of eggs, and all the eggs will look the same. Individual birds within a group of pure-bred chickens can vary quite a bit in their laying habits. For example, one may lay 180 eggs a year and another lay 250. Also, the eggs will be very different from each other in color, shape, and size.

One advantage of raising pure breeds is that you can replace and improve your flock with your own breeding program and eat the birds you cull. If you take the time to learn about chicken breeding, you can steadily improve your flock. Unfortunately, it is difficult to profitably produce enough eggs for market without at least some production hybrids, but we're working on it.

Bantams Lastly, we must at least mention bantams, the toy poodles of the chicken world. Typically, they are one-quarter to one-fifth the size of the standard varieties of whom they are miniature versions. Like their canine counterparts, bantams are all about personality. They are active foragers and famously self-reliant. Bantam hens are such devoted brooders that they are often enlisted to set and hatch clutches of eggs laid by more lackadaisical standard hens. They're also vigilant mothers to their own chicks.

Although you could certainly keep them for their small eggs, bantams are usually kept for show and as amusing barnyard pets rather than for utility. As in the world of toy-dog fanciers or the subculture of miniatures collectors, there are folks whose entire lives revolves around bantams.

Raising Chickens for Meat

In some ways, it's even easier to raise chickens for meat than to keep egg layers. For one thing, it's a short-term relationship. For hybrid broilers, we recommend slaughter at 4 lb. to 4½ lb. live weight. Dressed weight (the weight of a bird after it has been plucked, eviscerated, and cleaned) is approximately 75 percent of live weight, so the finished birds will weigh in at 3 lb. to 3⅓ lb., perfect for a roast chicken dinner. A well-managed batch of hybrid broilers on pasture will attain this weight in about six weeks, if you start with chicks. You'll only need a 10-ft. by 10-ft. space and/or small backyard. If you want bigger birds, just keep them longer (up to nine weeks). You won't save money

Cornish × Rock

The penultimate meat hybrid is the Cornish × Rock, a cross between White Plymouth Rock and Cornish. All the big hatcheries have their own strains of this hybrid. Our favorites come from Murray McMurray and Mt. Healthy.

For the first two weeks of life, the chicks look like fuzzy yellow Peeps® and are adorably cute, but that doesn't last long. As they grow, their features become coarse, and their carriage grows clumsy. By the time they reach slaughter weight, their white feathers have become disheveled, and they've developed such top-heavy breasts that they resemble wobbling bowling balls. Most people are repulsed by the Cornish × Rock when it is alive, but everyone loves this chicken when it's dead and on the plate.

Because of their preternaturally rapid growth, if not managed properly, these birds can develop deformed legs and heart problems. They are bred for a short life, not for the long haul. They lack endurance and vigor. This characteristic is another mercy that makes you glad to see them go. Their white feathers, yellow skin, and short blocky frame yield a carcass that is much easier to pluck (and looks much nicer in the package later) than the narrow-breasted and dark-feathered pure breeds.

All these traits add up to make an aesthetically challenged bird that grows fast and produces a very juicy, tender, and tasty meat for as little expenditure of money and effort as possible.

(compared to the cost of store-bought factory-farmed chicken), but the meat will be much tastier and better for you.

The hardest and, indeed, most unpleasant part of raising meat birds is killing and processing them. It's not so much the actual killing—that part is pretty straightforward and a lot less traumatic than killing a pig or steer—it's the processing. Getting the feathers off is messy and can be difficult or impossible if you don't do it just right. You have to dunk the carcass in scalding hot water, at exactly the right temperature, for the right amount of time, in order to loosen the feathers enough to pluck them. You pluck them either (laboriously) by hand or (quickly) by machine, but, either way, it's a chore.

You may want to try killing your own chickens yourself at least once. Before you go solo, however, we recommend that you offer to help someone who already knows the process. If you can't find that person, don't be afraid to stumble through on your own. It's not that hard. You'll figure it out, and the results will probably be edible.

If you prefer to avoid the whole mess, you can pay someone else to do the dirty work. It's fairly easy to find custom chicken processors, but that wasn't always the case.

Where to Buy Chickens

There are three places to buy chickens: your local feed store, your local farmer, and mail-order hatcheries. There are pros and cons to each source. We have bought from all three at different times for different reasons.

• If you want day-old chicks of an unusual breed, hatcheries are your best bet.

• If you want chicks of a common variety, check out your local feed store (availability may vary by location). Feed stores often have better prices than the hatcheries, and, if you get there early on delivery day, you might have "the pick of the litter." Whenever possible, we buy from our feed store, even if I can get the same variety online for a bit less. Buying locally is important to us, especially because we charge premium prices for our premium local product. Buying local is our way to complete the circle.

• Look for buying groups and farming organizations that pool their purchases. Sometimes these groups buy livestock together. Start your own group if you can't find one.

• Local farmers often have started pullets and older hens for sale. You can find small breeders and farmers through the American Livestock Breeds Conservancy (ALBC), in local papers, and online. Craigslist.com has a very active animal-exchange network that we use frequently. Again, be sure to follow good biosecurity protocols when buying and selling animals.

• February is not too early to be thinking about May chicks. Order your chicks early to ensure that you get what you want. The best hatcheries sell out early.

Hatchery chicks are shipped to your local post office, which will contact you to let you know that there's a chirping package waiting for you. Give the post office a call a few days in advance of delivery to give them a heads-up. Turn the heat lamps on and fill your waterers at least 24 hours ahead of the expected arrival date so that both the surroundings and the water will be up to temperature when you bring the chicks home. By then, the birds will have been without food, water, or heat for two or three days, and even though they appear lively, they'll be fairly stressed.

For a while, they were as scarce as hen's teeth. Now that more people are raising chickens, there are more people in the business of killing chickens. (*Mirable dictu!* That's just how capitalism is supposed to work.)

Our son, who keeps chickens in Santa Barbara, California, told us about a 16-year-old girl who bought a small scalder and plucker and went into the business of killing and cleaning chickens. Even though she charges a whopping $15 a bird (five times the usual fee in Vermont), she is so busy that customers have to make appointments months in advance. (If there are professional chicken killers in

Santa Barbara, there are probably chicken killers where you live, too.)

New chicken transport crates are pricey, so most folks borrow crates from a neighbor or even from the chicken processor—although this could be a penny-wise-and-pound-foolish economy. Unless the crates have been thoroughly disinfected between cargoes, you could introduce disease into the rest of your flock. (If you are only raising a single batch of birds, of course, this won't be an issue.)

The easiest way to catch the birds in order to get them into the crates is to first herd them in their pen. Then corral them into a corner with a piece of plywood and lift them out, one at a time, to a helper who will load them into the transport crate. Always handle the chickens as carefully, gently, slowly, and respectfully as possible—you owe them at least this courtesy in exchange for their gift to you. Calm them by holding them against your body, with their wings folded down. Never grab or move them by the wing or a single leg, both of which are easily broken. Don't pack more than 10 to 12 birds in each crate—they will already be so stressed that overcrowding could cause them to drop dead of heart failure, even on a cool day. Keep the crates shaded in hot weather.

In contrast to hybrid chickens, purebred meat chickens (New Hampshire Reds, for example, and any of the new boutique breeds, such as French Red Ranger) will spend time foraging for food beyond the grain in front of their beaks. Moreover, you don't have to worry about them doing something stupid like drowning in the water dish. Heritage breeds, however, take at least 12 weeks to reach their market weight and so tend to be tougher than the faster-growing hybrids. The meat will be a bit more tender if, instead of letting the birds range openly, you confine them to a small pen that you move about the pasture.

As long as you know how to cook them, hybrid and heritage chickens are equally delicious. We raise and enjoy both. At present, the market will not bear the cost of slow-growing heritage chickens. As a result, many pastured poultry farmers are trying to develop breeds that combine the best qualities of both hybrid and heritage breeds.

Building Your Egg-Laying Flock

When you're starting your laying flock, the big question is this: Do I start with day-old chicks, adult layers, or pullets at "point of lay" (when pubescent hens are just about to start laying)? Like everything else in homesteading (or in life, for that matter), it depends.

Chicks Starting with day-old chicks has several advantages. First of all, choosing chicks is fun, and you'll have a great variety of choices. You'll also get to know your flock from day one and can watch it grow. Kids get a big kick out of raising baby birds. Chickens raised by hand—especially little hands—are very tame, much easier to handle, and, therefore, worth their weight in gold. In addition, if you buy your chicks from a reputable source, you won't bring diseases onto your farm, which may happen if you get older birds (and their bugs) from another farm.

The main disadvantage of starting from scratch (as it were) is that you'll have to wait several months before you eat your first egg. Chickens begin laying when they're four to five months old, and it can take another month before they make full-size eggs. Pullet eggs (the small eggs laid by a young hen) are fine to eat, but they're harder to sell than large eggs. Regardless of its size, when you find that first egg, pillowed in the nest box like a crown jewel, you'll be as proud as the hen that laid it.

Caring for chicks does takes a little more skill than caring for grown birds. They need a dry, breeze-free, secure area that can be kept warm (95°F) for at least a month. For the first week or so, you also need to check on them three or four times a day. By the time you find that first egg, you'll have learned quite a lot about chickens and will feel justifiably confident in your ability to manage your flock.

Pullets If patience is not your strong suit or if you lack the facilities to brood chicks, you can also buy pullets, aged anywhere from 10 weeks to point of lay (about 17 weeks). At the time of this writing, day-old chicks cost about $2 to $3 each, depending on the variety, sex, quantity, and shipping method. An 18-week-old pullet could cost as much as $15.

The jury is out as to whether it is cheaper to raise your own birds from day-olds or buy pullets. There are arguments in favor of both positions, which leads me to conclude that it's another one of those "six of one, half-dozen of the other" choices.

The biggest drawback to buying started or grown birds, of whatever age, is the possibility that they may carry disease and parasites from someone else's farm to yours. If possible, before you buy, visit the farm from which you're getting your birds to observe the farm's biosecurity protocols. Some farms prohibit visitors, or the farm may be too far away to visit, but, in either case, try to find out what kind of a reputation it has. I once took birds from a hardscrabble homestead because I felt sorry for the overcrowded chickens. My sentimentality brought leg scales to my flock. It took a lot of work to get rid of the affliction. I won't make that mistake again.

Hens If you don't have an existing flock, you don't run the risk of contamination. If this is the case, you have an option that can get you started quickly and on the cheap. Start with hens. Some farmers replace their flock around the molt every year, and they might be willing to part with their "used but not abused" birds for little or nothing. If well managed, two- to three-year-old "rescue" hens still have a lot of eggs left in them—especially true in a backyard as opposed to a production flock.

While you're at it, buy a batch of day-old chicks. Or you could keep the hens until you feel confident in your chicken husbandry and buy the day-olds later. (You should keep the two groups separate, as explained on p. 326.) This approach will allow you to have eggs right away and build your own flock from scratch, too. By the time your chicks are ready to lay, you'll be an old hand at managing chickens. You can recycle the old girls into chicken stock or dog food when you move the youngsters into the scrubbed and disinfected coop to start laying. You could also keep the older hens, if they are laying well, and add pullets to the flock.

Living Accommodations

Chickens are arguably the most versatile animals on the farm (some argue in favor of the pig) and certainly the easiest to care for. They require only a small living area and the most modest accommodations.

Almost any outbuilding will do. You can retrofit almost any old building into a chicken coop for very little money or you can spend thousands buying or building a top-of-the-line chicken palace. We've done both, and find that portable coops are the most useful. A small fleet of coops on wheels (wooden coops built on old travel-trailer frames, like ours, for example) is more versatile than a large stationary structure. Portable coops allow you to rotate pastures and work the garden in the spring and fall. If your yard is large enough, the coops can stay parked most of the year but are movable if you need to clean or address unexpected problems.

Mount a nest box or two on the wall and set a perch 2 ft. to 4 ft. off the ground. A galvanized-steel 30-gallon garbage can provides rodent-proof storage for feed. A recycled metal cabinet, hung from a wall, makes handy storage for miscellaneous supplies. If you've got money to burn, you could buy one of the myriad movable shelters or prefabricated coops that are now widely available. Or, if you'd rather, you could build more-or-less elegant and spacious accommodations from the plans that are featured in most of the many books on chicken husbandry.

In our opinion, nothing beats an old travel trailer for cheap and serviceable mobile chicken housing. It can often be had free for the hauling if it's no longer roadworthy and will get you by until it rots away, at which time you can build a more durable coop on the salvaged frame.

Bottom line: If you have a square yard of extra floor space in your garage, you can comfortably keep three or four hens that would provide you with more than a dozen eggs a week. (They'll also appreciate a small fenced outdoor run.) Three or four birds cost almost nothing to keep. They'll need only a small amount of commercial feed and will eat almost any kind of table scraps. If allowed to range in the summer, chickens will hardly even touch their grain.

Trough space Chickens like to greet the sunrise and be outside at the first hint of dawn. They rarely eat or drink during the night, so they'll want some water in the morning before they head out to scratch and peck. Often, they'll skip their feeders in favor of foraging, especially when there's a new pasture to explore.

Chickens don't eat a lot at once; they nosh a little ration here and there all day. Nevertheless, provide plenty of trough space at the feeders, or there will be fights. Chickens are very cliquish; like teenagers in a high school cafeteria, certain hens won't eat with certain other hens. If you spend a little time watching them, it will soon be apparent who are the Cripps and who are the Bloods. If you have more than 10 hens, you'll need two small feeding and

Top: Cornish × Rock meat birds ready for transport to the slaughterhouse. Bottom left: Day-old Cornish × Rocks under the broader lamp. Bottom right: A couple of Speckled Sussex laying hens.

watering stations set at least 10 ft. apart. If you've provided enough space and distractions, there's less chance of war between the rival gangs.

Floor and perch space If your chickens free-range or if you have a large fenced yard and weather that allows them to be outside most of the year, their coop can be fairly small. They'll only use it to sleep at night and lay eggs in the morning, so a floor area of 1 sq. ft. to 2 sq. ft. per bird will suffice. If they must spend a lot of time confined, however, the more space you can give them, the better (10 sq. ft. per bird for confined heavy-breed chickens, for example).

For humane indoor confinement of even a fairly small flock of chickens, you should have a rather large structure—more like a hoop-house barn than a backyard coop. This facsimile of a "free range" will protect layers from weather and predators, but it's still better to let chickens outside as much as possible. Here in northern Vermont, we leave the coop doors open on all but the worst subzero or stormy days. The hens come and go as they please.

Whether they're inside or out during the day, most chickens want to perch at night. Like everything else chickens do, finding a place to roost is determined by the flock's pecking order. The highest roosts are the most prestigious, and so the top hens get

to sleep there. Add to each adult bird's floor-space allotment another 8 in. to 12 in. of perch space. Young birds need less, but only temporarily—even the slowest-maturing pullets are nearly full-grown in four months.

Pastures, Yards, and Fencing

In the early 1900s, all chickens were raised outdoors, often totally free-range, without fencing of any kind. Although the exact nutritional needs of poultry weren't known at the time, farmers knew that chickens needed "greenstuffs." Later research showed that laying hens did far better when allowed to forage a portion of their own food. They also found that, even without grass to graze, the chickens benefited just from being outside. Give your chickens the largest area you can.

Pastures and yards both serve as outside accommodations. Stationary henhouses typically have adjacent yards, and if there's enough area, pastures beyond the yard. Unlike yards, pastures have enough grass and other vegetation to provide some food for the animals. Without significant maintenance, after a while chicken yards can become barren lots of packed dirt that, when it rains, ripen into stinking, muddy havens for disease. Keeping yards clean is a challenge. Spreading a few inches of hay or straw will help. Replace the hay or straw with fresh material every few days and add the old material to your compost pile. Wash away any manure deposits on the lawn adjacent to your house with a hose to keep the grounds a bit cleaner.

Four-Door Chicken Coop

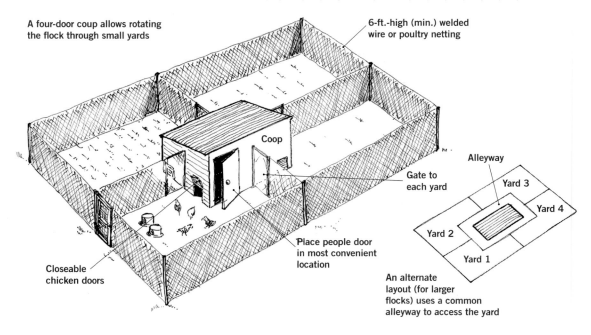

A four-door coup allows rotating the flock through small yards

6-ft.-high (min.) welded wire or poultry netting

Coop

Gate to each yard

Place people door in most convenient location

Closeable chicken doors

Alleyway

Yard 3

Yard 4

Yard 2

Yard 1

An alternate layout (for larger flocks) uses a common alleyway to access the yard

The key to maintaining sanitary conditions in a chicken yard is to set up a system of subyards through which the birds rotate throughout the summer, giving each area a chance to recover (see the drawing above). Provide the coop with two to four chicken doors, each opening into a different subyard. If you have space for only one yard, cover the ground with a thick layer of sand that can be washed down or raked from time to time.

If you have just a few chickens, let them range throughout your lawn and only fence them out of off-limit areas—like your young gardens, which they'll rip

up, trample, nibble, and otherwise wreak havoc upon. A few chickens (no more than four) ranging in mature gardens for short periods, however, can be beneficial for both the garden and the animals.

For larger flocks, good management requires a bona fide pasture and its associated fencing, range shelters, and sturdy feeders and waterers. Range fencing serves two purposes: to keep chickens in (although chickens only wander about 100 ft. from their shelter) and, more important, to keep predators out. Pastured birds need portable shelter and some sort of covered area for shade

> *"Chickens are very cliquish; like teenagers in a high school cafeteria, certain hens won't eat with certain other hens."*

and for protection when eating in the rain. Trees and shrubs will keep your birds out of the sun, but the areas around vegetation will get trampled and ruined if you don't rotate the birds often enough.

Chickens cannot sweat and so are vulnerable to heatstroke. If you see birds lying immobile and panting hard, they are too hot. Spray the area around the pen with a hose to cool them off. Be sure they have plenty of cold, fresh water, especially in the middle of the day. If there is no natural shade, you'll have to build it for them.

Inexpensive backyard shade canopies are ideal for providing shade (if you foreshorten the legs). To keep them from overturning in a strong breeze, anchor the canopy corners with tent stakes. (Don't try to employ the same structure to shade your turkeys, as we did. Turkeys have a passion for heights, and the flimsy pipe framework of our canopies crumbled under the weight of three or four half-grown poults as they attempted to roost on the canopy.)

Bedding Materials

Birds in confinement need bedding. It should be absorbent, inexpensive, plentiful, and readily compostable. It should also not pack down easily. We find that wood shavings make the best bedding. Wood shavings are the large curls and chips cut from planed boards. Although sawdust is easier to find, do not use it as bedding. Sawdust—fine, dusty wood particles produced by sawteeth—will irritate the birds' lungs.

We use our home office shredder to turn all our junk mail, scrap paper, and envelopes into bedding. Paper is not as absorbent as wood shavings—and leaves a lot to be desired in the aesthetics department—but it does break down rapidly in the compost pile and gives us the satisfaction of recycling on-site. Ground corncobs, rice and buckwheat hulls, and chopped straw are also good options. Use whatever is most available and cheapest in your area.

Instead of straw, we also use low-quality hay for bedding. Straw is the residue left after the seeds have been removed from grain crops. It has no nutritional value and, at one time, it was just burned in the field. Now that straw bale building is more common, baled straw is much sought after and pricey. Hay is dried cut-grass stems that have the nourishing seed heads still attached. Depending on the weather during the haying season, the price and availability varies greatly. If the hay is rained on before it can be properly cured, it spoils and is unsuitable for feed. Spoiled hay makes good bedding material and is also an excellent garden mulch. We use hay in the outdoor pens for the meat birds and for chickens we house on the ground. We also spread hay in front of the hen-houses to keep mud puddles from forming.

When I was a kid, straw and shavings were waste products—cheap and often free for the hauling. It was a big treat to go with my dad once a week to the local lumberyard where we would fill the dump truck with shavings and sawdust that the sawyer was only too glad to be rid of. Those days are long gone. Any kind of bedding material is expensive today. We use hay and wood shavings because that's what is locally available at the lowest cost. You can buy bales of straw or shavings from the feed store, but you'll pay boutique prices compared to the wholesale prices at your local sawmill.

Ask other farmers how they deal with their bedding. Unfortunately, you may discover that their solution only compounds your problem. They may have already contracted for all the shavings and sawdust the local sawmills produce. At best, you might get put on the bottom of the waiting list. In northern New England, you can buy shavings in bulk from Canadian dealers—but we're talking serious bulk, tractor-trailer-load minimums. Even if you pooled buyers, the average small farm or homestead can't store more than a pickup truck's worth of bedding at a time. So, feed-store shavings or spoiled hay may be your only practical choice. If you own a shredder/chipper that can handle the job, running the hay through the machine will greatly improve its absorptive capability.

Regardless of the type of bedding you use, it is critical to keep your animals very clean. Cleanliness is the number-one defense against disease. There are different schools of thought regarding bedding management and cleaning. One method is to shovel the bedding out on a more-or-less daily basis and replace it with clean bedding (the method typically used to keep large animals like cows and horses clean). The litter for baby chicks should be changed daily—and even more often for hybrid meat birds.

In the second method, called deep litter, you continuously add and mix new litter on top of the old litter and clean it out entirely only two to four times a year (see facing page). The deep-litter system is well suited for most poultry. For meat birds, however, you completely clean out the litter between batches of birds, so the bedding would never accumulate to any significant depth, as it does for laying hens. The method is also suitable for critters like sheep and goats, which produce dry, pellet manure. This method also works well with hogs, providing that the litter from the "bathroom" corner of the pen is removed daily. Lately, dairy and beef farmers have begun to utilize deep bedding management in free-stall barns to build up prodigious reserves of compost.

Chicken Feed

Feeding your birds properly helps them develop strong immune systems and promotes general good health. Always buy the highest-quality feed you can afford. Don't scrimp and buy the cheap stuff. Find other ways to economize rather than on nutrition. We fully support local feed

The Deep-Litter System

We use the deep-litter system in our henhouses because it keeps the coops clean with the least amount of bedding and bother. The system relies on a mix of bedding and manure to create a self-sanitizing compost system. Here's how it works:

1. Start with a clean coop.
2. Spread about 8 in. to 12 in. of new bedding material over the floor.
3. Mix in a few handfuls of garden lime or rock phosphate.
4. Add more bedding more or less every week. When you have achieved the proper balance, the litter will be fluffy and dry and (relatively) odorless.
5. Use waterers that limit the opportunity for spillage. (To prevent disease and anerobic conditions, remove soggy bedding under waterers as soon as it accumulates.)

Getting the balance right does require some trial and error and perseverance. Crowding too many chickens into too small a space can also affect the balance. Keep the birds outdoors most of the time, especially during the warm months.

Adequate ventilation definitely improves the balance at all times of the year. We've learned that, even in winter, so much heat is produced between the bedding and the birds themselves that we have to leave the coop windows open except on the most frigid nights. If we don't, the water vapor that our birds exhale condenses to form a fog that saturates the bedding, knocking the cycle off-kilter and kicking up the ammonia level. Usually, you can restore the balance by adding more shavings and lime. This system can require quite a lot of bedding material.

If you let the litter get too far off balance, you'll have no choice other than to clean it all out and start again. Ammonia is poisonous, and, if your birds are forced to breathe it, they'll develop major respiratory problems and could go blind. Fortunately, you can get your chickens to contribute to system maintenance by scattering some "scratch" feed (a high-calorie mix of cracked corn and other whole grains) and table scraps over the litter. They'll aerate the bedding as they scratch for their treats.

If your bedding is properly balanced, you shouldn't have to clean it out more than two or three times a year. Whenever you clean out bedding, be sure to scrub down the entire coop with a disinfecting bleach solution.

Don't bother using the deep-litter bedding system with hybrid broilers. They won't be in the picture long enough, and, furthermore, they produce so much manure relative to their size that it's difficult to maintain the chemical balance that the microbes need to do their job.

producers, but do your homework before you experiment on your animals. When in doubt, use a brand-name feed. Avoid medicated feeds. If you think your birds need an antibiotic, provide the drugs separately so you can control the dosage.

Always feed the bird the recommended amount of protein for its age. Birds like table scraps, but if they're getting a significant amount of scraps (bread from a local bakery, for example) in lieu of a standard ration of feed, you need to consider how that affects the overall percentage of protein they're ingesting. If the scraps are only served as treats, however—less than the flock will eat in 5 to 10 minutes—don't worry about protein levels.

Game-bird feed is both high in protein and free of medications. If you want to go organic, you'll be sure to get high-quality grain, but be prepared to pay about twice as much as for nonorganic feed. If you're already gardening organically, you might also want to raise your meat and eggs organically —which is easy enough if you are simply providing for your family and not raising poultry or eggs for market. In order for your products to be certified organic, you cannot treat your chickens to table scraps or let them forage on pasture, unless every morsel they eat is from certified organic sources. The certification necessary for legally labeling your produce as organic is an all-or-nothing proposition.

Commercial chicken feeds are available in three different textures: mash (fine), crumble (medium), and pellet (coarse). You can also buy whole or ground grain. Chicks should be fed either mash or crumble. Pellets are less wasteful for larger birds, because the birds tend to eat any pellets that fall from the feeders rather than tread them into the litter as they do finer feeds, which, it also takes them longer to get their fill of. For the first four weeks, you should feed all chicks, whether meat birds or layers, mash that is at least 22 percent protein. After that, their nutritional needs vary, although all chickens need fresh greens, fresh air, and fresh water.

If your birds eat only commercial mash, crumbles, or pellets, they need access to grit. Grit is pieces of small stone, usually granite, which stays in the chicken's gizzards, grinding food into small, digestible particles (chicken don't have teeth). Free-ranging birds naturally pick up enough grit as they graze.

Feeding egg layers Egg layers have special nutritional needs. Among them are calcium, vitamin D3, and vitamin A. These nutrients enable the chickens to make eggs while maintaining their own health. Indeed, these rules apply to all animals. When the animals are gestating (or lactating, in the case of mammals), the nutrients go to the offspring first. The mother's needs come second.

Good layers have a productive life of three or four years, although they have a lifespan of up to ten years. The various physiologic modifications they undergo during their lifetimes determine their nutritional needs. As chicks, they require a high-protein (20 to 22 percent) starter mash. At about six to eight weeks, switch them to a 14 to 16 percent "grower"

The Pearson's Square

The Pearson's Square is a handy device for calculating how to mix various feeds to get the desired amount of a given ingredient in the proportion you want. For example, you've been feeding your birds 28 percent protein crumbles and you want to lower the amount of protein to 16 percent because the birds are older and need less protein. You can add scratch that is 8 percent protein to your regular feed to make a 16 percent feed, but you need to calculate how much of each product you need to get the right mix.

A Pearson's Square lets you figure this out. (Or you can also use algebra, if you remember any of it from school.) Draw a square. In the center, write the percentage of protein you want your finished feed to have (16 percent, in this case). In

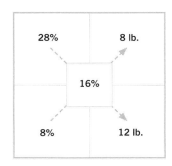

Center square = desired % of protein in finished mix

Upper left = % of protein in current feed

Lower left = % of protein in supplemental feed

Lower right = amount of original feed to mix

Upper right = amount of scratch feed to mix

the upper left corner, write the percentage of protein in the feed you are using (28 percent). In the lower left corner, write the percentage of protein in the scratch you are going to add (8 percent).

Now move diagonally downward, from upper left to center, subtracting the lower number from the higher number. Write the total in the lower right corner. Then move diagonally upward from left to center, subtracting the lower number from the higher number. Write the total in the upper right corner.

The number in the upper right corner will give you the parts in pounds that you need of the original feed (8 parts, or 8 lb.), and the lower corner will give you the number of parts in pounds (12) of the scratch feed to add. So, in this case, you need 8 lb. of 28 percent feed and 12 lb. of 8 percent scratch to yield 20 lb. of feed that is 16 percent protein. Don't try to substitute volume (for example, number of scoops)—this calculation works only by weight.

ration. Alternatively, you can add whole oats or scratch to the starter feed at about a one-to-one ratio. Use the Pearson's Square, described above, to figure the exact mix for the ingredients you have.

Once pullets start laying, their protein needs ramp up to about 16 to 18 percent.

As the birds mature, you need to reduce the amount of protein in the feed to prevent the pullets from growing too fast, which could cause them to begin laying before they are fully mature. If their feed is too high in carbohydrates and too low in protein, they get fat and become poor layers of small eggs. If their ration is too rich in protein, their overall health suffers, and they are at risk for prolapsed uterus, which marks the end of their egg-laying days.

There are many brands and types of chicken feeds available for layers. They differ according to geographic area and the prevalence of poultry farming/business in that area. Most brands have their own feeding regimen, and your feed store staff can explain the specifics. At my store, I always talk to Emily about every new animal I get. (Besides learning a lot about feeding animals, I'm updated on the latest gossip—the real "local" news.)

Well-fed birds are healthy birds, and healthy birds are productive birds. Eggs are mostly protein and fat, and, without an adequate intake of both, your hens cannot lay. Weather also affects how the birds take in these macronutrients. In hot weather, hens won't eat as much as they normally do, so their total protein intake decreases. If you live in a region where long hot summers are normal, increase the protein content of your feed to ensure that, even though they are eating less, your birds still get the total amount of protein they need. Switch from your standard layer ratio (16 percent) to game bird feed (typically around 22 percent) and supplement the feed with some added calcium and vitamin A for the season. If you live where summers are cooler, you can simply throw your hens a little super-high-protein cat kibble and oyster shells (which are high in calcium) during that week of hot weather in August.

Extra nutrients All layers need extra calcium and vitamin A, and a good com-

mercial layer mash contains both. (An eggshell is nearly 100 percent calcium, and the shell is 10 percent of the egg.) You can start your pullets on layer rations any time after 18 to 20 weeks to ensure a maximum store of calcium for egg production. Think of the early start as prenatal vitamins.

There are times, however, when your hens may need supplemental calcium. Hot weather, the rate of egg production, and a decrease in storage capacity of the hen may all lead to a need for increased calcium. To be on the safe side, provide extra calcium in the form of oyster shells, so the chickens can feed "free choice," eating as much or as little as they want. Alternatively, you can add oyster shells to their feed. Some people save their eggshells, dry and pulverize them, and feed them back to their chickens. The shells must be finely ground so the hens do not recognize them as eggs, however. Otherwise they'll get into the habit of eating their eggs before you get the chance to eat them. Some people caution that chickens will suffer if fed a high-calcium diet before they begin to lay. This is nonsense. Chickens have kidneys, and kidneys easily excrete any "extra" calcium. Roosters, who, as we know, do not lay eggs, eat the same feed as layers and appear no worse for it.

Chickens, just as we do, also need vitamin D3 to utilize calcium, and they need vitamin A to make good egg yolks—both of which they get from greens and sunlight. Chickens love to eat table scraps, greens from the garden, fruit (especially anything red), meat, and bones. In the summer, these treats are easy to provide.

Come winter, it's a bit more challenging, especially if you have more than just a few hens. Growing extra cabbage and winter squash is one solution. A head of cabbage suspended inside your henhouse in the morning will be gone by evening. Cut a squash in half and lay it on the floor, seeds and all. For an extra-special treat, cook the squash in the oven or microwave first and watch the birds celebrate. These extra nutrients will keep your hens healthy and the yolks of their eggs bright yellow all winter.

Farming books from the early 1900s describe farmers growing barley and rye grass shoots in sprouting trays for flocks of 100 to 200 hens. Can you imagine commercial egg producers today going to that much trouble for their hens? Farmers at that time believed that greens and sunlight were essential to keeping their flocks in peak condition. They were right.

Keep an eye out for off-homestead sources of chicken food, too. Cheese producers, especially the small artisan producers that are popping up everywhere these days, need to get rid of their whey. Chickens love whey and all dairy products. Sometimes restaurants and bakeries will let you have their leftovers. Contrary to popular belief, chickens are not vegetarians —after all, they eat bugs and just about any other small creature they can catch—and they love meat scraps. A supply of clean meat scraps will save a lot on your grain bill, as meat is largely pure protein, the most expensive part of any ration. Thoroughly cook any animal products before feeding them to your chickens. When we slaughter our meat birds, we save the livers (there's only so much chicken liver we can eat or give away) lungs, hearts, gizzards, and necks. We boil them and toss the scraps into the laying-hen yard. When they see George approach, carrying a black-enameled pot, every bird in the coop drops what it is doing and rushes the fence.

All animals, including chickens, need more energy to stay warm in winter. Carbohydrates supply the extra boost. Add carbs to your hen's diet by giving them some scratch (cracked corn mixed with whole oats and barley) or just plain cracked corn as a bedtime snack. If you scatter the grains over the litter instead of putting them into the feeder, the chickens will turn over the litter as they "scratch" for the grains, helping to keep it loose and dry.

Chickens will not overeat. Keep feeders full and check as often as required to ensure they do not run out of food or clean water. In hot weather, birds drink two to four times more water than they do in moderate temperatures. Chickens are fussy—they will not drink water that is much over 50°F to 55°F. They would die of dehydration standing next to a full pail of warm, dirty water. So check and change water often in the summer. Keeping water in the shade is a surprisingly effective approach. In winter, keep water from freezing with one of the many heating devices available. In a well-insulated coop, the body heat produced by a flock of chickens is more than enough to keep their water from freezing, except on the coldest nights.

Day-old chicks explore their world.

Is it enough? How can you tell if you are feeding enough of the right stuff to your birds? Simple. They grow. Just watching how they grow isn't enough, however—they can fool you. If they stop growing or are growing too slowly, you might not detect it until it's too late. Weigh a few pullets every week or two and record the results until they are fully grown. Animals that are growing at the expected rate are almost certainly healthy. Light breeds eat less than heavy breeds by about 1 oz. a day, and laying hens eat twice what a nonlaying pullet eats. For example, a Leghorn pullet eats about 2¹/₂ oz. of feed a day. At full production, she will eat 4 oz. As a pullet, a dual-purpose hen eats 3 oz. a day; when she starts laying, she eats 5 oz. a day.

Caring for Broilers

Broilers simply do not tolerate stress, so do not overcrowd your birds. We raise no more than 100 birds per batch, and we put them outside as soon as possible. We find they do best if they always have food and cool water, light, and warmth. The biggest (fastest-growing) birds tend to be the most trouble free.

As do all chickens, broilers like to perch. They're too heavy for standard perches, however. They like piles of hay or logs laid on the ground or wide boards set 3 in. or 4 in. off the ground. You can raise broilers indoors for their entire 6-week lifespan, or you can put them on pasture after 2 or 3 weeks. Broilers kept indoors require more attention—it's not uncommon to add clean bedding two or three times a day; if they're outdoors, add bedding once a day.

Broilers raised in confinement need a minimum of 1 sq. ft. per bird—and 2 sq. ft. is better. Standard-breed broilers will not thrive if kept indoors in such cramped quarters for the 3 months they need to reach finished weight, however. They do best if they have a small house, just large

Heat Lamps

Be very careful with heat lamps and don't take shortcuts. Never put an infrared bulb into a plastic socket. Use only porcelain sockets; standard sockets cannot withstand the high temperatures. Make sure that the lamp is hung securely, but surround the bulb with a guard to protect the chicks and bedding if the light should fall. I learned this the hard way. A carelessly hung heat lamp that had no bulb guard fell, fried a couple of hapless chicks, and nearly burned down the barn. It's a horrible feeling to kill an animal, even one little chick, because of negligence.

enough for them to roost at night, and a yard that gives them 2 sq. ft. to 3 sq. ft. per bird. Ideally, any such house and yard should be movable so your birds have plenty of opportunity to forage.

mals, and chickens are no exception. The management of your flock at this stage is called brooding. If a mother hen does it, it's called natural brooding. If you do it, it's called artificial brooding. Obviously,

"Victor Borge had just completed the purchase of a chicken farm. 'Do you know anything about breeding chickens?' asked a friend, astonished to learn of this new acquisition. 'No,' replied Borge, 'but the chickens do.'"

The meat of chickens that spend some of their lives outside has a better flavor than that of those raised indoors—and it has a higher ratio of omega-3 to omega-6 fatty acids, so is healthier for you, too. If you can't put them on pasture, supplement their grain diet with grass clippings and with weeds and greens from your garden. Hang the greens in bunches at the chicken's eye level—or make a makeshift manger. Staple chicken wire to the wall at both ends and along the bottom of the pen and stuff the greens into the top, bending it slightly forward for easy access.

Heavy standard breeds raised for meat will do fine if you slowly lower their protein level after eight weeks. Switch to a finisher ration or mix enough oats or scratch feed into their broiler feed to bring it down to about 18 percent protein. You can calculate exactly how much of each to mix with the Pearson's Square (see p. 305).

Managing Your Flock

The first couple of weeks in the world are the most critical time for most ani-

natural brooding requires a broody hen—quite simply, a hen that has finished laying but continues to sit on eggs to hatch them.

Brooding hens will raise any kind of egg you give them. It's quite comical to see a hen with a baby goose. In this case, mother hen and baby part ways early on, when the gosling, now bigger than its "mother," takes off for the nearest body of water.

Natural brooding Natural brooding is much easier than artificial brooding, especially if you want to only raise a few chicks. The hen does all the work. Give her no more than 8 to 10 fertile eggs and provide her with a safe, quiet place to sit for about a month. Be sure she has food and water positioned about 10 ft. away from her nest so she will get a little exercise. One day you'll wake up to a batch of baby chicks.

Two or three days after the first chick hatches, discard any unhatched eggs. If you simply provide the family with its basic needs, you'll soon discover from whence the term "mother hen" comes and will never use it in a pejorative manner again. The chicks hatch under the hen

A Simple Brooder Box

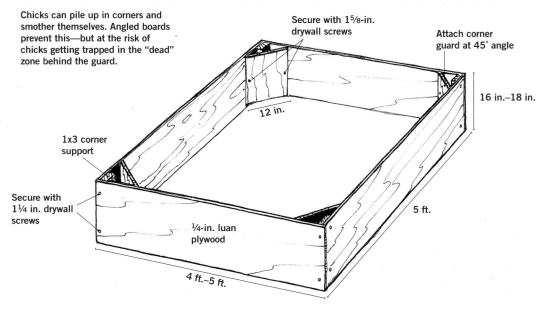

Chicks can pile up in corners and smother themselves. Angled boards prevent this—but at the risk of chicks getting trapped in the "dead" zone behind the guard.

Secure with 1⅝-in. drywall screws

Attach corner guard at 45° angle

16 in.–18 in.

12 in.

1x3 corner support

Secure with 1¼ in. drywall screws

¼-in. luan plywood

5 ft.

4 ft.–5 ft.

and stay in the nest for up to 72 hours, until they dry off. After most of the eggs have hatched, the chicks venture out in search of food and water.

After a few days in seclusion, the hen introduces her charges to the rest of the flock. The adult birds will accept and maybe even watch out for the babies. Slowly, the chicks start to stray a short distance from the hen—to eat, drink, explore, and then run back under mother's wing for warmth and protection. As time goes on, they spend less and less time under wing until, when they are 3 or 4 weeks old, they are well feathered and no longer need the extra warmth of their mother.

Artificial brooding If you don't have a brooding hen or if you want more than 10 chicks, buy day-olds and brood them artificially. The method is more or less the same whether you are raising meat birds or egg layers. You can keep the two types of birds together for the first week, but they must be separated as soon as the meat birds begin to grow larger than the layers. It's better for all concerned to keep them apart from the start.

For the first week or two, chicks require ½ sq. ft of space per bird. If you have fewer than 10 birds, a good-sized cardboard box will suffice. For more than that, you'll need to build a simple brooding pen. We make ours from 16-in.-wide, 5-ft. lengths of ¼-in. lauan plywood.

Twenty-five to fifty chicks can be comfortably brooded in a 5-ft. by 5-ft. enclosure, set up in any space that can maintain a temperature of 95°F. We have corralled as many as 100 day-olds in the greenhouse/sunroom off our dining room for the first critical weeks (and were serenaded by chirping chicks as we ate our supper). Any room that does not get too hot or too cold—such as a mudroom, bathroom, workshop, guest bedroom, or basement—can serve as a home for a batch of chicks in a cardboard box. A draft-free outbuilding that can be secured against predators is another choice for a brooder site. At various times we've brooded birds in an unoccupied henhouse, old travel trailers, a bay of our garage, the floor of our guest cabin, and the stalls in the horse barn (when the horses were out on pasture).

Chicks are covered in down rather than true feathers, so they cannot maintain their body temperature. They require supplemental heat for three or four weeks, until their feathers grow in. (Fast-growing broilers feather out about a week earlier than pure breeds.) To provide adequate heat for a cardboard 10-chick brooder, you can hang a standard 100-watt lightbulb and inexpensive reflector about 12 in. to 18 in. above the bottom of the box. Preferably, and certainly for a larger brooder, we recommend that you buy one or more 250-watt infrared brooder heat lamps at a feed store or hatchery.

Infrared bulbs are either red or clear. The red lamps last longer and discourage pecking (see p. 324). If you opt for red, you'll also need to provide a white light source, as chicks need bright light for at least 12 hours a day to thrive. There are much more elaborate (and correspondingly expensive) brooding setups, but the cheap and simple arrangement in the drawing on p. 311 works well for batches of up to 100 birds per enclosure.

For the first week, the brooding pen should be kept at about 95°F. Thereafter, reduce the temperature by 5°F a week. Lower the temperature by raising the heat lamp about 6 in. at a time. Use a cheap thermometer from the feed store (your new home away from home) or an instant-read kitchen thermometer to measure the temperature under the lamp at ground level. Adjust the lamp height accordingly. You only need to check the temperature a few times at first. Soon the chicks will let you know if their pen is too hot or too cold. If they're huddled together under the light, they're too cold. If they're smushed up against the walls, they're too hot. If they're evenly spread around the brooder and seem content, the temperature is just right. At about the fourth week, when your chicks have most of their wing feathers, they will be comfortable at ambient temperature and can go outside if the weather is warm.

Timing Successful brooding is a matter of common sense. When starting chicks, your timing is important. Consider the weather and the number of birds you are raising and what kind of shelter you have. For example, if you have a lot of birds and only an uninsulated garage for shelter, you

Brooder-Box Temperature and Chick Distribution

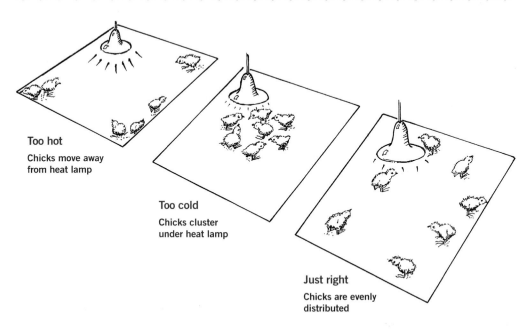

Too hot
Chicks move away
from heat lamp

Too cold
Chicks cluster
under heat lamp

Just right
Chicks are evenly
distributed

might want to wait until the weather is reliably warm so you can keep the brooding area at the right temperature. Likewise, it's difficult to keep young birds cool enough under a tin roof in the heat of summer.

As you gain experience in brooding chicks, you can modify the plan based on how your chicks are doing. If the weather is warm enough and the chicks are well feathered, you might be able to turn off the heat lamps sooner. (Running a battery of 250-watt lamps for 24 hours a day adds more than a little to your electric bill.) If you are raising layers, keep in mind they won't start laying for 20 to 25 weeks. If

they reach point-of-lay in the fall, you'll have to provide them with artificial daylight. A little planning goes a long way.

If you start hybrid and standard meat birds together, separate them after the first week. By the time the hybrids weigh about 8 oz., they'll park themselves at the feeding troughs and not let the smaller standard birds anywhere near the food. You can, however, raise layer pullets (both light and heavy breeds) and standard meat birds together until the cockerels are ready for slaughter—about 12 weeks old. The pullets will start laying at 18 to 24 weeks, depending on the breed.

If you want to raise meat birds and layers, one good strategy is to buy a batch of straight-run chicks (typically, 50 percent males and females) of a dual-purpose breed, like New Hampshire Reds. Raise the pullets for eggs and the cockerels for meat. (If you want to develop your own strain, save the biggest and fastest-maturing roosters. The next year, put your best hens and roosters together at a ratio of four hens to a rooster and hatch the eggs. Do the same in successive years, and soon you will have a stunning flock of your favorite breed.)

Pen conditions Day-old chicks, especially hybrid broilers, need sure footing. It is very easy for them to slip and permanently injure their legs—and chicks with splayed legs rarely recover. Spread wood shavings on the bottom of the pen, a couple of inches deep. For the first day or two, until the chicks learn the difference between bedding and food, lay paper towels (not sheets of newspaper) on top of the shavings to prevent slipping. Remove the paper towel when all the chicks are eating from their trough.

Some folks like to raise their chicks on wire mesh. Mesh allows droppings to fall through the holes and, theoretically, keeps the pen cleaner, but there are several disadvantages. First, wire mesh is hard on the chicks' little feet. Second, some of the droppings stick to the wire and are hard to remove (so much for cleanliness). Third, you must cover the wire with paper for a few days to a week until the birds' feet grow bigger and tougher. (I just don't like this method. I think it's cruel. Chicks that are allowed to live on litter and peck around build strong immune systems more quickly. Disease is not just a matter of the pathogens an animal encounters, but of how capable the animal's immune system is to resist them.)

Water Brooding chicks need watering devices of varying sizes, commensurate with their stage of growth. Like all other accessories, these devices are sold by hatcheries or your feed store. Begin with the 1-quart waterer. In five to seven days, switch to a 1-gallon waterer. It is unwise to skip the first step and go straight to the 1-gallon size to save money. The chicks only need the small waterers for a week or less, but baby chicks can either drown in a large waterer or get soaked, chilled, and then die. Any small tray—such as a pie tin or a plastic egg carton with the top cut off—will work as well as store-bought chick feeders for the first few weeks. After that, opt for the larger plastic or metal feeders or one of the do-it-yourself versions shown on p. 391.

For the first day or two, we add about $1/3$ cup of sugar to each quart of water to help the chicks recover from the stress of shipping and of having no food or water for several days. We also like to augment their water with commercial vitamins and probiotics for the first week. If you purchase probiotics, be sure they are specifically intended for poultry. You can also dilute live cultured yogurt that has lactobacillus and other fermentation bacteria. Mix the yogurt with an equal amount of warm water and add the solution to your chick's drinking water. Probiotics and vaccination can help prevent serious diseases, including the most serious, coccidiosis.

Coccidiosis is a ubiquitous protozoan that, when out of balance with the other naturally occurring microbes that colonize a chick's guts and environs, can kill your whole flock. Chicks between the ages of 3 and 16 weeks are most at risk. If your hatchery offers a vaccination against this disease, have your chicks inoculated. Vaccines work by artificially boosting the immune system to resist the targeted bad bugs. Probiotics tip the balance toward the good bugs right from the start. In addition, chicks raised on litter, as opposed to wire mesh, will gradually develop a resistance to coccidiosis and other harmful microbes, such as E. Coli, salmonella, and campylobacter.

Feeding chicks Some people advocate using a starter feed that is medicated with coccidiostatic (an antibiotic that slows the growth of the protozoa). If your chicks have already been vaccinated, however, medicated feed will counteract the vaccine. Medicated feed is neither organic nor "natural," and the prophylactic use of antibiotics contributes to the development of antibiotic-resistant "superbugs," which is why we won't use it—but we do vaccinate. It can be difficult to find starter feeds that don't contain antibiotics but have the necessary high protein levels. If medicated feed is all that is available or if you cannot find starter feed with a protein content of at least 22 percent, game bird feed is the best alternative.

By the time your chicks are three to four weeks old, they should be almost fully fledged (feathered but for their heads and necks) and comfortable enough without supplemental feathers to move outdoors to graze.

Real Eggs

Once you get used to what my grandkids call "real" eggs, you'll wonder how you ever ate anything else. There is one downside to truly fresh eggs, however: They do not peel easily when hard-boiled. But, if you cannot abide the extra minute or two it takes to peel a fresh hard-boiled egg, you probably need to reexamine your life.

There's no more perfect food than an egg. One egg has about 6.25 grams of complete protein, with all the essential amino acids; it has 4.5 grams of fat and is high in vitamins A, D, and E. The notion that eating eggs raises your cholesterol has been thoroughly debunked, yet there are still some lingering myths about egg nutrition.

Despite what many people believe, white, brown, and even green eggs have the exact same taste and nutritional value. So do fertilized and nonfertilized eggs. All eggs have about the same amount of protein and fat, including cholesterol. You can, however, definitely see and taste the differences between eggs from chickens raised on pasture and eggs from chickens raised in confinement.

To see the difference, crack open an egg from a pastured chicken and a commercially grown egg and compare them. The homespun egg will have a big, plump, bright yellow (almost orange), and almost perfectly centered yolk. The commercial egg will have a pale, flaccid, off-centered yolk. The white of the homegrown egg may be a little cloudy, but it will be thicker. The egg will also be more compact and won't spread out on the plate as much as its store-bought counterpart.

There are two main reasons for these differences. The first is that homegrown eggs have more vitamins and are higher in omega-3 essential fatty acids. The bright yellow/orange yolks of eggs from grass-fed chickens comes from carotenoids, the pigments that give fruits and vegetables their color. Carotenoids are the precursors of vitamin A. The brighter the yolk, the higher the content of vitamin A and the companion vitamins D, E, and K.

The second reason for the difference is that homegrown eggs are much fresher. A fresh egg has dense albumin (the egg white) that holds the yolk up high and keeps it centered within the shell. The albumin in a very fresh egg, one that is still slightly warm, may appear cloudy because the carbon dioxide has not yet dissipated. As it ages, albumen thins and does not hold the egg together as well. Store-bought eggs are often three or four weeks old. As quickly as possible, store clean, dry, fresh eggs, with large ends up, in the refrigerator in a clean papier-mâché egg carton. Paper cartons are inexpensive—or even free if you collect them from friends and neighbors. (We market our multicolored "rainbow" eggs in the clear plastic cartons made from recycled soda bottles to boost their customer appeal.) For best results, keep the cartons inside plastic bags

and at the back of the refrigerator. Eggs stored in a normal household refrigerator at 45°F and 70 percent humidity will keep for four to five weeks. One day on the counter equals one week in the fridge. An egg with a cracked shell is still good for a few days as long as its inner membrane is intact. If the inner part of the egg is exposed to air (in other words, if you have a "leaky" egg), feed it to the dog, cook it, or chop it up and feed it back to your birds, shell and all.

You can estimate an egg's age by floating it in a bowl of water. A very fresh egg will immediately sink to the bottom and rest on its side. A fresh egg sinks because it has very little air inside the shell. As eggs age, air accumulates within the shell, creating a bubble at the large end. A one-week-old egg will rest at an angle, large end up. An egg that stands on its small end is a couple of weeks old. If the egg floats on top of the water, it is very old. You can view the air cell by shining a flashlight through the egg in a darkened room, a process called candling, which is used to measure embryo development when incubating eggs.

The bacteria most likely to contaminate eggs are *Streptococcus*, *Staphylococcus*, *Pseudomonas*, and *Salmonella*. Cooking readily kills all of these organisms. These bacteria are ubiquitous, yet the number of healthy people who get sick eating "undercooked" eggs is very small. Nevertheless, the USDA recommends that people cook their eggs and egg dishes to 160°F. At that temperature, the yolk is no longer runny. I'd rather take my chances than give up over-easy eggs from my own chickens. The *Salmonella* on a commercial egg has already survived some very powerful antimicrobials and has likely developed a resistance, so infection is difficult to treat. Homegrown *Salmonella* is likely to cause a mild diarrhea and then clear on its own.

Gathering Eggs

Proper egg handling begins with clean nest boxes. Straw, hay, or recycled shredded paper are better than wood shavings. (Little paper ribbons sometimes stick to the eggshells, but they wash off easily.) Bedding should be kept free of manure at all times (you may have to change or at least turn and shake out the bedding daily). If necessary, as long as there is adequate roosting spaces, you can discourage hens from sleeping in the nests by covering them at night. Collect eggs at least twice a day to keep the eggs clean (the hen has less time to poop on them).

Clean the shells by rubbing them with a dry, scrubbing dishcloth or an emery cloth. A freshly laid egg has a thin outer cuticle, called the bloom, which seals out bacteria and dirt, protects the integrity of the shell, and prevents evaporation. If you are in the coop when a hen is laying and you pick up the egg immediately, you'll notice that it's damp. This liquid layer is so thin that it will completely evaporate in a few seconds before your eyes. The bloom is very fragile and comes off with washing or even rubbing. Wash eggs only when necessary, with water at 110°F to 115°F. Colder water will cause the inner membrane to shrink away from the shell, opening pores to the air. Keepability is diminished when the eggs are washed. If you have an especially dirty egg, dip it in

Chicken Facts at a Glance

- It takes approximately 4 lb. of grain to produce 1 dozen white eggs and a little more to produce brown eggs. (The American and English breeds that lay brown eggs are bigger birds, so they eat more grain.)
- A good egg producer lays 250 eggs per year.
- It takes 25 hours for a hen to produce one egg.

- Pullets start laying eggs at 20 to 22 weeks of age.
- Hens reach peak egg production at 30 to 34 weeks.
- After peak, production declines by 2 percent per month.
- At peak production, a full-grown laying hen eats about 4 oz. of feed per day.
- Refrigerated eggs keep for 4 to 5 weeks.

- Hybrid broilers take 6 weeks to reach market weight; pure breed birds take 12 weeks.
- The conversion ratio for hybrid broilers is 2 lb. of feed to 1 lb. of live weight.
- A chicken's dressed weight is on average 75 percent of its live weight.

a weak water-and-bleach solution to kill surface germs.

Egg production Chickens will lay eggs almost every day. They do not like to lay eggs at night. Most will lay their eggs by 9 or 10 a.m. It takes 25 hours for a follicle (egg yolk) to leave the ovary, make its way through the various stages of egg development, and end up in the nest. In order to keep on her morning schedule, a hen will have to skip a day from time to time. This 25-hour cycle is why hens never quite lay an egg a day.

The record for egg production is more than 370 eggs in one year, but a hen that lays more than 250 eggs is considered a very good layer. Pullets start laying between 18 and 25 weeks of age, with peak laying at around 30 weeks. Productivity drops off about 2 percent per month thereafter. Once their routine is established, some hens will continue laying until they die of old age, at about 10 years. Others will quit laying years before their natural death. Either way, all hens become steadily less productive over time, with a big drop-off after three years. Every hen is born with about 4,000 ova, but less than 10 percent of those will develop into mature eggs—partly for biological reasons, but mainly because few chickens live long enough to die of natural causes.

Several factors determine chickens' egg productivity:

Genetics There is, unfortunately, no list of the breeds that lay the most eggs. Some breeds are more prolific than others are, some strains within those breeds are even more productive, and certain individuals within a strain will lay better than other individuals. Hybrids are supposed to be more fruitful than purebreds, but I have had individual Speckled Sussex, a breed that some call "sluggish," that outlaid all my hybrids.

Light In order to lay at maximum capacity, chickens and other poultry need 15 to 16 hours of light (either natural or artificial) each day. (The animal's pineal gland, located deep in the middle of the brain, relies on light to produce melatonin, which affects various reproductive hormones.) Use a timer to keep an accurate schedule.

Some experts say that lights should come on in the coop in the morning but that the hens should have a natural sunset. Apparently, it's easier for them to adapt to instant light than to instant dark. If the lights go off abruptly at night, the birds don't have a chance to settle in and find their best perch. Our birds have adapted very well to evening lighting, however. Our lights are set to switch off at 9:30 p.m., and by 9:15, every hen is on her perch. Some people do not give their hens any artificial light at all and just accept reduced egg output in the winter.

Whichever system you opt for, stick to it. Don't add light one day and none the next. Changing the photoperiod changes your hen's hormone levels, and the inconsistent light patterns are very stressful for the birds. Most of all, poultry are creatures of habit. They prefer to do the same thing every day at the same time. If you are able to accommodate their predilections, your birds will flourish.

Do You Need a Rooster?

The short answer is no. Most, if not all, domestic male birds (and male animals, in general) are a nuisance. Hens will lay eggs whether there's a rooster on the premises or not. In truth, the only real reason to put up with a rooster is for breeding your own stock, an enterprise that is much more expensive, time-consuming, and complicated than buying day-old chicks from the hatchery. Otherwise, there is no need to have a rooster, although you might want one just because you like the way they look or like to hear them crow. (Roosters crow not only at the crack of dawn, but throughout the day and sometimes at night.)

Your preferences notwithstanding, there are probably more reasons not to have roosters than there are to have them. For example, you may like crowing, but your neighbors may not. Second, an adult rooster is aggressive and may attack anyone who comes near his hens. Don't be fooled by the docile demeanor of a young rooster who has not yet reached sexual maturity. As soon as his testosterone reaches the right level, he'll start strutting his stuff. It is, after all, his job to breed and protect. If there's more than one rooster, one will stand out as the most assertive, and the rest will remain submissive. Don't think that eliminating the kingpin solves the problem. If you do away with him, a new pretender will claim the throne of the former tyrant, and you'll be back where you started.

I like to watch and hear roosters, but I try to keep their number to a minimum. It's a nuisance to fend off their attacks whenever our paths cross. Although a rooster can't seriously hurt an adult (unless it hits an eye), I have nine grandchildren and several friends with young children who could be injured.

Food and water A constant and reliable source of food and water may be even more important than light to egg production. Some breeds lay reasonably well during short photoperiods, but no chicken does well without daily food and water. If a hen doesn't have enough water one day, it takes another full day for it to recover. If she is deprived of water for 36 hours, she will go into molt and may never fully regain her original laying schedule. Follow your feeding program religiously and never allow your ladies to go without.

Stress General stress can affect egg production, too, but it will impinge less on the production of birds of good breeding that are fed and housed well. Stressors for chickens are the same as for any animal and include filthy surroundings. I am convinced that all of my birds know the difference between a clean house and a dirty one. When I add new bedding to their pens, they all come running as if for food. They will scratch and peck the floor while making the cooing sounds indicative of contentment. It is likewise clear

Culling Your Chickens

Don't fool yourself into thinking that just because you keep laying hens or a milk cow instead of broilers and beefers you have sidestepped the moral quandary of killing animals. Nobody likes to do it, but if you don't kill substandard and sick birds, you'll have trouble on your hands. Being a responsible steward of barnyard animals means not only husbanding your stock but also improving the gene pool. If you are opposed to killing animals, you shouldn't keep animals, even laying hens.

Sooner or later, you'll be faced with culling a sick or injured bird, an extra rooster, or just replacing a worn-out layer. Broilers are especially susceptible to leg deformities, for example. If a bird develops leg problems, euthanize it. Leg deformities are painful, and a bird should not have to endure the pain.

Never eat a sick bird. Recycle it into the compost heap. Injured or old birds, however, are worth at least the effort of soup and stock in exchange for their faithful service.

that they know their regular handlers from strangers.

The molting cycle Once a year, usually in the fall as the daylight hours begin to dwindle noticeably, chickens molt—that is, they shed and replace their old feathers. During the molt, egg production either slows or stops altogether. Good layers start molting late in the season and get through it in a couple of months or less; poor layers begin molting earlier and take longer to finish. Production hens tend to slow down while pure breeds are more likely to stop laying altogether.

Hens lose their feathers a few at a time, not all at once, so the birds never really look naked. In fact, unless you look closely, you might not notice any change at all, but a decline in production coupled with lots of feathers scattered about the coop is a sure sign that your birds are molting. After a young hen has gone through her first molt, her production picks back up and should be stronger than it was before (although not as good as at her peak). Egg quality and size also tend to improve after the first molt. With excellent care and a flock of good birds, the molting cycle will repeat the following year.

Time Many farmers, if not most, replace their flocks every year. A few will go 2 years, when production, and therefore, profit, drop sharply. If you are raising eggs for your family, a good flock can easily produce for 3 or 4 years.

Some experts recommend replacing your flock all at once rather than a few birds at a time. If, however, you have only a half-dozen chickens or so, it doesn't make much difference. You can either dispose of your old hens and brood up a new batch (or buy some pullets) in the same spring, or you can more continually add and subtract chickens. The drawback to replacing gradually is that adding new birds is generally a stressor to the whole flock (and the flock owner), although a small flock can probably take the introduction of a newbie more or less in stride.

Keeping Your Birds Clean and Healthy

There are no tricks to keeping your birds clean. Just use your nose and common sense. Your coop should never smell of ammonia. Keep the litter dry and fluffy by adding fresh litter regularly. Remove wet material and droppings that pile up around feeders, under roosts, and in front of doors. Scrape roosts often to prevent the droppings from accumulating.

Even if your flock has 100 acres to range across, they will beat down the area surrounding the coop, destroying any trace of vegetation. So, the chicken yard should be subject to the same sanitary regime as the interior of the coop. Rake the yard often, spread hay or straw when the weather is wet or the ground frozen, and, in warm weather, spray the hay with a hose. Most important, relocate the coop or the yard each year to minimize problems with parasites.

Watching your birds, holding them, and petting them are the best parts of having them. This is also your best weapon against disease. If you know what your birds look and act like when they're healthy, you'll quickly notice a bird that is off just a bit and can catch a small problem before it becomes a large one. If you don't have

time to spend time with your birds, frequently, you probably have too many.

To be a good steward to your chickens, you should have at least a basic understanding of chicken physiology. Most basic books on chickens discuss this subject. For example, *Storey's Guide to Raising Poultry* by Leonard Mercia (Storey, 2000) has a very good chapter on anatomy.

The good news is that the problems that your birds might encounter are surprisingly few. The bad news is that the first symptom of many of these problems is death. Therefore, your focus truly should be on prevention and on saving the next victim. I don't mean to imply that chickens drop dead regularly. They don't. Chickens are very hardy and, when well cared for, are relatively free of disease, but there will be times when you enter the coop in the morning and find a hen that was just fine yesterday stone-cold dead, and you won't have a clue as to why.

Common causes Chickens occasionally die for no apparent reason, so if this happens rarely, there's no need to worry. If you lose two or three chickens within a few days, however, you need to find the reason fast. If you can't find the likely culprit in your veterinary handbook, consult your vet or the county extension agent. Common antibiotics and other medications are available at your feed store.

Bring home a sick bird from another farm (as I did), and you could lose your entire flock. (My birds got leg scales two years ago, and I'm still mad at myself.) We rarely buy adult birds, but when we do, we isolate them for several weeks before adding them to the flock, even if they look okay. Impatience can be a severe teacher.

Here is a list of common health problems that could affect your flock:

Parasites Lice and mites are not usually serious problems, unless they get out of control. Mites live around the hen's vent. You can see them under strong light—they're tiny and either grey, red, or almost transparent. Harder to see are the mites that forage on the chickens at night and retreat to the cracks in the woodwork during the day. The hens actually pull out their own feathers to relieve the irritation and itching the parasites cause.

Prevention: Keep flock isolated from other birds; remove bird feeders, as wild birds are prime vector for transmission.

Symptoms: Chickens look unthrifty and are losing feathers; show weight loss and a decrease in egg production.

Recommended remedies: Dust the chickens and coop with pyrethrum. If the flock is small, bathe each bird in flea shampoo (used for dogs or cats). For severe infestation, clean coop out and wash walls, nests, and roosts (and, in particular, crevices) with water-bleach solution. Spray dry walls with insecticide and close up coop for 1 hour, then open all doors and windows for at least 1 hour. Repeat if necessary.

Worms Worms are as ubiquitous as mites but seldom a serious problem with healthy birds. Many worms have alternate hosts, such as earthworms and grasshoppers, so chickens pick up intestinal worms while grazing—although chickens with access to the outdoors early in life seem to develop resistance to these parasites. The worms may be present in most flocks, but the problems they cause may not be.

Prevention: Every now and then, I mix a handful of diatomaceous earth into the flock's ration (the microscopically sharp dust repels worms). Others suggest adding garlic (chopped or liquid extract), alone or in solution of apple cider vinegar, to the ration.

Symptoms: If your flock is listless and egg laying is diminished (and you can find no other obvious ailments), take a stool sample to your vet.

Recommended remedies: Solutions vary depending on the type of worm.

Leg scales These nasty little devils are mites that live and multiply under the leg scales of poultry, causing the scales to lift up and loosen, which is very irritating to the birds. They'll peck at the scales relentlessly. My chickens never had leg scales until I accepted a bunch of "rescue" chickens. I was able to get the infestation under control, but not until it had infected a number of my birds. I no longer take other people's birds without a thorough inspection of both the animals and their habitat.

Prevention: Cleanliness and good flock management will help prevent scales.

Symptoms: Scales that harbor the mites accumulate a light brown debris; birds peck at scales continually.

Recommended remedies: Coat the birds' legs with petroleum jelly or dip them in a mixture of mineral oil and kerosene. Then remove any loose scales and the underlying debris. A small amount of bleeding is possible, but of no consequence. Repeat a few

How to Tell a Layer from a Slacker

Nonlaying layers are freeloaders. If you have just a few birds and you love them all and are happy with the four eggs a day you are getting, who cares? If you are trying to make your birds support your farm hobby, it might be important to get rid of freeloaders. If you're breeding your hens, it's best to build up your flock with eggs from productive hens.

It's harder to tell good layers from sluggish layers than it is to determine whether a hen is laying at all. Assume your flock of replacement pullets has reached maturity, and eggs are beginning to appear. How to tell who is laying or who isn't?

Look at the hen's headgear. A laying hen's comb and wattle are plump, large, and waxy. If, when you try to pick her up, the hen assumes a squatting stance with her wings held out to the side but not unfurled, she's ready to start laying.

The condition of her vent will reveal if she has laid any eggs yet. After a hen starts laying, the yellow pigment will start "bleaching" out of her skin and shift to the yolk of her egg. The bleaching sequence can actually tell you approximately how many eggs the hen has laid. Before laying begins, the skin surrounding the vent is very yellow. After she has laid two

or three eggs, it is nearly white. In a week or two, the color has completely bleached out.

If you want to find out if an older hen is a good layer or not, you'll need a trap nest—which, as the name implies, traps a hen in the nest. Check these traps at least every half-hour. If you keep records for a week, you'll know exactly how your hens are performing. This technique is easy if you have a small flock. Cull large flocks by examining the hens, using the criteria in the list below to distinguish good layers from low producers. Combine this test with the trap nest method until you feel confident.

Characteristics of Layers and Nonlayers

Anatomy	High Production	Low Production
Head furnishings	Large, plump, waxy	Small, pale, dusty looking
Vent	Pale, full, moist	Flat, yellow, dry
Abdomen	Soft, full	Hard, shallow
Pubic bone	Flexible, three fingers wide	Stiff, < three fingers wide
Head	Clean, bright red, no feathers	Yellowish, dull, with feathers
Eye/eye ring	Bleached	Yellow
Plumage	Worn, dry, tired looking	Bright, shiny
Molt	Late, fast	Early, slow
Overall	Active, alert	Dull, tired

more times until the legs are mostly clear; repeat the next season if necessary.

Cannibalism When chickens are crowded, bored, or really stressed, they may actually start eating each other alive. Low-ranking birds in the pecking order will be the first ones attacked during times of stress. (Chickens take their pecking order very seriously—and so should you.) Typically, the bird being attacked will run and hide, but when cannibalistic conduct is in the air, the victim refuses to defend herself. She allows the aggressor (and, soon, a coterie of aggressors) to peck her relentlessly. If you don't rescue the bird, the torture continues until death. The underlying circumstances must be very stressful to foster cannibalism. The most common cause is overcrowded winter quarters in tandem with prolonged artificial light. During winter, boredom (or what you might call Gallinaceous Seasonal Affective Disorder, or GSAD) can trigger behavioral problems.

As my passion for chickens grew from a hobby to an enterprise, our coop was soon too small for my multiplying flock. Each morning in midwinter, we began to find horribly maimed and dead birds. We added a second feeder, installed red lights and more roosts, and tried everything we could think of to stop the mayhem, but it did not subside until a dozen hens, a full third of the flock, had been killed off. This harsh adjustment in population density was an equally harsh lesson for us in flock management.

Prevention: Make the coop as large as you can, so there's enough room for the flock, and control size of flock to avoid overcrowding. Reduce boredom by varying the terrain of the yard and the roosts. Hang strips of red cloth, greens, whole cabbage, or other edibles at a height that requires effort to reach. Scattering scratch on the litter (adding whole seed grains in winter). Let your hens outdoors on all but the harshest days.

Symptoms: In young birds, the behavior can start with toe pecking; in adult birds, it may escalate to pecking out the entire vent area and viscera.

Recommended remedies: Remove any injured hens from the coop and put them in a hospital cage (a wire dog-transport cage works well). Clean and protect wounds with antibacterial ointments. Treat infections with antibiotics dissolved in the bird's drinking water. Do not return the injured hen to the flock until she has healed completely, as the slightest remaining scab or wound will stimulate the other birds to peck it open. If, despite everything, your birds persist in killing each other, give away or slaughter enough hens so the conditions are no longer crowded.

Biosecurity Biosecurity is a strategy to prevent the spread of disease within your flock and throughout your farm. The term *biosecurity* is relatively new and was probably invented by a government bureaucrat in response to avian influenza. The term may be new, but the concept is not. Anyone who is serious about animal husbandry has thought about how to keep animals healthy. If your operation consists of just you and a few laying hens, a written agenda isn't necessary. If you have several animals and several people who handle them, consider developing a written protocol of safety procedures—and maybe post it on a wall somewhere—so that everyone is aware of them.

- Keep people away from your birds. Don't let just anyone in to see them, even though you want to show them off. If guests must come in, have them don disposable coveralls and, especially, booties.
- Quarantine new additions for two weeks before adding them to the rest of the flock.
- If you buy used equipment, before you use it, be sure that it has been disinfected with bleach, ammonia, or commercial disinfectant (just don't use them together!).
- Rinse out your waterers every day and disinfect them once a week.
- Cull birds that appear sick. You can baby an injured bird, but not one with a disease. If in doubt, cull.
- If two or three birds die in a short time span, get suspicious. If you can't figure out what's going on yourself, seek help.
- Know the signs of infectious bird disease:
  Sudden death
  Diarrhea
  Decreased egg production
  Respiratory symptoms (coughing, nasal discharge, other breathing problems)
  Lack of energy or appetite
  Swelling about the eyes or neck
  Discoloration of head furnishings
  Tremors, droopy head or wings, twisting of the head, paralysis
  Unusual appearance or behavior (trust your intuition)

Catching Chickens

Chickens can seem pretty dumb until you try to catch one. They run very fast and change direction with erratic and infuriating ease. Just when you think you finally have that hen cornered, she'll dart between your legs and get away. Of course, if you've handled your hens from the day they arrived, you can sometimes call them to you and simply pick up the one you want. If, however, your birds are not especially tame, they'll never let you get close enough to snatch them. Sometimes, even the tame ones will forget you're their friend.

There are a few tricks for catching chickens during the day, but if you're not in a hurry, it's a lot easier to wait until dark. At nightfall, birds go into a near-trance, and even the nastiest rooster can be picked up without a struggle. During the day, if you can get close enough to the bird, you have two options.

The first option is to snare or corral the birds with a poultry net—basically, a large butterfly net at the end of a 6-ft. pole. The second option is to hook the bird with a poultry hook, which is basically a 4-ft.-long, 1/4-in. steel rod with a handle at one end and a squiggly, U-shaped hook at the other. You catch the bird by snaring one of its legs in the hook and then pulling back while lifting upward (like playing a fish). Grab both of the bird's legs with one hand, release the hook, and cradle the chicken between your arm and body, securing both wings.

If the birds you're trying to catch are already within the yard or pasture—or can be coaxed in—have two or three people each hold a 2×8 panel of foam insulation (aka blueboard) in front of themselves horizontally. Then all should advance slowly toward the bird, driving it toward the poultry fence. As the bird nears the fence, bring the panels close together. The goal is to trap the bird against the fence so you can reach down and pick it up. The same group approach works pretty well without the foam boards, if you have more helpers. (Get the kids involved—they're usually better at it than adults.)

Once you have caught your bird, take a few minutes to soothe her. Even a skittish bird will eventually calm down. Always talk to your birds. Whenever you are around them, sing or hum or make any other type of sound that lets them know that all is well. From the time they are chicks, whenever you feed them, call them in the same way. Then, when full grown, they'll come running when they hear your call, no matter how far away they are—very handy.

Introducing New Chickens

Chickens don't like change. They want today to be exactly like yesterday. They also don't like making new friends. Chickens of different ages should not be housed together. Chicks without the protection of a mother hen will not survive in a flock of adult hens. There will, however, come a time when you have to introduce pullets (either homegrown or newly purchased) to the older hens. You can sometimes mix batches of chickens if the new birds somehow have an advantage over the old ones—for example, if the new chickens are bigger than the older ones or the new birds outnumber the old.

Be sure you'll be around for a few days after the merger to watch the chickens carefully. Introduce the new birds at night. (Birds put everything on hold when the lights go out.) By morning, the two groups should have become somewhat accustomed to each other. Many times, this trick and a little "tincture of time" is all that it takes.

Another trick is to spray all the birds with a strong aromatic (garlic, for example) at night. Apparently, odor is important for chicken recognition, and if everybody smells the same, there's nobody to fight. I have never tried this, but it sounds reasonable. At any rate, don't be surprised if there's some pecking and fighting at first. After all, the pecking order must be reestablished.

We've never had serious problems mixing birds because we have not mixed birds of different sizes or rushed the process. We often have two flocks that each live in their own coop but share a common pasture. They intermingle without conflict during the day and then segregate themselves at night when they return to their home coops. Eventually, they begin having sleepovers at the other coop, and the two former flocks meld into one.

....

Top: Children are usually better than adults at handling chickens. Bottom left: Relocating the portable chicken coop. Bottom right: Chickens enjoy a good dust bath.

Chickens and Eggs

Prior to the 1930s, there were no large commercial egg producers. You either kept your own hens or bought eggs from a local farm. Fresh eggs were, historically, a seasonal item—plentiful in summer and scarce and expensive in winter (chickens need 15 to 16 hours of daylight to keep up their production). Year-round, large-scale egg production became possible only after the Rural Electric Administration program brought electricity to the farm and artificial lighting to the henhouse. By the 1950s, the once-ubiquitous backyard chicken range had been replaced by patio barbecues and manicured lawns. We've come full circle. Every day, more and more folks are raising chickens for eggs and meat—in backyards and garages or on small farms.

Urban Homesteading

You likely have limited space, or zoning requirements may limit the number of birds you can keep. You need a minimum of three hens to supply a household of two adults with eggs (and don't swap out a hen for a rooster, even if zoning allows you to have one). Expect at least two eggs a day from your three hens—at least a dozen a week, which is probably all you'll need. Hard-boil or pickle the extras. They make a nutritious snack—either for yourself or for your dog. You could even crush them, shells and all, and feed them back to your chickens.

With this tiny flock, you'll need only a handful of grain each day to supplement their primary diet of kitchen scraps (even meat scraps!) and whatever they can forage in an outdoor yard. If possible, let your chickens range on the compost pile. They will aerate and improve the pile with their manure as they scratch it up and turn it over.

Suburban Homesteading

Consider sharing a medium-size flock with your neighbors or as part of a community garden. You'll probably have to keep your birds penned up most of the time, but try to find a way to let them free-range for at least a few hours a day. They'll benefit from the exercise and the opportunity to forage.

You can pay for your grain bill and some of the upkeep of the flock by selling eggs to one or two additional families. The basic rule of thumb is to sell eggs for twice the cost of production. An oft-quoted rule of thumb is that it takes 4 lb. of feed to make a dozen eggs. If a bird consumes 4 oz. of feed per day, it would eat 4 lb. in about 16 days. At peak, even the best hens won't lay every day, and many will lay every other day, so you can figure that the bird will fill an egg carton in 16 days or more. Organic feed is more expensive and pretty much doubles the retail price of the eggs. You also need to account for the cost of the bird itself, whether raised as a day-old chick or purchased as a pullet. Also consider those initial months, before the layers hit their stride and start reliably producing marketable eggs.

To reduce feed costs, set aside part of your garden or community plot to grow sunflowers, cabbage, winter squash, and comfrey to supplement your bird's diet. A cabbage hung from a string in the coop during the winter is both nutritious and stimulating for the birds.

The Mini-Farm

A medium-sized flock of 100 to 200 laying hens—for many years, the typical size of the chicken division of a diversified farm operation—can turn a modest profit ("egg money"). Because everyone and his brother is selling eggs these days, you need to develop some sort of clever marketing strategy to distinguish your eggs from the rest of the pack and attract customers.

Hobby farming and homesteading magazines may lead you to believe that you can sell your eggs and produce at the local farmer's markets. These markets are indeed becoming more plentiful, but you can't assume they'll be your ticket to success. As the new kid on the block, you'll likely discover that the markets are closed to new vendors—and there's a multiyear waiting list for the best ones. Also, the local market may have too many vendors of the same products

who compete for the same few customers. Unfortunately, in most communities the locavore movement is still too small to support truly profitable markets for more than a few core vendors.

We recommend developing a wholesale market for your products among locavore restaurants instead. There are solid opportunities for producers of artisanal meats and poultry—although fewer for vegetables. You could also contract to supply an established and growing CSA (Community Supported Agriculture) network. You might also consider going into business supplying heritage-breed started chicks or point-of-lay pullets to your local market. Bottom line: Find an unoccupied or underdeveloped niche and fill it.

Brown, white, and green eggs make up a carton of our "rainbow" eggs.

chapter xiii

....

Turkeys & Other Barnyard Birds

urkeys are the joke of the poultry world. They're the birds that
supposedly drown looking up at
the rain and drop dead for no discernible
reason. They are clumsy, and filthy, and
seem basically just too stupid to live, unless
they're safely penned in a small wire cage,
protected from the world, and themselves.

Keeping an animal in close confinement goes against our nature, so, for
a long time, we never even considered
raising turkeys—but our experiences have
taught us that not everything you read or
hear is true. Why would Ben Franklin have
promoted the turkey over the eagle as the
preferred symbol of the newly fledged nation? How stupid can they be?

Domestic turkeys are only a few hundred
years removed from their wild ancestors. In fact, at first glance, it's hard to
tell a domestic turkey of the Bronze breed
from an individual of the Wild Eastern
strain. If they were as vulnerable as legend
reports, why would they still be around?
As further testimony on their behalf, the
Wild Eastern turkey has made a remarkable
comeback (with a little help from wildlife

management experts) after being hunted
to near extinction. Once rare, large flocks
now dot the edges of woods and cornfields
everywhere. Something just did not add
up. We decided to find out the truth about
turkeys for ourselves.

One thing we learned from raising
chickens is that the more you let chickens
be chickens and do chicken things, the
happier and healthier they are. Animals
that are happy and healthy are easier to
care for. We figured that turkeys were
probably similar to other animals in
this respect. Maybe, we thought, those
wire cages were the reason turkeys fared
so poorly.

To prove the theory, we got 20 Giant
White turkeys (the commercial hybrid
type) and raised them mostly outdoors,
the same way we raise chickens. Eighteen
turkeys survived to 13 weeks and reached
good slaughter weights. We sold a few at a
profit, and the rest went into our freezer
whole, cut up, and ground.

....

*Jane sets out fresh bedding hay for her flock of heritage
and standard turkeys.*

We discovered that turkeys are curious, friendly, and self-sufficient. Given the opportunity, they are great foragers and will search out and eat tremendous quantities of bugs and vegetation. They are fun to raise. If you have even a little extra space, consider raising a couple of holiday turkeys. If you have a little more space, think about raising a few more to keep on hand in the freezer.

"Turkey, n. A large bird whose flesh when eaten on certain religious anniversaries has the peculiar property of attesting piety and gratitude. Incidentally, it is pretty good eating."
—*Amborse Bierce,* The Devil's Dictionary

ardent grazers and will busily forage in the fields all day. They even eat small snakes. Given enough range, they come to the troughs only to eat grain in the morning and at early evening.

Turkeys have a wide repertoire of sounds, from their famous gobbles to hisses and yelps. With the strutting and display of the toms, the pecking order antics, and the nighttime perching habits, they are fascinating creatures. Rather than dim-witted weaklings, we found them to be affable and resilient. They are more interactive than chickens or ducks, love to follow people around, and stick their beaks right into the action. You could even keep turkeys as pets. Before you get the idea that they're perfect, however, we have to confess that one of the negative perceptions about them is true. They are, indeed, dirty. The bigger they get, the harder it is to keep them clean.

Despite this shortcoming, however, we appreciate turkeys more and more with every batch. They are easy and a lot of

Raising Turkeys

Most of the turkeys we've raised so far have been the commercial white strain, the Broad Breasted Giant White. Like their counterpart in the chicken world, the Cornish × Rocks, this breed grows much faster than others, with a conversion ratio under 2:1 for most of their life (that is 2 lb. of feed to produce 1 lb. of live bird). The Giant White toms grow so huge, they cannot mate naturally. The tom's huge breast makes him too top-heavy to successfully tread a hen. The hens must be artificially inseminated. Now there's an interesting job!

We recently added several heritage breeds, too. (In fact, there is a renegade Narragansett hen chirping on my bedroom balcony right now.) The smaller, narrow-keeled heritage turkeys, in addition to being very good layers and mothers, are capable of mating naturally—and they make mighty fine eating. Narragansetts and Bourbon Reds are touted as the tastiest turkeys of all. We have raised these

Turkey Breeds

There are two basic categories of turkey breeds: commercial and heritage. The two commercial breeds are the Broad Breasted Giant White and the Broad Breasted Bronze. The toms of these breeds are huge, often weighing 40 lb. at maturity. Most, if not all, of the turkeys sold in supermarkets are Giant Whites. Homegrown, pastured birds are much tastier—eating grass and bugs makes all the difference.

Heritage turkeys are from one-half to three-quarters of the size of commercial turkeys.

The heritage breeds include the Standard Bronze, Narragansett, Beltsville Midget (aka Midget White or Beltsville Small, which are basically the same bird), Black Spanish (although not recognized as a breed by the American Livestock Breeds Conservancy [ALBC]), Bourbon Red, and Royal Palm.

At the time of this writing, these heritage birds are on the ALBC's threatened and watch lists, which means they are in danger of becoming extinct. The only way they can survive and contribute to the diversity of the genetic pool is for farmers, homesteaders, and backyard hobbyists to continue breeding them. Fortunately, there are quite a few hatcheries and boutique breeders that specialize in rare and exotic breeds of domestic livestock of all stripes. Actually, to generate some revenue for your enterprise, you might consider finding a compatible breed to specialize in and promote it yourself.

two breeds, White Midgets (so-called because they are only 12 lb. to 15 lb. at market weight), and Holland Whites. They all taste equally great.

Whichever you choose, consider raising a breeding pair. They will grow you a nice brood of birds for your holiday table and for year-round eating. Turkey burgers are a family favorite here.

If you want to just raise a few poults (baby turkeys) without the mom and dad, you would brood them basically the same way as you would chicks (see pp. 310–315). You could even brood the two species together if you are short on space or if you have only a couple of poults that would otherwise have trouble staying warm.

Risk of disease Although you can brood poults and chicks together, keep poults away from adult birds of other species. Chickens, guinea fowl, and game birds can harbor cecal worms (*Heterakis gallinarum*), whose eggs carry a protozoan (*Histomoniasis meleagridis*) that causes the highly lethal disease known as blackhead or histomoniasis. The eggs that carry *H. meleagridis* are also found in everyday earthworms.

Chickens and game birds, which are often carriers, evince no signs of disease,

but turkeys become sick and die within a few weeks of exposure. The prevalence of blackhead seems to have diminished somewhat over the years. Some believe the drop is due to the fact that turkeys are most often strictly isolated from other poultry and are rarely raised outdoors, where they are more susceptible to infection from any earthworms and worm eggs found on the ground where other birds have grazed.

Symptoms of blackhead include sulfur-yellow diarrhea, listlessness, and a change in head color to dark blue, after which the animal dies. There is no vaccine and no effective treatment, although some recent studies suggest that cinnamon oil, garlic oil, and rosemary oil can help in the prevention and treatment of blackhead. The disease primarily attacks the intestines and liver and depresses the immune system, so the birds often get secondary bacterial infections. Antibiotics can be helpful against the secondary symptoms. If you suspect you have a sick bird, isolate or cull it immediately and burn the carcass and feces. Histomoniasis mostly affects young birds, so once they are old enough to be out of the brooder and onto pasture full-time, they will have built up enough resistance, and you will likely be home free.

Because of the risk of disease, there's some controversy about whether you should raise chickens and turkeys together. Most of the books about turkeys recommend (some more strongly than others) that turkeys be isolated from all other avians at all times. Some experts assert that the two birds should not inhabit the same farm within three years of each other. The conventional wisdom used to be that turkeys should never even be kept on land that has had chickens or game birds—*ever*.

Many homesteaders keep their turkeys and chickens together with impunity, however. Our turkeys range freely and, although they don't graze in the chicken yards, they would certainly be susceptible to the disease if it were present on our farm, but we've never had a case of blackhead—and I've never met any other poultry grower who allows interspecies cohabitation who has had an outbreak. As with all infectious diseases, it's not just the infecting organism that causes illness. The health and condition of the host animal is at least as important, if not more so. Raising birds on litter, not on wire, helps them build strong immune-system responses to common infections.

Feed for turkeys Turkeys require higher-protein feed at the start of their lives than chickens do. Turkeys that are day-olds through 6 weeks require feed that is 27 to 29 percent protein. From 6 weeks to the last 2 weeks before slaughter, reduce the amount of protein to 20 to 22 percent. During the last 2 weeks, feed them a ration that has about 16 percent protein and extra carbohydrates (cracked corn or scratch feed will do nicely).

Feed the birds standard turkey or game bird feed, adding corn and oats (scratch) or plain cracked corn in proportion,

Top: The Goose Posse, headed up by #9, on patrol. Bottom left: A pair of Wild Eastern turkeys (domestic strain). Bottom right: Jane with one of her Muscovy ducks.

calculating with the Pearson's Square (see p. 305). Alternatively, if your feed store carries an antibiotic-free turkey feed, use that regimen and simply follow the manufacturer's recommendations.

"If it looks like a duck, and quacks like a duck, we have at least to consider the possibility that we have a small aquatic bird of the family Anatidae on our hands."

—Douglas Adams, from Dirk Gently's Holistic Detective Agency

Unfortunately, it's difficult to find turkey feed that doesn't have antibiotics added. For this reason, we've made do with game bird feed from start to finish. We've had good luck, even though game bird feed is a little low on protein (22 percent) for the starter phase. We give the poults greens (chopped grass, comfrey, and vegetables) from the time they are just a few days old. Be sure that if you're feeding poults this way you also provide chicken grit, free choice (in other words, leave out in a bowl so the birds can indulge as much as they want, whenever they want). Because part of our free range includes the graveled roadway, during the normal course of their daily circulations all of our birds get all the grit they need to keep their gizzards in tip-top operating condition. Weather permitting, we give our birds access outdoors from their second week on. As soon as they no longer need an external heat source, they are out on pasture full-time.

Processing Turkeys are slaughtered, plucked, and dressed the same as chickens. Because these birds are much bigger than chickens, however, the processing requires larger equipment. Our scalder and plucker can comfortably handle five chickens at a time but can accommodate only one turkey, so the processing of turkeys is slower and less efficient. That fact—and the fact that there's enough profit in a big bird to cover the cost of off-farm processing—is why, even though we slaughter all of our chickens on the farm, we always send out our turkeys.

On the other hand, if your birds are for home use rather than for market, you'll probably only have a few to kill. A 5-gallon pail with a hole cut in the bottom for the head makes a serviceable turkey-size killing cone. Be careful handling the big toms, as their wings and feet can do some damage in a struggle. Whether you kill your turkeys yourself or send them out, don't forget to age them at least three days before you eat or freeze them (as for chickens).

Ducks and Geese

If you live in a suburban area, with a limited amount of space, waterfowl may not be the best choice for you. All geese and most ducks are quite noisy. They are also messy, scattering lots of feathers about wherever they go (not to mention generous amounts of sloppy stools.) These waterfowl don't absolutely need water to swim in, but they greatly appreciate it, and because they leave their aforementioned calling cards in and around the water, the water quality is likely to suffer.

Geese (especially ganders) are aggressive and make great "watchdogs." The problem is that often geese don't discriminate between strangers and family—they go after everyone. This policy of equal-opportunity harassment sometimes includes the person who feeds them. They also love to get into your flower gardens and wreak havoc. Geese have very strong personalities. For most people it's a "love 'em or hate 'em" affair. Both of my daughters detest my geese. Molly, the daughter who shares our farm and has close encounters with them more often than she would like, refers to the gaggle as the "geese-stapo."

Ducks are not as troublesome as geese. They are shy and prefer to keep a comfortable distance between themselves and any human admirer. Fortunately, they are self-sufficient and enjoyable to watch and listen to, kind of like waddling animatronic lawn ornaments.

Admittedly, there is a downside to ducks and geese—and for many people, there is no upside. To make matters worse, ducks and geese are hard to find homes for, if you decide they are not worth the trouble.

Duck Breeds

All ducks, with the exception of the Muscovy, originated from the wild Mallard. The most common duck breed in the United States is the Pekin, which are large white ducks also known as Long Island ducks or green ducks. They are raised mostly for meat because they grow fast and big, and their white plumage makes them easier to pluck.

Pekin ducks are popular meat birds because their meat is milder and less gamey than that of other types of ducks. There is a sizeable number of folks who like to eat Mallards and other dark-meat birds, however. Muscovy ducks are also raised for the table. Some folks consider them to have the best meat of all. They are leaner and lack the substantial layer of subcutaneous fat that chefs prize for confit.

The Indian Runner was bred in China to weed rice paddies and to eat the bugs that are pests of the plants. Farmers would herd the ducks to the paddies in the morning and then herd them back to the duck pens at night. These fascinating creatures are also called Bottle-Neck ducks because they stand straight up, creating a silhouette reminiscent of a tall bottle. Like Khaki Campbells, they are prolific egg layers.

Feeding Habits of Waterfowl

Waterfowl do not peck their food as chickens do. Instead, they scoop up the mash with their spoon-shaped bills, leaving as much on the ground as they take into their mouths. After a few mouthfuls, they scurry to their water and take a swig or two, swishing the water up and around their nose and sinuses repeatedly. Often they will stick a whole head in the water and vigorously shake it around in order to rinse every speck of leftover feed out of the nasal passage and mouth.

Ducks and geese can actually choke to death on grain if they don't have enough water to wash it down. For this reason, be sure your waterfowl, young or old, never have grain unless there's water close by—and make sure that the water dish is deep enough that they can dunk their entire heads.

For this same reason, they are easy and cheap to buy. Unless you have plenty of space and everyone in the family is on board for the adventure, think carefully before you bring home waterfowl. They are tricky to brood and don't like confinement. If you have toddlers or young children, you absolutely should not keep geese. Ganders feel threatened by small bipeds and will relentlessly and aggressively defend themselves against the perceived threat. Sometimes you can work out these problems, but don't count on it.

For those of us who truly love barnyard birds, however, the beauty and personality of waterfowl more than compensates for their less-endearing traits and habits. Waterfowl can be great additions to a farmstead. Geese are wonderful grazers. We put a small flock of Buff geese in our raspberry patch and have never had to weed it. They also keep the grass around our house and vegetable garden mowed.

We do have to fence in the flower gardens and the area around the house, however, to keep it untrammeled and unfertilized. The ducks don't eat as much grass as the geese do, but they devour bugs and especially love slugs.

Bedding Although the deep-litter system (see p. 303) works for turkey poults, we use low-quality hay as bedding for our geese and ducks. Their manure is wetter and more plentiful than chicken or turkey manure, and we've found that hay is more absorbent than wood or paper shavings. Waterfowl litter will never stay dry. Just keep piling fresh hay on top of the old soiled hay every other day or so. (If you chop the hay by running it through a chipper/shredder first, it will be more

....

Top: Guinea fowl are self-sufficient and independent; they eat huge numbers of bugs. Bottom: Jane talking to the geese (who prefer to stay outside, even in winter).

absorbent.) The bottom of the pile will compost and release heat. We can go quite a while between muck-out sessions, but the waterfowl system is not as elegant as the deep-litter system we use for chickens and turkeys. Ultimately, you end up with a deep pile of soiled hay beneath a thin, clean surface layer—but at least the birds are clean, too. As long as the pile doesn't begin to reek of ammonia, you can let it build up or clean it out as often as you like.

ers, but they also track water throughout the whole pen. Within a few hours, there is not a dry spot to be found. Ducks are much worse than geese in this regard. Goslings and ducklings have similar table manners, but goslings are less interested in swimming and so are not quite as messy.

> "To get your ducks to lay their eggs in the nests you've provided for them, close them in the barn for a few days—they'll figure it out."

Brooding waterfowl Artificially brooding waterfowl is quite different from brooding other farm birds. It can be frustrating and a lot of work. Just like any other baby birds, ducklings and goslings have to be kept warm and dry. The problem is that, unlike chicks or poults, all they want to do is get wet.

Ducks and geese that brood under their mother's wings have a thick, oily coating over their down. When you hold them, they feel as if they've been dunked in a vat of lard. Thus waterproofed, they can withstand rain and cold just like the adult members of the flock.

Artificially brooded babies don't have that protection, and so they can get soaked. They don't know this, of course, so they constantly try to immerse themselves in any drop of water they can find. Not only do they stand or sit in the water-

Build your waterfowl brooder about twice the size as you would for the same number of chicks. Cover the area with a thick bed of shavings and divide it in two. Build a 2×2 wood frame covered with a piece of hardware cloth (closely spaced galvanized-steel wire mesh) that is large enough to cover half the brooder floor. Place the food and water troughs on the frame.

Place the food in any flat container that is large enough to accommodate the ducklings' bills. The water container must permit the birds to submerge their bills at least to the nostrils. In addition to dunking their heads in water many times throughout the day, waterfowl drink four or five times the amount of water that chickens drink.

Hang a heat lamp at a height sufficient to maintain 90°F over the bedding area so the babies stay warm when they sleep. Hang at least one more lamp near the feed and water area at a height of about 18 in. to keep the birds warm while they eat and drink.

Waterfowl Brooder Setup

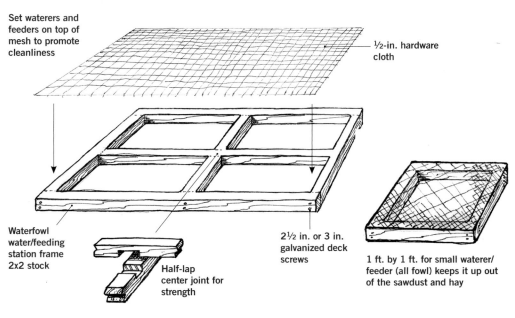

Set waterers and feeders on top of mesh to promote cleanliness

½-in. hardware cloth

Waterfowl water/feeding station frame 2x2 stock

Half-lap center joint for strength

2½ in. or 3 in. galvanized deck screws

1 ft. by 1 ft. for small waterer/ feeder (all fowl) keeps it up out of the sawdust and hay

Even with this setup, it isn't easy to keep a duck pen dry and clean. You'll have to refresh or change the water and bedding several times a day. If you wait until the weather is reliably warm before brooding ducks or geese, you'll save yourself a lot of work. The babies can go out after a week or two as long as they can retreat inside to warm up under the lights. The brooding pen will stay cleaner and drier if you can keep the feed and water outside.

Feeding It's not easy to find starter feed that's made specifically for waterfowl. Game bird feed (20 to 22 percent protein) is a more-readily available substitute.

By the third or fourth day, begin supplementing the starter feed with chopped greens and grass. You can also start your birds on broiler ration that's augmented with a little moistened cat food or fish or blood meal to boost the protein level. In any case, at about 8 weeks, gradually change to a maintenance feed of 16 to 18 percent protein or so (we mix scratch grain with the game bird feed to lower the protein, but you could also use a premixed 18 feed). Compare the protein contents of the feed and calculate what you need with the Pearson's Square (see p. 305) or ask your feed store guru.

Ducklings require about twice as much niacin as chicks do. They should have 35mg of niacin per pound of feed at 0 to 2 weeks and 30mg from 2 to 10 weeks. Some chick starter feeds provide adequate niacin for ducklings, too. Check the label. If it does not specifically say that the feed can be fed to ducklings, or if the nutritional analysis does not list the amount of niacin appropriate for ducklings, add 100mg to 150mg of niacin per gallon of water. (You can get niacin at the drug store in a pill form that will dissolve in water.) Once your ducks are eating green feed on pasture, they'll get plenty of niacin. Geese follow pretty much the same dietary regimen as ducks, but because they are prodigious grazers, they require less feed than ducks do. A lush lawn will go a long way toward reducing your bill for summer feed for geese.

Given the difficulties of artificially brooding waterfowl, make sure you are up to the task before you get involved, but you'll never know how much you might like these birds until you raise a batch. You could test the waters, as it were, by buying some adult birds. Adult ducks and geese are indestructible and almost maintenance free, at least during the summer months when they are busy mowing and fertilizing your lawns.

Maintaining your flocks Ducks are good egg layers. Some varieties are as prolific as moderately good laying hens. Nutritionally, duck eggs are equivalent to chicken eggs, but they're larger. Goose eggs are much larger ("gi-normous," in fact, as our granddaughter puts it). Some bakers swear they make excellent meringue.

If you want duck eggs, get either Khaki Campbells, a hybrid egg-laying variety, or Indian Runners, if you have enough space for them. Ducks need to have a nesting box at ground level in which to lay their eggs, which they will do more or less consistently if you train them. Chickens naturally want to lay their eggs in nests, but ducks have to be convinced that it is a good idea. When ducks get broody, they will often hide their eggs until they're ready to set on them. To get your ducks to lay their eggs in the nests you've provided for them, close them in the barn for a few days—they'll figure it out.

Geese, on the other hand, lay a limited number of eggs for a relatively short period of time, beginning in late winter and on into late spring. As long as you remove the eggs from the nest daily (assuming you can find it—a laying goose typically seeks a secluded outdoor spot to make her nest), she will continue laying an egg every day or so, producing 30 to 40 eggs over the course of the season. If you leave her alone, she'll stop laying and start brooding as soon as she amasses a suitable clutch. Chinese geese are the most prolific layers, producing 40 to 65 eggs in a season. Embden are the runners-up. Most other breeds, especially those favored for meat (such as the Tolouse), produce 20 to 30 eggs per season.

Top left: Day old ducklings (the yellow birds are Muscovies, the dark birds are Runners). Top right: Young goslings, almost fledged. Bottom: Turkey toms showing off for the camera.

"If you feel the urge, don't be afraid to go on a wild goose chase. What do you think geese are for anyway?" —Will Rogers

Mature waterfowl require minimal shelter. They need only a place that's dry and out of the wind. A small flock (you should never have only one bird; two is the minimum) will be happy to have a corner of your barn and a pile of clean hay. Even in the worst weather, ducks and geese prefer to be outside. In the depths of winter, even on a windy, -10°F day, we have to work to convince our water birds to come inside.

Ducks and geese have fragile legs. Never catch or carry a duck or goose by their legs, as they break and injure easily. Ducks are easily frightened, and when they're scared, they become hysterical. The first casualty is always a leg. If the leg injury is a fracture, the duck will likely die. Sometimes a lame duck can be saved if you put it in the "duck hospital" (also known as the "chicken hospital" or "turkey hospital," as the occasion demands). Our "hospital" is a wire dog crate, which we use to isolate any injured bird from the rest of the flock while it recovers—or not. If you must pen a duck or goose to help it rest and recover, consider putting a friend in with the patient. Separation from the flock can be so stressful for an individual bird that it can slow or even prevent healing. If, for whatever reason, there's only room at the inn for one (sometimes two birds just won't get along or won't fit in a tight space), we set the hospital cage in a corner of the coop or outdoor yard so the isolated bird can at least see its buddies.

Processing ducks If you're thinking of raising ducks for the table, you should know that they are a real pain to dress. To start, there's only a narrow window of time in which to slaughter them. At around 6 weeks, almost immediately after becoming fully fledged, they molt. At the beginning of the molting season, before feathers start falling out in large quantities, tiny pinfeathers start to grow on their breasts. These feathers are almost impossible to pluck, even after double-dunking the bird in the scalder. The plucker will tear the skin and rip the wings and legs apart without any noticeable effect on the pinfeathers. At 8 weeks (for Pekins and some other breeds) and again at 12½ weeks, the pinfeathers will have matured into true feathers that can be plucked, either by hand or machine.

Still, even under the best circumstances, plucking a duck is never easy. The feathers are more tightly held than those of a chicken. The natural oils that keep ducks waterproof also keep soapy, scalding water from penetrating through the feathers and down to the skin in order to loosen them. This waterproofing is so effective that when you remove the carcass from the scalder, the down beneath the surface layer is almost perfectly dry. Some experts say that the scalding water for ducks should be hotter, 160°F, compared with 143°F for chickens, and that the carcass should be dunked for no more than 60 seconds. We've found that these higher temperatures tend to liquefy the subcutaneous fat, leaving a mottled skin that is both unappetizing and unmarketable. With ducks, you usually don't have the option of farming the job out to a professional. The professional's solution to the plucking problem is either not to accept ducks for processing or to skin the duck entirely, removing the wonderful layer of self-basting fat that makes the meat so tasty (and is so sought after for making duck confit).

Consequently, if you want to raise your own duck for the table, you're going to have to slaughter, pluck, and dress the animal yourself. Faced with this situation, we embarked on a quest to find the secret to duck plucking on a small scale. We searched everywhere for the secret, elegant method that we knew had to exist, but we never found it—even on the Internet. We're still looking. In the meantime, our duck-processing technique has evolved empirically, by trial and error.

We scald the carcass once to loosen the biggest feathers, hand-plucking as much of the underlying downy feathers as possible to allow water to penetrate to the skin on the second scalding. This double-dip method, coupled with a run through the plucker, successfully removes the bulk of the feathers. To remove the remaining pinfeathers, we dip the carcass in hot paraffin wax and then dunk the carcass in cold water. When we peel off the wax,

feathers come with it. It can take three or four of these "bikini wax" treatments to obtain a clean carcass. Even then, we still need to do some remedial work with tweezers. If our timing was off, and the duck was in full molt, we might spend hours trying to get the rest of the pinfeathers off of the breast, where they tend to remain.

Even with practice, it takes us at least 20 minutes to scald and pluck a duck versus $1^{1}/_{2}$ minutes to scald and pluck a chicken—but it's worth it. Pasture-raised duck is far superior to the commercial product. That fresh, juicy roast duck is so tasty, we readily forgive the bird for the effort it took to get it onto the platter—but it's never quite forgotten.

We've never had any desire to eat a goose, but everyone tells us that it's even harder to pluck a goose than it is to pluck a duck. There are certainly a lot more feathers on a goose. If you want to save the down from either bird, it's best to dry pluck—that is, pull the feathers out by hand without first scalding the carcass. The clean, fluffy down will come off fairly easily. (If you attempt to save down that's been through the scalder, you'll end up with a useless, soggy, smelly mess.) After you have plucked all the down you want, the remaining feathers on the semi-denuded carcass will be more responsive to the scalder. Fortunately, with geese, as with turkeys, it's unlikely that you will be processing more than one or two birds on a given occasion, so hand processing—although tedious and time-consuming—will not be an overwhelming task.

Waterfowl and Guinea Hens

Ducks, geese, and guinea fowl are among the easiest domestic birds to raise. When it comes to hardiness and ease of care, they have it all over chickens and turkeys. If you're attentive, a small flock will almost never have problems with disease or parasites. They are practically immune to cold and wet and require minimal shelter. Their clumsiness on land makes them vulnerable to predators, however, so enclose them at night for safety. Geese are superb foragers and can obtain 100 percent of their nutritional needs from your lawn; ducks and guineas do almost as well. So the cost of keeping a few around is not excessive, and their antics will be a source of unending amusement. They do make a mess, however, and geese and guineas can be extremely noisy—so loud that, unless you live way out in the boonies, they may antagonize your neighbors.

Geese are fine weeders.

Urban Homesteading

Usefulness and charm notwithstanding, ducks and geese are not the best choice for the urban poultry fancier. Because these waterfowl forage extensively, they're happiest when they have room to roam—not a characteristic of most urban environments. Unless you really want to annoy your neighbors, don't even think about guinea hens. They make a lot of noise. A couple of turkeys, however, provide a great way to raise a lot of really tasty meat in a small backyard. One medium-size tom turkey yields as much good eating as five 3-lb. chickens.

Suburban Homesteading

Ducks, geese, and turkeys—unlike chickens—are easy to herd, which makes it easy to manage a small, free-ranging flock. Simply walk behind them and use an extended sapling like a magic wand to direct their line of travel. Once the birds get used to the routine of returning to their enclosure at night, just showing up in their vicinity at twilight is usually enough to get them moving into their shelter or enclosed yard area.

Muscovy is probably the breed of duck best suited to the suburban homestead, at least for meat purposes. The Muscovy is much leaner than the Pekin duck, the more common meat bird. Muscovy drakes (males) grow to a huge size, dressing out at 6 lb. to 8 lb. at 12 weeks, almost twice the size of females. These ducks are also placid and pretty much mute. Although the females quack, they are not as likely to disturb the neighbors as chickens would be. If you'd like to keep ducks for eggs, a Khaki Campbell will outlay even the most prolific chicken, and the eggs are 30 percent larger. Ducks on forage, without a lot of supplemental grain, will produce more than enough eggs, although 30 to 40 percent fewer than those not foraging.

Ducks delight in keeping your gardens free of slugs. Just be sure to fence off lettuce and other tempting, tender greens. Enrich your compost pile by running your pulled weeds through your ducks first—they absolutely devour lamb's quarters and purslane and many other leafy green weeds and grasses. Duck manure is high quality and worth all the straw or spoiled hay bedding it will take to collect and preserve it.

Indian Runner ducks are specialists in insect control, but they do live up to their name. They are fairly high strung, and their mouths never stop running. The susurrus of their alarmed voices in concert is endless. Even in the middle of the night, they find something to worry or complain about.

The Mini-Farm

Guinea fowl are best raised on a fairly large spread. These birds have an incredible repertoire of sounds—most of them loud and some almost earsplitting—so they will really annoy neighbors and fend off visitors. Their penchant for sounding the alarm will alert you that a stranger is in the dooryard long before you are aware of the visitor yourself. Guineas also have a tendency to attack automobiles and generally come out the worse in the encounter, so you'll want to keep them far from a busy road.

Guinea fowl originated in Africa, where they are raised for their meat, which is dark and slightly gamey. Unlike chickens and turkeys, guineas are very tolerant of hot weather, and yet as long as they have a chance to get out of the wind, they winter well in even cold climates like that of Vermont. They are also excellent aerialists, capable of long-distance flight, so it's never a good idea to bring home adult guineas if you'd like them to stick around. The moment that there is an opportunity for them to slip out the door, they'll take off like a shot and never look back. If you want to keep guinea fowl, raise the birds from chicks, and they'll stay more or less close to their nest or shelter.

One really good reason to keep guineas is that they will clear your property of ticks, which is their favorite food. They'll also do a number on Japanese beetles. Guineas really don't like vegetables, so your garden will be safe from their foraging—although wait until the plants are well established because they like to take dust baths in nice clean dirt, like the soil around your newly planted or just-sprouted corn.

chapter xiv
....

Pigs, Cows & Other Farm Animals

E mu, ostriches, minks, llamas, alpacas, beefalo, water buffalo, bison, yaks, yeti—every niche animal has its fervid fans. As the inimitable M. G. Kains recommends, we prefer to raise "staple" animals, "whose meat or milk you can surely sell." Good ol' M. G. never imagined the near future that is today's boutique agricultural market. Here in Vermont and elsewhere throughout the country, there are plenty of small farms— and even a few large ones—profitably raising exotics such as elk and venison (and, yes, even yak) or making mozzarella and ricotta cheeses from water buffalo milk.

We're not suggesting that you shouldn't raise beefalo, frogs, tilapia, or any of the other critters that M. G. calls "freaks." We're only saying that, before you do, you should perfect your husbandry skills by raising some of the more common and familiar animals. Make your mistakes with

....

Top: Feeding Billy Bob, our veal calf, his milk.
Bottom left: Piglets begin foraging a few days after birth. Bottom right: Ginger, a Guernsey heifer, is the family milk cow.

pigs, goats, rabbits, cattle, and sheep first. (That way, as you learn, you'll have the opportunity to try to make sense of not only the conflicting advice in the books you've read, but also the conflicting advice from more experienced growers and breeders.) Before you commit to keeping any animal, regardless of the type, learn as much as you can about its unique characteristic and care.

The Pig: The Homestead's MVP

If you're going to get serious about raising meat, raising a pig (or two) is the best way to begin. Pigs are amazing creatures. Adaptable, versatile, hardy, and charismatic, they are probably the easiest and most economical meat animal you can raise.

Most books you pick up about pigs will point out that, contrary to popular opinion, pigs are not dirty. In fact, after cats and dogs, pigs are one of the cleanest domestic animals. (They can even be toilet trained.) They probably got their bad rap from their notorious love of mud and of rooting in the dirt. Pigs cannot sweat and so keep themselves cool in hot

349

weather by wallowing in mud. Cool mud cools them much better than water alone does, because it sticks to their bodies and evaporates more slowly (and, incidentally, protects them from biting flies).

If there's dirt and water around, pigs will wear mud. So pigs are often, quite literally, "dirty." When we talk about animals' being dirty, however, we're really referring to feces. Pigs do produce a lot of them, but, when given enough space, pigs will piss and poop in one area and keep the rest of their pen and bedding tidy. Unlike most other barnyard animals—who relieve themselves wherever they happen to be, thereby requiring you to muck out the entire pen each time you clean—pigs only require daily cleaning of their potty area; you can clean the rest of their stall once every week or two. (The dirtiest animals on our farm are those pretty white ducks. We clean their truly disgusting pen at least twice a day, as they seem to poop nonstop everywhere.)

Buying a piglet is a rural rite of spring. Beginning in late April or early May and through the first week of June, farmers and breeders just about anywhere here in the North will have six-week-old piglets for sale. By late October or mid-November, that cute little piggy will have transformed itself into 250 lb. of pork-to-be. In between your pig's arrival and departure, all you have to do is provide it with minimal shelter, with or without some kind of enclosure, and enough feed. Any shelter you build can be reused for next year's pig and all pigs thereafter.

Buying your piglet Historically, there were two basic types of pigs: bacon (long

and lean) and lard (short and fat). Back in the 19th and early 20th centuries, when vegetable-based cooking fats were either scarce or too costly, a pig that yielded a lot of lard and fatback was highly prized. These days, it's next to impossible to find a lard-type pig.

Most of the piglets you'll find for sale today are not pure breeds, but rather a mixture of two or more breeds. With the increasing popularity of small pasture-raised herds, there is a renewed interest in the older breeds, like the reddish Tamworth, brownish Duroc, black Berkshire, and white Cheshire and Yorkshire. These varieties were common back in the days when all pigs were raised outdoors. Mixing and matching these old breeds, if done well, produces pigs that are sociable, well adapted to the local climate, and excellent foragers. These cross breeds also yield high-quality meat. Once you've tasted home-raised pork of any kind—but especially the meat of heritage-breed crosses—you'll never touch commodity pork again.

Until recently, when we decided to begin raising our own pigs for market, we never paid much attention to the breed of piglets we bought. We always found our piglets in the local want ads or on Craigslist.com. Chances are, the farmer didn't even know the breed. If an unknown breed is the only kind of piglet you can find, that's okay. The foraging, feeding, and finishing—not the breed—are what give the meat its taste. The premium you'll pay for purebred genetics isn't going to be worth much in a pig that won't be around long enough to contribute to the breeding pool. Unless

"The hog on the range in many ways functions as a free agent. It isn't a wild or uncontrolled animal, but in some respects the hogs do get closer to nature and their animal origins."
—Kelly Klober, from Dirt Hog

you plan to start breeding pigs for market, a "field run" feeder pig or two will fill the homestead larder just as well as it's fancified cousins—and will save you money, too. If you just ask around at the feed store or look in the right newspapers, you usually find more-or-less-generic pink and maybe black-and-white, lean-type pigs.

Pigs farrow (give birth) in spring and fall. If you live in the North, buy a spring pig. If you live in the South, a fall pig may be better. If you can, buy your piglet from a farmer who raises pastured pork or feeder pigs (pigs raised to a 200-lb. market weight). You may pay a little more, but you'll get a better animal and one that has been bred especially for the way you intend to raise your pig.

The overall condition and disposition of the animal is more important than its breed. Whenever possible, visit the farm and see the litter and the dam (mother). Avoid buying at an auction or from the guy who drove to Pennsylvania and came back with 100 feeder pigs to sell. It's not that the auction or that guy is dishonest, it's just that you can't tell anything about your pig's litter mates or mother or how they were treated or raised.

Pick the most active and curious piglet of the batch. You can feel sorry for the quiet one in the corner or love the cute little runt, but don't take it home with you. Your pig is only going to live for 4 to 6 months, so it doesn't much matter if the piglet is male or female. Males may be a bit more aggressive, so they'll tend to eat more and, therefore, may grow a bit faster, but not so much faster that it makes any real difference. Clearly, you don't want an animal that is limping or shows some other deformity or injury. Bottom line: Pick the biggest, most active piglet you can find.

Piglets are generally weaned at 4 weeks and sold at 6 to 8 weeks. A 6-week-old pig should weigh about 20 lb. to 30 lb.; at 8 weeks, from 30 lb. to 40 lb. Many farmers give newborn pigs iron shots, and some also vaccinate them. If your pigs root around on pasture or dirt, they will ingest plenty of iron. If they will spend most of their lives in the barn, it may be a good idea to get the shots.

The males are usually castrated, and most have had their needle teeth clipped. The traditional wisdom is that the meat from boars (anatomically intact male pigs) tastes rank and smells bad because of a quality known as "boar taint." This assessment may be more myth than fact. We know farmers who never castrate their male piglets and swear that they have never had any complaints. We also know others who say that once you've smelled boar taint you'll never forget it. Not all boar meat carries this elusive (or illusive) taint. Some pig farmers theorize that taint has to do with the boar's age at time of slaughter; some claim it's more pronounced in some breeds; others say that it's only a problem if the boar has been with a sow in estrus. We've never smelled or tasted boar taint— and we have eaten plenty of boar meat, including meat from an 800-lb. 2-plus-year-old. His meat, like all boar meat, was darker than barrow (castrated male) meat, but it was just as sweet and mellow as any we've ever had.

As far as growth rate is concerned, castration does not seem to make much difference. Because it's not exactly a benign procedure, castration can set a piglet back or even cause a fatal infection. Feeder pigs are butchered at 5 to 6 months, at which point they're not mature enough for testosterone to cause taint or any other kind of problems (such as aggressive behavior) that can make the animal hard to handle. So it probably doesn't matter whether you buy a castrated or whole pig, unless you decide to keep your boar for breeding instead of eating.

Living areas Factory pigs are raised crowded together in large buildings with just enough space and food so that, with the addition of regular antibiotics and growth hormones, they will reach market weight before they die of stress. They live on slotted or concrete floors with no bedding and no opportunity to do piggy things, like root around for grubs and wallow in the mud. Little or no regard is given to the animal's comfort or quality of life. The fact that they can survive under such conditions is a testimony to how hardy pigs really are.

Given the deplorable living conditions of commercial hogs, anything would qualify as better. The more space you can give your pigs, the better. If you have some pasture or at least a patch of ground where your hogs can root, great. Small farmers often run their hogs on fields or wooded lots in small herds.

You don't need a lot of land to raise your family pork, however. If you have a 10-ft. by 20-ft. area, your pigs will do just fine. Just be aware that they will turn any small piece of ground into a mud hole, without a single blade of grass or a root left in place—which can be a good thing. If a corner of your property is overgrown with some particularly noxious weed, like Japanese knotweed, you can put your pigs there, and you'll never see that weed again.

We've raised several pairs of pigs in a 4-ft. by 10-ft. pen in the back of an outbuilding. The pen opened onto a 10-ft. by 16-ft. outdoor corral, which had a cement "patio" for sunning and a patch of ground for digging. In hot weather, we watered the dirt to make a big wallow. It wasn't a pasture, but those pigs seemed contented. They could get warm and dry inside, lie in the sun, and dig in the dirt. We never had to clean the indoor pen. They designated one corner of the corral as their latrine. The problem with this arrangement, however, is that it works fine for a single season. If we keep pigs the next year, we wouldn't put them on the same ground they rooted up the previous year, as that would increase their chances of parasite infection.

Space permitting, you could solve this problem by arranging four paddocks (enclosed mini-pastures) in a U shape around the central barn. In addition to the pigs, the paddocks could also house a flock of layers or a batch of broilers. One pasture is always planted with grass or another forage crop, recovering as the pigs follow the chickens in rotation through the paddocks. (The rotation cycle for each paddock is chicken, pig, grass, and around

again.) Sound familiar? This system is just a large-scale variation on the idea of the four-door chicken coop (see p. 300). Barn doors can open directly into each of the paddocks or onto a common alley that services the paddocks, which can then be at some distance from the barn.

You can house pigs and chickens in separate pens in the same structure, and they will also happily coexist in an outdoor paddock, but don't think for a moment that they can share the same indoor pen. I've never forgotten the night when—responding to an alarming ruckus in the barn where we kept our pigs and

Livestock Barn & Paddock Rotation System

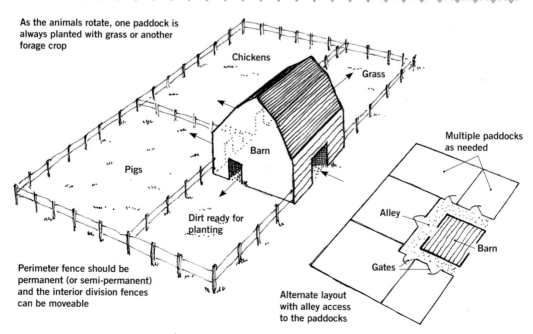

As the animals rotate, one paddock is always planted with grass or another forage crop

Chickens

Grass

Barn

Pigs

Dirt ready for planting

Perimeter fence should be permanent (or semi-permanent) and the interior division fences can be moveable

Multiple paddocks as needed

Alley

Barn

Gates

Alternate layout with alley access to the paddocks

chickens, separated by a partition of chicken wire and boards—I switched on the light to discover the partition in shambles and saw chicken feet sticking out like toothpicks from the jaws of a very contented but suddenly guilty-looking pig. Outdoors, chickens have room enough to avoid any pig that gets too close for comfort. Just make sure your pigs are always well fed. They are, after all, omnivores.

Shelter Whether freely ranging or penned, pigs need some sort of minimal shelter that furnishes them with a dry place to sleep and protection from the elements. Even pigs on pasture should have access to a small doghouse or lean-to, with or without a floor, to provide shelter from the worst weather. In open fields, be sure to provide shade to protect them from the hot sun, too.

Despite their relative hairlessness (compared to horses or cows), pigs are amazingly hardy creatures. Their thick layer of insulating fat enables them to withstand cold. As long as they have a thick bed of dry hay to burrow down into and a lean-to and roof of some sort to block the wind and snow, they can winter outdoors, even in northern New England. In a dry climate, a simple floorless roofed pen may be all the shelter they need.

We've spied more than a few old truck caps recycled as pig shelters around here. When the pigs are small, the cap simply rests on the ground. As the pigs grow, the farmer raises the corners of the cap up on stakes that have been driven into the ground. One pig farmer we know excavates a cavity in the hillside, roofs it over, and lines it with a wall of hay bales. His pigs stay warm and dry as they munch their way through their winter quarters.

If you get a lot of rain or if the ground inside your pig pasture is wet, you should provide some sort of floor or platform—even just a couple of pallets covered with scrap boards or plywood—to keep your pigs comfortable. A comfortable pig is a pig that's packing on pounds with those expensive feed-store calories rather than just burning them to keep warm. Another inexpensive and easy-to-build all-purpose pig house is a three-sided shed, or A-frame, which you set on top of a floor platform attached to a pair of timber "sled runners." You can move it around the pasture or into the garden after harvest to put your pigs where their services will do the most good and where they will always have fresh ground to turn over.

Pigs on the move The "pig tractor" is a time-honored and incredibly efficient method for clearing and improving land. It's also a way to provide pigs with an opportunity to indulge in rooting and foraging when you don't have a pasture large enough for your pigs to range in and tear up. The two basic options are a portable enclosure or a portable pen.

The portable electric-fence systems originally developed for controlling sheep in New Zealand have been adapted as fencing for poultry and other classes of livestock. These systems are economical and extremely versatile. For a portable electric-fence system suitable for containing hogs, you'll need a roll of conductive

Pig Pen with Built-In Shelter

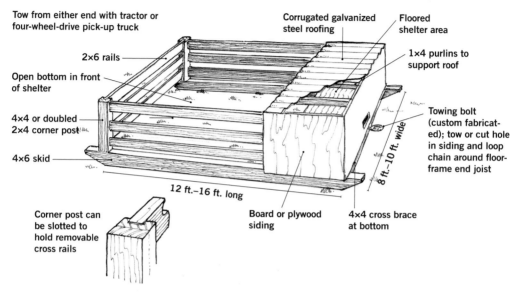

Tow from either end with tractor or four-wheel-drive pick-up truck

2×6 rails

Open bottom in front of shelter

4×4 or doubled 2×4 corner post

4×6 skid

12 ft.–16 ft. long

Corner post can be slotted to hold removable cross rails

Corrugated galvanized steel roofing

Floored shelter area

1×4 purlins to support roof

Towing bolt (custom fabricated); tow or cut hole in siding and loop chain around floor-frame end joist

8 ft.–10 ft. wide

Board or plywood siding

4×4 cross brace at bottom

polyester ribbon (strands of stainless-steel wire are interwoven into an ultraviolet-light-stabilized plastic ribbon), slender 4-in. fiberglass rods and plastic lock-on insulators to support the ribbon, and a fence charger (either plug-in or battery or solar powered).

Choose the area you want to enclose as a pig yard. Before you set the posts, mow the grass along the proposed fence line down to bare ground with a weed whacker to keep the grass from touching (and thereby shorting out) the fence. It's easy to push the fiberglass rods into the ground by hand, but be sure to wear gloves, or your palms will be peppered with painful fiberglass splinters.

Pigs don't jump (well, they can if they really have to, but they don't like to admit it), so, for this low fence, you'll only need two strands of ribbon. Set the lower strand about 4 in. off the ground to discourage rooting along the fence line. Set the upper strand at snout level, which will change as the pigs grow, so at 8 in. to start and later at 12 in. and 18 in. (see the photo on p. 359). The idea is to prevent the pig from sticking its head between the ribbon strands with impunity, which might encourage the rest of its body to follow.

The top ribbon will be low enough for you to step over, so there's no need for a gate (although you might want one—if the pigs ever escape, as you attempt to herd them back in they'll refuse to step across a ribbon or walk under one). Sometimes, the pigs' learned aversion to electric fences is so strong that they won't cross a ribbon on the ground even if it's completely covered with hay. A covering of plywood might fool them, but an especially suspicious pig with a long memory will likely mistrust the board or any other cover-up and stay away from the area where he knows there used to be a painful fence. They seem to just naturally assume you're up to something disreputable.

Check the fence often, as plants grow back and pigs push furrows of dirt and roots onto the ribbon, grounding out the fence. If you hear a rhythmic snapping sound, that's the sound of a short. Somewhere, a clod of dirt or the stem of a weed is touching the ribbon. Follow the sound to locate and clear the offending object.

If you enclose a relatively small area and leave your pigs in it long enough, they'll eventually plow up every square foot, pushing up the stones, digging out roots, consuming the weeds and witchgrass, and leaving you with very well fertilized bare dirt. After your four-legged rototillers have finished prepping the area, relocate the fence and the pigs to the next area that you've slated for improvement. Pick the stones, level the wallows and furrows they've left behind (with a mechanical tiller), and seed the former pig yard to a cover crop or pasture grasses.

Portable enclosures work well when you have a number of pigs that can work a fairly large area relatively quickly. If you have only one or two pigs and/or a small area to work, you could dispense with the fence entirely. Instead, keep the pigs inside a wooden pen (or "pig tractor") that is sturdy enough to pull with a tractor or four-wheel-drive truck (see the drawing on p. 355). Build a 3-ft.- or 4-ft.-wide floor platform across one end of the corral and roof it over so the animals will have a dry, clean, and shady place to sleep and loaf. In a few days or less, the pigs will have thoroughly churned through the remaining enclosed ground, and you can pull the pen elsewhere to repeat the process.

Feeding Feeding pigs can be very economical, as they are omnivores and will gobble up the food that people throw away. This "garbage" can be table scraps from your kitchen or plate scrapings from a local restaurant (ideally, one that serves locally grown and or/organic food). It can be day-old bread from a local bakery, spent brewer's mash from microbreweries, or whey from a cheese plant (although it's questionable that a diet heavy on old doughnuts, beer, and stale white bread would be any better for a pig than it would be for you). In any case, whatever you feed your hogs should not be spoiled or moldy. Never allow any pig food to be contaminated by rodent droppings, which can harbor trichinosis organisms and salmonella.

Pigs will forage for up to one-third of their total nutritional needs. Count your blessings if you live where oaks are plentiful. You can fatten a pig magnificently on acorns and nothing else, and the taste of the meat will be smooth and rich. If, however, you're a small landowner and are

How Much Does My Pig Weigh?

Convincing a pig to step onto a bathroom scale would be an interesting challenge. So, how can you determine the weight of your pig without the help of a scale?

A pig is basically an amazingly dense cylinder. Assuming a value for the average density of pork, it follows that the weight of a pork-filled cylinder is proportional to its volume.

This calculation is reputed to be accurate within 3 percent.

With a flexible tape, measure the animal's heart girth (HG), the circumference of the pig just behind the front legs, in inches. Then measure the animal's length (L) from the base of the ears to the base of the tail, also in inches.

Square the HG number and multiply the number by L.

Divide the result by 400 for the total estimated weight of your pig.

$$(HG^2 \times L) \div 400 = \text{approximate weight}$$

(You'll be amazed at how much porcine poundage is packed into that low-slung frame!)

providing good pasture, spoiled vegetables, garden waste and weeds, and as many table scraps as you can, your pigs will still require at least some commercial feed to balance their diet—although not as much as they would without the food sources you're providing.

How much feed is enough? You can find all sorts of tables and charts that, theoretically, provide the optimal answer (which might, indeed, be valid for the strictly controlled environment of a CAFO barn). Out on the range, however, or even in the backyard pen, the multifarious variables of age, weight, weather, social arrangements, and the availability and quality of forage are so unquantifiable that you may as well hand your pigs a printed menu and ask them to make their own selections. As you might expect, appetite is proportional to weight. A 50-lb. to 100-lb. growing pig will eat, on average, 3½ lb. of concentrate or its equivalent per day. When the pig weighs from 100 lb. to 150 lb., the intake will average closer to 5 lb. From that weight to market weight (from 200 lb. to 250 lb.), the animal's average daily needs increase from about 6 lb. to 6½ lb. of feed. Feed utilization (fuel economy) improves as the pig grows. In other words, pound for pound, the animal eats less per each additional 100 lb. of live weight—one of the most admirable qualities of their species.

The rule of thumb on our farm is strictly empirical. We feed our pigs enough to maintain good table manners—that is, although they may be hungry by feeding time, they shouldn't ever be *ravenously* hungry. Decorum for hogs at the trough is a relative concept, of course, but once you've experienced the alarmingly cacophonous and insistent rush of a gang of very hungry pigs, you'll know the difference. Properly fed pigs will amble rather than scramble toward the trough. If there are leftovers after feeding, you're feeding the pigs too much. If they're still lingering and complaining at the empty trough, you need to feed them more.

Mature sows are either gestating, lactating, or recouping their strength after a litter, so you should feed them a full ration of concentrates, regardless of whether they're on pasture or not. For sows, forage is basically a beneficial diet supplement. Feeding gets a little complicated, if you have a mixed group of sows and their weaned piglets (which is why pig farmers separate the mothers from their young 'uns after weaning). If you feed to the needs of the sow, however, everybody will do fine—assuming you don't have a breeding boar in the group.

Boars are kept separate from the sows until you want them to breed. Once that business is concluded, the boar can remain with the sow throughout her pregnancy until shortly before farrowing, when the boar is removed, and the cycle begins anew. You should dial down the feed for boars so they don't grow too big too fast—which is easy enough to do during their solitary confinement, but not so easy when they're running with the ladies. Or you could introduce a young boar to a group of older sows. The sows run the show, so he'll be lucky and grateful for any scraps they allow him—if they don't beat

him up in the meantime. Rather than own a boar, you could instead rent one.

If your homestead includes a milk cow, you're probably getting a lot more milk (and butter and yogurt and potted cheese) than you and your family can use. The skim milk left from butter making will raise very fine pigs. In the Northeast, the apple trees are at their peak at just the time we are "finishing" our pigs. There's nothing quite so fine as homegrown pastured pork, finished on milk, apples (wild or orchard drops), or acorns.

Pig management A fellow from down country asked his farmer neighbor, "How do you move a pig?" The old timer replied, "Any way you can." Pigs are, by nature, suspicious animals. Their guard goes up easily and comes down hard. Just like that stereotypical old Yankee farmer, they don't like change—especially when you want to get a pig to go somewhere it doesn't want to go. Maybe you can lure it along—as you could a cow—by dangling a bucket of its favorite food under its snout? The pig will stick its head down into the bucket all right, and maybe even take a step or two toward it as you back away, but, with pigs, instinct always trumps appetite. That pig just knows something's up, and whatever it is you're sellin', it ain't buyin'. Inevitably, you'll make the mistake of dumping a little of the contents on the ground just to show it there's nothing to be afraid of. "Look, it's your favorite!" You might as well dump out the rest because that pig has faked you out.

There is some hope, however. You can eventually convince a pig to trust you— at

Training to the Fence

If it so chooses, any pig (like any other critter) can push right through an electric fence. To prevent this from happening, piglets must be "trained to the fence." Simply put, they have to touch the fence soon after they're put behind it to learn that the fence "bites." Pigs are smart—usually it only takes only one or two applications of this shock treatment for them to get the idea. Thereafter, they will keep their distance from the fence.

Some folks believe you should just let the piglets discover the power of the fence on their own. Others suggest leading the piglet to the fence and gently pushing its snout against it until the animal gets the idea. This second method can achieve the desired results, but it can also make the animal afraid of you. It can also spook the pig badly enough to make it dart right between the ribbons and, in fact, teach exactly the opposite of the intended lesson. As an unexpected bonus, if you're touching the pig when it touches the fence, you'll get a shock, too.

We push a food dish with something very tempting in it (like bread and milk) halfway under the fence and then put the piglet down near the dish. When it attempts to reach the food, the piglet touches the fence (and shocks its very sensitive snout). After it's gotten the message, you can give the animal its treat away from the fence.

Always be sure your pigs are calm before you put them inside the fence for the first time. If your new charges are all riled up when you let them go, they may dash off through the fence before you have a chance to teach them anything. Once a pig (or any animal) learns that the electric fence doesn't hurt that much if it runs through fast enough, getting it to respect that fence can be very difficult or even impossible to achieve. Test the fence to be sure it has a good jolt—preferably with a fence tester (avoid deliberately touching an electric fence; the sensation is way too much like sticking your finger into a live wall outlet).

least to associate your presence with the appearance of its dinner. Without this connection, you'll never be able to get close enough to an escaped pig to coax it back into its pen—hence, the raison d'être for hog calling. When you feed your pigs, always call them to the bucket. It doesn't matter what kind of a call you make, as long as the call is always the same. The idea is to get the sight and sound of you and the sight and sound of the slop bucket to meld in the pig's mind so that you become the dependable bringer of good things.

The next step is to get the pig to allow you to intrude into its comfort zone. Approach slowly while the pig's alarm system is temporarily disabled by the food in the trough. Try to touch the animal on the back of the neck or lightly scratch it behind the ears, along the back, or shoulder. At first, your touch will trigger the alarm, and the pig will jump away startled, but if you patiently continue to make contact, the pig will gradually not only tolerate your touch but welcome it. Pigs really enjoy being scratched, so much so that they'll actually collapse onto their bellies with a grunt of pure pleasure. The whole business is a lot easier to accomplish with one pig. With a bunch of them, the suspicion quotient multiplies, and

Top: George and Winky share a pleasant moment after a good scratch. Bottom left: Circe, our Tamworth/Old Spot sow. Bottom right: A pig keeps cool on a hot day.

the zone of comfort shrinks. You'll need a lot more patience and perseverance to overcome their mistrust.

Eventually, your pig will discover that, if it pushes up enough sod to bury the bottom ribbon, the fence doesn't bite any-

"You can eventually convince a pig to trust you—or at least to associate your presence with the appearance of its dinner."

more. The problem is that a pig explores by rooting stuff up and that exploration may include your flower bed, the garden, or the lawn. Pigs can run amazingly fast when they have to, and the last thing you want to do is upset an escaped pig. If the pig isn't hungry enough to respond to the call of the slop bucket, approach the animal slowly and calmly. You can usually steer the pig in the direction you want it to go by lightly prodding it behind the base of its ears with a long pole. If there's no gate in your fence, you may actually have to take down or relocate a length of the fence before the pig will reenter the enclosure.

Unlike other domestic animals, pigs have no necks, so you can't just slip a rope or halter over their heads and tug on it. If you're clever and quick and the pig is calm, you can loop a rope over its head and then behind its forelegs with a half-hitch to make a harness. Again, unlike other animals, pigs won't be led. Their instinct is to back away from a restraint. You can use that instinct to your advantage by holding a bucket over the pig's head and, as it tries to back away from the bucket, steering its opposite end in the direction you want it to go (a good job for a helper). The bucket trick works pretty well, as long as the pig's head isn't too big to fit entirely inside the bucket (and you can manage to hold the bucket in place, which ain't all that easy). Otherwise, you'll just have a very annoyed pig trying to shake off both you and the bucket. You can also direct a pig backward by holding a scoop shovel or a plywood panel in front of it.

Processing The hardest part of the whole pig-raising enterprise is that last bad day, when the pig becomes pork. (Fortunately, one reason why pigs are a good choice for raising meat is that by the time a pig has to be killed, it's pretty likely you'll be ready to kill it. One day, you'll look at that creature who almost bowled you over to get at the food you dumped in the trough, and you'll see bacon instead of brute.) Putting aside for the moment the emotional component of the act of killing,

The Killing Dilemma

If you raise your own meat animals, you have to come to terms with killing them. There's no way around it. It's a nasty job, but someone's got to do it. I believe (and this is just my opinion, take it or leave it) that the someone should be you—at least, the first time.

When you choose to eat meat, you are intimately involved in the cycle of life and death. If the consequences of that choice remain a poetic abstraction rather than a visceral, blood-spattered reality, you have shortchanged yourself. The whole point of self-sufficient living is to take responsibility for your

choices and actions, including giving that wonderful animal the decent and kind death it deserves by your own hand. Paying someone else to do the job is acceptable if you're there to participate; paying to keep your distance isn't. I don't understand a person who says, as he wipes the grease from his chin, "If I had to kill this pig myself, I could never eat it." That is exactly the kind of thinking that creates CAFOs, those animal prison camps. I don't want my animals dying in a strange place, alone and terrified. I want their last moments to be pleasant. When I kill a pig, I'll set out a shallow

basin of its favorite food on the floor and wait until the animal is blissfully preoccupied before I shoot it.

The hardest part of killing any animal is the moment when you pick up the knife or the gun. Part of you doesn't want to do the deed at all and wishes someone else would do it. The other part knows what has to be done and remembers to give that animal a silent thank-you. After the trigger is pulled or the cut is made, it's all process. The knot in your stomach dissolves, the tension releases with your breath, and you get to work, making meat to feed your family.

the main difficulty with slaughtering a pig yourself is logistical.

A market-weight hog (what farmers call pigs at the point of optimal balance between additional weight gain and additional feed cost) is a big, heavy animal, especially when it's literally dead weight. It's about as much weight as two strong men should safely handle. At the very least, you'll have to engineer a way to hoist the carcass. There's also the question of scalding or skinning, that is, whether to remove the coarse hairs that cover the hog's skin (by dipping the carcass in a tank of scalding hot water and then scrapping off the hairs, a major operation in itself) or to remove the skin and hair en masse with a knife, which is easier, but less desirable if you prefer your pork cooked up with a crisp and tasty rind. Once you've made the necessary arrangements, the process of turning your dead pig into four quarters of hanging pork isn't as difficult. With an adventurous spirit and a good book as a guide, even someone whose previous experience with home butchering involved carving a roast at the table could do a reasonably good job of it. Just the same, I'd recommend you offer a friend or neighbor who's done the deed and knows what he's doing a six-pack or two to show you how it's done.

You could instead hire someone to slaughter the pig. There are traveling butchers who will come to your place to kill and quarter your hog or any other large animal for a very reasonable fee. Some will also haul the carcass to a custom slaughterhouse for cutting, wrapping, and (for the hams and bacon) smoking.

The other major logistical challenge of at-home butchering is storage. You probably already have a chest freezer that is large enough to hold your year's meat. The problem is finding a safe place to hang the carcass for proper aging before cutting and wrapping it. In the north country, we wait to kill our animals until the cusp of October/November, when the days are consistently chilly and the nights cold enough, but not so frigid that the meat freezes solid, and we hang the carcass in an outbuilding. The carcass is more likely to be safe from scavengers and less likely to freeze or overheat if it's hung from a beam in the barn or shed than outdoors. On our farm, we hang quartered carcasses from the ceiling of our root cellar. You could also (although just barely) accommodate a quartered pig in an old refrigerator that has most of the shelves or bins removed.

If you find the entire process too overwhelming, you could simply haul the live pig to that custom slaughterhouse yourself, kiss it good-bye at the gate, and, a few weeks later, pick up your pork, bacon, and hams, all neatly wrapped, labeled, and freezer-ready. Just remember to book your date at the slaughterhouse months in advance, as most are straight-out busy come the fall season—and the same is often true for the traveling butchers, too.

Veal Calves

You don't need as much land as you might think to grow your own beef. In fact, you don't need any. Veal calves require less space to raise than either chickens or pigs.

A 6-ft. by 6-ft. pen per animal is entirely adequate. To get really tender meat, your calf needs to be confined, so don't make the pen any larger than 10 ft. by 10 ft. The pen should be protected from sun, wind, and rain, but it should also allow for as much natural daylight and fresh air as possible. We put our veal pen under the shed roof attached to the horse barn, where we store hay in the winter. A corner of your garage would work just fine.

Any dairy bull calf will make good veal (or beef). Most books will suggest you get a Holstein calf because they grow bigger and have white fat (most commercial veal is Holstein). You can also raise Jersey or Guernsey calves. These breeds are smaller, and the meat has yellow fat, which looks different but doesn't taste different. Some people will pay a premium for Jersey meat, which they say has a distinct, sweet taste. (We can't tell the difference.)

Newborn, dairy-breed bull calves are downright cheap to buy. You might even be able to pick one up in exchange for a plate of brownies, if (as is common in some areas) farmers have to pay to have their day-old calves hauled away. Contrast this to the high prices you might pay for a weanling beef-breed calf. (Even if you want to raise a calf to 400 lb. or 500 lb. for beef, you're probably still better off buying a dairy bull calf—unless you plan to start a beef herd, in which case you should buy the best beef calves you can afford.)

Feeding Once you've struck your deal and have agreed to take the calf, most farmers are amenable to keeping a newborn for at least three days so that it can get colostrum milk from its mother. (The new mother produces this antibody-rich immune-system booster for the first few days after calving.) Failing this, ask if you can take the colostrum home—farmers can't mix it with the rest of the milk and will just throw it away anyway.

There's a bit more day-to-day effort in feeding veal calves than in feeding broilers or pigs. You have to bottle-feed the animal, either with milk replacer, which you'll need to mix twice daily, or with culled milk, which you'll need to fetch from a dairy farmer, store, and warm up. Some people teach their calves to drink out of a pail, with or without a nipple attachment. This feeding method may be less trouble for you, but it's not so good for the calf, especially a newborn. The pail setup encourages the calf to eat too fast. Large curds will then sit in the rumen (first stomach), and the calf cannot digest them. Dirt and fecal material can get into the bucket, too, causing severe illness. Initially, it's more work to bottle-feed, but, in the end, it decreases the risk of disease—and it's kind of fun, too.

The best way to raise a veal calf is to feed him real milk from a local farm. Dairy farmers frequently have milk that they cannot sell for one reason or another. If you arrange to pick it up at the farmer's convenience, you could maybe get it free for the hauling. Or you could offer a trade (some veal, perhaps?).

If you can't find a source for real milk, you'll need milk replacer (powdered milk proteins derived from whey with supplemental vitamins and minerals). Be sure

The Veal Dilemma

If, like us, you pride yourself on raising your animals "naturally" and humanely, there are some issues with raising veal. First, in order to ensure that its meat is tender, the calf is kept in a small area and gets as little exercise as possible. Second, a calf typically begins to eat hay, grass, and a little grain within a few days after birth. To feed it only milk for three months makes the animal anemic—which is why meat is white and not red or pink.

The way we can justify these "unnatural" (some even say immoral) practices is by considering the otherwise bleak prospects for a bull calf born into a dairy herd. Bull calves are often shipped to processing plants within a day or two, if not hours, after birth. Which is worse, ending up as dog food right away or living three comfortable months in a pen before slaughter? Either way, there is no future for 99.9 percent of dairy bull calves. We are fully aware that this is a justification, but it's one we're willing to live with. You have to decide for yourself. If you decide to raise a veal calf, resist the temptation to get attached to the animal. Certainly, be gentle and kind. Just don't get sentimental. It's hard enough to kill a pretty calf without making a pet of him first.

the replacer is not medicated. (If you can't get milk or unmedicated replacer, you may want to scrap the idea of raising veal. Look into the options before you get your calf.) You can feed the animal a combination of milk and milk replacer, as need be. It does no harm to the calf to switch back and forth between them.

Feed the calf as much milk as it will drink in one sitting, twice a day. After two to four weeks, you can offer the calf a little grain if you want. Always have water and a salt block available.

Treating scours The main health problem of calves is calf scours, a severe, potentially life-threatening diarrhea. It is usually caused by a combination of stress and one or two of several bacteria, including *E. coli*. Scours is very common and, if caught early and treated immediately, it's easy to cure. After three weeks of age, the risk of infection goes way down.

Scours can be scary, but it's not as bad as you think. If you see loose, grayish stool in a calf that is three days to three weeks old, slow down his feed and check on him every two hours. If he doesn't improve, stop feeding the animal milk and instead feed it electrolytes in water. (Electrolyte solutions are available at the feed store.) If the calf is no better in one to two days, start oral antibiotics. (Some purists balk at resorting to antibiotics, but when the choice is between losing a calf or compromising principles, we choose life.) If the animal is still not better in a day or so, or at any time gets worse, call a veterinarian.

Processing When your calf is 12 weeks old, it's time to butcher him. With a handy instruction manual, determination, and a setup for hoisting the carcass, you can kill, skin, gut, and portion the calf yourself. (Don't forget the shank cut for osso bucco.) Of course, you can always hire someone to do the job at your place or send the animal to the custom slaughterhouse.

Beef Cows

If you want to grow that dairy bull calf into dairy beef instead—or raise a beef cow—you'll need anywhere from 1 to 10 acres of pasture per animal (depending on how good the pasture is). Animals improve pastureland, so you might be able to find someone who is willing to let you graze your animals on their unused meadow.

Raising just one beef animal isn't a good idea. Cows, like all herd animals, hate to be alone. A solitary cow will be unhappy and will always try to get out of its pasture. A goat or a horse can help alleviate its loneliness, but another cow is even better. At roughly 500 lb. of dressed weight per cow, two cows is a lot of beef. Sharing the project with a few other families is one option. Another would be to keep animals of different ages. Beef cattle are slaughtered at 18 to 24 months, so staggering the ages of your beef animals will assure that you have meat each year.

We recommend that you have some experience and competence with raising other meat animals before you try to raise a beef cow. Cattle are big and can be difficult to handle, alive or dead. Unlike pigs, chickens, or calves, beef cows are a long-term project; they have to be overwintered at least once. Keeping large animals over the winter requires a quantum leap in your farm's infrastructure and support. In cold climates, beef cattle will need a barn or shed and a good deal of hay or silage. If you can't raise your own winter feed, you'll need to buy it. (Our rule of thumb is 200 square, 40-lb. bales per cow per winter—at the current price of $3 each, that's $600 per cow. To provide insurance against a long winter and slow spring, we might put up 250 bales and recycle any leftovers for bedding and mulch.) New farmers often fail to account for the overhead of shelter and winter feed when they're figuring how much they'll save raising their own meat animals.

Any bull calf that you intend to raise for beef should be castrated as early as possible. (Veal calves don't live long enough to warrant castration.) Bulls are dangerous and not to be trusted. They can be perfectly friendly for their entire lives and, then, in a split second, seemingly without reason, they can turn vicious, possibly maiming or killing someone. The least-traumatic way to turn your week-old bull into a steer is with an elastrator. This plier-like device expands an elastic band so that it can be slipped over the base of the animal's scrotum, pinching off the blood supply and thereby causing it to atrophy and fall off. A botched job can cause gangrene, however, so novices would be better off hiring a vet, who will use an emasculatome, aka a Burdizzo, which is a device that safely crushes the spermatic chord and associated blood vessels. Elastrators are relatively inexpensive, but emasculatomes are not.

It's a good idea to get friendly with your beef critters. Let the kids take the calf out and play with him. Get him used to a halter and lead. It's a lot easier to move a tame beefer than a wild one. Even under the best of circumstances, beef breeds are not so much domesticated as they are docile and predictable. Unlike dairy cows, they really don't trust humans and will tend to move away as you approach. You can overcome this aversion to some extent by calling them to the grain bucket. If you're raising grass-fed beef, however, the grain should be "for medicinal purposes only" and not the basis of their diet. (We're talking Crunchy 16 here, cow candy—not corn.) Think of the occasional grain treat as a bribe that will keep you in their memory and good graces when they're out on pasture during the summer. Try to spend time with them every day, too, to keep them friendly throughout the summer.

Feeding In the beginning, you'll feed beef calves as you would veal calves. At about 2 weeks old, however, offer them hay and grain. Feed the animals the highest-quality food you can to ensure good strong gains in the first couple of months—it will pay off in the end. Calves can go out to pasture at about 3 or 4 months. Don't put them out to pasture too fast, or they can get the bloat resulting from gas produced by organisms in the digestive tract and a potentially life-threatening condition. In winter, they'll need good hay and some grain (14 to 16 percent protein). A young cow cannot be outside alone all winter, but if you have a small herd that has access to a three-sided shelter, they'll do fine.

You can grow beef to almost any age you want, although 18 to 24 months is best. The flavor and texture of beef improves greatly if the animal is fattened for a month or two before slaughter. During this time period, give them feed that is high in carbohydrates—for example, forages of high-sugar-content grass or a grain mixture that is heavy on corn. Farm manuals from the early 1900s offer detailed feeding and finishing formulas for homegrown rations that are well suited to the needs of today's small farmer.

Milk Cows

The decision to keep a milk animal puts you on a whole new level of homesteading. Chores now become superchores. You will rarely be able to leave your farm for more than a few hours, for a very long time. Don't even think of getting involved with milk animals until you're completely comfortable with doing chores and raising everything else on your farm—after at least three or four years of the routine.

Nevertheless, raising your own milk is arguably rewarding enough to be worth the crimps it puts in your lifestyle, and there are a few things you can do to lessen the burden. A cow gives enough milk for more than one family, so consider sharing a cow. You and the other family will need to live near each other, of course. (It definitely helps if you're related or nearly so, as the venture is akin to running a business together.) You might find a reliable teenager (a seeming contradiction in terms) and, after a training period, hire the youngster to milk one or two days a week in exchange for milk or cash. Having a backup will give you a reprieve when you need it.

I'm sure you've heard that cows are finicky and will not tolerate more than one person milking them. This statement is not entirely true. Cows will tolerate two to four milkers, as long as (and this is key) they milk her on the same schedule and in more or less the same manner. Recently, there has been a trend toward milking only once a day instead of twice—which also might make it easier to find help milking. Cows milked just once daily, however, will give slightly less milk and may be more prone to mastitis, an inflammation and infection frequently associated with freshening (dairy talk for the phase when a cow resumes or begins milk production after giving birth to her calf). Even if milking only once a day, you still need to feed and check on the cow twice a day.

For some people, never leaving the homestead may be exactly what they wish for. Other folks may discover that what seemed like a great idea at the time has become involuntary servitude. Think very hard before you commit to a dairy cow (or goat). You might be better off buying raw milk from a neighbor. Consider taking care of someone else's family cow when they want to go away in exchange for fresh milk.

About Milk Replacer

Until very recently, milk replacer commonly contained spray-dried blood and blood plasma—which are now banned—potential vectors for the transmission of Bovine Spongiform Encephalopathy (BSE, aka Mad Cow Disease). Any organic producer that feeds its calves milk replacer—except in an emergency situation—will lose its certification. Organic dairies are required to feed calves whole milk only.

At this time, there is no approved source of organic milk replacer in the United States (although there is in Europe). To further complicate matters, although milk replacer is made from whey and whole milk proteins, there is no way of knowing its provenance. For example, the replacer could well be derived from the milk of cows that have been treated with bovine growth hormone— someone, somewhere is buying that milk! Feeding a calf reconstituted instant industrial milk instead of fresh, whole, mother's milk sort of undermines the whole concept of self-sufficient sustainability. Until organic milk replacer becomes available in this country, we'll just have to learn to share our fresh milk with baby cows and get by with a little less for a while.

Artificial Insemination

Gone are the days when dairy farmers routinely kept bulls. Some farmers with herds of 50 to 100 head might keep a bull to run with the heifers, but most do their serious breeding by artificial insemination (AI).

With AI, you can upgrade your "herd," even if it's with only one or two cows. You can even pick the sex of your calf. If you want to have a good cow to replace a merely average cow or if you want a calf to sell, then get high-grade heifer sperm. If you want to eat the calf, breed to a good beef bull (not one too much bigger than your dam, though, or she could have trouble at birth).

The trick to a successful AI session is knowing when the cow is receptive. Cows come into estrus every 21 days, but only remain "open" for one day or less. A heifer in heat will be more active than usual—almost edgy—and will bawl even when the other cows are quiet. She will usually attempt to ride other cows or let other heifers ride her. A sticky, clear, mucus discharge from her vulva is a definite sign of openness, and sometimes the vulva will be reddish and swollen.

When you think you've confirmed the signs of heat, schedule an appointment with the AI technician for 21 days hence. Be forewarned: Even with careful observation and record keeping, AI is hit or miss. The technician may not get it right, either, which is why we borrowed our neighbor's young bull. He's a lot better at knowing when our heifer is open than we'll ever be.

Milk production Nothing beats fresh milk, cream, and butter (and homemade cheese, yogurt, and ice cream). Expect to get 7 gallons of milk or more a day from an average, freshened Guernsey and about 5 gallons from a Jersey. (We're not alone when we say that these are the two best breeds for a family cow.) That's a lot of milk, more than enough to keep a family of four awash in dairy products and still supply leftovers for the pigs.

A cow's milk production will gradually dwindle down to nothing over the 12 to 24 months after she gives birth (which makes sense, because, left to herself, the cow would eventually wean her calf). You'll want to dry her off long before that, however. Drying off is the process of intentionally shutting down a pregnant cow's milk production so that she has some time to put her energy into the calf before she gives birth. To dry off the cow, you reduce her concentrates and stop milking.

Milk cows need extra protein. In winter, they like a legume hay and a 16 percent concentrated feed. Silage (fermented chopped corn) or haylage (fermented chopped grass) can replace grain if you have a grass-based operation. In summer, a good pasture with a little grain will work fine. You'll know whether or not you're feeding your cow enough by her milk production. Production slowly declines with time, but a sudden drop signals that something is wrong.

The milk supply A heifer (cow that has not had a calf) can be bred at about 18 to 24 months and will freshen about 9 months later. After she calves, she is called a first-calf heifer. (She isn't a full-fledged cow until she has had her second calf.) Her calf should get all of her milk, which is mostly colostrum for the

> *"The cow is of the bovine ilk: One end is moo,*
> *the other, milk."* —Ogden Nash

first 2 to 4 days (although there may be enough for the pigs, too, so feed them whatever the calf doesn't take). You can keep the calf with its mother for the first 12 to 46 hours, but then you should separate them and start bottle-feeding the calf. Don't be tempted to keep them together longer—it's much easier on everyone to separate them early. Keep the calf way away from its mother, so they can't hear or smell each other. If the calf and mother are in visual or olfactory contact, they will keep up a constant bawl.

The conventional wisdom is that if you leave the calf on the mother, the calf will get all the milk, and there won't be much left for you or anyone else. Milk production will also start declining, because the calf will never completely empty even one-quarter of the cow's udder (each of the four quarters of the udder has its own teat). Some farmers will leave the calf with

its mother on pasture by day, separating them only at night. They skip the evening milking, but milk the following morning for the family's supply. Other farmers reverse the schedule—milking in the evening and then allowing mother and calf to spend the night together. There's no one ideal or correct approach.

At first, you'll have enough milk to feed the calf and your family, but, as the calf grows, it will need more milk. If you don't want to surrender your share of the milk supply, substitute milk replacer until the calf is ready to be weaned (but see the sidebar on p. 368). In any case, give the calf as much milk as it will drink in one sitting, twice a day. Offer grain and hay or fresh pasture within a week. Then switch over to all replacer when you want to keep all of the milk for yourself. If you have a heifer calf that you want to raise for sale or as a replacement, reserve the lion's share of the milk for the calf until it is weaned (do the same if you are raising a veal calf).

In order to maximize milk production, dairy farmers "breed back" their cows 12 weeks after their calves are born, so that they'll freshen every year. Once the cow has "settled" (meaning that the artificial insemination took, and the cow has

....

Top: "Civilizing" the heifer. After a winter hanging out with the beef cows, it takes some coaxing with treats to get her used to people again. Bottom left: Winky and Dinky in love. Bottom right: Desdemona does a great job clearing brambles.

Butter Wars

A French chemist invented margarine in 1869, but the stuff did not catch on in the United States until World War II forced the country to ration dairy products. In the 1950s, "oleo" (as my mother called it) was sold, by law, as lardlike white gunk, made palatable to consumers with a hand-mixed-in squirt of yellow food coloring. The yellow was a compromise; an earlier New Hampshire law mandated that margarine be pink. Regardless of whether the substance were yellow or pink, aftermarket coloration laws were supposed to appease dairy farmers like my parents, who worried that customers would mistake the new concoction for the real thing. To them, margarine was a product of the devil.

The general population, however, was impressed. Margarine was cheap and was touted as "better than butter." The dairy industry lost the battle, and margarine captured the market. Millions of kids grew up without ever tasting real butter. The irony of watching our neighbor, who was heir to five generations of dairy farmers, slathering his white bread with "nondairy spread" would be comical if it weren't so horrifying.

become pregnant), she is dried off 4 to 8 weeks (often less) before she has her next calf. If you're just feeding your family, you don't need maximum production; you just need good production. Consider breeding your cow to freshen every second year, with a dry season that's a bit longer. You'll still get plenty of milk. For several months, your production could go down to 1 to 2 gallons a day. Then there will be a couple or three months with no milk. During the dry season, check your cow for health, worm her, trim her hoofs, brush her coat, and check her udders and teats. The dry season is when you take that vacation. Your cow will be healthier and far less stressed—and so will you.

Milking You learn hand milking by doing. The first few times can be a painful ordeal for both you and the cow and might take an hour or longer. The work gets easier and faster after you build up your milking muscles and perfect your technique. Fortunately, most cows are infinitely patient animals.

You might consider buying a milking machine, especially if you intend to milk more than one cow. There are quite a few dairy supply companies that specialize in milking equipment for the family cow. At the very least, you'll need stainless-steel buckets (at least two), a milk strainer with paper filters, and gallon glass jugs to store the milk. An electric butter churn or large standing mixer with a slow speed is another vital accessory—and then, there's the cheese-making equipment, of course. If you milk goats instead of cows, you will need all of the above, plus a cream separator.

Goats

Goats are all about personality. They are lively, curious, user-friendly, and definitely interactive. They truly love people and would live inside your house, next to the family dog, if you would let them.

Goats, of course, give much less milk than cows, and the milk tastes different. For some people, the taste takes some getting used to. Goat's milk is famously great for cheese making, but you can't get goat cream or butter without a cream separator. Unlike cow's milk, goat's milk is naturally homogenized, so the cream will not separate without mechanical assistance.

The utility of goats as browsers—and effective land clearers—lets your goat earn his keep and live long and prosper on the homestead. Goat meat is pretty tasty, too. Any male kids (baby goats) should be castrated as soon as possible. Bucks (aka Billy goats) are not only aggressive, but uniquely, pungently odoriferous, especially during the breeding season.

Care and feeding The breeding and care of goats is similar to that of cows. A goat's gestation period is shorter—150 days. A goat will give about a gallon of milk a day (give or take a quart or two) for about 200 days out of the year. Goats tend to dry up faster than cows, so stretching out the time between freshening doesn't work as well.

Dairy goats eat the same feed as cows, just not as much. The big difference, however, is that goats are browsers. They prefer to eat brambles and leaves and, in fact, will eat grass only if there is nothing else to eat. They would rather eat twigs. The best thing about goats (next to their personalities) is their penchant for browsing. We keep two, Desdemona and Ophelia. We aren't presently milking them, however (although we have not ruled that out). We keep them to browse. In combination, goats and pigs will restore any land. If you have noxious weeds like knotweed, poison ivy, bamboo, or brambles, your goats will clear them out in one or two seasons. Goats provide virtually the only way to get rid of poison ivy without resorting to nasty herbicides. They devour the stuff, which is one of their favorites. (As a bonus, drinking milk from ivy-eating goats reduces your skin reaction to the plant.)

Unlike cows, goats are very easy to keep clean. Goat manure is almost identical to rabbit turds, little pellets that just get lost in the hay. The manure is rich, but there is not much of it, and it's mixed with a lot of bedding, so it's a lot slower to compost.

Accommodations Goats don't need much in the way of shelter. Either a stall in the barn or any closed-in shed that offers protection from the wind and cold will suffice. You do need a protected space for milking, however, and, if you use a milking machine rather than milking by hand, you'll need a heated washroom where you can clean and store the equipment without risk of freezing. Most milking machines have attachments for milking goats.

Until recently, the expense in time and effort to put up adequate goat fencing was enough to keep many a homesteader from keeping this charming and very useful animal. Goats love a challenge, and they can climb on anything. It's not uncommon to see a goat perched on a low-hanging branch that is just barely stout enough to hold its weight. Thankfully, now you can use portable electric fencing that is reasonably priced and easy to set up. You can also move it as needed.

Rabbits

Some homesteaders love to raise and eat rabbit. (We are not in this demographic. We don't like the meat and don't like to raise animals in small cages. They call them "hutches," but they look like cages to us.) People who like rabbit meat describe it as tasting a lot like chicken, but better. Rabbit is technically game meat. It is all light meat and, when raised properly, has very thin skin and tiny bones. Any preparation you can do with chicken, you can do with rabbit. If you like the meat and don't mind keeping animals in cages, rabbits are an economical addition to your homestead.

Rabbit raising is cyclical. One doe can have a litter of 8 to 10 kits (sometimes many more) after 31 days of gestation. She will nurse her babies for 57 days. At that point, the babies will be ready for slaughter and will each yield from 3 lb. to 5 lb. of dressed meat, about the same amount as a broiler chicken (they are even called broiler rabbits). Because an 8-week-old rabbit is still nursing, rabbits have a very high conversion ratio. It requires only 1 lb. to 3 lb. of feed to raise a broiler to slaughter weight. The best breeds for meat are the medium-size breeds, such as Californians and New Zealand Whites (the most common).

Living accommodations Rabbits are generally raised indoors in 36 in. by 30 in. by 18 in. wire cages. They eat a combination of concentrated feed (20 percent protein) and legume hay. Alternatively, you can feed them alfalfa pellets instead of hay. There is also a combination feed available that includes high protein and roughage. Rabbits must have at least 20 percent roughage in their diet to stay healthy. Dry does and bucks do not require as much protein.

Some farmers, most notably Joel Salatin of Polyface Farm in Virginia, are experimenting with raising rabbits on pasture. Salatin claims that his pasture provides from 20 to 40 percent of his rabbits' food. At 8 weeks he puts the litter on pasture in a "hare pen," which is similar to the portable pens he uses for his broiler chickens.

Apparently, as soon as the bunnies are able to dig burrows, they want to. Natural rabbits, living in the wild, like little hidey-holes, as open spaces are dangerous, and therefore scary, to a rabbit. Salatin's rabbit pens are floored with wooden slats, which keep the rabbits from burrowing into the ground and escaping under the walls while also allowing the bunnies to graze the grass that is accessible between the slats. In the winter, Joel's rabbits live with the chickens in hoop houses. The chickens scratch around under the cages, keeping everything clean and free of unwanted bugs. Some people raise worms under their rabbit cages. The worms digest the rabbit manure and turn it into rich compost.

If You're Considering Sheep

Sheep are probably not the best choice for a novice homesteader. They have been domesticated for so long they have forgotten the basics of self-preservation and do not fare well on their own. In addition, they really are not very bright. Sheep are one of the few animals that will readily eat poisonous plants, have trouble lambing on their own, and do some very stupid things.

The number-one problem with sheep is fencing. Lambs are defenseless against all of their predators, which is why sheep ranchers have sheep dogs (ironically, dogs are the worst predators of sheep). With the advent of portable electric fencing, raising sheep has become much easier. The same fence that encloses your goats will work with sheep.

Sheep are much easier to deal with if you have a small farm—one or two will fit right in. If you're hell bound to have sheep, ask yourself, "Do I want wool, meat, or both?" Some breeds of sheep are best for one purpose or another; there are also dual-purpose breeds

(which, I don't think are good for either purpose).

If you're raising animals for your family's use, you can solve your meat/wool quandary in many ways. You can, for example, have one wool ewe, such as a Merino, and breed her to a meat ram, such as the neighbor's Suffolk. Breed the ewe in late fall. In the spring, the ewe will lamb and will also need shearing. You'll have meat and a nice fleece to card, spin, knit, or weave. (You can send the fleece out to be spun and dyed.) Most sheep produce from 6 lb. to 10 lb. of wool. Or, you can buy one or more spring lambs to put out on good pasture for the summer and butcher them in the fall. The point is to avoid lambing, which always comes at the wrong time and has a predictably uncertain outcome.

Sheep do very well feeding exclusively on good pasture, especially if they are not breeding. These grazers pull up grass with their teeth, and, as a consequence, they eat it right down to the ground. This habit makes them more susceptible

to infection and parasites carried by insects and microbes that live in the soil. Liver fluke is a common health problem, particularly if the sheep are pastured on wet land. Flies are another problem. If you don't keep the fleece in the perirectal area of the sheep trimmed, feces moistened with urine can build up on the wool and supply the ultimate environment for fly eggs. The maggots, which burrow into the wool and are not readily visible, will multiply and thrive on the poor animal's backside. You have to stay vigilant if you raise sheep.

In winter, sheep can remain outside as long as there are enough of them to keep each other warm. They also must have at least a lean-to as shelter. If you have just one or two animals, put them in the barn. In cold climates, sheep need good hay and a little grain, but don't let them get fat.

Sheep are probably harder to raise than any other farm animal, save horses. Befriend a sheepherder to learn more about it before making the commitment.

chapter xv

....

Shelters & Fences

I'm pretty sure that when most people hear the word "farm," the scene that springs to mind includes a big red barn. The barn is certainly an archetype of the farm. In his book *The New World Dutch Barn* (Syracuse University Press, 2001), John Fitchen describes the barn as the "most essential and indispensable building of the rural homestead, counted on to accommodate and preserve and shelter both animals and crops against freezing cold and deep-drifting snow and howling blizzard." When you commit to keeping livestock, you commit to ensuring their comfort and security, which certainly requires providing shelter—although that doesn't necessarily mean a full-blown, bona fide barn. A prefabricated shed purchased from your local big-box home-improvement store may be all that it takes.

If you're the sort of person who finds satisfaction in having "a place for everything, and everything in its place," you'll never feel at rest until you've erected your barn. Building your own small barn is an good way to learn or improve your carpentry skills, especially if you hope to someday build your own house. Building a large barn may have to wait until you can save or borrow enough to pay for it, however.

One advantage to buying (or renting) a property with an existing barn is that you can repair it or restore it (or, blessed be, use it as is). If you don't have an existing building, there are alternatives. For example, you'd be amazed at how many different types of animals you can house in the average two-car garage. A typical 24-ft. by 24-ft. garage can be subdivided into four 8-ft. by 12-ft. or six 8-ft. by 8-ft. stalls with a 4-ft.-wide center aisle. In the winter, your vehicle will suffer far less outdoors in the driveway than your hens, goats, piglets, calves, and other critters would.

Determining What You Need

A general-purpose barn may be more practical than a cluster of individual,

....

Top left: Old-style electrified wire fence. Top right: Electrified plastic poultry netting keeps chickens in and more important, predators out. Bottom: George moving one of our portable chicken shelters for our meat birds.

species-specific sheds. From a caretaker's point of view, it's certainly more convenient to house all one's critters in a single building. In fact, in many cases, barns may be more necessary for the farmer than for the animals. (An added benefit: The cost of a single-purpose livestock structure

concern. Either a pole barn (simply a roof supported by four poles) or a shed roof extension on another outbuilding will serve as covered protection.

Species As long as they can stay dry and out of the wind, most livestock require surprisingly little shelter, even in cold

"There is no more beautiful sight in the world than a collection of buildings either on a farm or a large city lot that are harmonious one with the other." —William A. Radford

can be depreciated, whereas you can only include the cost of general livestock housing in the basis used to compute capital gains, should you ever sell the farm.)

Before you decide what type of shelter your animals require, consider four essential criteria: the climate in your area, the species of animals, the number of animals, and, of course, your budget.

Climate The classic barn originated in response to the difficulties of keeping livestock in cold climates, as a means to provide protection from the cold while also providing safe storage for winter feed. Actually, the amount of barn area dedicated to animal housing is quite small relative to the area devoted to storage of hay and other forage.

Even if your animals can pass the winter outdoors, their feed still requires some sort of shelter—even if only pallets laid on the ground and covered with secured tarps. In temperate or hot climates, shade from the withering sun is the primary

climates. A roofed, three-sided shed, preferably floored, is more than adequate for pigs, beef cattle, horses, and sheep (with the possible exception of lambing ewes). Wintering outdoors doesn't have to be stressful for the animal. Given enough bedding, an outdoor burrow can actually be warmer than a stall in an unheated barn. Pigs, being social animals, may actually be happier outdoors in social groups than they would be indoors, isolated in roomy, individual stalls.

Ducks and geese have much better natural insulation than chickens do, so they also thrive with rudimentary shelter. For waterfowl, the concern is deep snow, which makes them more vulnerable to predators because they can't get the running start they need to launch themselves into the air. Chickens will happily venture out of the coop on all but the windiest and most nastily cold days.

Unfortunately, in snow country, we have to take our electric poultry netting down for the winter (the deep snow bends and snaps the flexible fiberglass posts, and the netting gets trapped in ice and shorts out), which leaves birds vulnerable. Come winter, we "circle the wagons"—we move all of the coops to an area within 25 yd. of the house and arrange them in a semicircle. We scatter seedy, old, mulch hay on top of the snow to give the birds something to occupy their time during the day and lock them into their coops for the night. So far, predators have kept their distance during the day. If you have only a small flock, you could enclose the coop within a permanent 6-ft.-high welded-wire fence to create a secure winter yard. (Be sure to include a gate that opens into their summer range and that is protected by portable electrified netting.) To deter raccoons and other predators from scaling the welded wire, install electrified tape or twine on standoff insulators along the bottom of the fence. You can either clear the fence line to keep it free of snow or raise the insulators as the snow deepens.

Number Obviously, the more animals you have, the more shelter you need to provide. As Nathaniel Tripp observed in 1881 in his book *Barns and Outbuildings and How to Build Them* (Lyons Press, 2000), "The proper and economical erection of Barns and Outbuildings requires far more forethought and planning than are ordinarily given to their construction . . . the error is usually on the side of too small structures, as the thousands of lean-to sheds, 'annex' stables, and hay stacks, etc., through the country testify to." One option is to build a large enough barn to house all your animals at the outset. Another is simply to add more shelters as your herds or flocks grow.

For poultry, there are two related reasons that we believe it's better to build more coops as flocks increase rather than add onto an existing coop. The pecking order is disrupted when you combine flocks, and you need to regularly replace superannuated laying hens with fresh pullets. It's much healthier for the birds if you have a fleet of small mobile coops that you can rotate through pastures than it is to confine them within a single fixed coop and surrounding yard area.

The most practical accommodations for cows, sheep, or goats are a single fixed structure that is large enough for all of them or a smaller one that is easy to expand. In any case, it's better to build in some excess capacity at the outset rather than build too small. Animals tend to multiply. The temptation to add new members to the family is hard to resist. In less than a year, our hobby flock of a dozen laying hens morphed into a serious enterprise, employing some 500 full-time professional hens, and, very soon, finding a solution to the hen-housing shortage was on the Things To Do list.

Budget As the story goes, a farmer hit the lottery jackpot big-time. When the television reporter asked him what he planned to do with his windfall millions, he replied, "Well, I guess I'll just keep on fahmin' 'til I use it up."

Our laying hens more than pay for their feed and bedding, and so do our meat birds. When you factor in the costs of the materials for their mobile coops, the feeders, waterers, fencing, and processing equipment, however, there's an exponential imbalance between what we've spent on infrastructure and what we've seen in profits. Whether you're trying to be a full-time farmer, a self-sufficient homesteader, or just a backyard or rooftop hobby farmer, a market grower, or a patio gardener, it's all about the infrastructure. No matter how carefully you try to estimate, and even if you do all the work yourself, what with buildings, structures, hoop barns, greenhouses, row covers, mulches, tools, equipment, and machinery, your enterprise always costs more than you expected.

Hoop Barn: The Barn in a Box

Hoop barns are galvanized steel arches covered with fabric, a building technology borrowed from greenhouses. First introduced in the mid-1990s, they have become increasingly common features of the rural landscape. Indeed, many initially skeptical farmers have become converts, extolling the virtues of the hoop barn over traditional timber-frame or modern steel-clad barns. These structures offer many advantages that conventional steel or wood structures do not, including the following:

- low initial cost
- quick to erect
- subject to little or no property tax (unlike permanent structure)
- built directly on ground, no foundation
- can be made portable by adding wheels or tracks
- provide natural interior daylight (due to translucent covering)

- easy to take down, relocate, and resell
- no interior supports or obstructions
- easy to expand
- easy to ventilate (providing healthy indoor environment for animals)
- cooler in summer and warmer in winter than ambient air
- frames made from recycled steel; covers also recyclable
- require no maintenance or painting (other than repair of rips and tears)
- multiple uses (available in wide range of sizes, in various shapes, with different-style coverings and end closures, and with optional accessories)
- compatible with organic farming methods (deep winter bedding packs to make excellent compost; animals "free range" indoors in winter)

Hoop barns also solve the conundrum of outdoor shelters versus conventional stall barns. Some homesteaders set up winter hoop houses directly over their garden so their pigs can fertilize and prepare the soil for planting during the off-season. Laying hens would be happy to have the same opportunity—but don't be tempted to house chickens and pigs under the same hoops, as the pigs will be quite delighted to collect the eggs for you. A herd of pigs can socialize as they "free-range" the hay bedding, nesting where they choose and making daily deposits into the compost bank account. Dairy and beef cattle also do well in stall-free hoop barns, provided they are given fresh bedding daily. Depending on the number of cows you have and the area in which you position the hoop barn, by spring, when you return

> *"He was a very inferior farmer when he first began . . .*
> *and he is now fast rising from affluence to poverty."*
> —*Mark Twain,* from Rev. Henry Ward Beecher's Farm

the cows to pasture, the compacted and composted bedding that has built up over the winter can be as muchas 6 ft. deep.

You can use hoop barns as greenhouses, season-extending high tunnels, hay or equipment storage areas, livestock free-stall barns, movable chicken tractors and poultry houses, garages, heated work spaces, processing facilities, and more. If there are any serious drawbacks to these fabric structures, they appear to be a well-kept secret. Yes, the covering, stabilized for ultraviolet (UV) light, has a service life of only 4 to 5 years, but replacement is easy and inexpensive.

Modifications Some headroom is lost due to the curved walls of the most common design, but you can remedy this issue by constructing a concrete- or wood-framed, vertical, partial "pony wall" to raise the hoops. Without the pony wall, the fabric can also be damaged by poultry pecking it and other livestock chewing on or pushing against it. If you don't build a pony wall, you'll need some kind of protective interior partition or wire fence panels. In the North, unless we shovel the area to keep it clear, snow piles up at the base of the fabric and can exert enough pressure to collapse the frame—another argument in favor of a pony wall.

You also need to protect any watering systems in the hoop barn from freezing,

although with the heat given off by enough animals inside and by the composting bedding, freezing is less frequent than one might expect. Some experts consider the costs of the extra bedding the animals require and the labor it takes to remove the bedding to be drawbacks to the hoop barn—but they're overlooking the added value of that self-composting bedding for building organic matter for the soil, ready to be spread on the fields in the spring.

Encounters with reality For me, the problem with hoop barns is that, when it comes to buildings, I'm a stubborn traditionalist. I don't believe in life-cycle cost analysis. The way I see it, the "service life" of something as important as a barn (or a house) should be calibrated in centuries, not decades. I also want what I build to be, if not always a thing of beauty, at least not a blight upon the landscape. Wood weathers, but plastic (even UV-stabilized plastic) degrades. All function and no form, a fabric-covered hoop barn has nothing remotely beautiful about it.

Yet, we really need a good-size barn and we really don't have the wherewithal to build with wood right now. So we decided it would be a "barn in box" for us after all—but with a sop to my conscience. Our hoop barn will be a stopgap measure, expedient and strictly temporary.

Top: This simple shed on skids is easy to move and serves as three-season shelter for our goats.
Bottom left: Where it all started: This chicken coop was originally for Jane's hobby flock, but we soon outgrew it. We use it now for brooding and as a duck house. Bottom right: Simple latch hardware also works for barn doors.

....

Despite extensive ditching to improve drainage, the level field directly across the road from our house is so wet and stony that it will never amount to much more than marginal pasture. It does have convenient access to power and water and a good gravel roadway, however, so, all things considered, it was the best location for our temporary hoop barn.

My plan was simple: Strip off the muck topsoil down to the hardpan, spread a layer of crushed stone to keep out the water, and top it with sand or gravel to make a well-drained base for the concrete-slab foundation of our 30-ft. by 72-ft. hoop barn. We also planned to position a 30-ft. by 30-ft. slab 20 ft. from the far end of the barn and put a roof over it so we could store and compost manure and bedding. Valuable nutrients in unprotected piles would no longer leach away and into the ground.

After the bulldozer had stripped almost 1,000 yd. of rich but bony topsoil and pushed it into huge windrows to dry out, we began spreading the coarse rubble-stone base. My initial estimate for the necessary trucked-in fill was some 250 cu. yd., and, indeed, it took 252 cu. yd. to cover the 120-ft. by 40-ft. base area. I did a great job of estimating, except for one small but

crucial oversight. Although our field looked level, it actually sloped almost 4 ft. from the top to the bottom of the barn site. It had never occurred to me to actually shoot a level line along the site to determine the grade. A trompe l'oeil of sorts—and one that would take some 330 cu. yd. of trucked-in sand to level out!

Between the machine time and the extra fill, our budget for the entire barn was maxed out. Our barn in a box remained in its box until the next year. I took consolation in the fact that the sand base would be well settled by the following spring, saving us the expense of renting a soil compactor.

When it comes time to replace the hoop barn, we'll buy timbers, boards, and roofing to build a real barn. We'll transplant the hoops onto a new gravel base and buy new greenhouse covering to transform our hoop barn into a hoop greenhouse. Who knows? When that time comes, I may have become a convert to this new technology. I am not such a Luddite that I can't see the advantages of season-extending hoop houses in the garden. We'll use a few of those without reservation. That's appropriate technology.

Considerations for Barn Builders

Several considerations go into the design of a useful barn—no matter how big or small it is. Among them are the site, the mode of construction, use, the crops and equipment to store, the type and number of livestock to house, the availability of water and power, the availability of access roads for vehicles and farm equipment, proximity to pastures, yards, and the house, and, finally, your budget. What follows is an overview of some of the most important design criteria:

Location When deciding where to position your barn, you might want to consider these practical features and conveniences, which can make your day-to-day life run a little more smoothly.

Convenient to house and pastures. You don't want to trek halfway across your land or up a steep hill to do your daily chores. Consider the prevailing wind, too. You want to be sure the house is upwind of the barn, to avoid both odors and flies indoors. The barn should not be too convenient to the house, however (as in the "big house, little house, backhouse, barn" style of connected structures, which, while surely convenient for winter chores, is way too close in the event of a fire).

Accessible by vehicles year-round. A steep, icy drive or a muddy yard can ruin your day. You should allow adequate room around the barn to turn vehicles and equipment or back them up to a loft or door. Provide well-drained gravel roadways and make sure there is somewhere for the plow to push or pile up snow banks, other than against the walls of the barn.

Convenient to power and water. As the length of a power-line extension (whether overhead or, better yet, underground) increases, the size of the cable must increase, too. It may be less costly, therefore, to extend power from a new service drop at a conveniently located utility pole rather than from the house or garage. Check with your electric company for clearance specifications if you intend to run a water-line extension in the same trench as an underground power line.

Access to phone line. You'll be spending a lot of time out in the barn, so you might want to have a phone there. If, as in many rural areas, cell service is sketchy or nonexistent, add a telephone-line extension to your underground utility trench.

Sloped site. A sloped site allows "bank barn" design (with stables and stalls on the lower level and bermed into the hillside, with access to the hay loft from grade). Classic barns were built into hillsides with a "cellar" opening on the lower ground level at the rear of the barn. This opening eliminated the need to build a wagon ramp up to the main floor and hayloft. Farm equipment could enter on the ground level at the front. The underground portion of the lower level served as a root cellar for storage of winter fodder.

Foundation You have some choices when it comes to foundations, depending on the mode of construction you choose for the barn itself. Whichever type of foundation you decide upon, the floor of the barn—whether packed gravel or slab-on-grade—should be at least 8 in. above the surrounding grade, and the grade should be sloped to drain surface runoff away from the foundation and/or structure.

No foundation. For pole barns, sink the vertical treated poles that support the walls and roof structure of these inexpensive and utilitarian structures at least

4 ft. into the ground. The floor can be either packed gravel or a concrete slab poured on packed sand over a well-drained gravel base.

Hoop barns can be set directly on gravel or lag-bolted to treated wood planks or timbers. The hoop structure is typically secured against wind uplift with ratcheted tie-downs that are attached to "earth anchors" (which, like giant corkscrews, are turned into the ground). You can build a pony wall (less than full height) from treated heavy timbers and set them on a gravel base or on slab or a conventional concrete-wall foundation.

Slab-on-grade. This least costly concrete option is ideal for warm climates and adaptable to cold regions. Good drainage is critical to its durability. The edge of the slab should be thickened (turned down) to support bearing walls of a conventional timber or wood-frame barn (not necessary for a hoop barn). A slab floor can incorporate radiant-heat tubing to keep livestock-stall floors warm in winter.

Frost wall (with or without slab-on-grade floor). This first-class foundation is less likely to fail than a slab foundation, but it's much more costly. Excavate a trench to below frost line and then pour footings and a concrete wall to grade or to the height of a pony wall. You'll need perimeter drainpipes along the footings. (On level land, finding an outlet for the drain can be problematic.)

Tenant needs When building a barn, the number and type of livestock you want to have will guide you through the decision-making process—but be sure to plan ahead. If you intend to grow your farm over time, think about those future needs as you build.

Modular stall design. Modular stalls provide a flexible system that will accommodate various types of animals. For example, you might consider 10-ft. by 10-ft. stalls on both sides of a center access aisle that is wide enough for a tractor or cart to pass along and that has a door at each end to facilitate manure removal and fodder and bedding distribution. Consider providing the animals with access to outdoor yards from each stall. Stalls can be subdivided or doubled as needed, depending on the number or type of livestock they enclose.

Free stalls. In a free-stall barn, animals roam free on deep bedding. If you keep only cows, goats, or sheep, a free-stall design makes more sense than a stall barn with modular pens. Chickens can roam freely with any of the inhabitants of a deep-bedding free-stall barn. Unlike stall barns, which must be cleaned every day, free-stall barns require only a single spring cleaning—but that cleaning will be quite the job as the composted bedding will be deep and densely packed.

Feed storage. Traditional barns required cavernous hay mows to accommodate loose hay. When square bales became available, much more hay could be stored in a much smaller area (although the risk of spontaneous combustion from tightly packed bales that were put up too "green" greatly increased). Nowadays, many farmers put up their hay in giant round bales that are wrapped in plastic and so can be left outdoors all winter. As a result, a hayloft is no longer a necessary element of livestock-barn design. You can pile round bales in the barnyard and feed them one at a time to your animals. Baled hay is just as easily stored in a pole barn or in an open shed attached to another structure. Any grain storage bins should be rodent proof. If you grow root vegetables, winter squash, or other bulky winter fodder crops, store them in a cool place.

Manure storage. In traditional "tie stall" dairy barns, the cows spent the winter and milking time in stanchions. These barns featured a shallow depression between the center aisle and the stanchions, which facilitated the shoveling of manure into wheelbarrows or dump barrels on overhead tracks. Manure was often left piled against the wall of the barns, however, which would rot the wall—and exposure to the elements would not only leach the nutrients from the manure but also invited rats to colonize the piles in winter. (Later, chain-driven gutter cleaners were installed to convey manure outdoors.) Consider building a roofed-over slab where manure can be stored and composted.

Milking parlors, etc. If you milk more than a few dairy animals, you'll either need a milking parlor or a heated room to house the milk-storage bulk tank, wash sinks, water heater, vacuum pump, and pipeline controls. If you milk one or just a couple of dairy animals, you can milk by hand directly into a pail or you can use a portable vacuum milker that attaches to the pail. In either case, it's very handy to have a heated washroom. You can design

the washroom as an insulated box in the corner of an otherwise unheated barn (see "Heat," below).

You may also decide you want or need other ancillary service areas—for example, for animal slaughter and processing, for washing vegetables, or for freezing and refrigeration. A toilet with a washbasin would be quite a luxury, indeed.

Utilities Your water, heat, and electrical needs will depend on the type of structure you have, the type of farm you have, and on the barn tenants.

Water. Decide whether your water supply needs to be year-round or seasonal. If your barn is unheated, you'll require some kind of freeze protection. You can't use systems that pipe water to troughs and drinking bowls in an unheated barn where there is danger of freezing (if you have a herd of 40 cows in a tie-stall barn, however, their body heat would keep the water from freezing). A frostless hydrant located inside the barn provides the simplest way to fill water buckets, especially if you also use heated watering pans—you'll eliminate the hassle of breaking ice out of buckets each morning.

Heat. To create a small, enclosed, insulated room inside an otherwise unheated barn—for a washroom, milk parlor, etc.— you might consider an LPG (liquefied petroleum gas) space heater. To heat the entire barn, insulate the walls and ceiling. (Hay storage in a loft provides ceiling insulation for a traditional stall barn.) Although they are expensive, efficient biomass furnaces or outdoor boilers that burn wood chips, pellets, corncobs, straw, or other waste products can supply hot air or hot water to in-floor radiant-heat piping. Because of their translucent coverings, hoop barns offer the advantage of solar gain, trapping heat like a greenhouse.

Power. A dedicated meter simplifies farm bookkeeping. You'll need a minimum of 100-amp service, which may require a new service drop from the nearest utility pole or an underground extension from the garage or house, if there's adequate capacity. Use BX (steel jacketed) cable, Greenfield (flexible armored conduit), or EMT (electrical metallic tubing or "thin wall") steel conduit for all exposed wirings. Never use Romex (plastic-coated cable) in stables or barns, as livestock might chew on it. Fit light fixtures with protective cages so that the animals cannot break them. Check for compliance with code, even if no inspection is required.

A word about wiring: Be fastidious about proper grounding. If you aren't, animals standing on damp concrete or earth can be exposed to deadly shocks or, even worse, to stressful chronic and constant low-level current leakage (which you would experience as only an unpleasant tingle unless you had to endure it day in and day out). If you're building a new barn with a reinforced concrete-slab floor, bond the ground wire from the service panel to the slab rebar.

Coops, Sheds, and Feeders

There are advantages to housing a flock in small, individual shelters and coops rather than housing all your livestock in one general-purpose barn. The chief advantage is flexibility. You can design small structures so that they are relatively easy to move should the need arise, as it often does.

Our first chicken coop was built on the hill in back of our house. I designed the floor frame to be supported on concrete blocks under its corners rather than on a permanent foundation. When we decided to move it to its present home across the road from our house, all I had to do was jack up the corners, remove the concrete blocks, wrap a chain around the base of the coop, and tow it down the hill with our tractor. I now build our mobile chicken coops on recycled travel-trailer frames.

As we've said before, homesteading is an expensive hobby. It sometimes seems that building the road to self-sufficiency and sustainability requires pavers of bullion (and we don't mean chicken bouillon). It's not only the big-ticket items—the barns, sheds, garden or farm tractor, chainsaw, rototiller—it's the endless myriad of small stuff that bleeds you slowly and steadily, without quite killing you: all those feeders, waterers, nesting boxes, storage containers, veterinary tools and supplies, rakes, shovels, hand tools, carts, and wagons. Mindful consumption, especially on a reduced income, is in some ways even worse than mindless consumption, because, unlike the latest fashionable gewgaw, you really cannot do without that garden cart.

The point is, scrounge or build as much of your ancillary equipment as you can. Why pay $900 for a nifty fiberglass backyard chicken coop when you can build your own for a few hundred dollars in materials? Build your own troughs, mangers, and range feeders (see p. 391). Make it a habit to religiously scan the farm, garden, and building-materials sections of your local online or hard-copy classifieds for secondhand materials and equipment. Remember the three R's: Reuse, Repair, Recycle.

Fencing Materials

Back in the mid-1990s, when I built my garden and livestock fences, welded wire ("sheep fencing"), chicken wire netting, barbed wire, and electrified smooth wire were pretty much the only options for fences. All of these fences were material- and labor-intensive. One could spend days, if not weeks, erecting and repairing fences each spring—cutting and pointing fence posts made of heavy cedar (or other rot-resistant local wood) or buying them at the farm store and trucking them home, setting and pounding them into the erratically yielding earth, stringing and stretching wire, and then stapling wire to posts or attaching it to porcelain or plastic insulators. In the North, each fall, if your fence runs parallel to the roadside, you also have to take it down, pull posts, and set the fencing aside, lest it be destroyed by the snowplow, and rebuild the fence in spring.

New Zealand, or Australian, fencing was developed in the late 1970s in response to the need for an affordable permanent fence that provided reliable protection for the vast acreages of sheep ranchers. This high-tensile, smooth-wire fencing was heralded as the ultimate stock fence. So

strong that wildlife, livestock, or falling tree branches could not break it, it was the cheapest permanent fence you could buy. It is long lasting, requires as little as one line post every 40 ft. on level terrain, and is strung with multiple strands of electricity-free wire. The most difficult part of building the fence is the installation of the deep, extra-strong, braced corner posts needed to resist extreme tension on the wires—but building any high-tension fence is a lot of work.

Electrified plastic netting, rope, polytape, and twine Lightweight, portable, electrified plastic netting, which can be put up and taken down within hours as needed, has no posts to drive or wires to tension. Since the turn of the millennium, new materials have revolutionized plastic fencing. Electrifiable netting, poly tape, twine, and rope (which are all basically plastic fibers interwoven with a number of stainless-steel conductors) are supported by nonconductive fiberglass line posts or various styles of plastic insulators for standard wood or steel T-posts.

There is a wide variation in the durability and conductivity of electrifiable plastics. The best products interweave copper-coated conductors with stainless steel to reduce resistance, at the same time increasing the shock per unit of energy input from the energizer. This feature is

Top: Chickens dine at our homemade range feeder, which holds about 100 lb. of grain. Bottom left: Commercial galvanized-steel nesting boxes mounted to a plywood stand in our hen hoophouse. Bottom right: Tess enjoys a run in her paddock.

especially important in fences that are more than 1,000 ft. long or that come into contact with weeds. The longest-lasting plastic filaments are made of polyester and remain intact for up to 25 years. Polyethylene monofilament lasts about 10 years, and the least-expensive polypropylene-based products start to disintegrate in about 3 to 5 years. Longevity is why one particular product may cost three to four times the price of a similar-seeming competitor—of course, this doesn't mean you should always opt for the most expensive or longest-lasting fencing material. Your choice should depend on the intended use. Use the best materials for permanent fences— for example, the energized conductor on a wire boundary fence. For temporary fences that you move frequently and use only a few months a year and then store, the economy version may be all you need.

The only real problem we've had with plastic netting is its tendency to sag between posts and the tendency of the posts themselves to bend, particularly at corners or angles, where the fence line changes direction. Also, particularly on sloping or uneven ground, it's difficult to keep the bottom (nonenergized) strand close to the ground and keep the first conductor from sagging and touching the ground between posts. We've solved this problem by positioning rigid, plastic-coated, steel rods (or stiffer 5/8-in.-dia. fiberglass) next to the sagging posts and securing them to each other with electrical tape.

Also, we install 3/8-in. fiberglass rods with clip insulators at midspan between the built-in posts to stretch the netting tightly and remove the sag from the lower conductors. There's also a more costly, semipermanent netting that addresses the problem of bending posts and sagging netting by offering stronger, larger posts and longer ground spikes, but for the price, I'm content to stick with my jerry-rigged system.

Despite its utility, electrified netting does require some maintenance. Because the bottommost energized conductor of most netting is close to the ground (the Poultry Net, for example, is a mere 2 in. above the ground), weed control along the fence line is critical. Encounters between netting and a weed whacker are not pretty, so be sure to move the plastic posts in back of the line as you mow. Weed control is a little less demanding with the ElectroStop® netting we use to enclose our goats; the lowest conductor is 4 in. from the ground. This netting also has vertical stays that prevent it from sagging, but I use the fiberglass rods, especially on slopes, to close any gaps at the bottom and reinforce corners and angles to keep them straight.

Ultimately, the flexibility and ease of installment—and its superior effectiveness as a deterrent—makes electrified netting hard to beat. Although permanent fences of barbed, high-tension, or woven wire have their place—especially along boundary lines or as enclosures for stock, such as elk or deer—most often livestock fencing is of a more temporary nature, especially with a system of frequent pasture rotations. (We simply use a single strand of electrified twine and rope to keep our beef cattle on pasture and the wider, more visible,

$^1/_2$-in. electrified poly tape to corral the horses.) Permanent enclosures can be easily subdivided as needed with temporary or semipermanent fences. If you live in a northern climate, you need to take down your temporary and semipermanent plastic fencing so it isn't buried by winter snowfall. Continued exposure to sunlight also eventually causes plastic fencing to degrade.

There are a few other places on our land that would be better served by a permanent fence. Netting and woven wire do not adapt well to the uneven terrain of the rocky and wooded hillside where we summer our adult hogs. A seven-strand barbed-wire fence, with wires spaced at 3 in., 10 in., 17 in., 24 in., 32 in., 40 in., and 48 in., is not only "hog tight," but is also able to contain goats and just about any other animal we might consider containing. As with high-tension fences, the key to a successful, permanent, barbed-wire fence is rigid corner bracing.

Wood fences If you buy good boards to build a wooden fence, you'll have a pretty good-looking and pretty expensive fence, in other words, a fence with a double-strength drawback: high materials cost and a high expenditure of labor to put it together. Today, it makes sense to buy wood fencing only if the material is available for little or nothing, and you have the time to build it at your leisure. Sawmill slabs and edgings, coupled with the usual barbed or

"Three-bag" Range Feeder for Chickens and Turkeys

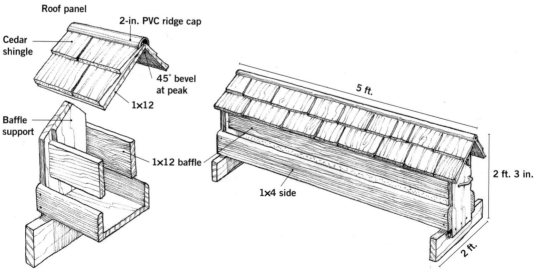

Roof panel
Cedar shingle
2-in. PVC ridge cap
45° bevel at peak
1x12
Baffle support
1x12 baffle
1x4 side
5 ft.
2 ft. 3 in.
2 ft.

Top: Ajax, our breeding boar, outside his apartment. Bottom left: An outdoor roofed poultry feeder shelters both the critters and the feed. Bottom right: A multipurpose shed is supported by treated poles set on the ground.

....

electrified bottom and/or top strand, will make a low-cost but pleasing and effective fence. Over the years, I've enclosed pastures with fences made of horizontal sawmill slabs and have enclosed gardens with vertical edgings.

Slabs are the long, tapered, convex trimmings created when a round log is cut square. Edgings are the remnant natural edge left when a board or plank is trimmed to width with a double-bladed edging saw. Slabs can be anywhere from a few inches to a foot or more in width and taper as much from end to end. As when building a cabin with natural logs, you alternate the taper of the slabs from end to end and between courses, for best appearance and more-or-less regular spacing. Don't cut the slabs to length to try to make them all break on the center of the post—you'll waste wood and have a weaker fence. Instead, stagger the joints so that some run past the posts and others break on it, like coursing board sheathing or brickwork. No two joints should fall next to each other. With a chainsaw, cut the thick butt ends of the slabs to make a half-lap joint. To splice the thinner ends, cut a flat face on one of the slabs.

Cedar posts will last longer if the bark is stripped off before you set them in the ground. Even naturally rot-resistant cedar posts will last little more than a decade or

so, except in the arid Southwest, where the air is too dry for wood to rot when in contact with the ground. If you can obtain pressure-treated (but not sawn) round posts from your local farm-supply store, it's unlikely that you would have to replace them within your lifetime. So-called landscape treated timbers, with two flat and two natural edges, are another lower-cost alternative to squared 4×4 treated wood posts, which I'd suggest you reserve for really important, permanent fences.

When I built my first edging fence around our vegetable garden, I thought I was being really frugal by using hardwood saplings for the horizontal rails. Those sapling poles, especially the bottom ones, rotted away in a few years, and I had to tear down the entire fence. If I build another fence in this style again (which I plan to do), I'll splurge on treated 2×4s for the top and bottom rails. Then, I could conceivably replace several sets of these rustic pickets over the years, while the rails remain sound.

I used the same strategy to build a privacy fence along one edge of our Maine village homestead. I cut post-length cedar in half with my chainsaw and fastened the slabs, butted tightly against each other, to the horizontal treated rails. Alternating the tapers top to bottom, I made a tight and secure fence.

Fencing for Animals

As the old prescription for a legal fence ("horse high, bull strong, and hog tight") suggests, different kinds of livestock react to fences in characteristically different

Slab-Fence Construction

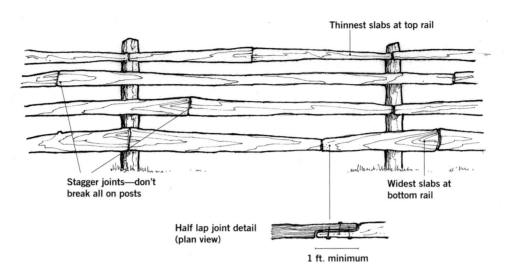

Thinnest slabs at top rail

Stagger joints—don't
break all on posts

Widest slabs at
bottom rail

Half lap joint detail
(plan view)

1 ft. minimum

ways. From the fence builder's point of view, the only solution is to build a different kind of fence for each kind of livestock, which is exactly how farms were traditionally fenced.

Cows Cows push on fences. They keep on pushing at the same spot until the spot weakens and then they push through the fence or trample it down. A fence that relies solely on its strength to withstand this patient bovine battery would eventually succumb to the animal's brute strength. A wood fence that is strong enough to contain cattle needs to have massive, firmly anchored posts and heavy planked rails at least 4½ ft. high. If the rails are nailed or bolted to the fence, they should be on the inside, to keep animals from push-

ing them off. Although the intelligence of cows is questionable, they at least know enough not to lean on something sharp, which is why a few strands of barbed wire strung between flimsy posts will restrain an 1,800-lb. steer more effectively than the heaviest rail or board fence.

Horses Horses invariably prefer the greener grass on the other side of the fence (no matter what color the grass may be on their side), so they eventually break down wire fences to get at the inviting repast yonder. Although barbed wire is as off-putting to horses as it is to cows, horses have a hard time seeing it. They are easily spooked for no apparent reason so will often maim or even mortally wound themselves when they bolt full-speed into barbed wire. This tendency of theirs explains why, on the modern farmstead, one still finds horse fencing made of wide board rails, painted white for visibility.

The posts and rails in a horse fence don't need to be quite as rugged as they would be in a cattle fence, because the horses won't lean on them, but there must be more of them and they need to be placed higher—at least 5½ ft. high or the height of the horse's shoulder—to thwart the over-the-top and under-the-line grazing habits of equines. The specific number and spacing of rails isn't critical as long as the fence is "hoof proof": The spaces between the rails in the lower 3 ft. of the fence and between the bottommost rail and the ground need to be either wide enough so that a pawing horse can withdraw its hoof without getting hung up on a hock or should be too narrow for the hoof to fit through in the first place. The top rail is often capped with a perpendicular board (a "strongback") to stiffen it.

Horses destroy top rails by cribbing (chewing) on them whenever they have nothing better to do, which, unless you work them hard, is most of the time. Creosote, the traditional antidote to cribbing, discouraged the habit a little too well—it also poisoned the horse. A strand of electrified wire running along the top of the rail is a kinder repellent.

Sheep and goats The challenge with sheep is not so much keeping the sheep in as keeping their predators out. Barbed wire can snag and tear fleece. The ability of woven wire mesh to deter dogs and coyotes makes it the preferred choice

among sheep people. The horizontal wires are spaced closer together at the bottom, both to prevent lambs from getting their heads stuck between them and to keep out raccoons or gopher-size pests.

A 3½-ft.-high rail or board fence would also work just fine for sheep, as long as the bottommost rail is close enough to the ground to keep a lamb or frightened ewe from squeezing under it or, worse, getting stuck. Given the acrobatic abilities of most predators, however, an overall height of 4 ft. to 4½ ft. is probably a wiser choice for sheep fencing. Their persistence justifies a strand of barbed wire about 1 in. aboveground and perhaps another strand of barbed wire, or a strand of electrified smooth wire, along the top of the fence. Unless there's a direct hit to the nose, single-strand electric fencing won't deter sheep, as wool is an excellent insulator. An electrified wire spanning the 6-in. gap between the bottom of the lowest rail and the ground will discourage an intruder from insinuating himself under the fence. As long as sheep have good pasture, they won't be tempted to graze under the fence line.

Both welded-wire and board-rail fences will work with goats, which aren't as vulnerable or intimidated by dogs and coyotes as sheep are. The top of a goat fence should be at least 4 ft. or, even better, 5 ft. high, as goats can jump. We use 4-ft.-high ElectroStop netting to enclose our goats and have had no problems with escapees— unless we leave the energizer off for a while (goats have an uncanny ability to sense when you've forgotten to turn the energizer back on). The danger is not so much that they will escape as that they will become entangled in the netting in the attempt.

The possibility of deadly entrapment when animals are first introduced to energized netting is likely enough that you should monitor their behavior until you are sure that they have learned to respect the fence. They can become entangled and strangle themselves in their attempts to push through the fencing.

Pigs When it comes to fencing, hogs are the epitome of barnyard incorrigibles. They can lift an amazing amount of weight with their snouts. Levered under a bottom rail, they've been known to topple entire fence panels, posts and all. A determined and hungry hog (a tautology) can root under any fence or even squeeze between loose barbed wires. The old-timers, well acquainted with the earth-moving capabilities of free-ranging hogs, bound their owners by law to fit pigs with yokes or snout rings to keep them from rooting during growing season. For the same reason, these farmers set the bottommost rails of wood fences close together. If they get really excited, hogs can jump over a low fence (or, more accurately, climb up on and pull themselves over), so a top-notch hog fence should be between 3 ft. and 4 ft. high. I've had really hungry, really big hogs just about straddle a waist-high fence in their lust to reach the slop bucket before I could fill their trough.

The ideal hog corral could also serve as a prototype all-purpose, heavy-duty, maximum-security stock fence. (Although not absolutely necessary, an understanding of the criminal mind and prison construction can be an asset for livestock-enclosure design.) Start with a 4-ft. hog-weight (heavy 9- or 10-gauge) welded-wire fabric. Stretch the fabric tight and staple it to 5½-ft.-tall 6×6 treated posts, set on 10-ft. centers. Position peeled poles or 2×6 plank rails at top and bottom to anchor the wire and stiffen the posts. Cross-brace the terminal and gate posts with tensioned cables and, for good measure, add a strand of barbed wire above the top rail, a strand of smooth electrified wire at midlevel on projecting stand-off insulators (to deter loitering and lounging), and, finally, a single strand of barbed wire at the bottom of the fence (to defend the gap and convince any potential rooter or burrower to think otherwise). This fence is truly "horse high, bull strong, and hog tight"—and sheep- and goat-proof, too!

Chickens Welded-wire poultry fencing is like sheep fencing, only higher and with smaller holes. Poultry netting that is 6 ft. high will keep birds in and vermin out. The bottom of the wire should be stapled to treated 1-in.-thick boards set in and staked to the ground to close any gaps. (Although folks do it all the time, burying the bottom of the netting in the ground will cause it to rust.) Another option is to run a strand of electrified wire along the outside of the fence, just above ground level, to discourage dogs and other pests (like skunks) from digging underneath the fence.

As already mentioned, on our farm we depend on semipermanent electrified Poultry Net to protect our birds on pasture. We enclose their portable coop within a rectangle of electrified netting, energized by a solar-powered charger. The birds can range safely throughout the day and return to their coop at night. The electrified netting has so far protected them against all ground-based predators (and, fortunately, they have not yet ever been attacked by hawks). After the chickens have thoroughly worked over their current range, we relocate them to fresh ground. We then add lime to the well-manured ground of their previous yard, run the rotovator lightly over it, and reseed. Our chickens do most of the work, and we get the benefit of improved pastures.

Although feathers and down provide excellent thermal and electrical insulation, frightened ducks, geese, and turkeys can become inextricably entangled as they attempt to bolt through the netting. If you're lucky, you'll rescue them before they strangle themselves or break a wing or leg. For safety reasons, never leave poultry netting unenergized when the birds are out and about.

Consider the Gate

If you've built your fence right, it's apt to stay where you put it, unless something too big and strong gives it a shove. That which does not love walls and fences seems to have a particular animosity toward gates.

Fundamentally, a stable gate is an impossibility—the laws of physics conspire against it. In the battle against gravity, all of the builder's art and artifice amounts to a rear-guard action to slow the fall from the grace of plumb and true, and the only

hope is a Pyrrhic victory. Quite simply, gates sag, and when they do, they don't work right anymore. They pinch against the latch post, the latch mistakes the strike, the very boards and battens that had once nestled comfortably seem to acquire repulsive magnetic charges, and they twist apart, warp, and split.

Other things being equal, gates sag because the gatepost shifts or the gate frame racks under the force of its own weight. Only a diagonal cross-brace can confer the stiffness that enables the gate to resist. If you remember any of the physics you never learned in high school, the causes of gate slouch and the appropriate prophylactics are, as my high school physics teacher was wont to say, "obvious to the reasonably intelligent observer." Judging by the many gates whose diagonal brace runs from the top at the hinge-post side to the bottom at the gatepost end, quite a few fence builders apparently are as unfamiliar with high school physics as most people are.

Consider how a downward load on the end of a gate, such as the weight of a 10-year-old boy who is swinging on it, is transmitted along the diagonal brace from the bottom at the latch side up to the top at the hinge side. Assume that the gate is attached to the post, at top and bottom, by hinges, which, if correctly installed, are firmly anchored. Next, imagine how the gate's spine (the vertical frame member at the hinge side of the gate, analogous to a fence post) is pushed sideways, augmenting the already considerable upward force on the hinge post. Consider how that leverage is compounded by its application at a point high up on the post. Is it any wonder that downward pressure at the end of the gate leads to a tendency for the bottom hinge to rip away from the post and for the post to rise up out of the earth?

When a wooden brace runs from the bottom of the gate at the hinge post to the top at the latch-post end, however, the downward load is exerted against the strongest and most stable point of the post. The fulcrum is too close to the handle of the lever to gain enough purchase for a good lift. In fact, there's a tendency for the load to push the gatepost downward. The gate might tear from its hinges, but it won't sag, and the gatepost, if well footed, will remain steadfast and true. The reason this brace angle works is because, in this position, the wooden brace is under compression, and wood under compression is extremely strong.

A gate can also be braced by tension, that is, by pulling rather than pushing together opposite sides. To make a tension brace, attach a threaded steel rod or cable diagonally from the hinge-post end of the gate to the latch-post end, in exactly the opposite direction to the direction you would use for a wooden brace, as shown in the drawing below. As you tighten the central turnbuckle, the tension pulls the corners of the gate together and upward. If well built and hung, a tension-braced gate will withstand downward forces without sagging.

If you have a heavy farm gate, increase the height of the gatepost and reinforce it with a turnbuckled tension brace that runs from the top edge of the latch end to a point high up on the post. The steeper the angle of the diagonal, the greater the bracing effect. Because the leverage that

Bracing a Gate

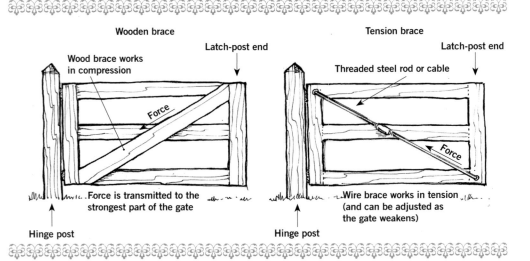

Wooden brace
Wood brace works in compression
Latch-post end
Force
Force is transmitted to the strongest part of the gate
Hinge post

Tension brace
Threaded steel rod or cable
Latch-post end
Force
Wire brace works in tension (and can be adjusted as the gate weakens)
Hinge post

tends to pull the post toward the gate while kicking out its bottom increases with height, tension braces can actually bend the top of the gatepost, which is why this bracing method requires a stouter, thicker-than-normal gatepost.

Solid anchorage is the highest priority. In unstable or wet soils, increasing the depth of the posthole may not keep a heavy gate from pushing a post out of line at bottom. Provide extra anchorage or a strain plug. To make the strain plug, insert two parallel lengths of rebar in the base of the post and cast the base in concrete.

Considering all the work involved in hanging wooden gates and building permanent wood, welded-wire, or

barbed-wire fences, it's not hard to understand why electrified netting and electrified wire gates have become so popular. For permanent, multistrand, high-tension, or woven-wire fences, however, proper gates are a necessary evil. Whether you build one of wood (and string barbed wire across its braced frames) or buy a factory-made galvanized steel gate, building and hanging the gate so that it doesn't sag is always a challenge. If the gate is set in an electrified fence, bury double-insulated wire to conduct the electricity between the gatepost and the hinge post.

Fences

If you keep animals, you need fences. Even if you don't keep animals, you'll still need to fence freebooting critters out of your garden. (Raccoons seem to know exactly when the sweet corn is ripe for picking and will clean out a patch the night before you plan to harvest it.) Whether you're in the city, suburbs, or country, you'll find that a significant part of your time and money will be devoted to fencing critters in or out.

Urban Homesteading

Urban homesteaders are often challenged by predator problems that would flummox their rural counterparts. Poultry (especially baby chicks) must be protected from neighborhood dogs, feral cats, and city rats, whose reputation for ferocity and rapacity is well deserved. Skunks and raccoons have adapted well to a life of urban plunder and pillage. In some cities, coyotes have been sighted lurking about.

In most urban environments, netting or other kinds of electrical fencing are usually impractical, illegal, or liable to invite lawsuits. Chain-link fencing is not a barrier against rodents and fence climbers, so some urban gardens employ three-dimensional security measures—netting suspended on poles to keep out birds of prey and other predators who manage to scale the fence.

The most fearsome urban predator, however, is *Homo sapiens* var. *criminalis*. Some folks can't grasp the idea that vegetables, fruits, and poultry are not free for the picking, and vandals delight in destruction for their own sake. As a result, in some urban settings, chain-link fencing garnished with concertina wire substitutes for board fencing. Lock tools and equipment at private and community gardens in a secure place. You could also ensure security for the backyard homestead or rooftop garden with a privacy fence, which is more attractive and often just as effective as the chain-link variety.

Suburban Homesteading

All 50 states still have laws on the books that protect livestock from people and property or vice versa. In some states, owners are legally liable for any damage their animals might do if they escape the fence; in others, animals are allowed to wander, and landowners must fence them out (and can only collect damages if the fence the animal breaks through is judged to be "sound").

The perimeter fences of a suburban homestead likely double as boundary fences, and their placement is almost always governed by local laws. Codes and ordinances vary greatly from town to town and state to state, however. Building codes typically define basic design and construction requirements, so before you make plans to build or replace a fence, check with your local planning office or building department for requirements, restrictions, and necessary permits. At the very least, there will be regulations regarding the height and location of residential fences, including hedges and tree plantings. Typically, the height of backyard and side-yard fences is limited to 6 ft. to 8 ft.; front-yard fences cannot exceed 3½ ft. to 4 ft. Some towns prohibit the use of what they consider hazardous fence materials, such as barbed wire. Others try to set minimum aesthetic standards.

Things can get a little complicated when a boundary fence straddles the legal property line. Unless otherwise specified in the land deed, the boundary fence is considered jointly owned. Even if your boundary line is entirely within your property lines (as many often are), common sense and neighborly etiquette suggest you discuss proposed alterations, construction, or maintenance with your neighbors—especially if you're the new kid on the block. A little courtesy can prevent a lot of ruffled feathers and possibly even a lawsuit.

The Mini-Farm

The weakest points in the defensive perimeter of any fence are the top and bottom. If a wood fence is to last, its bottommost rail (or the bottom ends of its pales) must be at least 3 in. or so above the ground, or the wood will soon rot. Small animals are able to easily infiltrate this bottom space. A strand of barbed wire will usually discourage coyotes, dogs, and skunks, which are adept at digging under fences. The wire also keeps lambs from crawling or getting stuck under the bottom rail.

Barbed wire is a better choice for closing the gap at ground level than electrified wire or poly twine, which—although initially quite effective—is quickly shorted out by unchecked grass and weed growth. (The only way to avoid frequent patrols with the weed whacker is to spray the fence line with an herbicide, which is not an option for organic practitioners.) Whether you choose electrified or barbed wire, do not succumb to the temptation to double-team the two as an electrified barbed-wire deterrent. An animal or unwitting human—shocked by the wire, caught on the barbs, and unable to disentangle—could be seriously injured.

For the same reason that birds and squirrels can perch on high-voltage wires without harm, a strand of electric fence wire running across the tops of the fence will have no effect on any creature whose feet are not touching the ground. If you want to keep raccoons and other climbers out of your garden or chicken yard, build a fence with woven wire. Ground the wire fabric at 20-ft. intervals by connecting it to 3-ft.-long galvanized steel or copper-coated rods that are driven to their full length into the ground. Set electrified wire on standoff insulators above the top of the wire fabric. When the intruder touches the hot wire, it will receive a shock because it will also be in contact with the grounded portion of the fence.

Books

Philosophical and polemical musings and thoughts about home-steading, husbandry, ecology, and the ills of modern factory farming

Berry, Wendell. *The Unsettling of America.* New York: Avon Books, 1977.

Bright, Jean Hay. *Meanwhile, Next Door to the Good Life.* Dixmont, ME: BrightBerry Press, 2003.

Carpenter, Novella. *Farm City: The Education of an Urban Farmer.* New York: Penguin, 2009.

Coperthwaite, William S. *A Handmade Life: In Search of Simplicity.* White River Junction, VT: Chelsea Green, 2002.

Goodall, Jane. *Harvest for Hope.* New York: Warner Books, 2005.

Hanson, Victor Davis. *Fields Without Dreams.* New York: Free Press, 1996.

Kains, M. G. *Five Acres and Independence.* 1940. Mineola, NY: Dover, 1973.

Kunstler, James Howard. *The Long Emergency.* New York: Atlantic Monthly Press, 2005.

MacFadyen, J. Tevere. *Gaining Ground: The Renewal of America's Small Farms.* Austin, TX: Holt, Rinehart, and Winston, 1984.

McKibben, Bill. *Deep Economy.* New York: Henry Holt and Company, 2007.

Nearing, Scott and Helen. *Living the Good Life.* New York: Schocken Books, 1987.

Pollan, Michael. *The Omnivore's Dilemma: A Natural History of Four Meals.* New York: Penguin, 2006.

Stewart, Keith. *It's a Long Road to a Tomato: Tales of an Organic Farmer Who Quit the Big City for the (Not So) Simple Life.* Emeryville, CA: Marlowe & Company, 2006.

Practical advice and helpful information

Burch, Monte. *Building Small Barns, Sheds & Shelters.* Charlotte, VT: Garden Way, 1982.

Cesa, Edward T., Knots, J. Howard, and Lempicki, Edward. *Recycling Municipal Trees: A Guide for Market-ing Sawlogs from Street Tree Removals in Municipalities.* Washington, DC: U.S. Department of Agriculture Forest Service, 1994.

Coleman, Eliot. *Four-Season Harvest: Organic Vegetables from Your Home Garden All Year Long.* White River Junction, VT: Chelsea Green, 1999.

Fitchen, John. *The New World Dutch Barn: The Evolution, Form, and Structure of a Disappearing Icon.* Syracuse, NY: Syracuse University Press, 2001.

GeRue, Gene. *How to Find Your Ideal Country Home: A Comprehensive Guide.* New York: Grand Central Publishing, 1999.

Gibbons, Euell. *Stalking the Wild Asparagus.* Chambersburg, PA: Alan C. Hood & Company, Incorporated, 1962.

Grandin, Temple. *Animals Make Us Human.* New York: Mariner Books, 2010.

Khan, Lloyd. *Shelter.* Bolinas, CA: Shelter Publications, 2000.

Mercia, Leonard. *Storey's Guide to Raising Poultry: Breeds, Care, Health.* North Adams, MA: Storey Publishing, 2000.

Nash, George. *Wooden Fences.* Newtown, CT: Taunton Press, 1997.

Salatin, Joel. *Pastured Poultry Profit$.* Swoope, VA: Polyface, 1996.

Sherill, Sam. *Harvesting Urban Timber: A Complete Guide.* Fresno, CA: Linden Publishing, 2003.

Woll, F. W. *Traditional Feeding of Farm Animals.* Guilford, CT: Lyons Press, 2004.

Antique Classics

Modern sustainable farming practice is basically a reboot of 19th-century methods (sans the petrochemicals and petro power), so farm journals and books from that century are a great resource. You can search and download them for free from online libraries like Google Books (*www.books.google.com*). If you prefer actual books, browse an online antiquarian booksellers' site, such as Abe Books (www.abe.com). Samuel Deane's *The New England Farmer*, published in 1790, and reprinted in 1972 by Arno Press (but now out of print) still contains a surprising amount of practical and useful information—although it's amalgamated with folklore and quaint but harmless superstition.

One good thing about timeless wisdom is that it doesn't go out of date—although some of those old farm manuals do promulgate recipes and practices that range from dubious to downright dangerous, so

be wary of the "scientific" pest-control advice.

We highly recommend the reprints of these classic handbooks from the 19th and turn-of-the-20th centuries as a source of still useful and valuable information for today's homesteader and small farmer:

Beard, D. C. *Shelters, Shacks, and Shanties: The Classic Guide to Building Wilderness Shelters.* 1914. New York: Dover, 2004.

Cobleigh, Rolfe. *Handy Farm Devices and How to Make Them.* 1910. New York: Skyhorse Publishing, 2007.

Dwyer, C. P. *The Homestead Builder: Practical Hints for Handy-Men.* 1872. Guilford, CT: Lyons Press, 2007.

Martin, George A. *Fences, Gates and Bridges: A Practical Manual.* 1887. Charleston, SC: Nabu Press, 2010.

Radford, William, A. *Radford's Combined House and Barn Plan Book.* 1908. General Books, 2010.

Starbuck, R. M. *Standard Practical Plumbing: An Exhaustive Treatise on All Branches of Plumbing Construction Including Drainage and Venting, Ventilation, Hot and Cold Water Supply and Circulation.* 1910–1923. Charleston, SC: Nabu Press, 2010.

Tripp, Nathaniel. *Barns and Outbuildings and How to Build Them.* 1881. Guilford, CT: Lyons Press, 2000.

Magazines

Backwoods Home Magazine
P.O. Box 712
Gold Beach, OR 97444
541-247-8900
www.backwoodshome.com

Countryside & Small Stock Journal
Countryside Publications
145 Industrial Drive
Medford, WI 54451
800-551-5691
www.countrysidemag.com

Hobby Farms
Hobby Farm Home
Urban Farm
P.O. Box 8237
Lexington, KY 40533
888-245-3699,
ext. 4053
www.hobbyfarms.com

Mother Earth News
Ogden Publications
1503 SW 42nd Street
Topeka, KS 66609-1265
800-234-3368
www.motherearthnews.com

Websites

www.backwoodsliving.com
Information for rural and urban homesteaders

www.gopherbrokefarm.com
Our website

www.hearth.com
Information about gas fireplaces, wood stoves, gas logs, pellet stoves, fireplaces, chimneys, and hearth products

www.metaefficient.com
MetaEfficient: The Guide to Highly Efficient Things

www.michaelbluejay.com/electricity
Michael Bluejay's Guide to Saving Electricity

www.nfpa.org
National Fire Protection Association

www.oasismontana.com
Source for residential solar electricity and renewable-energy power systems

http://websoilsurvey.nrcs.usda.gov
U.S. Department of Agriculture, Natural Resources Conservation Service

www.woodheat.com
Information about wood-, pellet-, gas-, coal-, and corn-burning stoves, fireplaces, and inserts

www.woodnotoil.com
Wood boiler reviews and resources

Insulation, 84
Intercropping, 149–51, 160, 194
Interplanting, 148, 181, 183, 212, 213

J

Japanese beetles, 139, 347

K

Kale, 186–87, 210
Kitchen, 234–61
  about: preparing food, 234–36
  baking bread, 258–61
  canning, 256–57
  cooking ranges, 239–41
  design criteria, 237–39
  essentials, 236–42
  freezers and freezing, 252–56
  harvest (outdoor), 238
  storing food, 247–52
  toolbox, 242–47
  wood cookstoves, 241–42
Knives and sharpeners, 242
Kohlrabi, 186–87, 249

L

Lamb's quarters, 41, 158
Land, 32–42. See also Location
  building barns and, 383–87
  evaluating, 17–20
  lay of, 34
  pastureland, 27
  productive types of, 26–27
  slope, 44
  tillable, 27
  value-adding traits, 34–36
  woodlots on, 27
Leach field. See Sewage systems
Lead paint, 84, 86
Leeks, 194, 197, 210
Legumes. See Beans; Peas
Lettuce, 143, 177, 183, 186, 189–90
Lifestyle, 20–22, 23
Lilaceae (lily), 194–97
Loam, 37, 156, 177
Location, 14–31. See also Land
  buying the best land, 24–25
  cardinal rules, 16
  climate, weather and, 17–20

cost of land and, 24–26
farms, 25–26 (see also Farming)
goals and, 14–17
lifestyle and, 20–22, 23
neighbors and, 22–23
proximity to civilization and, 22, 93–95
renting, 26
search process, 17–19
types of productive land, 26–27
urban/suburban sites, 28–31

M

Manure
  chicken, 161, 168, 286
  first-year garden and, 165
  green, on small scale, 161
  importance of, 270–71
  improving soil with, 156–58, 270–71
  managing, 271
  storing, 386
Masonry stoves, 124–25
Meat, eating, 267–69. See also Processing animals; specific animals
Meat grinders, 246
Meat slicers, 246
Melons, 190–93, 210, 254
Milk cows, 367–73
Milk replacer, 364–65, 368, 370
Milking parlors, 386
Minerals. See specific minerals; Trace minerals
Mini-farms. See Urban/suburban homesteading and mini-farms
Mixers, standing, 245
Mobile homes, 88–90
Mulch
  for berries, 220, 221, 224, 225, 229
  controlling weeds with, 69
  first-year garden and, 165
  improving soil with, 155, 156–58, 163
  managing, 157
  materials, 168, 191–92
  slugs and, 186–87, 212
  watering, moisture and, 69, 144–45, 157, 177, 190, 211

weeds and, 140–41, 144–45, 162–63, 191–92, 211–12
Mustard, 186–87

N

Neighbors, 22–23
Nitrogen, 159–60
NPK, 159–60. See also Nitrogen; Phosphorus; Potassium

O

Onions, 175, 194–97, 210, 251–52, 254
Organic farming, 136, 144–46
Outbuildings. See Barns and outbuildings

P

Pantry, 251–52
Parsley. See Apiaceae or Umbellefeae
Pastureland, 27
Pathways, 158, 183
Pearson's Square, 305
Peas, 161, 175, 193–94, 210, 236, 254
Pellet stoves, 121–22
Peppers, 160, 170, 172, 199, 204–06, 209–11, 254
Permaculture, 68, 143, 148, 151, 157, 173, 181
Pesticides, 137–41, 144, 146
Pests, controlling, 173, 191. See also specific pests
Pests, in house, 73–74, 76
Phosphorus, 160
pH, 41, 42, 154, 156, 158–59, 229, 257
Pigs, 349–63
  appeal of, 349
  boar taint and, 351–52
  boars and sows, 358
  buying piglets, 350–52
  calculating weight, 357
  castrating males, 351–52
  chickens and, 353–54
  corn intake, 213
  developing trust with, 358–61
  farrowing, 351, 358
  feeding, 356–58